Undercurrents of Power

THE EARLY MODERN AMERICAS

Peter C. Mancall, Series Editor

Volumes in the series explore neglected aspects of early
modern history in the western hemisphere. Interdisciplinary
in character, and with a special emphasis on the Atlantic World
from 1450 to 1850, the series is published in partnership with the
USC-Huntington Early Modern Studies Institute.

Undercurrents of Power

Aquatic Culture in the African Diaspora

Kevin Dawson

PENN

UNIVERSITY OF PENNSYLVANIA PRESS

PHILADELPHIA

Published by
University of Pennsylvania Press
Philadelphia, Pennsylvania 19104-4112
www.upenn.edu/pennpress

Printed in the United States of America
on acid-free paper

10 9 8 7 6 5 4 3 2 1

Library of Congress Cataloging-in-Publication Data

Names: Dawson, Kevin (Historian), author.
Title: Undercurrents of power: aquatic culture in the African diaspora /
    Kevin Dawson.
Other titles: Early modern Americas.
Description: 1st edition. | Philadelphia: University of Pennsylvania Press,
    [2018] | Series: The early modern Americas | Includes bibliographical
    references and index.
Identifiers: LCCN 2017032704 | ISBN 9780812249897 (hardcover: alk.
    paper)
Subjects: LCSH: African diaspora—History. | Africans—America—Ethnic
    identity—History. | Slaves—America—Social conditions. | Aquatic
    sports—Africa—History. | Aquatic sports—America—History. | Boats and
    boating—Africa—History. | Boats and boating—America—History.
Classification: LCC DT16.5 .D39 2018 | DDC 305.896/070903—dc23
LC record available at https://lccn.loc.gov/2017032704

To the waters of the Atlantic world and those enslaved Africans
who suffered and endured so their story might be told

Contents

Waterscapes of the African Diaspora

Our story begins in the Pacific, off the island of Hawai'i, in Kealakekua Bay. Here, on January 22, 1779, surgeon's mate David Samwell wrote an early account of surfing, an account capturing Western apprehensions of water and other people's affinity for gliding through liquid infinities: "These People find one of their Chief amusements in that which to us presented nothing but Horror & Destruction, and we saw with astonishment young boys and Girls about 9 or ten years of age playing amid such tempestuous Waves that the hardiest of our seamen would have trembled to face." The sailors "looked upon this as no other than certain death." Like other Europeans, Samwell viewed surfing as mere "amusement," failing to comprehend non-Western cultural understandings of water. Conveying Western land-oriented perceptions, he reveals how anxieties about swimming caused white people to misconstrue Hawaiian aquatic traditions, while regarding water as an unnatural element and swimming as a life-threatening pursuit. The playground of Hawaiian youth was a place of "Horror & Destruction" for white men who had just spent three years at sea.[1]

Societies carve diverging identities from their interactions with and historicization of the same ocean. In many important ways, Westerners are terracentric—"landlocked, mentally if not physically"—treating waterways as empty, cultureless, historical voids. In 1620, William Bradford, governor of Plymouth Colony, captured beliefs concerning humans' natural relationships with land as he witnessed the landing of Pilgrims who "fell upon their knees and blessed the God of Heaven, who had brought them over the vast and furious ocean and delivered them from all the perils and miseries, again to set their feet on the firm and stable earth, their *proper element.*"[2]

For more than a millennium, there has been a concerted effort to suppress the sea with religious, scientific, and historical perceptions beginning and ending on the terra firma. Scripture tells us humanity began in the

Garden of Eden, while seas symbolized the unfinished chaos predating civilization, a metaphor for God's vengeance, and a perpetuation of the Great Flood. Scientists explain that humanity emerged long after our common ancestor flopped ashore. Historians favor land-bound studies over maritime ones; occasionally using Atlantic voyages to frame accounts of Pilgrims, priests, conquistadors, colonists, and slaves.[3] Terrestrial perspectives treat water as a border for land-bound events and an intercontinental highway, concluding that cultural creation was restricted to land.

Water covers some 70 percent of the earth. Most people live near water. Water dominates much of Atlantic Africa.[4] Stretching from Senegal to Angola, this region is rimmed by thousands of miles of coastline, bisected by rivers and streams, and pockmarked by lakes, while the Niger River's sweeping arch frames its northeastern limits and the Congo plunges through its southern reaches. Here, Africans maintained intimate interactions with water during work and personal time; regarding it as social and cultural spaces, not as intervals between places. Scholars regularly encapsulate societies into binary reductive spheres, treating individuals as land people or mariners; farmers or fishermen—not both. Societies were not dichotomized into discrete terrestrial and maritime worlds and water people equally understood land and water.[5] Many Africans were fishing-farmers and farming-fishermen who wove terrestrial and aquatic experiences into amphibious lives, interlacing spiritual and secular beliefs, economies, social structures, and political institutions—their very way of life—around relationships with water.[6]

Undercurrents of Power: Aquatic Culture in the African Diaspora examines aquatic fluencies to consider how African-descended peoples charted cultural constellations onto New World waterscapes while forging similar communities of practice and meaning. African-born and country-born (or those born in the Americas) slaves re-created and reimagined African traditions as they cast cultural anchors into ancestral waters while interlacing diverse ethnic valuations upon New World waterscapes. Grounded in the eighteenth century, this book extends from 1444, when the Portuguese first entered sub-Saharan Africa, to 1888, when Brazil became the last New World society to abolish slavery.

Like watermarks on paper, aquatics can leave ineffaceable impressions on cultures, on memories, and on one's sense of place and identity. Water was a defining feature for African-descended peoples living along seas, rivers, lakes, and estuaries as immersionary traditions enabled many to merge water and land into unified culturescapes. Accounts indicate many were adept swimmers, underwater divers, and canoeists.

In Africa, the construction and use of dugout canoes was imbued with spiritual and secular meanings. Canoes were a central means of conveyance, possibly moving more goods than any other method. Men and women preparing to use them for fishing, market voyages, visiting family members and friends, and warfare made offerings to water deities and dugouts, asking for guidance and protection.

The Atlantic slave trade created a cultural watershed, channeling traditions to the Americas where slaveholders clustered Africans into ethnic enclaves. Imported Africans constructed cultural beachheads, exercising muscle memories that provided New World waters with echoes of home. Sources suggest that captives used African-informed canoe designs and swimming and canoeing techniques to maintain ethnic traditions while forging new identities in multiethnic communities of belonging.

Aquatics enabled unwilling colonists to forge semiautonomous cultural worlds as they traveled more extensively than previously assumed, gaining privacy away from white authority. Parting blue and green waters while swimming and canoeing, many African captives enjoyed their exploited bodies while temporarily escaping the gray monotony of agricultural bondage. Many leveraged their expertise for lives of privileged exploitation.

Maritime retentions resulted from converging phenomena. During free time, saltwater (or African-born) captives of the same ethnicity purposefully re-created traditions, while members of diverse groups reimagined and merged customs. Slaveholders forced some to maintain traditions when members of the same and discrete ethnicities constructed and crewed dugouts or formed underwater dive teams. Multiethnic labor forces faced communication obstacles. Still, similar customs, spiritual beliefs, building techniques, and aesthetic valuations seemingly permitted waterscapes and dugouts to possess meanings for all as traditions coalesced.[7]

Undercurrents of Power expands traditional interpretations of how we examine the past. The Chesapeake, for instance, is one of the most examined regions of America. Historian Rhys Isaacs broadened our historical understandings, explaining how "Virginians of different ranks experienced their surroundings as they went through them, heading out from home along ways that connected them." Cutting through fields and woods, bondpeople gained subtle knowledge of their "alternative territorial system."

Traveling by road, planters experienced the "landscape differently—from a vantage point some three feet higher." They observed fields, slaves, and great houses, encountering white and black people who showed them signs of deference, reaffirming their social status.[8]

Isaacs vibrantly illustrated how landscapes shaped human experiences. But what about water? What about the Chesapeake Bay? We would be remiss to ignore how geographic features, like mountains, urban settings, and agricultural fields, as well as the types of crops grown in them, informed human experiences. Still, we only consider a portion of the environment slaves intimately understood, forgetting the thousands of square miles of water that dominated this region, as well as the Caribbean, Latin America, and the rest of North America.[9]

Colonization redefined New World landscapes physically and conceptually, treating them as a savage wilderness that needed to be cultivated into civilized gardens evocative of Europe.[10] Colonists did not culturally conquer water. This allowed captives to impose African meanings upon waters that were once known only to Amerindians, using them to "maintain distance, distinctiveness, and some sense of ownership" over their lives.[11]

The term *waterscape* expresses how freshwater and saltwater systems actively informed group identities while articulating how water and land were interlaced into amphibious culturescapes. Waterscape extends the idea of "seascapes" beyond its saltwater confines into freshwater systems.[12] African-descended peoples "enlisted" water "as a player in the historical drama," treating it as dynamic multidimensional spaces.[13] Indeed, waterscapes invite scholars to slide into the drink to reconsider how people who are traditionally treated as members of land-bound societies interacted with local and distant waterways. This approach dramatically expands our historical perspective, adding tens of thousands of miles of culturescapes above and below the water's surface.[14]

At the same time, Atlantic history extends our understanding of the early modern (c.1500–1800) world; terrestrial perspectives ground it in an intellectual valley, limiting its horizons to landbound events.[15] Oceans largely remain a literary mechanism bookending terrestrial histories, prompting historian W. Jeffrey Bolster to observe that "modern people" are "riveted to a land-centered geography" and "have difficulty imagining the oceanic areas" as early modern people did, challenging scholars to "put the ocean in Atlantic history."[16] We equally forget to add water to the Atlantic, assuming maritime history primarily existed on the decks of Western ships or along the docks and wharves of European cities and their colonial outposts, relegating Africans' immersionary experiences to intellectual backwaters. We must avoid making "the historical experiences of Europeans" the "normative standard against which judgments about Atlantic people and their histories are made."[17] Those willing to take the intellectual plunge will find vibrant histories below the surface, in the curl of breaking waves, and seated in dugout canoes.

In this regard, scholars of Oceania offer possibilities for integrating water and aquatics into Atlantic paradigms. In 1993, Epeli Hau'ofa charted Oceania, borrowing concepts of cultural geography from scholar-activists writing in the wake of African independence who forged broad integrative frameworks to correct the historiographic fragmentation that broke Africa into "a historical jigsaw puzzle" by ignoring human relationships with their environment. Stressing that previous studies similarly misconstrued Oceania by concluding that islanders were sea-locked peoples stranded on islands, Hau'ofa rejected the "belittling" tendency of "continental" scholars who shrank this expanse by focusing on human relationships with dry areas, ignoring how Oceanians holistically understood their space, which Europeans had carved into Polynesia, Micronesia, and Melanesia. Water was not a confining barrier, nor a liquid void. Seas and islands formed a seamless culturescape—a "sea of islands." "Oceania" signifies human connections to the sea. While this sea of islands suffered "a colonial tsunami," it did, as historian Nicholas Thomas stressed, "remain an Islanders' world."[18]

This book is constructed at the intersection of Atlantic history and the African diaspora. Atlantic history uses a comprehensive approach for examining the past by tracing connections across webs of transnational engagements that emphasize movements and interactions. Scholars of the African diaspora evaluate how captives "*remembered* Africa intentionally and deliberately" while "creating new and vibrant cultures informed by memories of Africa." They convincingly argue that the slave trade and slaveholders' purchasing preference congregated Africans from specific ethnic groups and regions, with James Sweet stressing that bondpeople "were arriving in coherent cultural groupings that shared much in common," allowing many customs to be re-created "in nearly pure structure." While cultural amalgamations routinely began in Africa, traditions retained their original meanings, providing ethnic hallmarks while forging links with new communities.[19]

Scholarship on the African diaspora relies on understandings of African cultures and how they influenced African-descended peoples in new environments and circumstances. It was greatly informed when Africanists cut deep intellectual inroads into Atlantic history, integrating Africa and the diaspora into a single unit of analysis that follows cultural paths into the Western Hemisphere.[20] Scholars increasingly examine how the Atlantic slave trade connected captives from specific ethnic groups or regions to particular New World destinations.[21] Biographies, composite biographies, and micro-histories facilitate the consideration of trans-Atlantic patterns and minutia of individuals' lives as they created their own space, identities, and experiences.[22] Many sources are separated by considerable time and distance, precluding this book from fully engaging this productive line of inquiry.

Scholars increasingly evaluate how cultural resilience served as a mechanism of resistance. According to one historian, even as European expansion swept Africans to the Americas, "European domination was never a forgone conclusion, particularly in those spaces where Africans and their descendent figured prominently in the overall population." Sources suggest that slaves purposefully retained and insinuated their cultural exactitudes onto New World societies.[23]

The documents used to compose *Undercurrents of Power*—travel accounts, slave narratives, diaries, newspapers, plantation records, government documents, and ship logs—are familiar to scholars of bondage. My experiences perhaps offer new perspectives. As a multiracial person of African descent who has spent decades swimming, surfing, underwater diving, and sailing, I found accounts of black aquatics to be striking, especially as popular misconceptions contradict historical sources by claiming African Americans were averse to water and aquatic activities.

Sources provide a sound analytical foundation, often permitting empirical examinations. Unfortunately, they do not always definitively link African and slave traditions. Accounts of cultural practices routinely appear in clusters rather than neatly spaced across generations, constraining considerations of change over time and sometimes forcing an impressionistic, even synchronic, approach.

White-authored accounts regularly racialized African-descended people while richly chronicling black aquatics. Whenever possible, documents produced by African-descended people are used, allowing nameless voiceless characters to tell their histories. Slave-authored accounts are routinely held to higher standards of scrutiny than white-authored ones. Still, they are often our best sources for understanding captives' experiences.[24] The spelling and syntax in primary-source quotes remains true to the original text and "sic" is not used to prevent cluttering. Historical images enhance this book's analysis. Some images reveal Western aquatic anxieties, while careful observers produced informative representations. All extend our historical understandings.

PART I

Swimming Culture

Chapter 1

Atlantic African Aquatic Cultures:
A Cross-Cultural Comparison

The first recorded interaction between Europeans and Sub-Saharan Africans occurred in the water. Off Senegal in c. 1445, Portuguese sailors, coming from a maritime culture that devalued swimming, were astounded by the aquatic expertise of Wolof-speaking fishermen. Sailors lured fishermen in six canoes close to their ships to capture and interrogate them. As a Portuguese longboat overtook one dugout, the fishermen "leapt into the water." It was with "very great toil" that two were captured, "for they dived like cormorants." Though the incident occurred well offshore, the others rapidly swam ashore.[1]

From the fifteenth through the late nineteenth century, the swimming and underwater diving abilities of African-descended peoples regularly surpassed those of Westerners. Most white people could not swim. Those who could were inexpert. To reduce drowning deaths, some philanthropists, beginning in the mid-nineteenth century, advocated swimming as a means of self-preservation. In 1838, *Sailor's Magazine,* a New York City missionary magazine, published the inscription of a city placard titled "Swimming." It read: "For want of knowledge of this noble art thousands are annually sacrificed, and every fresh victim calls more strongly upon the best feelings of those who have the power to draw the attention of such persons as may be likely to require this art, to the simple fact, that there is no difficulty in floating or swimming." Regardless, in 1899, swimming advocate Davis Dalton lamented: "Few persons know how to swim."[2]

Sources indicate that many Africans were proficient swimmers who learned at a young age. Aquatics were woven into people's spiritual beliefs, economies, social structures, political institutions, and worldviews, shaping societal relationships with waterscapes. A comparison of African- and European-descended peoples reveals striking differences in valuations and practices that suggest the African origins of slaves' aquatics. Swimming pervaded Africans' muscle memory. Along with walking, talking, and reading, swimming becomes virtually intuitive, once learned, and was one of the easiest skills to carry to the Americas.

Ancient Europeans were proficient swimmers, but from the medieval period until the modern period and for numerous reasons they discouraged swimming. Christian texts characterized the ocean as the unfinished chaos preceding civilization and "realm of Satan," while stories of the Great Flood and drowning of Pharaoh's army depict water as an "instrument of punishment." Catholic and Protestant epic stories of colonization described Satan dispatching sea monsters to destroy Christian colonists seeking to expand Christendom. Writers routinely equated water to hell and swimming to eternal torment, describing it as a futile act and an allegory for the loss of salvation. Jesus, for example, admonished His followers to be "fishers of men," pulling them from waters of damnation. In 1602, a Jesuit compared sinners to "a swimmer who, extending and contracting his arms, displays the gesture of a man utterly vanquished and in despair. Thus Saint Jerome, Adam, &c., compare [the ungodly] with a shipwrecked swimmer in the sea because, just as such a one is tumbled about in the depth of the sea, so the ungodly, being shipwrecked from salvation, are tumbled about in the abyss of Gehenna," or "hell."[3]

Medieval swimming was regarded as a fruitless struggle against nature, while changes in warfare favoring knights precipitated a shift in attitudes regarding its utility.[4] Doctors discouraged immersion, as water purportedly upset the balance of the body's humors, causing diseases. Since swimming was generally performed nude, Catholic officials admonished it for moral reasons.[5] Furthermore, many believed waterways were filled with "noisom vapours" and ravenous creatures. By the fourteenth century, the crawl was virtually forgotten.[6]

White authors indicate that few European-descended people could swim well enough to negotiate moderate turbulence. Advocates recognized that some could swim if permitted to strip nude and enter calm waters while keeping their heads above water. They encouraged proficient swimming in which individuals resurfaced if submerged during maritime accidents and swam until rescued.[7]

More specifically, Europeans preferred variants of the breaststroke, concluding it was the most civilized and sophisticated stroke. When performed correctly, both arms are extended forward and pulled back together in a sweeping circular motion, the legs are thrust out and pulled together in circular frog kicks. Early modern whites used forms akin to the dog paddle, keeping their heads above water, letting their legs drop almost vertically, which reduced speed and endurance. During the sixteenth century, theorists began publishing treatises that advocated elementary versions of the breaststroke, believing that swimming should be graceful and sedate.[8]

Theorists neither swam themselves nor consulted swimmers. Instead, theories largely evolved as analytical speculation on "ideal forms of swimming" that had little influence on swimming practices.[9] Many speculated on how swimmers could cut their toenails, catch birds, or perform other still unperfected activities. Some considered how to escape unlikely scenarios like "lions, Bears, or fierce dogs lurking in the river" Thames.[10]

Observers, including Benjamin Franklin, referenced the breaststroke as the "ordinary," or white, method.[11] White people became averse to the crawl, also called the "freestyle" or "Australian crawl," because it generated splashing, and they felt swimming "should be smooth and gentle." The crawl was judged savage while the breaststroke, which was relatively basic, was deemed refined and civilized.[12] During the 1830s, George Catlin documented Amerindian culture in print, drawings, and paintings, revealing how whites appreciated the crawl's speed while dismissing it as uncivilized. In North Dakota, he wrote: "The mode of swimming amongst the Mandans, as well as amongst most other tribes, is quite different from that practiced in those parts of the *civilized* world, . . . The Indian, instead of parting his hands simultaneously under his chin, and making the stroke outward, in a horizontal direction," used the "bold and powerful" crawl.[13]

Fear of submerging one's face prevented many whites from becoming proficient swimmers. In 1587, theorist Everard Digby guided readers into the water. Paraphrasing Digby, Franklin encouraged readers to "walk coolly into it till it is up to your breast, then turn round, your face to the shore, and throw and egg into the water between you and the shore." The real test came when readers were told to submerge their faces "with your eyes open" while retrieving the egg. Annette Kellerman, an early twentieth-century movie swimming performer, believed swimming was an ideal sport for women. She too encouraged people to relinquish their fear of water by

Figure 1. Dongola Men. This image depicts Dongola men in the Sudan using the "high elbow" of the crawl while crossing rapids, illustrating the widespread use of this stroke within Africa. These men were part of a British military expedition. British troops apparently could not swim well enough to traverse the river and were shuttled across in boats. "The Nile Expedition for the Relief of General Gordon," *Illustrated London News,* 85 (October 4, 1884), 316; article on 318. Author's collection.

getting wet: the first hurdle in transforming land-bound people into swimmers.[14]

In contrast, Africans created immersionary cultures that valued aquatics, which we must consider since humans do not instinctively swim. Swimming transforms water into a "mystical medium," permitting swimmers to glide weightlessly through liquid infinities as body and water slip into fluid motion. Africans treated swimming as a life skill and a method of personal cleanliness, devising efficient techniques for traversing surface and submarine strata. Swimming was a sensual experience, blunting some senses while accentuating others to provide an otherworldliness. It was a rhythmic, dynamic pursuit that defied terrestrial forms of locomotion, stimulating the skin's nerve endings as they came in contact with warm tropical waters and cool surface breezes. "Swimming cultivates imagination," permitting people to focus their thoughts or set them adrift. It has long been described as "poetry in motion;" allowing humans to feel "almost capable of soaring in the air." One advocate felt that the "experienced swimmer when in the water may be classed among the happiest of mortals in the happiest of moods, and in the most complete enjoyment of the most delightful of exercises."[15] Yet, we must not romanticize swimming. Unlike walking, swimming is a struggle for survival, and, in the Americas, became a form of exploitation.

Africans perfected variants of the crawl, concluding that its alternate overarm stroke and fast scissors kicks, which make it the strongest and swiftest style, was the proper method. Nearly every white traveler was amazed by Africans' fluencies. In 1455, Venetian merchant-adventurer Alvise da Cadamosto relayed that those living by the Senegal River "are the most expert swimmers in the world." He asked if "anyone who could swim well and was bold enough" would "carry my letter to the ship three miles off shore," as storm-swept seas prevented dugouts from making the passage. Two volunteered for what Cadamosto believed an "impossible" task. After "a long hour," one "bore the letter to the ship, returning with a reply. This to me was a marvelous action, and I concluded that these coast negroes are indeed the finest swimmers in the world."[16]

Other travelers agreed and routinely claimed that Africans were better swimmers than Europeans. Dutchman Pieter de Marees described Gold Coast Africans' crawl during the 1590s, writing that "they can swim very fast, generally easily outdoing people of our nation in swimming and diving." Comparing the Fante's crawl to Europeans' breaststroke, Jean Barbot asserted, "The Blacks of Mina out-do all others at the coast in dexterity of swimming, throwing one [arm] after another forward, as if they were paddling, and not extending their arms equally, and striking with them both together, as Europeans do." Similarly, Robert Rattray said Asante "are very fine swimmers and some show magnificent muscular development. They swim either the ordinary breast stroke [like Europeans] or a double overarm with a scissor-like kick of the legs."[17]

Impressed white people frequently compared African-descended peoples to marine creatures, tritons, and mermaids, often proclaiming them amphibious. In 1600, Johann von Lübelfing averred Africans "can swim below the water like a fish." Thomas Hutchinson concluded, "The majority of the coast negroes . . . may be reckoned amphibious," proclaiming women "ebony mermaids."[18] New World slaves were similarly likened to aquatic animals. Edward Sullivan concluded that black Bahamians were "an amphibious race." In 1796, George Pinckard observed a Barbadian slave, exclaiming: "Not an otter, nor a beaver, nor scarcely a dolphin could appear more in his element." After remaining submerged "for a long time" he surfaced, appearing "as much at his ease, in the ocean, as if he had never breathed a lighter, nor trodden a firmer element." Others equated them to nymphs, mermaids, and tritons.[19]

Many Africans believed drowning was dishonorable, with maritime disasters juxtaposing African and European abilities. Typically when boats sank, those of African descent saved themselves. One of two things usually happened to whites: African-descended peoples saved them or they drowned. U.S. Naval officer Horatio Bridge provides examples of both. In 1836, ten U.S. sailors drowned when their boat swamped and capsized in the Liberian surf. In 1843, Bridge noted that marines disembarking in Liberia upset the canoe they traveled in. "Unable to swim, [at least one] was upheld by a Krooman." One year later, five whites and five *Kru* were aboard a boat that "capsized and sunk. The five Kroomen saved themselves, by swimming, until picked up by a canoe; the five whites were lost."[20] No account of a white person swimming to save a drowning African has been found.

Some Africans used spiritual beliefs to explain high rates of white drowning, concluding that deities drowned Europeans for their transgressions. In 1887, Alfred Ellis learned that peoples along the Gold Coast believed in "Akum-brohfo, 'slayer of white men, whom he destroys by upsetting their boats.'" He felt this deity was "apparently introduced to account for the number of instances in which boats are capsized, the white occupants, encumbered with clothes, and either unable to swim or less powerful swimmers than the black crew, are the only persons drowned. Since the blacks, though equally thrown into the water, escape, while the whites perish, it is evident to the native mind that the god has a special dislike for the latter."[21]

Africans similarly construed shark and crocodile attacks. Some believed that whites provided a line of defense against attack, as their skin shimmered in the water like fishing lures. While on the Gambia River, Richard Jobson noted that canoemen refused to swim until he "leapt into the water," saying "the white man, shine more in the water, then they did, and therefore if Bumbo [crocodile] come, hee would surely take us [whites] first." Likewise, peoples in Sierra Leone believed sharks were attracted to whites.[22]

Some Westerners equally sought religious explanations for African aquatics. The Great Flood narrative was used to facetiously explain Africans' expertise, as reported by an American woman in East Africa: "Respecting the amphibious traits of the natives in Africa, an English officer exploits the fiction that some antecedent of the African race was crowded off the ark and had to swim or drown."[23]

One striking difference between African and Western aquatics was that many African women were strong swimmers, while most white women could not swim. After describing men, de Marees noted, "Many of the women here can swim very well too." Likewise, Rattray wrote that Asante women were "as expert as the men, and this I quite believe, as I used to see whole family parties alternately wading and swimming along the lake shore instead of following the road running between the villages."[24]

White women tended not to swim, as Western mores prohibited them from publicly disrobing. African-descended women were not so constrained.[25] Because Africa is hot and humid, many people did not completely clothe themselves. More important, Africans believed their bodies were gifts from their creator that should be proudly exhibited. Shaka, ruler of the Zulu Empire, expressed as much, saying, "The first forefathers of the Europeans had bestowed on us many gifts . . . , yet had kept from us the greatest of all gifts, such as a good black skin, for this does not necessitate the wearing of clothes to hide the white skin, which was not pleasant to the eye."[26]

We would be remiss to conclude that the fluencies of saltwater captives were learned in the Americas. Just as Muslim slaves transmitted Arabic reading and writing skills to the Americas, aquatics were as transportable as walking. Atlantic Africans maintained similar swimming techniques and valuations, while sharing similar, spiritual beliefs concerning water. In the Americas, saltwater slaves from diverse ethnic groups established beachhead cultures where kindred traditions coalesced as they forged communities of belonging and meaning.[27]

Accounts of bondage are embroidered with descriptions of African- and country-born swimmers and underwater divers. When New York professor William Miller visited the Bahamas in the 1820s, he was impressed by the *"Expertness of the negroes in swimming,"* relating that many remained submerged for "two to three minutes." Some portrayed Africans as virtually unsinkable, with Miller exclaiming: "The stories of the feats performed by the negroes in swimming are almost incredible—They will remain near 24 hours or more without sinking." Descriptions of the swimming valuations and techniques of African-descended peoples scattered throughout the Atlantic world by the currents of bondage are remarkably similar.[28]

In fact, some slaves taught whites to swim, transmitting affirmative values of swimming and water that promoted limited white swimming. John Clinkscales's father owned a Low Country, South Carolina plantation. There, he and a bondman named Essex formed a friendship partially cultivated on swimming. Essex was "the best swimmer on my father's place" and possibly in the county. Believing it was a "disgrace for a 'ge'man' to be unable" to "swim with ease," Essex taught Clinkscales.[29] Essex's statement suggests slaves viewed swimming inabilities disgraceful, while expertise was a source of pride.

African-informed valuations of swimming were seemingly transferred to white Bermudians shortly after the colony's settlement in 1609. In Bermuda and the Bahamas, African-descended peoples apparently prompted whites to revise swimming perceptions and practices, making them the only societies where white swimming was valued and many whites were proficient enough to save themselves during maritime disasters. The English did not value swimming. Yet in these colonies, black and white boys and girls swam together, allowing Bermudian Governor Robert Robinson to exclaim, in 1687, that they were all "blissfull in swimming." By the late seventeenth century, most white men and women were proficient swimmers.[30] During Bermuda's formative years, colonists imported significant numbers of underwater divers from Africa and the Caribbean. They apparently inserted an important plank into Bermuda's maritime culture—a tradition permitting whites to save themselves during maritime calamities.[31]

The significance of Bermudian swimming culture is overlooked unless the colony is situated in an Atlantic context, which reveals descriptions of white swimmers mirroring those of African peoples. Robinson explained that the colony's children "chiefly exercised in fishing, swimming and diving" and most women were proficient. Equally, in 1778, Philip Freneau penned that Bermudians "from the time of their birth, are familiarized to the water to such a degree, that by the time they are five, six or seven years of age, all the boys and many of the girls can live under the water and in it, pretty near as well as the fish, to which they seem to be of a congenial nature." Africans were commonly measured against marine creatures. Nowhere else were such comparisons made about whites.[32] Interestingly, early generations of captives sometimes established traditions that subsequent generations "adopted in their new environments." All Bermudians seemingly followed this pattern.[33]

Waterscapes also challenged racial perceptions, values, and hierarchies in other ways. For example, they provided captives with a medium for defying white claims to their bodies. Women used waterways to prevent white men from sexually abusing them. Simultaneously, men and women used water to steal their bodies when they swam to freedom.

Water was a sanctuary from unwanted sexual advances. Even as African mores permitted public nudity, water obscured their bodies from white voyeurs. White men lustfully gathered along beaches to observe the aesthetic qualities of women's nude, agile bodies gracefully parting waters the men dared not enter. Depicting these objects of their sexual desires as mermaids and nymphs, white males wished they could swim so that they might better appreciate their suppleness and beauty. Richard Ligon lusted over the "round, firm, and beautifully shaped" breasts and other exotic charms of young African "Nymphs."[34]

African women on both sides of the Atlantic quickly understood how affirmative African beliefs regarding nudity made them the objects of white lust. Just as quickly, many realized water could preclude unwanted sexual advances. For example, several nude women swam through the surf to sell palm wine to British sailors anchored off Fernando Po Island (now Bioko). One clambered aboard, where a sailor, thinking himself in luck, put "his arm around her neck." Perturbed by his advances, she "dived under the boat, and, reappear[ed] at some distance on the opposite side." Amused by the sailor's "surprise and disappointment" she "swam, laughing, to the shore." Aboard ship, where European notions of nudity and wine prevailed, African standards placed the woman in an undesirable position. Aquatic acumen rescued her.[35]

Bondwomen understood how white men objectified them. Country-born girls came to realize that rape could be their cruel rite of passage into adolescence. Ashore, white men could exploit women almost at will, blaming victims for the assaults. In water, women could parlay white advances in a manner that hopefully would preclude future wrath. Touring Jamaica in 1823, Cynric Williams and a group of male companions covetously studied at least twenty nude saltwater women in Turtle Crawl River, "some

washing clothes, some washing themselves, flouncing about like nereids."
When the men were discovered, the women "on shore dashed into the
water. . . . When they were, according to their own notions, far enough
from our masculine gaze, they emerged one by one, popping their black
heads and shewing their ivory mouths as they laughed and made fun of
me." On land, they had reason to fear white sexual assault. Swimming abilities afforded protection unparalleled ashore. They flaunted their sexuality.
Allowing the men to see silhouettes of their bodies while the water distorted
the intimate details, they provocatively sang about a white preacher who
"cross de sea" to "make lub [love]" to slave women. Like Sirens, they
enticed the men to swim out and fulfill their sexual cravings. Williams
thinly veiled his desires, dubbing the song's composer "Proserpine," a
Greek/Roman goddess raped by Hades. For the men, this was a scene of
double taboo: one of intercourse with African women in a sensual but
unnatural element that claimed many white lives. The women remained in
control of their nude bodies even as men a few feet away sought to sexually
dominate them. The men prudently resisted the femme fatale's song.[36]

Swimming allowed many to appropriate their bodies. Some swam during physical altercations with white authority. Others did so while hiding
in secluded areas or while fleeing the realms of bondage.[37]

Swimming permitted some to distance themselves from white pursuers.
Bondpeople in the Danish West Indies, comprised of St. Thomas, St. Jan
("St. John" in English sources), and St. Croix, paddled and sailed eastward
to freedom in Puerto Rico and Vieques. After Britain abolished slavery
in 1834, captives from Danish and French islands voyaged to the British
Caribbean. Many Danish slaves swam or used paddleboards to reach these
Spanish possessions, at least fifteen miles away, and the much closer British
Virgin Islands. "From several points of St. John's to the English Island of
Tortola, the distance is scarcely a mile. Many negroes could swim across;
and, with the aid of a few bamboos, could carry their families along with
them." In 1840, five St. Jan slaves embarked for Tortola in a canoe, trigger-
ing an incident that strained Danish and British relations. They were intercepted and fired upon in British waters by a Danish patrol boat. A
bondwoman was killed and a mother and child captured, while two others
swam to freedom.[38]

Many fugitives in the American South swam to avoid recapture. For
three years, Essex, who Clinkscales praised, remained hidden "in the
swamps and forests on both sides of the Savannah [River], not many miles

Figure 2. Meeting of Fugitive Slaves in the Marshes. After General Butler's Union Forces seized Fort Monroe in Hampton, Virginia, during the American Civil War, so many slaves fled to his lines that surrounding slaveholders reportedly prohibited them from openly communicating. This image depicts surreptitious meetings held in water to preclude even the stealthiest white authority figure from overhearing their furtive plans. "Meeting of Fugitive Slaves in the Marshes," *Le Monde Illustré*, 9 (August 3, 1861), 492; account is on 486. Author's collection.

from the City of Augusta, Georgia." Frequently pursued "by the best-trained dogs," Essex "wanted no better sport than to slip into the river and kiss good-by to hound and hunter." Likewise, Octave Johnson of New Orleans lived as a maroon "for a year and a half" with twenty-nine other fugitives. "Eugene Jardeau, master of the hounds," tracked them. On one occasion "twenty hounds came after me; I called the party to my assistance and we killed eight of the hounds." The fugitives swam off using their aquatic environment to destroy the dogs. The "dogs followed us and the alligators caught six of them," which made an easy meal.[39]

As American fugitives struck north for freedom, many swam across obstructing waterways. Those fleeing Kentucky and Virginia traversed the Ohio River. As James Adams and his cousin Benjamin Harris fled Virginia for Canada they negotiated several bodies of water. When Charles Lucas and "two companions" fled their Virginia slaveholding, they "waded and swam, changing our ground as the water deepened."[40]

Bondmen knew that water allows strong swimmers to overpower poor-swimming antagonists who were stronger than them. When J. H. Banks of Virginia was sold away from his home he fought everyone conspiring against him. The battle began with Banks wrestling his overseer and a slave trader, both "able-bodied men," into the Shenandoah River. "But still our sinful propensity to fight was not washed away," declared Banks, who "stood waist deep in the water," dunking anyone who drew near. Banks eventually "surrendered." However, he demonstrated to the slaver that he must be treated with respect; if he weren't, the slaver would have to beat his new possession so severely that, according to Banks, he could not "sell me at a premium," leveraging his swimming abilities and pecuniary value to gain concessions.[41]

Frederick Douglass observed how field slave "Bill Denby or Demby" attempted to use water to blunt white dominance. As overseer Austin Gore whipped Demby, he "broke away" and "plunged into the creek, standing there to the depth of his neck in water, he refused to come out at the order of the overseer; whereupon, for this refusal, *Gore shot him dead!*" Gore justified his actions, asserting, "If one slave refused to be corrected, and escaped with his life, the other slaves would soon copy the example." There were surely other factors at play. Demby seemingly knew Gore would not pursue him into the river; yet he did not believe Gore would shoot him. Gore surely knew Demby was forcing him into a duel that would tarnish his authority and dishonor him. Like the femme fatales who tempted Cynric Williams, Demby goaded Gore while remaining just beyond reach. Ashore, Gore and Demby were apparently equally matched. In waters precluding sure-footing, Gore would suffer humiliation if beaten, dunked, and perhaps drowned. In the Old South, "most 'dueling encounters' never involved bullets" and were conducted among white equals as a "ritual that embodied the values and language of honor." Demby asserted himself into a duel with a superior. Knowing he could not win, Gore shot him, restoring his honor, terrifying slaves, and enhancing his reputation as his "fame as an overseer went abroad."[42]

Enslaved Africans drew on the cultural and muscle memory of their liquid worlds to create new communities of meaning and value in the Americas. Most people of African and European descent increasingly came to regard each other as aquatically different: as swimmers and nonswimmers, imposing group—even racial—identities upon themselves and those whose practices differed from theirs.

Chapter 2

Cultural Meanings of Recreational Swimming and Surfing

Africans valued swimming as a skill capable of extending fortunes and saving lives. Parents inculcated aquatics into children at a young age, transforming waterways into safe play spaces. Toddlers were taught after learning to walk, between the ages of ten and fourteen months, or after they were weaned, at approximately two to three years of age. "Once the children begin to walk by themselves, they soon go to the water in order to learn how to swim," wrote Pieter de Marees. William Bosman commented that "Mother gives the Infant suck for two or three Years" then they went "to the Sea-side to learn to swim."[1]

After teaching children the fundamentals, parents promoted expertise through play. Boyrereau Brinch, who was probably raised along the Niger River in what is now Mali, explained that Bow-woo, or Bobo, peoples regarded swimming as "a usefull" and "pleasing amusement." His "father and mother delighted in [his] vivacity and agility; on this occasion, every exertion on their part seemed to be made use of, to gratify" him. Many societies affixed spirituality to gliding through this potentially deadly element, creating charms to guard against drowning and marine creatures. Brinch's father gave him "ornaments," instructing him to "not get drowned." Safeguarded by prowess, amulets, and buddy systems, parents encouraged children to explore their liquid worlds.[2]

Africans did not divorce swimming from bathing, with both facilitating socialization. When F. Rankin was in Sierra Leone, he watched a group of Bullom people "indulging in the luxury of bathing" in a tidal river. Similarly, at the Hot Springs of Mtagata in what is now northwestern Tanzania,

Henry Stanley observed people from throughout the region visiting these springs. Mtagata's waters were a place of socialization as "merriment and cleansing, bathing and lounging" intertwined.[3]

Although men and women swam nude together, bathing places could be gender-segregated, providing gender-specific social spaces. According to the Islamic traditions of the Susu of Guinea and Sierra Leone, they punished "by slavery a man who looked upon the fair sex 'cleaning' itself."[4] Gendered waterscapes provided women with important intimate social settings, requiring more scholarly attention.

Swimming washed away much of the day's grime. Still, cleanliness did not end here. People scrubbed their bodies once, often twice, each day and washed their hands before eating and handling food, and after going to the bathroom and handling the dead.[5]

Play is a liberating pursuit and group swimming facilitates bonding and socialization. Along the coast, youth used beaches as playgrounds, frolicking in the surf and swimming along inland riverbanks and lakeshores. At Elmina, Barbot watched "several hundred . . . boys and girls sporting together before the beach, and in many places among the rolling and breaking waves, learning to swim," concluding that Africans' dexterities "proceed from their being brought up, both men and women from their infancy, to swim like fishes; and that, with the constant exercise renders them so dexterous." Sierra Leonean children were "as fond of playing in the water as ducks, and spend much time in that way, when not otherwise engaged. They seem to be perfectly at home in the water, and swim about for hours without any signs of tiring." Similar scenes unfolded in the interior. Near Timbuktu, Réné Caillié "amused" himself "by observing a group of young negroes of both sexes, who were bathing, dancing and gamboling about in the water."[6]

Parents prefer safe, controlled play environments; children favor spaces affording adventure, creative play, and at least the illusion of danger. Beaches met these criteria. Coastscapes (the area bounded by the surf and seashore's inland reaches) were important playgrounds, providing an ever-shifting milieu of land and sea. Youth played *with* the sea, interacting with surf, currents, and tides while learning its rhythms and hydrography (marine geography, including seas, lakes, rivers, and the influences of waves, currents, and tides). The sea's energy is integrally connected to surfing, requiring youth to learn surf patterns, wavelengths, and how to catch breakers—valuable skills when bringing canoes through surf as adults. In waters that reflected clouds, meandering birds, and slave castles, youth socialized, fabricated group cohesion, and developed aptitudes, like leadership, loyalty, and responsibility. Bobbing in the surf, they watched fathers stow goods in trade canoes, haul fishing nets through surf with their canoes, and catch waves. Children played with toy canoes, replicating the actions of fishermen and canoemen.[7]

Coastscapes, especially intertidal zones, were liminal, in-between, playgrounds always in flux. Rising and falling tides shrank and expanded beaches as surf and tides continually altered shorelines and seafloors. Situated between land and sea, coastscapes afforded settings for transitioning from childhood to adulthood.[8]

Some games played in coastscapes surely reflected the realities of adult life. Leaping over and ducking under crashing surf, the children learned the physics of breakers, a useful skill when launching surf-canoes. During other games, girls and boys pretended to be sharks pursuing playmates, while clumps of marine vegetation became ravenous creatures.[9] Play also provided adults with vivid, childhood memories as they continued to merge swimming and socializing, while imparting these skills to their children.[10]

The arrival of Europeans and construction of shipping infrastructure made play spaces more dangerous and attractive. A Kenyan account mirrored scenes that surely transpired throughout Atlantic Africa: "On the Mombasa wharf and shore, hosts of nude boys and girls were plunging into the water from the framework of a pier over seventy feet high, giving vent to hilarious shouts of delight and vying with each other. They dive feet down, and are most expert swimmers."[11]

Vibrant maritime societies similarly thrived in Africa's interior freshwater systems. Along the Niger River's Great Bend, maritime societies flourished on the cusp of the Sahara. Natural environments impose rules on humans, forcing them to yield to their will. Inland animist and Muslim communities adapted themselves to their waterscapes.[12] Olaudah Equiano commented that many in Nigeria's interior were proficient swimmers, saying he was "astonished to see some of the women, as well as the men, jump into the water, dive to the bottom, come up again, and swim about."[13]

Asante living around Lake Bosumtwi, located about one hundred miles inland, were expert swimmers. They were adept in the crawl and breaststroke, which facilitated fishing, as the "anthropomorphic lake god," Twi, prohibited canoes on the lake. Keeping with divine sanctions, people swam or used paddleboards, called *padua* or *mpadua* (plural). Fishermen wove reed traps, called *Ntakwa*, that were "oblong-shaped mat[s]" folded into cones. A "fisherman dives into the water, drags it along the bottom or among a shoal of fish, and keeping water pressure against the pocket-end keeps the fish that enter till he comes to the surface." Several *Ntakwa* were woven together to make *Kotokuo Keses*. Five or six fishermen on *mpadua* scared fish into *Kotokuo Keses* by lining up "about twenty yards from the net and then simultaneously start off at top speed, yelling '*padua! padua!*' and splashing and beating the water." Reaching the net, they dove underwater, grabbing its bottom lip to close the trap.[14]

Mungo Park's two interior journeys (1795–1797 and 1805) are equally illustrative. When crossing the Senegal River in 1795, a "few boys swam after" Park's horses, urging them on. Near the Bambara capital, Sego, located more than five hundred miles inland, Park observed a fisherman diving underwater to set fish traps. The man's lung capacity permitted him to remain submerged "for such a length of time, that I thought he had actually drowned himself."[15]

During Park's second expedition, forty-three Europeans accompanied him—many drowned. After crossing the Bafing River about three hundred miles inland, a canoe carrying three soldiers overturned. Africans "swam to their assistance, yet J. Cartwright was unfortunately drowned." They "recovered two muskets, and Cartwright's body." Park and the surviving Europeans drowned during a battle on the Niger River against Africans. Only an enslaved canoeman and the interpreter and guide, Amadi Fatouma, lived to carry Park's journal to British officials.[16]

Peoples of the Upper Congo River were equally expert. "Riverine people can remain under the water for a long time while attending their fish-nets, and this habit is gained from those infantile experiences," wrote John Weeks. Edward Glave observed ivory merchants hide tusks underwater to prevent theft, penning: "It was curious to see a native dive into the river and fetch up a big tusk from his watery cellar for sale," a task requiring considerable ability since they could weigh more than one hundred pounds.[17]

Responding to environmental and human pressures, some riverine and lacustrine societies were built upon the water. Water overwhelmed flood plains during much of the year, compelling people to raise the earth into islets or build structures on stilts. Residents swam between dwellings, as they tended fish traps and went to agricultural fields. Peoples of the Middle Congo River Basin adapted to the ebb and flow of biannual flooding that transformed the region into Africa's largest swamp. Amphibious societies existed as people fished and farmed during different parts of the year.[18]

Some societies moved onto waterways to guard against slave-raiders. During the eighteenth and nineteenth centuries, diverse peoples erected the stilt-village of Ganvié on Lake Nokoué, in what is now Benin. Nokoué and its marshlands provided a defensible sanctuary from Dahomean slavers. They created the Tofinu ethnicity, meaning "men on water"; Ganvié translates to "safe at last." Today roughly seventy thousand water people live in Nokoué, existing primarily on fish. In this "amphibian environment," canoeing and swimming were the only means of traveling.[19]

Others similarly developed lacustrine societies. In 1874, Verney Cameron observed "three villages built on piles" in Lake Mohrya, situated on the Lualaba River, a headstream of the Congo River. Structures were "raised about six feet above the surface of the water, supported on stout piles driven into the bed of the lake. . . . Underneath the platforms canoes were moored, and [fishing] nets hung to dry." People swam and canoed throughout the villages and to lakeshore farms.[20]

Evidence of aquatic expertise is preserved in accounts of slave-ship disasters. After the Atlantic slave trade was outlawed, and before English and American laws regulated the seizure of illegal slave ships, slavers could only be confiscated if captives were found aboard. Slavers pursued by naval vessels could avoid impoundment by throwing bondpeople overboard. In 1830, two Spanish slavers jettisoned captives in the Bonny River while pursued by British ships. "During the chase, they were seen from our vessels to throw their slaves overboard, by twos, shackled together by their ankles, and left in this manner to sink or swim, . . . Several managed, with difficulty, as may be supposed, to swim on shore."[21]

When slave ships sank, captives sometimes swam ashore. Though many could not verbally communicate with each other, their passages ashore illustrated shared cultural understandings. According to tradition, a marooned Angolare community was formed in 1544 when a slave ship carrying Angolans wrecked on the southern coast of São Tomé, an equatorial African island. "The slaves being able to swim, got safely to shore" to form fortified villages.[22] The ethnocultural group known as Black Caribs (also known as Garifuna and Callínago) similarly developed on St. Vincent Island in the Caribbean. In 1675, a slaver bound from the Bight of Benin to Barbados apparently "wrecked on the coast of Bequia, a small island" near St. Vincent, and the

Figure 3. Lake Dwelling on Lake Mohrya. This stilt-village was built in Lake Mohrya, situated on the Lualaba River, a headstream of the Congo River. Residents swam or canoed between structures and to shore to tend their fields. Note the swimmers' use of the crawl with the swimmer in the foreground turning to breathe. "Lake Dwelling on Lake Mohrya," *The Illustrated London News* (April 22, 1876). Author's collection.

slaves swam ashore. Caribs convinced them to go to St. Vincent, where members from both groups intermarried.[23]

Scholars generally believe the first account of surfing was written in Hawai'i in 1778. They are only a hundred and forty years too late, and some ten thousand miles off the mark. The earliest written record was penned on the Gold Coast during the 1640s. Swimming expertise enabled Africans to independently develop surfing in what are now Senegal, the Ivory Coast, Ghana, Cameroon, Liberia, and West-Central Africa. Atlantic Africa shares traits that inspired surfing in Oceania, including thousands of miles of warm, surf-filled waters and seagoing water people who knew ocean rhythms and surf patterns and were powerful swimmers.[24] Surfing was only developed by societies with deep aquatic connections. It gauges African understandings of fluid environments and aquatic valuations.

Surfing was developed throughout Atlantic Africa, Oceania, and Peru. Today, one surfs while standing; traditionally, one surfed in prone, kneeling, sitting, or standing positions, while canoe-surfing was a related activity. Even in Hawai'i, where surf culture became the most developed, many surfers sat, knelt, or lay.[25]

Several factors restrict our understanding of African surfing. First, only four known early accounts of African surfing exist. The uninitiated early European eye did not know what to make of African surfing. Comparatively, Europeans traversed Oceania for centuries before documenting surfing and did not express a concerted interest in it until the early twentieth century when Jack London romanticized the Hawaiian surfer as a masculine, muscular "black Mercury" whose "heels are winged, and in them the swiftness of the sea." By then, surfing in Africa and Oceania had nearly been drowned beneath the bow waves of colonialism and Christianization, which decried naked surfers as the articulation of savage cultures.[26]

Michael Hemmersam, who was a superficial observer, provided the first known account of African surfing. Believing he was watching Gold Coast children learn to swim, he wrote that parents "tie their children to boards and throw them into the water." Barbot penned the next known account in 1679, noting that children at Elmina learned "to swim, on bits of boards, or small bundles of rushes, fasten'd under their stomachs, which is a good diversion to the spectators."[27] Such lessons would result in many drowned children, not proficient swimmers. Africans learned to swim at an earlier age and surely with more positive reinforcement. These children were certainly catching waves.

Later accounts are unambiguous. In 1834, while at Accra, James Alexander wrote: "From the beach, meanwhile, might be seen boys swimming into the sea, with light boards under their stomachs. They waited for a surf; and came rolling like a cloud on top of it. But I was told that sharks occasionally dart in behind the rocks and 'yam' them."[28] In 1861, Thomas Hutchinson observed surfing in southern Cameroon. Fishermen rode small dugouts "no more than six feet in length, fourteen to sixteen inches in width, and from four to six inches in depth." Describing how work turned into play, Hutchinson penned:

During my few days stay at Batanga, I observed that from the more serious and industrial occupation of fishing they would turn to racing on the tops of the surging billows which broke on the sea shore; at one spot more particularly, which, owing to the presence of an extensive reef, seemed to be the very place for a continuous swell of several hundred yards in length. Four or six of them go out steadily, dodging the rollers as they come on, and mounting atop of them with the nimbleness and security of ducks. Reaching the outermost roller, they turn the canoes stems shoreward with a single stroke of the paddle, and mounted on the top of the wave, they are borne towards the shore, steering with the paddle alone. . . . Sometimes the steerer loses the balance of his guiding power; the canoe is turned over; its occupant is washed out. . . .

Yet despite . . . these immersions, no one is ever drowned, as they are capital swimmers—indeed, like the majority of the coastal negroes, they may be reckoned amphibious.

In their piscatorial excursions, it sometimes happens that a prowling shark, tempted to pursue the fish which the fisherman is hauling on the line, comes within sight of the larger bait of the negro leg and chops it off without remorse. A case of this kind has happened a very short time before the period of my visit, and the poor victim had died; but this did not diminish the number of canoes riding waves, nor render one of the canoe occupants less energetic or daring than before.[29]

Alexander and Hutchinson document Africans' passion for surfing. Like many Hawaiian surfers, the Africans were ardent enough to enter waters known to contain sharks. Neither Alexander nor Hutchinson seemed aware of Oceanian surfing. However, their accounts anticipate the prose used by Mark Twain, Jack London, and others who described Hawaiian surfing.[30]

Surfing illustrates discrete understandings of marine environments and abilities to transform surf zones into social and cultural spaces. As surf conditions improved with shifting tides and changing winds, Cameroonian fishermen transitioned from work to play. Risking one's life in shark-infested waters surely enhanced one's honor and masculinity. Refusing to surf could blemish one's manhood, compelling compatriots to disparage those who refused as unmanly or feminine.[31]

Coastscapes and riverbanks were cultural frontiers. They tested mettle, as frontiers do, and they were not cultural peripheries and social margins. Greg Dening's theoretical model of Marquesan cultural exchanges with Westerners in *Islands and Beaches* elucidates these liminal experiences. The Marquesas Islands provided "cultural worlds," where "signs that expressed institutions and roles were very particular." Beaches were narrow "cultural boundaries" around the Marquesas Islands and individuals, affording room for contact and interaction. They were structureless places between cultural frontiers, providing liminal experiences as people shifted from one stage to another in their lives. African coastscapes similarly provided settings for cultural interactions between Africans and Westerners.[32]

Seasides and riversides were transnational "contact zones." Aquatics situated African youth at the vanguard of this interplay, making them among the first to spy strange white-winged birds skimming the horizon and pale creatures emerging from the sea. As Europeans became familiar sights, swimming and surfing children surely looked shoreward at these white men, learning these travelers' habits, and interacting with them. Coastal populations reflected evolving cross-cultural dynamics as they became home to growing numbers of multiracial children.[33]

Surf breaking in the long shadows of African slave castles has long been a place of cultural interaction that provided lessons of the world. Here, the miseries and pleasures of the sea intertwined as the Atlantic slave trade unfolded within play spaces. Throngs of swimming and surfing youth parted for canoes carrying captives to awaiting slavers, their laughter striking sharply against slaves' lamentations. Shoreward glances inevitably fell upon looming slave castles. Slavers dominated their seaward gaze. The bodies of jettisoned slaves that washed into recreational spaces brought this business into acute perspective.

People venturing from Europe understood that the swimming dexterities of darker-complexioned people surpassed their own. Joseph Banks marveled at "ten or twelve" Tahitian boys riding breakers "impossible for any European boat to have lived in; and if the best swimmer in Europe had, by accident, been exposed to its fury, I am confident that he would not have been able to preserve himself." African surf was equally terrifying. As Warren Henry approached Sierra Leone, he pled, in his best " 'pidgin' English," for canoemen to take care, exclaiming: "I know savvy swim." Later he lamented the dearth of calm waters for Englishmen to cool off in, saying, "We could frolic on the fringe of the surf, but not being born that way, could never go so far as to swim in it."[34] Play spaces too dangerous for white men remained places of excitement, learning, and memory for Africans and Oceanians.

Play for all children is more than just play: it allows youth to absorb societal values, as each generation internalizes inherited practices. Water-scapes provided settings for developing social skills, crafting a sense of group cohesion, and enhancing real-world aptitudes like leadership, responsibility, and loyalty. Brinch documented this socialization process. He and "thirteen of my comrades" swam in the Niger, where, a "perfect union prevailed; all had a noble emulation to excell in the delightful sport before us; we plunged into the stream, dove, swam, sported and played in the current; all striving to excell in feats of activity." Brinch also illustrates how swimming was conveyed to the Americas, as he and his swim-mates were kidnapped into bondage.[35]

Scholars have considered how slave ships provided cultural spaces where captives of different ethnicities shared traditions.[36] Swimming abili-ties and desire for freedom were among the first traits that many realized they shared. Presumably using multilingualism, hand gestures, or lingua francas, diverse peoples devised escape plans. Many did not regain shore. Those who did were undoubtedly re-enslaved by waterside peoples.

Slaves frequently took to the water during attempts to resecure freedom. Many leapt from canoes while heading toward the coast.[37] Men and women similarly jumped from slave ships lying offshore.[38] English sailors learned that most Calabar and Cross Rivers people were "expert swimmers the women as well as the men." Assuming women could not swim, they only shackled the men "to prevent them from swimming ashore." Before "we got out of ye River, 3 or 4 of them shew'd us how well they could swim, & gave us the ye slip. tho' we took one of them again, that could not shift so well as ye rest, being big with child."[39]

By accident and design, some slave traders used sharks to deter deser-tion. Slavers chummed the waters with human waste and the bodies of jettisoned dead and dying Africans, swelling shark populations. In many places, it was said that sharks attacked living and dead bodies the moment they parted coastal and littoral water.[40]

Sharks are "the invariable outriders of all slave ships crossing the Atlan-tic," wrote Herman Melville, "systematically trotting alongside, to be handy in case a parcel is to be carried anywhere, or a dead slave to be decently buried." They had good reason. As slave trader Richard Drake crossed the Atlantic, sharks trailed "as if they smelt the sickness." He noted the *Boa Morte*, or *Good Death*, "has been feeding the sharks with corpses for seven days past."[41]

Predation discouraged attempts to regain shore. William Snelgrave reported that after sharks "tore" two Africans "to pieces" while swimming ashore, the balance of his cargo became "very quiet," deterring subsequent escape attempts.[42] Some slavers deliberately attracted sharks by trolling living and dead Africans through the brine, as reported by an anonymous purveyor: "Our way to entice them was by Towing overboard a dead Negro, which they would follow till they had eaten him up." In this manner, Westerners unknowingly used African spiritual beliefs to deter passages to freedom. Those who believed sharks were deities had to consider if they would permit them to pass. No matter how pure one judged himself, spiritual convictions probably discouraged most.[43] Still some preferred sharks to bondage. As sailors from the Spanish slaver *Dianna* battled with a British warship in the Bony River, "many of our slaves," some of whom were probably Kalabari, "jumped overboard, into the jaws of sharks."[44]

Suicide could serve as a form of resistance, but it was more complex.[45] Slave-trading records document self-drowning, which must not be misinterpreted as evidence of swimming inabilities. In the absence of physical paths to liberty, suicide afforded spiritual passages. Many believed water was a sacred space and the realm of the dead lay at the bottom of the ocean or across a large body of water. To reach this realm, one crossed what scholars call the *Kalunga*—a watery divide between the here-and-now and the spirit world. Drowning funneled souls into channels of repatriation as water guided them home toward rebirth.[46]

The slave trade imposed a high rate of suffering on captives, resulting in elevated suicide rates. Knowing many preferred self-drowning because it facilitated repatriation, slavers encircled ship's decks with netting to prevent captives from leaping overboard.[47] Suicidal actions indicate that bondpeople were embarking on transcendental voyages. One sailor reported that a man who leapt overboard "went down as if exulting that he got away." As sailors in a boat pursued another, he "made signs which it is impossible for me to describe in words, expressive of the happiness he had in escaping from us." Likewise, when a slave-ship revolt was squelched wounded captives jumped to their deaths in "seeming chearfulness."[48]

It would be exceedingly difficult for swimmers to drown themselves, as Barbot learned from a woman exported through Akwamu. She leapt overboard at sea and it took over half an hour to pull her out. During this time, she "had done everything she could to make herself drown, but that she had not been able to succeed in this, nature obstructing her destruction and making her, in spite of herself, employ her swimming ability."[49]

Swimming becomes virtually intuitive, compelling captives to determine how to drown themselves. The most practical way was to dive deep and exhale, passing out before instinctively resurfacing.[50] Accounts indicate slaves did just this. Peter Blake recorded how one Gold Coast captive loaded at Winneba descended to death. On April 17, 1675, a "stout manslave" "Leaped Overboard & drowned himself." A ship's boat overtook him as "hee sunke downe Also my Cockswain runn down his oare Between his Arms but hee would not take hould of it & soe drowned himselfe." Likewise, in 1737 "above one hundred Men Slaves jump'd" off the *Prince of Orange* while anchored at St. Kitts. Thirty-three "would not endeavor to save themselves, but resolved to die, and sunk directly down."[51]

Others drowned themselves in the Americas. During the 1830s, a St. Vincent slaveholder transported a fugitive in a canoe. To prevent him from swimming away, a "heavy weight" was attached to an "iron collar." Yet, he did not want to swim. He "seized as he conceived, a favorable moment for escape, and leapt into the waves" to be "sucked into the vortex." The "momentary bubble of water announced that an immortal spirit was struggling to be free."[52]

The deaths of *Amistad* bondman Foone and Ibo Landing captives conform to this pattern. All the Mende slaves taken from the *Amistad* were "expert swimmers." After three years in America and believing he would "never see his wife & child," a depressed Foone walked into the calm waters of Pitkin Basin, Connecticut, and drowned himself. Seizing control of his destiny, Foone returned home.[53]

Ibo Landing captives apparently repatriated themselves. In 1803, Pierce Butler purchased several Ibo slaves. As they were shipped by three whites from Savannah to St. Simons Island, Georgia, the bondpeople "rose." The white men jumped overboard and "drowned." The Ibo "took to the Marsh" where "at least ten or twelve" apparently drowned themselves.[54]

Along with walking and talking, swimming was one of the easiest capacities to transport to the Americas, where abundant waterscapes provided arenas for recreating and reimagining aquatics, permitting captives to transpose African meanings upon the waters of the Western Hemisphere. It has been assumed that New World slaveholders discouraged swimming, as it could facilitate escape, and that they used water tortures to make captives afraid of water.[55] Some slaveholders prohibited slaves from learning "the art of swimming," as Solomon Northup discovered when kidnapped into Louisianan bondage. Alabama bondwoman Annie Davis explained how her owner attempted to beat aquatic desires from her body when he "took a bunch of willow switches" and gave her a "good tanning." Regardless, water was rarely incorporated into punishments, as it required elaborate contraptions, though it was occasionally used. In seventeenth-century Jamaica, white and black prostitutes were "carried to the ducking stole," to be dunked "six times." Some nineteenth-century St. Vincent slaveholders used "the immersions into tubs of water with the head downwards" as punishment. One especially sadistic planter placed a bondman into a barrel "the lid of which being closed down,—the sides were in a like manner pierced with sharp nails driven inwards." The barrel "was rolled down a precipice! {into the ocean}." Still, aquatic pleasures outweighed fears of drowning and physical punishment, as Caribbean and North American captives continued to swim. Indeed, Davis proclaimed, "every chance I got and no one around I went in the water."[56]

Country-born slaves throughout the Americas probably began learning to swim between two and four years of age. Many children roughly seven to twelve years old were strong swimmers, indicating they learned several years prior. For example, one of the first sights that greeted John Stedman's eyes as he entered the Suriname River was "groups of naked boys and girls promiscuously playing and flouncing, like many *Tritons* and *Mermaids*." Near Frederick Douglass's boyhood home "was a creek to swim in, . . . a very beautiful play-ground for the children." Likewise, John Washington recollected how the Rappahannock River was the favorite clandestine play spot for Virginian youth. They slipped off "to the river to play with some boat or other which I could always get or swim." Once they hurried, nude from the water, when a boy "cried out here comes the Overseer!" Unfortunately, they found refuge in "Pison Oak," paying a steep price for their adventures.[57]

As in Atlantic Africa, youth enslaved in the Americas witnessed the horrors of the Atlantic slave trade while engaged in aquatic play. The "*Tritons and Mermaids*" Stedman documented saw and smelled slavers ascending the Suriname River. The bodies of dead slaves tossed into harbors bobbed through play spaces as currents and tides carried them seaward. Dying Africans dumped overboard by slavers seeking to avoid import duties on humans that might not survive long enough to be sold possibly floundered past. Spectacles of the trade were not confined to seaports. Youth swimming in coastal waters and rivers saw captives deposited onto plantation landings or discarded overboard.[58]

Water provided many with Old and New World perspectives on aquatic play and the slave trade. Aquatics placed many African youth in isolated positions where some were enslaved.[59] While scholarship overlooks how enslaved youth transmitted traditions, they certainly brought aquatic games.[60]

Eighteenth- and nineteenth-century plantation slavery was "one of history's greatest episodes of destruction," as public exhibitions of brutality intimidated captives and economic systems consumed bondpeople at alarming rates. From the water, youth witnessed magisterial displays of human destruction played out along the waterfront. Captives fitted with medieval-like contraptions of corporal punishment tottered about while saltwater slaves bound for market were paraded past the mutilated bodies of executed recalcitrants hung on display.[61] In play, children were reminded of the adult lives awaiting them.

Parents, family members, and communities taught children to swim, just as they instructed them to procure food, cook, and emotionally and psychologically thrive in the heartless world of bondage. To facilitate communication and the shipment of slave-produced commodities to market, most plantations were situated on or near navigable waters that enticed children. Since swimming could prevent drowning, this was surely a skill parents imparted.[62]

For those subjected to New World bondage, aquatics seemingly took on new meanings, becoming a cultural marker and form of cultural resilience and resistance. Captives possibly regarded swimming as an ethnic marker and perhaps a characteristic in their new "African" identities forced upon them, distinguishing captives from their poor-swimming enslavers. Recent scholarship considers how African-descended peoples increasingly developed racial identities, perceiving themselves as "African," "Negro," or "black," transforming this new collective identity into a "source of pride and unity for the diverse victims of the Atlantic slave trade."[63] African martial arts "were living traditions" for many. Each ethnic group maintained discrete styles of fighting that yielded to synthesized "African" or "slave" forms of fighting distinct from the "gouging" or "rough-and-tumble" techniques of white Southerners. These styles provided members of ethnic groups and bonded communities with a sense of pride when their fighters defeated opponents in bouts organized by slaves or slaveholders. Ethnic groups did not seemingly develop discrete swim styles. Still, in relation to high rates of white drowning, slaves conceivably perceived their aquatic fluencies as an "African" cultural marker and a source of group pride, while drowning was deemed dishonorable.[64]

Slaves became strong swimmers despite the impositions of bondage. After fundamentals were learned, children's swimming skills improved through observation and advice. While parents were laboring, elderly slaves looked after many children, possibly providing shoreside instructions.[65] During harvesting season, most sugar-producing Latin American and Caribbean slaves were only permitted three to five hours of sleep a day. Still, most were adroit. During the 1760s, Christian Oldendorp believed Caribbean captives rivaled Africans, writing: "The Negroes are quite adept at swimming and dancing. As slaves, they do not have as much free time or enough opportunity to practice the first of these, as do the Negroes in Guinea. In spite of this, however, there are also excellent swimmers among the West Indian Negroes."[66]

Temperate waters did not discourage those in cooler climes. The waters of the American South, and especially of the North, could remain cold even during summer. For instance, Solomon Northup learned to "become an expert swimmer" in upstate New York's chilly waters. Free and enslaved Bermudians learned while cutting through the archipelago's temperate waters, enabling them to save themselves during maritime accidents. In 1701, a "Mulatto man, named Stavo" was washed overboard, run over, and would have "drowned, had he not been a good swimmer, for he swam, as we judged, three-quarters of a mile" through cold rough seas to regain the vessel.[67] It is assumed that black Bermudians did not maintain African traditions. Swimming seemingly served an outpost of African influence in the middle of the Atlantic, providing white Bermudians and Bahamians with traditions most whites did not possesses elsewhere in the Atlantic.[68]

Accounts signify that most captives could swim well enough to cross bodies of water and keep themselves afloat after maritime accidents. Francis Fedric, who was enslaved in Virginia and Kentucky during the mid-1800s, reported: "Unlike most slaves, I never learned to swim." When Robert Walsh traversed Brazil in 1828 and 1829, he labeled captives "amphibious," while reporting "white men are very rarely seen in the water."[69]

Many African- and country-born bondwomen were experts capable of out-swimming bondmen. Standards of modesty in the American South seemingly constrained adult women. Caribbean and Latin American slaves maintained many African mores. Consequently, most bondwomen probably faced little stigma when swimming nude. Stedman noted that Guianese adolescents swam "promiscuously, in groups of boys and girls, and both sexes exhibit astonishing feats of courage, strength and activity. I have not only seen a negro girl beat a hardy youth in swimming across the River Comewina (while I was in the party) but on landing challenge him to run a two mile race, and beat him again, naked as they were; while all ideas of shame on the one side and of insult on the other, are totally unknown."[70]

Learning to swim reduced drowning rates; still, mishaps occurred.[71] When captives drowned, others swam to recover their bodies. One July morning, William Still and other enslaved boys were playing in Spring Creek, Alabama. At some point, William went missing. The boys ran to get adults. "A crowd of men and boys hastened to the creek; and after diving for some time, they found him at the bottom." Likewise, a North Carolina bondman "refused to submit" to being whipped and ran into the woods. The overseer "set the hounds after him," driving him into a millpond where he drowned. "A fellow slave . . . swam in, and diving to the bottom, he found him, took hold of his clothes in his teeth, and brought him to the shore."[72]

Swimming was part of the daily milieu in which the sights, sounds, smells, and flavors reflected those of African waterside communities. Waterways afforded space for merging terrestrial and aquatic activities into amphibious culturescapes, and merging old and new aquatic worlds. The sights and sounds of children's and adults' afternoon swims merged with the thump of rice being milled, while the aromas of African-influenced seafood dishes wafted over slave quarters, which often resembled the built and social environments of African villages.[73]

In 1918, Annette Kellerman encouraged Americans to swim, penning: "For the woman who swelters in her kitchen or lolls in a drawing room, for the man who sits half his life in an office chair, an occasional swim does as much good as six months' vacation. That weary feeling goes away for once in the cool, quiet water. Tired men and tired women forget that stocks and cakes have fallen."[74]

Slaves understood the cathartic pleasures of sliding into the drink long before Kellerman lifted her pen. A brief plunge was often the only release for overtaxed muscles. When George Pinckard was in Dutch Guiana, he observed canoemen paddling upward of fourteen hours a day. After paddling "from half-past eight in the morning until seven in the evening," they became "extremely heated" and were permitted to "rest, occasionally for a few minutes." During respites, "they plunged from the side of the boat into the river, and swam about in order to cool themselves, and drive away fatigue."[75] Whites believed that, like beasts of burden, Africans were rejuvenated by these quick immersions during which they distracted their simplistic minds. Swimming could not dissolve daily abuses; yet, it afforded ephemeral relief.

Even as bondage constrained captives' ability to enjoy life and slaveholders transformed their bodies into edifices of suffering, bondpeople "worked hard to make their bodies spaces of personal expression and pleasure." Violating rules and laws, they took their bodies to unsanctioned parties, religious functions, and other communal spaces. "Enslaved partygoers had a common commitment to delight in their bodies, to display their physical skill, to master their bodies through competition with others, and to express their creativity."[76] Swimming offered similar pleasures; a way to demonstrate agility, strength, and stamina; a method for inventively expressing personal and group identities; and a means for subverting slaveholders' control.

Swimming equally allowed family members living on separate slaveholdings to visit each other, with or without their owners' approval. Richard, a Louisiana husband in an away-marriage, "would slip off" and paddle or swim across the bayou to see his wife, Betty. His enraged owner "told the patrollers every time they caught Richard on the plantation where Betty lived to beat him half to death. The patrollers had caught Richard many times, and had beat him mighty bad." Still he swam.[77]

Bondpeople ameliorated their grim circumstances by incorporating recreational swimming into beach cultures long before suntanning whites socialized in the sand. "We wucked in de fie'ls from sunup ter sundown mos' o' de time, but we had a couple of hours at dinner time ter swim or lay on de banks uv de little crick an' sleep," recalled Bill Crump of North Carolina. During a visit to Jamaica, Theodore Foulks saw bondpeople lounging on the beach with "others refreshing themselves by swimming in the tepid water."[78]

Captives similarly merged swimming and bathing, socializing as they scrubbed the filth of terrestrial labor from their exploited bodies. During late afternoons, they slipped into the water to cool off, relax, and wash away the day's troubles. While in British Guiana during the 1770s, John Stedman reported that swimming was slaves' "favorite diversion, which they practice every day at least twice or thrice."[79] George Pinckard equally observed the recreational aquatics of a Barbadian merge with his pursuit of cleanliness, saying he

> was amusing himself by exercises of uncommon agility in the sea. Not an otter, nor a beaver, nor scarcely a dolphin could appear more in his element. He was quite at play in the water, and diverting himself in all kinds of antic tricks, and gambols. He dived to the bottom—swam in a variety of ways—walked or paddled along like a dog—concealed himself for a long time under water—laid himself at rest upon the surface, and appeared as much at his ease, in the ocean, as if he had never breathed a lighter, nor trodden a firmer element.
>
> This expertness is much derived from an early habit of bathing, or, as it might be termed, exercising in the water.[80]

Hygienic waters were apparently gender segregated. Pinckard suggested that Barbadian men and women bathed at discrete "sea, or river" beaches. In 1823, Cynric Williams and fellow voyeurs ogled some twenty African-born women as they bathed and conversed in Turtle Crawl River, Jamaica.[81]

Hygienic swimming could promote socialization across the boundaries of race and bondage. When Stedman asked an old African-born slave named Caramaca how he maintained his health in Guiana's tropical-disease–prone environment, Caramaca replied, "Swimm every day twice or thrice, . . . This Masera, not only serves for exercise . . . but also keeps the skin clean and cool; and the pores being open, I enjoy free perspiration. Without this, by imperceptible filth, the pores are shut, the juices stagnate, and disease must invariably follow."[82]

Immersionary traditions transformed swimming into cultural markers for many Atlantic Africans, providing methods for understanding and conceptualizing waterscapes. Parents inculcated this means of self-preservation into children at a young age. As aquatics were integrated into work and recreation, experiential connections to water increased over one's lifetime. Swimming was included in some societies' judicial processes, while men used it to assert masculinity and honor.

Aquatic Sports and Performance Rituals: Gender, Bravery, and Honor

Accounts indicate that Africans carried not only swimming abilities but also a sense of competitive aquatics to the Americas, where these activities remained tied to deeper concepts of honor and masculinity. Swimming has long been a way for men and women to convert themselves into heroes. In art and literature, we find ancient warriors swimming into battle. Returning from Troy, Odysseus swam for three days through storm-swept seas stirred up by a wrathful Poseidon. For seven days, Beowulf and Breca raced across wintry seas battling demons. Swimming and surfing were central in Oceanian creation stories and are the fabric upon which the poetry, chants, legends, and proverbs of Oceania are written. Aquatics were equally woven into the folklore and legends of Amerindians and Aboriginal Australians.[1] Likewise, African-descended men swam for honor by engaging in ritualized aquatic blood sports when fighting crocodiles, sharks, and hippopotami, which permitted men to demonstrate aptitude, bravery, strength, and masculinity.

Historian John Iliffe proposes a minimalist definition of honor "stripped of cultural specificity and designed for cross-cultural comparison," characterizing honor as "a right to respect." Notions of honor have varied across time and place, yet in most societies the vortex of masculine honor pivoted on bravery, courage, strength, and prestige. Individuals could articulate honor through boasts of prowess reaffirmed by those of higher status. Societies eulogized honor through praise songs, poems, titles, and folklore.[2]

It has been argued that similar concepts of manhood have been imposed on males across cultural boundaries, allowing for cross-cultural considerations of masculinity. Societies typically erected boundaries around manhood, requiring boys to undergo a rite of passage. After attained, masculinity was routinely reaffirmed among peers and superiors; hence one's capacity to exist was publicly determined in self-empowering rituals, lest men were derided as "unmanly," "emasculate," or "effeminate."[3]

Water provided settings for Africans to attain and maintain honor and manhood while fighting marine animals that terrified most Westerners. Jean Baptiste Labat observed that "Negroes will venture to attack [a croco-dile] if he be in shallow Water: For this Purpose they wrap a piece of Ox-Hide about their left Arm, and taking a Bayonet, or Assagaye, in their right Hand," stabbed crocodiles in the eye or throat. A man near the fort at Saint-Louis on the Senegal River made "it his daily Exercise to engage these Animals wherever he saw them."[4]

Courage was equally exhibited while fighting sharks. Jacques Joseph Lemaire recorded how men killed sharks near the surface, saying, "As he turns on his Side, they dive underneath, and cut open his Belly." In Sierra Leone, the Bullom, and apparently others, fought "ground-sharks," which were possibly bull and tiger sharks. Likewise, "Fishmen" attacked "a shark in the water without hesitation."[5] "Fishmen" was a nineteenth-century Western designation for maritime peoples along the coast of Liberia and the Ivory Coast. According to one Englishman, "There are two grand divisions of native Africans on the Western Coast, the Fishmen and Bushmen; the latter being inhabitants of the interior; and the former comprising all the tribes along the sea-shore, who gain a substance by fishing, trading between the Bushmen and foreign vessels and laboring on shipboard."[6]

Others fought hippopotamuses, which are among the most dangerous animals to humans. Canoe-borne hunters sometimes harpooned hippopot-amuses, which dragged their boats as sperm whales pulled whalers on what were called "Nantucket Sleigh Rides." The exhausted hippos were easier to kill. Some capsized dugouts. To avoid being killed, hunters would dive "to the bottom of the river, and grasp a stone, a root, or anything that will keep them below the surface, and hold on as long as their lungs will allow them." When the hippopotamus "makes off," the hunters would emerge "half drowned." Some hunters swam into battle. Samuel Baker watched two men swim across a river to harpoon a bull hippopotamus basking on an islet. Submerging until a few feet from the hippopotamus, they rose and "hurled

Figure 4. "Negro Method of Attacking the Crocodile." This image illustrates how a man near the fort at Saint–Louis on the Senegal River frequently killed crocodiles to apparently showcase his strength, courage, and masculinity, affording him honor and respect. Wrapping a piece of leather around his left arm, he lured crocodiles close to stab them in the eye or throat. Frederic Shobel, *The World in Miniature; Africa, Containing a Description of the Manners and Customs, with Some Historical Particulars of the Moors of the Zahara, and of the Nations Between the Rivers Senegal and Gambia* (London: 1821); opposite 165. Author's collection.

their harpoons, and swimming for some distance under water, they came to the surface and hastened to the shore least an infuriated hippopotamus should follow them."[7]

If isolated from their social contexts, aquatic blood sports might be narrowly seen as unrelated moments that do not inform our understandings of African cultures. But these contests probably fulfilled many of the same functions as other performance rituals. While many frays were impromptu, some were apparently well-attended community events that promoted group cohesion and solidarity.[8]

These aquatic exhibitions conceivably functioned as rites of passage, marking the transition into adulthood, very much as manhood might be proven through warfare or wrestling or martial arts matches. Adults probably also used them to advance their status. Accounts do not illustrate how

Figure 5. Harpooning a Hippopotamus. This image is based on the observations of Samuel White Baker while he was exploring Central Africa. Africans and Europeans considered hippopotamus meat a delicacy. The hunters used their swimming skills to impress Baker, who watched from the safety of shore as the two men swam underwater until close enough to harpoon the herd's bull. The men then swam underwater to a safe distance. Once the hippopotamus tired itself out by dragging a buoy, hunters killed it with lances. Bayard Taylor, ed., *The Lake Regions of Central Africa* (New York: 1874); opposite 337. Author's collection.

aquatic battles were perceived, though victors were surely praised in poetry and song. Male honor was bound to heroism. Because these marine creatures posed a threat to humans and livestock, their destruction could have been seen as heroic acts.[9]

Aquatics probably permitted males to form intimate bonds as they reflected on maritime duels, connecting their deeds and those of community members to those of their ancestors. While defining themselves as individuals, men coalesced with their communities, uniting society members through shared rituals and beliefs. Waterscapes afforded platforms for bonding among members of the same clan, lineage, age, and ethnic group.[10]

Aquatic acumen surely elevated one's status. Competitive activities were a form of social selection that influenced a "boys' emergence as a leader." Champions often became family and community representatives. Parents lauded sons' achievements, preparing them for bouts by providing costumes, training, and special food. Aquatics offered similar functions. Boyrereau Brinch's parents "delighted in [his] vivacity and agility," which made him a peer leader. During match preparations, adolescents were adorned with some "conspicuous ornament of their father." Brinch's father, "with the Austerity of a Judge, tenderly took [him] by the hand, and said, my son conduct yourself worthy of me, and here you shall wear my cap," while his "brothers and sisters all assisted to ornament [him] and give [him] advice."[11]

Many societies divided the physical world into "the cultivated, built sphere made by people and the wilderness where mighty forces and untamable creatures reigned." Humans recognized the symbiotic relationship of these two environments. Manhood was pursued in wild, sacred regions when engaging in warfare, long-distance trade, and hunting. Aquatics probably afforded similar opportunities as those in the wilderness.[12]

In addition to these cultural functions, aquatic battles surely strengthened bonds to water deities. It has been conjectured that wrestling matches fulfilled spiritual functions related to agriculture. They often transpired in parched fields during dry seasons. Young, sexually potent wrestlers invigorated the earth, assisting priests and rainmakers in invoking natural and divine forces to enrich the soil and produce robust yields. Water people conceivably used blood sports to precipitate successful fishing, commercial voyages, and naval warfare.[13]

Female honor was typically attained through motherhood, agriculture, and trade. Societies in West-Central Africa, Bight of Benin, and Bight of Biafra honored female wrestlers and warriors. In Dahomey, women could exchange the honors of motherhood for those of a warrior, receiving honor from kings who praised their valor, devotion, and other capacities by awarding honorific necklaces, batons, shields, titles, and ranks.[14] Similar respect was seemingly extended to women who fought crocodiles with their scars visually proclaiming their right to honor.

Women do not seem to have willingly fought crocodiles, yet women and men learned to escape their jaws. On the Upper Congo, John Weeks encountered many fisherwomen bearing scars from crocodile attacks. When asked how they escaped, the "invariable" response was "I rammed my thumbs into its eyes." These battles and the related scars probably afforded women with honors similar to battlefield scars and those received during rites of passage. Community members knew one "needed great presence of mind" and strength to escape. Once free, they had to regain land before attacks were renewed.[15]

New World slaves similarly conjoined swimming and ritualized duels when fighting sharks, alligators, crocodiles, and manta rays. For instance, Stedman reported that Guianan slaves "attack and vanquish the alligator in his own element, notwithstanding his violent strength and unequalled ferocity, being particularly fond of human flesh."[16] Some slaves leapt on to the backs of manta rays—harmless creatures that Westerners had misperceived and dubbed as "devil rays" and "vampire[s] of the ocean—to impale them with harpoons before swimming back to a boat. Off Kingston, Jamaica, bondmen harpooned rays "after the manner practiced in the whale fisheries" and were "towed out some ways to sea." During the mid-eighteenth century, May, a saltwater captive enslaved on Parris Island, South Carolina, leapt upon a ray's back to put the "whole weight of his body to the force of the [harpoon] stroke," before swimming to the boat. William Elliott III described his grandfather's prized captive, exclaiming: "Had he belonged to the Saxon or Norman race, he had probably been knighted, and allowed to quarter on his shield the horns of the devil-fish, in token of his exploit!"[17]

In another performance ritual, they fought sharks. Describing a 1784 journey to Bermuda, Jean Hector St. John Crèvecoeur, a French-American writer, exclaimed: "There are perhaps no better swimmers, I have seen them display enough ability, coolness and audacity to attack sharks while swimming and to kill them with their knives." Likewise, in 1790, an anonymous traveler to the Caribbean penned: "Negroes have been known daring enough to go into the water, in order to give battle to a shark, and have returned victorious, towing their adversary." The chronicler was so overwhelmed, he bemoaned the demise of slavery, saying: "If they can go into an unnatural element, in quest of hideous monsters, for the sport of engaging with them, it will leave us to wonder at their submission to the yoke of slavery; to wonder that ever a rebellion can be suppressed; to wonder they do not prefer the gallows and the gibbet to the hoe and the whip."[18]

White people had mixed perceptions of aquatic clashes, which were informed by Western perceptions of water. Many were terrified of marine animals. Describing South Carolina's environment in 1769, a poet wrote: "Frightful creatures in the water / Porpoises, sharks and alligators." Historian Alain Corbin captured European fears, penning: "The ocean, that water monsters' den, was a damned world in whose darkness the accursed creatures devoured one another" and anyone who ventured into it.[19] Some whites perceived blood sport as primordial battles between man and nature, in which man prevailed, even if that man was deemed inferior, as Janet Schaw illustrated. Africans respected but were not terrified of crocodiles, which were more dangerous than alligators. When Schaw visited Wilmington, North Carolina, in 1775, she watched three bondmen kill an alligator. Inflating the alligator's destructive capabilities, she claimed it had "such a pair of jaws as might have admitted if not a Highland cow, at least a Lowland calf" and "is covered with a coat of Mail." Schaw, who had an unfavorable view of Africans, praised these slaves, saying: "The superior arts of man are more than a match for his amazing strength. Was superior reason never used to a more unworthy purpose."[20]

Whites applauded slaves' daring and strength at one level, while their race and status in white-dominated societies precluded their right to honor. Whites did not provide slaves with vertical honor used to elevate social standing in African and Western societies. The only time most whites exhibited any deference was when slaves restored their honor. Schaw viewed the alligator's destruction as "revenge" for eating "many a good goose" "stolen from her." Likewise, May was praised for killing a manta ray and restoring Elliott's honor, which the ray had assailed when it inadvertently damaged his docks, deemed a "bold invasion" upon his "landmarks." Still, slavery disrespected and dishonored May and his descendants.[21]

Most white people did not believe aquatic clashes demonstrated black bravery. Bravery hinged upon virtue, intellect, and reason; traits nonwhites purportedly lacked. Instead, African swimming and aquatic battles were deemed proof of animal-like savagery: that primitive people were unafraid of primitive creatures. Thomas Jefferson provided pseudo-scientific evidence that supported views on black bravery, writing: "They are at least as brave, and more adventuresome. But this may perhaps proceed from a want of forethought, which prevents their seeing a danger till it be present." This enabled whites to recast African bravery as instinctive ferocity, like that of a lion, not courage, as John Lawson illustrated. Arriving in what is now South Carolina in 1700, Lawson said: "Some Negro's, and others, that can swim and dive well, go naked into the Water, with a Knife in their Hand, and fight the Shark, and very commonly kill him, or wound him so, that he turns Tail, and runs away." To ensure that his readers did not conclude that these men were brave, Lawson averred that Africans were "savage, cruel, and . . . cowardly." In addition, whites minimized the dangers aquatic creatures presented to Africans by claiming that, unlike white people, black people have high, animal-like thresholds of pain. Hence, true virtuous bravery remained the domain of whites who downplayed threats to bondage that filled the anonymous Caribbean sojourner with distress.[22]

Likewise, Henry Stanley used racialized language to diminish the abilities of the inadequately fed African members of his West-Central African expedition. While chasing an antelope that had jumped into a river, the porters followed, so the river was quickly "dotted with the heads of the frantic swimmers." Stanley portrayed them as "savage men" and "madmen" unaware of the dangers their purported ignorance subjected them to. As if the perils of water were not great enough, Stanley claimed myopic imperceptions blinded them to the "poisoned arrow, the razor sharp spear, and the pot" of lurking cannibal. Always eager to portray himself as the great white hero, Stanley claimed the men "must assuredly have been drowned" due to their lack of forethought had he not dispatched canoes to rescue the "tired swimmers." Thus, what might have been the valiant feat of desperate white men was deemed savage African imprudence.[23]

Crèvecoeur offered a slightly more positive interpretation. He saw Bermudian shark-killers as civilized savages, "a race of men long since refined not only by their stay on this island but by education that they have received from their Masters." Despite these praises, he, like others, assumed Africans were uncivilized, and adopted the assertion of proslavery ideologues that bondage refined brutes by exposing them to the civilizing graces of Western culture.[24]

Blood sports also conformed to white perceptions of the barbaric diversions suitable for inferior peoples. As Douglass explained, even though slaves excelled in what were considered civilized sports, like horse racing and boxing, "everything like rational enjoyment was frowned upon, and only those wild and low sports peculiar to semi-civilized people were encouraged." Blood sports reaffirmed Africans' purported savagery, supporting Western racial and social hierarchies, allowing white people to assert that Africans were adept in unsophisticated sports in an unnatural medium.[25] Water became a stage for watching the uncivilized sports of Africans, providing a prelude to the ethnological shows that reached their zenith during the early twentieth century.[26] Still, blood sports were not performed for white people's pleasure, and they seemingly expressed African valuations.

Many Africans in the Americas participated in competitive swimming activities constructed on African-developed skills. In Suriname, John

Stedman observed many sports and games played by African-born slaves. Today, terrestrial games, like soccer and basketball, dominate national and international sport. According to Stedman, swimming was more popular among saltwater captives than were land-bound athletics, suggesting that aquatics also held sway in Africa. He observed men "cudgel and wrestle; . . . Most are strong and active. But swimming is their favourite diversion."[27]

Recreated swimming traditions remained hollow without the cultural richness and resonance of aquatic rituals as performance tied to honor and other cultural values. Captives participated in swimming contests and blood sports that transformed waterscapes into stages for "community performance rituals." After laboring for their owners all day, captives pursued ways to assert their self-worth and community identities. Slaves participated in boxing bouts and foot and horse races on land and in canoe races in the water, among other rituals, that could enhance self-esteem, demonstrate athletic mastery, and strengthen communal solidarity. Aquatics were similarly entwined with social and cultural meaning and could be rigorous and exhausting rituals that permitted women and men to demonstrate skill, courage, and finesse to attain honor among captives.[28]

Concurrently, while blood sports and spectacle enforced bondpeople's community solidarity in these ways, slaveholders manipulated bondpeople's desire for natural human experiences to meet their own interests.[29] Many slave owners twisted sporting events so that slaves vented frustrations without threatening the stability of bondage. Frederick Douglass articulated how sport served slaveholders' interests by distracting bondpeople from the "thoughts and aspirations short of the liberty of which they are deprived . . . keeping the minds of the slaves occupied with prospective pleasure within the limits of slavery," while providing settings where the "great wrestler could win laurels." Enslavers believed sports were "safety-valves, to carry off the explosive elements inseparable from the human mind when reduced to the condition of slavery."[30]

Though athletics often occurred away from white supervision, some slaveholders organized slaves' recreational activities for their own ends. Some Barbadian planters staged swimming competitions for guests' amusement. During the 1640s, Richard Ligon observed a game in which some of the colony's first slaves caught a "*Mufcovia*" duck. The captor was awarded the duck. The proprietor of these "recreations," Colonel Drax, "called some of his best swimming *Negroes*, [and] commanded them to swim and take this Duck, but forbad them to dive, for if they were not bar'd that play" they could easily capture the waterfowl. Describing their use of the crawl, breaststroke, and backstroke, Ligon said, "in this chase there was much of pleasure, to see the various swimmings of the *Negroes*; some the ordinary ways, upon their bellies [like Europeans], some on their backs, some by striking out their right leg and left arm, and then turning on the other side, which is a stronger and swifter way of swimming, than any of the others." The winner was a "*Negro* maid" who was absent when the rules were announced. She "put off her peticoat behind a bush, that was at one end of the Pond, and closely sunk down into the water, and at one diving got to the Duck, pull'd her under water, and went back again the same way she came to the bush, all in one dive." The duck would have been taken from her and the game resumed, but Ligon, who was impressed by her expertise and nude lithe body, asked that she be allowed to keep her trophy, and his request was granted.[31]

Planters wagered large sums of money during prearranged, interplantation boxing matches and races, for which captives undoubtedly received benefits from their owners. To hedge wagers, planters relieved competitors of hard labor in the days preceding matches while feeding them better than the balance of their malnourished property. High-stakes gambling brought elite planters together and created venues where they, as a numerical minority, cemented their solidarity while expressing competitiveness.[32]

Even as these contests benefited slaveholders, they could provide slaves with community-building opportunities. Group cohesion was cultivated along the waterscapes where blood sports were waged as they were surely festive events accompanied by food, drink, music, and dance, which enabled community members to cheer favorites. Matches could surely be used to settle disputes and were thus a method for maintaining community harmony. Interplantation competitions allowed those from different estates to solidify discrete identities while simultaneously creating a broader sense of solidarity by framing bonds with captives on neighboring slaveholdings. When slaves organized contests, they defined themselves as a community, reconstructing "African-based community-forming and individual-empowering rituals" that extolled their sense of gender and honor.[33]

Stedman documented how captives recreated an aquatic game in waters that were simultaneously used for coed, multiracial interactions with Amerindians and Europeans. He came across "Indians and black people of both sexes swimming at the back of Fort Zelandia." Joining in, "Donald Mac Neyl and myself completed the group, by stripping and getting in among them; I must confess I never beheld more surprising feats of activity in the water, than were performed by the negroes, who fought a *sham battle*, by plunging or rather tumbling like porpoises, when they struck each other with their legs, as they never used their hands; while the Indians, who were of the *Arrowouka* nation, swam and dove like amphibious animals." These Africans possibly used the Essequibo River to resurrect a game once played in home-waters—a game conceivably learned from their parents and that they hoped to play with their children at the playground of their youth. This scene reflects cross-racial cultural exchanges, with Africans and Indians teaching each other games as Europeans emulated both. Most of the Africans were apparently members of the same ethnicity. Those of different backgrounds could use their fluencies to participate.[34]

Blood sports could be "working socials" that brought community members together to cooperatively labor for their owners and themselves. Under slaveholders' direction, bondmen removed alligators that burrowed into levees surrounding rice fields, weakening them and posing risk to field slaves. Captives transformed these tasks into communal festivities. Males socialized while destroying alligators. Gendered divisions of labor enabled females to become more than spectators at otherwise male-dominated events.[35]

Bondwomen's culinary creativity permitted them to reinforce communal and familial bonds while actively showcasing their expertise. Henry Rogers of Georgia exemplified gendered labor during working socials, saying: "When a neighbor's house needed covering he got the shingles and called in his neighbor and friends, who came along with their wives. While the men worked atop the house the women were cooking a delicious dinner down in the kitchen. At noon it was served amid much merry making. By sundown the house was finished and the friends went home happy in the memory of a day spent in toil freely given to one who needed it." Corn-shucking and log-rolling were similarly followed by a "good hot supper" and "perhaps a dance." Gendered labor pivoted on hunting, with males killing and females cooking game, and probably reflected circumstances surrounding blood sports. Alligator was a favorite among many. After males killed alligators and other creatures, women surely prepared them, perhaps incorporating them into African-inspired dishes that expressed and reaffirmed communal bonds.[36]

In this way, swimming matches could create a sense of cultural continuity. Upon New World waters, some competed in familiar African contests with those of the same ethnicity, speaking the same language, and under-standing particular games without having to define their parameters. Parti-cipants could imagine themselves on home waters with friends and family members, as spectators encouraged them from shore. When members of different ethnicities participated together, they probably felt the bonds of both African and New World communities of belonging tugging them toward old and new identities. Yet these were ephemeral moments that evaporated when shoreward glances revealed white spectators.[37]

Maritime blood sports, in particular, presented unique opportunities denied ashore. For example, slaveholders often choreographed boxing and wrestling matches, flaming passions with alcohol and insults and breaking up bouts when contestants faced dire injury. Aquatics were not, and could not, be as closely regulated, especially in the light of differences between blacks and whites in aquatic comfort and skill. Furthermore, planters do not seem to have attended blood matches. Planters' adolescent sons and white travelers chronicled most blood matches, with neither inclined to leap into the depths to halt a fight, lest they be eaten or drowned, as illus-trated by Robert Mallard, the son of a Georgia planter.[38] While a teenager, he witnessed slaves wade and swim into rice fields to wrestle alligators ashore, where awaiting bondpeople decapitated the alligators with axes. These battles were well-attended venues where Mallard and slaves, from the safety of rice-field levees, observed bondmen conspicuously showcasing their strength and bravery. Combatants' egos and reputations were surely inflated when white people expressed fear, as when Mallard, who was "somewhat callow," took "to a tree until assured that the decapitation was a success!"[39]

Scholars have asserted that slavery nullified bondmen's advantages of being men in patriarchal societies by refusing them the fruits of their labor, destroying marriages, and prohibiting them from publicly defending their honor and asserting their masculinity. Even as slavery sought to dishonor and disrespect them, captives maintained African-influenced honor codes and engaged in aquatic battles seemingly as one way to demonstrate community-recognized masculine honor.[40] Bondmen conjoined swimming and ritualized duels when fighting sharks, alligators, and manta rays. By expanding definitions of heroism to include African notions of "heroic honor," we can consider how bondmen maintained their cultural heritage and concepts of masculinity in the New World. Contests stressed the heroic qualities of prowess, brawn, and bravery. To exhibit fear precipitated dishonor and ridicule. Incompetence caused injury or death.[41] Slaves of differing ethnicities apparently shared concepts of honor that rewarded masculinity. Combatants left no room for one to challenge their claims to manhood and honor. Regardless of the place of origin of the saltwater captives, they surely respected those who killed these creatures.[42]

Masculinity scholarship often focuses on provider–protector roles within the context of courtship and marriage to examine how bondmen hunted and fished to augment familial needs as slavery undercut their ability to protect family members from white abuse. Aquatic blood sports were part of this dynamic—and they filled other social and cultural obligations as well. They provided combatants and community members with tangible gains as the privations of bondage compelled captives to consume whatever they could. Slaves probably ate the meat from most vanquished creatures, while body parts were made into goods.[43]

In hunting narratives, Southern slaveholders "invariably placed themselves (or fictionalized representations of themselves) at center stage" and "portrayed the slave as an assistant or witness—often a frightened witness —to a master's ability to control death." These tales unfolded ashore. In the water, the opposite was true. There, admittedly fearful white men relied on captives to exert their masculinity while destroying creatures that terrified their enslavers. Hence, blood sports permitted slaves to temporarily invert traditional top-down social orderings. Bondmen became protagonists in stories they crafted and whites told, overshadowing and protecting cowering whites as they were woven into plantation legends and campfire tales.[44]

Joseph LeConte, a renowned natural scientist who founded the University of California, illustrates this process. LeConte came of age on his father's, two hundred–slave Georgia rice plantation during the 1820s. These slaves' amphibious culture helped nurture LeConte's interest in natural science. They taught him to swim, build African-style dugouts, and sail the dugouts across wintry rice fields. As a youth, he accompanied bondmen on alligator hunts, transforming those men into legends. In old age, he reflected on how he and his youthful brothers shot "small alligators, six and seven feet long." Larger ones were left to the *experts*—the captives. After bondmen killed a "fourteen foot alligator," LeConte noted: "It was a great sport, and I afterwards told the story to my children." Likewise, Richard Mallard lionized enslaved alligator killers, while he cowered in trees.[45]

White Southern society applauded risk-taking inherent in gambling and hunting, and regarded dueling as the "perfect gamble for a man of honor" as it "allowed him to demonstrate mastery of death." According to white standards: "A SLAVE CAN'T BE A MAN!" Despite white codes of honor and masculinity, bondpeople regarded risk-taking and heroism as worthy of respect. Aquatic blood sport functioned as performative duels, permitting males to display masculinity and independence even as slavery sought to dishonor and emasculate them.[46]

Virtuosos exhibited robust, agile bodies, esteemed by people of African descent. Emerging nude or seminude from the water, triumphant combatants' masculinity, prestige, and muscular physiques surely won the attention of potential spouses, serving as headwaters for love-based marriages. The previously discussed Essex seemingly used his renowned swimming status and position as plantation driver to compete with the more prestigious Griffin, a teamster and "aristocrat among the negroes," for the hand of Cindy. Marriages were overwhelmingly based on love, but women also selected husbands who could provide for them and their children. At gatherings, men frequently engaged in competitive activities, like dancing and singing, to catch a woman's eye. Likewise, African-descended men in Africa and the Americas incorporated martial arts into courtship routines to attract female attention and express their masculinity. Killing marine creatures surely served similar functions. Bondmen's ability to augment terse, bland rations and gain incomes through hunting and fishing were also desired qualities, with marine creatures providing large quantities of protein.[47]

Waterscapes were also used to defend loved ones by proxy, affording opportunities to fulfill gendered protector roles in white-dominated societies. Enslavers prohibited enslaved men from defending themselves and family members against white abuse, with scholars considering the anxieties and frustration this imposed on males. Blood sports created scenarios in which males publicly defended family members and white people, with Mallard, LeConte, and Janet Schaw illustrating how bondmen safeguarded whites from physical harm and restored desecrated white honor.[48]

The social dynamics of marine blood sports extended beyond provider and protector roles. It was a form of cultural volition removed from white interference that instilled a sense of control over bodies and immediate circumstances. Unlike sporting events arranged by slaveholders, slaves organized aquatic duels. Whites witnessed some, but slave owners probably did not encourage events that could have ruinous consequences on their human property. Like hunting, which was distinct from, yet bound to, everyday life, blood sports probably provided "a stage for the performance of an evocative drama" that indexed masculinity and honor. This permitted bondmen to claim masculine identities distinct from the influences of bondwomen and enslavers.[49]

Bondage afforded few opportunities for pride, while slaveholders' power subverted men's familial influences. Seeking to elevate their diminished sense of self-worth, some slaves took pride in their monetary value, others identified with the wealth and greatness of their owners.[50] Blood sports permitted bondmen to detach self-respect from associations with slaveholders, providing themselves with autonomy, honor, and prestige. Slaves could not articulate honor and manhood through gentlemanly duels—a "central ritual" in Southern white society that "embodied the core values of honor." Some sought respect through nonfatal, slave-versus-slave, martial arts matches. Marine battles extended opportunities for slaves while contesting their owner's authority. Indeed, "illicit use of the body must be understood as important and meaningful enjoyment, as personal expression, and as oppositional engagement of the body" that "insulted slaveholders' feelings of authority." Blood sports allowed slaves to speak the language of honor during unsanctioned exhibitions.[51]

Males learned to hunt as boys. After witnessing bondmen kill aquatic creatures in magisterial displays, enslaved boys undoubtedly took to marshy playgrounds in search of juvenile alligators. Though the tales of these episodes went unrecorded, they surely afforded youth with social meaning, providing hierarchies and honor, while enhancing group cohesion.[52]

Scars obtained during battles were probably badges of honor that distinguished African- and European-influenced valuations. For Southern gentlemen, scars, with the exception of those received in warfare, were marks of dishonor. The rough-and-tumble brawls of poor Southerners left discernible reminders of violent confrontations, including lost eyes and bitten off lips, noses, and fingers. Elites judged mutilated poor whites little different from whip-scarred slaves. For slaves, scars inflicted by marine creatures were probably considered symbols of masculinity.[53]

Like wrestling and storytelling, the hunting and killing of aquatic animals provided opportunities to eclipse compatriots. It is unclear if more than one creature was fought per day. By killing larger creatures or ones with fierce reputations, slaves probably trumped predecessors.[54]

Exhibitions of strength and bravery could elevate men into leadership positions recognized and respected in black and white society. Members of some communities throughout the Americas elected community leaders called "kings," "queens," "generals," and "governors" who exercised social, cultural, and political sway. Due to their standings within bonded communities, white people usually treated them with deference. Individuals' assent was sometimes attained through demonstrations of brawn and fighting skills. Blood sports possibly provided opportunities for such ascensions.[55] Blood sports also possibly served as rites of passage for boys, as males formed intimate bonds through mutual experiences. They could reflect on maritime battles, linking their accomplishments to those of community members in Africa and the Americas.[56]

Chapter 4

History from Below:
Enslaved Underwater Divers

Both in Africa and in the Americas aquatics undercut European attempts to project power across waterscapes. Europeans had hoped to conquer African polities. However, ecological advantages favored Africans who possessed iron weapons, forcing Europeans to treat them as equals and superiors as they largely controlled the terms of commerce into the late eighteenth century. They were powerful enough to control territorial waters, using swimming, among other things, to counter European incursions.[1] Waterscapes were thus inherent to water people's geopolitical spaces. They were also central to work and to the economy, as Africans incorporated aquatics into work routines, which became a central facet of contact with Europeans.

Among other aquatic labors, European slave traders employed African lifeguards to protect their investments. French slaver Theophilus Conneau hired Africans "to swim off whenever a canoe should capsize" in high surf. "Negro after Negro was rescued by the swimming party."[2] As canoes were launched, canoemen and fishermen often swam alongside to prevent capsizing by keeping bows pointed seaward. When dugouts overturned, they swam to save their own lives, and, as Barbot reported, "being excellent swimmers and divers recover goods."[3] Europeans equally appreciated when Africans saved them. When a dugout carrying Paul Isert overturned in the surf, he "had the unpleasant experience of being submerged with the canoe. I was tossed around in the breakers until a Black came swimming from the shore, pulled me onto his back, and thus drew me ashore."[4]

Others were underwater divers. Men and women harvested oysters for their meat and burned their shells to produce lime for construction. Carpenter Rock, Sierra Leone, was "celebrated for its excellent rock oysters, which are brought up in quantities by divers."[5] Divers played a central role in some states' political and economic development by obtaining forms of currency and export commodities. The Mbamba province in the Kongo Kingdom controlled Luanda Island and its surrounding areas, where *nzimbu* (cowry) shells were harvested for circulation. A sixteenth-century traveler reported that women harvested *nzimbus*, "Women dive under water, a depth of two yards and more, and filling their baskets with sand, they sift out certain small shellfish, called Lumanche, and then separate the male from the female, the latter being most prized for its color and brightness."[6] Others collected gold. Jean Barbot reported that the "Kingdom of Sakoo" produced "much gold, which the blacks fish for, diving under the rocks and into the waterfalls."[7]

The arrival of Europeans created new work opportunities. Many scraped barnacles from ship hulls. *Kru* watermen cleaned the *John H. Jones* in Monrovia, Liberia. An impressed Charles Stewart reported that we "employed them to scrape the barnacles from the bottom of the vessel several times, their power of remaining underwater being truly remarkable."[8]

By the late eighteenth century, Westerners ascribed *Kru* (also Kroo, Kroomen, and Krumen) as an identity for maritime people from what is now Liberia and western Ivory Coast. The *Kru* were members of discrete ethnic groups and did not identify themselves as such except when seeking employment aboard Western ships. They were maritime peoples renowned swimmers, canoe-makers, and canoeists who routinely paddled to newly arrived ships to sell fresh produce and seafood and to work as seamen.[9]

Diving was a spectacle for Westerners who watched Africans retrieve trinkets tossed overboard. William Bosman noted these displays on the Ivory and Grain Coasts, writing: "You are probably acquainted with the expert Swimming and Diving of these *Negroes*, which I have several times seen with Surprize. Whenever they were on Board, and I threw a string of Coral, or any thing else into the Sea, one of them would immediately dive after it, and tho' almost got to the bottom fetch it up again. This they seldom missed of, and were sure of what they brought up as their Reward." As James Holman's ship lay off Sierra Leone, sailors threw scrap iron into the blue and Africans "darted with the utmost eagerness into the water and exerted themselves most strenuously until on the luck to find it" on the bottom, some forty feet deep. An awestruck Stewart said *Kru* often dove from the "yardarm," about twenty-five feet above the water, and, "I threw

Figure 6. Somali Boys Diving for Money at Aden. There are no known images of Atlantic Africans diving for objects thrown from ships' decks. These Somali adolescents illustrate an activity pursued throughout the tropics, and not in Britain, which is why this expedition's special artist devoted considerable detail to its rendering and *The Graphic* devoted an entire page to the image, instead of the more typical half- or quarter-page. These youth paddled canoes out to newly arrived ships, calling to passengers to throw coins into the water, for which the boys dove. Note the use of the crawl by the boy near the bottom right corner, who is outstretching his left arm to breathe while raising his right arm. The artist sketched this image on location. *The Graphic: An Illustrated Weekly Newspaper* (November 27, 1875), 518. Author's collection.

the money would dive from his lofty perch and almost invariably recover it."[10]

Africans equally demonstrated their capacities when pursuing sea turtles; the meat was a delicacy and the shells were carved into jewelry. Observing *Kru* watermen, John Lawrence wrote: "The Turtle dived when they got within the space of forty or fifty feet. But the chase did not end here, and a submarine pursuit took place which was astonishing as well as amusing to witness; one would hardly suppose that men could acquire such perfection in swimming."[11]

Many sunken and grounded vessels became contested places, with both Africans and Europeans claiming ownership of them. Europeans wanted Africans to adopt Western salvage traditions, which dictated that ship owners maintained possession of stricken vessels while permitting salvagers to collect compensation for the recovery of goods.[12] Conversely, African rulers claimed that when Westerners lost control of their vessels they forfeited ownership of them, allowing Africans to appropriate distressed ships, their cargos, and, sometimes, crewmembers, who would then be ransomed. They typically dispatched male and female divers to extend their power over and salvage goods from shipwrecks. French officials in Senegal summarized European complaints: "The right of pillage rests on no other foundation than the claims of the Negroes, who have always maintained, that every vessel belonged to the sovereign of the country on the coast of which it might be wrecked."[13] In 1615, Manuel Álvares bemoaned that the Bijago averred "what arrives on the beaches belongs to the first who seizes it." If a vessel "wrecked on any of their islands, they consider it fair gain; and, . . . retain the unfortunate individuals whom they may have taken with it in captivity, until ransomed by friends."[14]

Men and women routinely stripped European shipwrecks. Some African rulers drew these salvagers into their attempts to suppress the slave trade. The Faloup of Guinea-Bissau, for instance, opposed the slave-trading activities of their Cassanga neighbors. They discouraged Portuguese slavers by attacking their vessels and selling shipwrecked mariners into slavery.[15]

Africans did not always appropriate distressed vessels. To ensure future trade, some oligarchs commanded citizens to recover goods and refloat vessels belonging to African, North African, and Western merchants.[16] Even when retaining ownership of grounded vessels, Europeans were compelled to employ African divers. During the 1850s, a British "man-of-war-steamer" went to Cameroon with *Kru* mariners to salvage a wreck. *Kru* divers raised some items as canoemen sent by "King William," an Isuwu ruler, furthered the effort.[17]

Others swam off with stolen merchandise. On the Grain Coast in 1600, a man with a "pewter tankard of beer in his hand and a soldier's helmet on his head, jumped into the water with them and swam thus a great distance underwater; then he re-emerged and jumped into his little boat." He seemingly knew Europeans could not swim well enough to capture him and that he would be ashore before they could lower a boat to catch him. Indeed, the Europeans remained transfixed by his ability to "swim like a fish" despite being impeded by ill-gotten gains.[18]

Slavery was a labor institution, and New World slaveholders realized they could exploit Africans' capacity to "swim like a fish." Divers had spent years tuning their minds and bodies. Just as training at high altitudes can improve athletic abilities, water pressure, oxygen apnea, and repeated prolonged immersion enhance divers' proficiencies. Slaveholders did not understand this physiological process but seemingly targeted members of ethnic groups known to possess strong swimmers.

Sources suggest that divers utilized African-derived skills. It is unlikely that neophytes quickly became experts, and there is no evidence that Indians taught Africans to dive. Enslaved divers exhibited their knowledge and wisdom during the length of a single breath. After African-born divers established beachhead cultures, they undoubtedly tutored country-born youth. Communities of African- and country-born divers were brought together to salvage wrecks throughout the Atlantic world.

Divers were highly skilled bondpeople, but, unlike other skilled captives, they did not spend the majority of the day in adept production. Most divers spent less than two hours a day underwater. Most could hold their breath for about two minutes; exceptional divers, three; and a rare few, four or more minutes. As fatigue set in, dive times decreased while recovery times increased. Making one dive every five to ten minutes, pearl and salvage divers worked from morning until about noon, when winds rendered conditions too rough. Completing four to seven dives per hour, divers worked approximately forty to eighty minutes each day and were typically not expected to perform other work during the balance of the day. It is perhaps surprising that aquanauts spent less than two hours a day beneath the surface while terrestrial bondage compelled captives to work ten to fourteen hours each day. Still, during brief moments beneath the sea, divers harvested valuables that made white people spectacularly wealthy.

Divers differed from highly skilled craftsmen in another significant way. Others' ascension into elite privilege hinged on their competency in Western artisanry.[19] Aquanauts' skills were developed in Africa. Western concepts of gendered labor strengthened male divers' positions. Skilled labor was a "gendered phenomenon" favoring bondmen as "enslaved women found themselves confined to the monotony and drudgery of the field more regularly than their male counterparts." Even though many African-descended women were expert divers, European claims that maritime labor was a male occupation precluded the exploitation of the women, at least in the water. In the absence of this gendered bias, slaveholders could have swelled divers' numbers to gain sway.[20] Westerners' inability to negotiate the deep and appropriate slaves' wisdom gave divers control over their profession and benefit-extracting leverage, with some perhaps organizing unofficial guilds.

Among other aquatic work, slaves were pressed into lifeguarding to reduce white drowning death rates. As George Pinckard toured the Caribbean and South America, he proclaimed that swimming ability "renders the negroes peculiarly useful in moments of distress, such as in cases of accident at sea or in the harbour." Slaveholders instructed some to watch and teach white youth, permitting them to escape arduous work.[21]

Captives usually found themselves rescuing white people on an ad hoc basis. In 1805, Barbadian slaveholder Robert Haynes sent his three sons to school in England, along with a slave named Hamlet, who "saved the life of my son George" when he fell "overboard whilst landing at Liverpool." Zamba, who was raised along "the river Congo" before being kidnapped into South Carolinian bondage, swam "like a seagull," using this ability to save Mr. Thomson. Toppling into Baltimore Harbor, a falling tide swept Thomson "far out in the harbour." Zamba dove in, and "after a few minutes' strenuous exertion," reached Thompson, keeping him "afloat until a boat" arrived. Likewise, a Brazilian sailor named Simão saved the lives of several passengers during an 1853 steamer wreck. "Twelve times had this noble fellow swam through the furious breakers on the coast, and each time returned bringing a victim from destruction." Hearing that a blind man remained aboard, "Simao again dived into the furious surf, reached the vessel, and brought the poor blind man safely to land, thus saving, by his noble and unaided exertions, no less than thirteen lives." The survivors rewarded Simão with "about £800" to which the "Emperor and Empress" of Brazil contributed an additional "nine hundred milreis," for a total of "£1,000." An equally dramatic rescue occurred during a 1792 flood on St. Kitts. Several "houses were carried into the sea" and a "Mrs. T–, with her house and family, was carried into the sea: she cried out, 'Lord have Mercy upon me.' A Mulatto, hearing her cries, ventured out, and swimming after her, caught her hair and saved her" and her son.[22]

Lifesavers received surprisingly small benefits. Those who watched white children temporarily escaped work and were possibly given food and clothing. When captives saved drowning victims, most received little more

Figure 7. "Uncle Tom Saves Eva." This scene documents the aquatic expertise of an African-descended man, while playing into stereotypes of slaves by portraying Tom as a simplistic self-sacrificing individual. Still, for readers to find it believable, it had to engage beliefs that African-descended people were stronger swimmers than white people, while reflecting the reality that black people were far more likely to save drowning whites than vice-versa. As Eva's father, who was apparently a poor swimmer, prepared to leap overboard after her, he "was held back by some who saw that more effectual aid had followed the little one" into the river. Harriet Beecher Stowe, *Uncle Tom's Cabin*, Florence Maplestone, illus. (1852; London: 1891), image on 24; account on 42. Author's collection.

than praise.[23] These were diminutive rewards for bondpeople who had preserved whites' most cherished possessions—their lives and those of their children.

Some received compensation. In Charleston Harbor on May 12, 1787, a "gale of wind" sank a rowboat carrying four white men, prompting General Christopher Gadsden to offer "two guineas to a negro, if he could save any of them; the negro immediately jumped into the boisterous element, and rescued one person from impending death." This was a considerable sum for a slave and a calculated risk. Indeed, he did not risk his life in the cool turbulence until enticed. The incident causes one to wonder why Gadsden specifically offered the reward to the bondman: was he a renowned swimmer; or was it assumed that *all* black people were expert?[24]

Perhaps most significant, Africans were crucial to dive operations from the fifteenth through the late nineteenth centuries. Dive communities were created and aquanauts were regularly moved about the Greater Caribbean. Some were taken to African, European, and Pacific waters.

In deeper waters, enslaved divers produced wealth and wielded their expertise, wisdom, and control over production to gain opportunities. Aquanauts possessed skills held by few in the Western Hemisphere. They were adept in what is ironically called freediving, which entails diving with only the air in one's lungs. Cloistering this wisdom so that only a few knew the secrets, they seemingly created semi-fraternal orders that prevented slaveholders from appropriating and propagating their wisdom, as had occurred with South Carolinian rice production. There, early bondpeople used their knowledge of tidal rice production to challenge the conditions of enslavement. "Once slaves demonstrated rice techniques, whether remembered from West Africa or developed to grow their own provisions, they lost the ability to restrain their dissemination or use of them as 'leverage to negotiate and alters some of the terms of their bondage.' Planters integrated African skills into applicable European farming strategies without the need to offer compensation."[25]

As Spaniards killed off indigenous divers, they unwittingly ceded increasing leverage to Africans. No known white people in the Americas ever mastered freediving. By the mid-seventeenth century, few Amerindian divers remained, and clusters of black divers—with what was now an even rarer skill—were scattered throughout the Caribbean, Bahamas, Bermuda, North America, and probably South America.

Spaniards along the Pearl Coast, which encompasses northern Venezuela and the islands of Margarita, Coche, Cubagua, and Trinidad, were apparently the first Westerners to exploit African expertise. Settling the region in 1498, they forced local Guaiqurí Indians to harvest pearls, augmenting their numbers with Amerindians imported from the Bahamas, the Caribbean, and South America. As diseases and harsh treatment decimated these divers, Spaniards began importing Africans in 1526, calling them "negros de pesca" or "concha," meaning "fishing blacks" or "shells" because, in the language of the day, they "fished" for pearls at "pearl fisheries."[26] Africans and Amerindians dove together for about the next fifty years, undoubtedly exchanging techniques.

Slaveholders understood that captives from certain ethnic groups possessed skills suited to specific labor demands.[27] Dutch and Portuguese travelogues seemingly alerted Pearl Coast slaveholders to Africans' aquatic fluencies, which motivated Spaniards to seek captives from regions known to possess divers. On January 6, 1534, they petitioned the crown for a license to obtain slaves. Slave traders apparently sought skilled Gold Coast aquanauts, delivering them to the Pearl Coast where they were marketed as divers.[28] During the 1590s, Dutch merchant-adventurer Pieter de Marees seemingly observed this process on both sides of the Atlantic, writing that Gold Coast Africans "are very fast swimmers and can keep themselves underwater for a long time. They can dive amazingly far, no less deep, and can see underwater. Because they are so good at swimming and diving, they are specially kept for that purpose in many Countries and employed in this capacity where there is a need for them, such as the Island of St. Margaret in the West Indies, where Pearls are found and brought up from the bottom by Divers."[29]

Sources suggest that slaveholders preferred to import skilled African divers[30] rather than train novices, a practice conforming to better-documented global practices.[31] Most sixteenth-and seventeenth-century Pearl Coast bondpeople were saltwater captives. As natural reproduction increased, African-born fathers and uncles possibly tutored country-born sons and nephews and nonrelatives.[32]

Pearl diving was seasonal, lasting from spring into fall. During the late sixteenth and early seventeenth centuries, Antonio Vázquez de Espinosa observed the working lives of Margarita's divers. Pearl fisheries, called *"rancherías de perlas,"* were established by those called *"patróns" "senore de canoa,"* or "canoe master" in English ("canoe" was a generic term for the vessels used). *Patróns* owned a sailing vessel and owned or employed "at least a dozen Negro divers, plus their captain who is a Negro expert in the profession." Many controlled upward of fifty divers.[33]

Diving required skill, endurance, and mental resilience. Each morning, vessels "set sail for the oyster bed or pearl fishery, which generally lies offshore 1, 1½, leagues or even more, and anchors at the bed . . . and this is in 8, 10, 12, and even 14 fathoms," or more than eighty feet deep. As shallow-water reserves were depleted, operations moved deeper. With sunlight penetrating clear waters to a depth of about 150 feet and visibility ranging from 60 to 180 feet, aquanauts worked depths of 40 to 120 feet. Most probably were submerged for one to three minutes. Visiting Margarita in 1582 and 1593, Richard Hawkins described aquanauts as "expert

Figure 8. "Canau pour Pecher les Perles" ("Canoe for Pearl-Fishing"), early 1590s. This image was produced on location by one of the artists who accompanied Sir Francis Drake's New World expedition. Off Margarita Island, they observed enslaved African pearl divers descend "in three or four fathoms [18–25 feet] of water" while carrying "a hoop-net," into which pearl oysters were placed. *Histoire Naturelle des Indes* (*The Natural History of the Indies*), early 1590s. Courtesy The Morgan Library & Museum, New York. MA 3900, f. 57.

swimmers, and great deevers," who, "with tract of time, use, and continual practice, have learned to hold their breath long underwater, for the better atchieving their worke." They held rock weights to quickly descend without expending oxygen. To counter buoyancy, many "use two stones tied together with a cord, which they placed over their shoulders" so they could walk on the seabed and rip oysters from reefs. At about sixty feet, the air in divers' lungs was compressed, creating negative buoyancy, causing them to sink, permitting gravity and increasing water pressure to concertedly pull and push them downward. Between dives, they frequently "receiv'd a glass of Wine and a Pipe of Tobacco" as refreshment, with the alcohol obscuring judgment as the day progressed.[34]

It took years to become a skilled swimmer, and many more to become a proficient diver capable of meeting the challenges of breath-apnea and water pressure. Africans began honing their minds and bodies during youth. Captives learned to descend to greater depths and cope with cooler waters. The appellations "diving negroes" and "negro divers" were regularly used in multiple languages to express the acumen of pearl and salvage divers. These titles articulate expertise and it is improbable that novices quickly gained this acumen.[35]

Limited medical research suggests how the physiology of enslaved freedivers adapted to prolonged submersion, water pressure, and oxygen deprivation, making them more proficient. The "diving reflex" or "mammalian diving reflex" optimizes respiration after one's face is submerged in water seventy degrees Fahrenheit or colder by slowing one's pulse and shifting blood from the extremities to vital organs. Freedivers develop large lung capacities and lean physiques. Their bloodstream possesses elevated concentrations of red blood cells and hemoglobin and reduced levels of carbon dioxide, increasing the circulation of oxygen while slowing its consumption. As on descends their spleen shrinks, releasing oxygen-rich blood into their arteries. Oxygen-deprivation also decreases heart, breathing, and metabolism rates. All these factors extend dive times.[36]

In addition, prolonged, recurring submersion changes the eye's lens shape, sharpening underwater vision up to twice the normal range while another adaptation possibly diminishes eye irritation to saltwater.[37] De Marees seemingly reported on this phenomenon, saying Africans "can dive amazingly far, no less deep, and *can see underwater*." This statement suggests divers possessed enhanced underwater vision rendered more acute by understandings of marine life.[38]

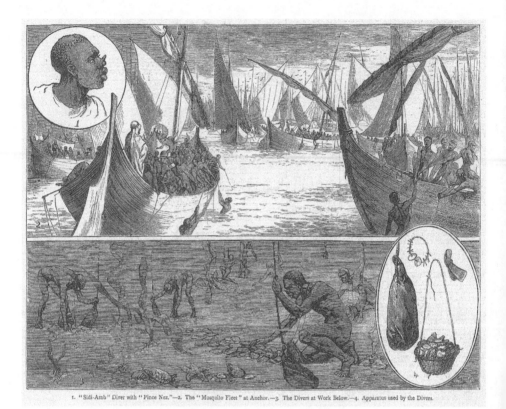

1. "Sidi-Arab" Diver with "Pince Nez."—2. The "Mosquito Fleet" at Anchor.—3. The Divers at Work Below.—4. Apparatus used by the Divers.

Figure 9. "The Pearl Fishery of the Persian Gulf Pearl Divers." This is the most detailed depiction of African-descended pearl divers. Although this portrays East Africans in the Persian Gulf, many of the diving techniques of Atlantic Africans were the same. Like Atlantic Africans, East Africans wore charms to protect against shark attack and other misfortunes. For Persian Gulf pearl diving, see Matthew S. Hopper, *Slaves of One Master: Globalization and Slavery in Arabia as in the Age of Empire* (New Haven: 2015). "The Pearl Fishery of the Persian Gulf Pearl Divers," *The Graphic: An Illustrated Weekly Newspaper* (October 1, 1881), 356. Author's collection.

Freedivers learned to pressurize their ears and effectively breathe. Instead of taking one deep breath, many inhale and exhale deeply, expanding their lung capacity and oxygenating their blood before taking one deep breath. As one descends, increasing water pressure compresses the middle and inner ear. If one does not equalize this pressure with surrounding water pressure by letting air into the Eustachian tubes, the eardrums (or tympanic membranes) can rupture, flooding the ears and sinuses, which can cause vertigo and temporary hearing loss. Though not fatal, this is painful and can cause disorientation, leading to drowning.[39]

Freediving requires one to remain composed while adjusting to variables in water pressure, temperature, visibility, and currents to preclude the release of oxygen-depleting adrenaline. Divers must also remain calm around marine creatures, especially when their sudden appearance can be startling. Nitrogen narcosis can cause a temporary decline of mental and motor functions, similar to that caused by intoxication, including impaired judgment, diminished ability to focus, vertigo, visual impairment, euphoria, and a heightened sense of tranquility. One risks drowning if unable to overcome these symptoms.[40]

Divers learned to negotiate oceanic forces that could make it exceedingly difficult to work while salvaging and pearling. Surge, or the underwater effects of waves forcing water into shallows, constantly pushed divers shoreward and then pulled them seaward. Simultaneously, currents produced by prevailing currents, wind patterns, and far-off storms produced stratified flows that moved in different directions at different depths, creating a perplexity of forces. To avoid overexertion, divers surely learned to calculate these forces by feeling the movement of their body and observing the movement of boats, fish, and submarine vegetation.[41]

Teams of "enslaved black divers" were imported into Panama, the Gulf of California, and perhaps the Pacific coast of Baja and southern California after apparently proving themselves on the Pearl Coast. In Panama, they largely replaced Amerindians. Seventeenth-century Africans worked the Gulf of California alongside Yaqui, Mayo, and other Indians. Circumstances in Baja California and Panama illustrate the practice of procuring rather than training divers and anticipated the practice of shipping teams of experts to shipwrecks.[42] The Seville-based Cardona Company considered purchasing divers from "Angola," "Cabo verde," or both, before concluding it was more efficient to obtain eighteen "Negro pearl divers" at Margarita. In March 1615, they were transported across Mexico to Acapulco. As they shipped north into the Gulf, Dutch pirates captured one of Cardona's three ships and eleven divers in October 1616.[43]

Documents dating to the 1520s indicate persistent desires for captives from African regions known to possess divers. While Senegambia possessed capable swimmers, a law passed on January 6, 1534, prohibited the importation of "blacks from Gelofe [Wolof]." On December 23, 1540, the king granted a "license to Francisquin Cristóbal and Diego Martinez," to "bring black slaves from the island of Cape Verde and Guinea and rivers which are the Kingdom of Portugal." On April 12, 1602, during a decline due to overfishing, a Margarita official reminded the king of the wealth Africans produced before requesting permission to obtain divers from "Guinea." Many were worked to death apparently under the assumption that they were replaceable. In 1621, another Margarita official recommended the importation of 300 captives to augment the island's 130 surviving divers.[44]

In 1551, it was reported that Pearl Coast wealth was obtained "at the cost of many Spaniards, many Negroes and many Indians." An oceanic trench channels cold water into the region, causing year-round surface temperatures to remain in the low seventies, making the waters "cold and the work difficult." As divers descended, temperatures plummeted, causing exposure-related disorders. Underwater pressure can cause cardiac arrhythmias and arrest, which occur at higher rates in colder waters. Divers sometimes damaged their eardrums and sinuses, so "blood gushed out of their Mouths and Noses when they came above Water to breath." When unable to obtain the desired quantity or quality of pearls, slaveholders locked the divers in "cells and punished them by beating them and flogging them in a cruel and savage manner." Pirates kidnapped, injured, and killed some. Dubious accounts claimed marine creatures devoured many. Bartholomé de Las Casas averred that "dolphins and sharks . . . swallow a man whole, kill and eat them." Drake reported that manta rays were "vicious; when the negroes dive into the sea for pearls it jumps on them to make them drown and afterward eats them." Predation was probably rare, and today sharks infrequently attack spear-fishing freedivers who hold bleeding thrashing fish. The disappearance of divers' bodies undoubtedly fueled assertions of predation. Yet most probably drowned as a result of shallow- and deep-water blackouts and other disorders, and currents quickly pulled bodies away. Physical abuse and forcing bondmen to dive when suffering pressure- and temperature-related ailments and illness heightened mortality rates.[45]

Slaveholders probably manipulated claims of predation to deflect culpability as officials, alarmed by high mortality rates, threatened to "let the fishery of the said pearls cease." Las Casas railed against abuses suffered upon Indian divers. In 1542, Charles V used the *New Laws of the West Indies* to command "the preservation of slaves working in said fishery."[46]

Illusions of freedom surely contributed to a mounting malaise and increasing drowning death rates. Contemplating past lives in tranquil depths, and perhaps gripped by the euphoria of narcosis, some probably

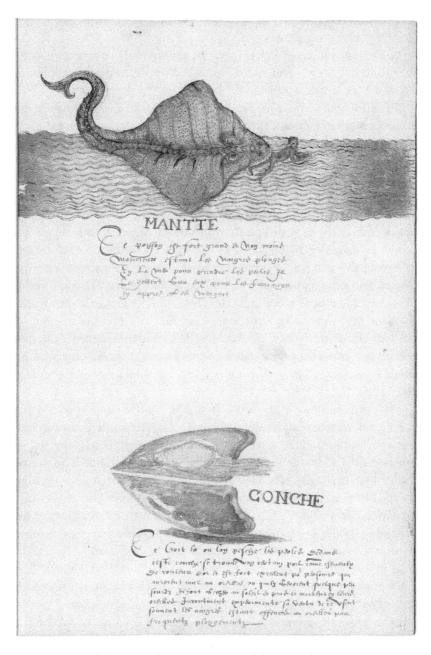

Figure 10. "Mantte" ("Manta ray"), early 1590s. One of the artists who accompanied Sir Francis Drake to the West Indies during the late sixteenth century painted this image of a manta ray catching an enslaved pearl diver. The accompanying caption translates to "this fish is very large and no less vicious; when the negroes dive into the sea for pearls it jumps on them to make them drown and afterward eats them." The artist did not witness such events, as manta rays do not eat humans, but this image expresses Westerners' fear of harmless marine creatures and perhaps recognizes divers' daring in the face of such dangers. *Histoire Naturelle des Indes* (*The Natural History of the Indies*), early 1590s. Courtesy the Pierpont Morgan Library, New York. MA 3900, f. 47.

embarked on transcendental voyages, permitting water pressure to draw them into the abyss.[47] Still, narcosis-induced drowning deaths should not necessarily be treated as suicide.

Pearl fisheries were an important source of Spain's wealth. Before the 1545 discovery of Peruvian silver, the Pearl Coast probably generated more wealth than anywhere else in the Americas. Most pearls were exported to Europe where some were re-exported to the Middle East; others were exported to Africa to be exchanged for gold, ivory, slaves, and other goods.[48]

Divers used their prowess to gain unusual privileges. They were entitled to a portion of the harvested pearls, which they sold to their owners, so "on certain holidays they lay on a table or elsewhere excellent suits of clothes or other valuable articles of clothing, and the Negroes come out with the clothes, and their masters with riches." Some accumulated enough wealth to conceivably purchase freedom. Most enjoyed little terrestrial autonomy. At night they were locked in dormitories, not to prevent escape but to preclude sexual intercourse. As Vázquez de Espinosa explained, "Chastity is necessary, to such a degree that if anyone among them did otherwise, he would be unable to fish or dive under water, but would stay on the surface like a cork."[49]

Pearl fisheries provided several firsts. The Pearl Coast was one of the first regions to receive slaves shipped directly from Africa. It was apparently the first location where slaveholders exploited African wisdom. These waters proved to be the first great source of colonial wealth. Here one of the earliest genocidal acts against Amerindians occurred as they were stripped from land and water and replaced by Africans.[50]

Slaveholders quickly realized that the same expertise that allowed pearl divers to produce spectacular wealth could be lucratively applied to other uses. Salvage divers sculpted their minds and bodies, learning to remain calm in harrowing situations. "Each vessel" out of Key West, Florida, "has a diver, who will go into the cabin of a ship, or to the bottom of the sea, if not over six fathoms [or thirty-six feet] deep and bring up goods." Just as one can gauge the presence of predators by the movement of small birds and mammals, divers surely recognized the presence of unseen sharks by the actions or absences of smaller fish and probably distinguished more aggressive bull and tiger sharks from less dangerous species, prompting one traveler to write that when Bahamians are "wrecking, or diving for sponges and conch pearls; they are the most marvelous swimmers I ever saw, and appear to have little dread of sharks." This expertise compelled one Bahamian to boast, in 1824, that he "has among his slaves divers who can go to depths of *sixty feet* & remain under water from *two* to *three* minutes." Salvors were reportedly the best divers in the Western Hemisphere with German botanist Johann Schoepff proclaiming: "It is the Bahama islands, next after the Bermudas, which are the most famous as furnishing the best and most skilful divers."[51]

For their part, Spaniards recognized that pearl divers could salvage shipwrecks. Spain amassed its looted wealth in Havana before dispatching treasure fleets to Europe during late summer or fall, sending galleons through the shallow, coral-toothed Florida Straits and Bahamas during hurricane season, precipitating many wrecks. These hulks became arenas where Spanish, English, Dutch, French, and Danish salvagers and wreckers exploited the aptitudes of saltwater and country-born divers. Salvagers obtained contracts to recover goods from shipwrecks. Wreckers did not. Operating on the cusp of legitimacy, they poached wrecks and cruised perilous waters for disabled ships, stripping those that could not be refloated of their masts and rigging, making them unseaworthy; actions opening them to charges of piracy. Many engaged in both.[52]

Diving bells and other European devices were expensive to fabricate and inefficient to operate. Hence, sixteenth-century pearl divers were circulated throughout the Caribbean, as Hans Sloane explained while describing Edmund Halley's bell: "Though the Money brought into *England* from the first Wreck was very considerable, yet much more was lost on Projects of the same nature. . . . Divers, who are us'd to Pearl-fishing, &c. and can stay under Water some Minutes, bought or hir'd at great Rates," proved more efficient.[53]

Early sixteenth-century Spaniards employed Indian divers, decimating their numbers by about 1550. They began using Africans, who initially worked alongside Amerindians. The nearly complete shift to enslaved Africans apparently occurred after the Tierra Firma Flota ("Fleet") of twenty-eight ships sailed into a hurricane on September 6, 1622. Three galleons, the *Nuestra Señora Rosario, Santa Margarita, Nuestra Señora de Atocha,* and several other ships were driven onto reefs in the Marquesas Keys, where they completely or partially sank. A five-vessel salvage fleet commanded by Gaspar de Vargas was dispatched. The partially sunken *Rosario* was located and her hull accessed. The *Atocha* was found in fifty feet of water. Slave divers recovered two brass deck cannons, but bolted hatches prevented access to the hull. Buoying the site, Vargas returned to Havana to obtain supplies.[54]

In January 1623, Vargas returned to the *Atocha*, but a storm had broken her up, scattering treasure across the seafloor and covering most with sand. Dragging the bottom with grapnels, divers descended whenever something was hooked. Salvaging was inhibited when Havana-based divers experienced pressure-related ailments. Vargas requested approximately thirty pearl divers, knowing they dove deeper. They recovered some silver but were unable to find the wreck, prompting Vargas to abandon the search.[55]

In 1626, Francisco Nuñez Melián obtained a contract to salvage the *Atocha* and *Santa Margarita*. Taking a contingent of Pearl Coast divers, Melián reached the Marquesas Keys in May, promising freedom to whomever found a galleon. On June 3, 1626, Juan de Casta Bañon, surfaced, shouting he found the *Santa Margarita*, while clutching a silver bar. As promised, he received his freedom. Using the free air that now filled his lungs he helped recover "350 silver bars, 74,700 pesos in reales, 8 pieces of bronze artillery," and other items.[56]

Spanish successes inspired other fortune-seekers to obtain African divers. Bahamians, Bermudians, Caymanians, Key Westers, and others began wrecking, or "Fishing upon the Wrecks," employing at least one slave who could descend upward of seventy feet deep. These maritime colonies lacked plantation systems while sharing similar economies that used bondmen as mariners and bondwomen as shoreside auxiliaries.[57]

Still maritime and terrestrial bondage remained compatible. In the 1640s, Richard Ligon observed that saltwater captives were "Excellent Swimmers and Divers they are, both men and women." Even as Barbados and, later, Jamaica were wedding themselves to plantation slavery, seventeenth- and eighteenth-century planters and would-be planters exploited Africans' diving skills. Unfortunately, no known sources document the use of divers around Barbados or reveal why the island was home to numerous aquanauts.[58]

Bermudians sought to establish pearl fisheries by importing Africans but quickly shifted to salvaging. In 1613, Richard Norwood, a diving bell designer, was brought to the islands to locate pearls. When this method proved unsuccessful, Governor Daniel Tucker turned to Africans, reporting in February 1615/1616: "Wee hold yt fitt and have given order that Mr. Willmot" should go to the "Savadge Islands," or Lesser Antilles, where it "is hoped he shall there gett . . . negores to dive for pearles," suggesting he sought to kidnap Pearl Coast divers. This was perhaps part of a larger imperial pattern. As mentioned above, Sloan reported on English acquisitions of pearl divers. In May 1683, Bermudian pirate Jacob Hall participated in a raid on Vera Cruz, Mexico, which possessed a pearl fishery. Seizing "1,230 Negro, Indian, and malato prisoners," he apparently sold some to Bermudian and Jamaican slaveholders. Gold Coast people were among Bermuda's unwilling immigrants. While anchored off Komenda in 1682, English slaver Charles Towgood complained that captives were diverted to a Bermudian slaving vessel that offered African traders better prices. Bermuda's aquatic culture was apparently distilled from African-influenced skills informed by Old and New World circumstances. Since Bermuda lacked pearl banks, captives were, by 1628, employed as salvors. For the next fifty years, Pearl Coast, Gold Coast, and Bermudian-born divers perfected salvaging techniques while stripping abandoned Spanish and Portuguese wrecks said to be the "Possession of the Devil."[59]

The recovery of Spanish galleon *Nuestra Señora de la Concepción* launched Bermuda's salvage industry, while convincing salvagers and wreckers to utilize African-descended divers. In 1641, the *Concepción* sank in forty to sixty feet of water on Ambrosia Banks (now Silver Bank) off Hispaniola. In 1686, future Massachusetts Bay governor, William Phipps colluded with Bermudian captains William Davis and Abraham Adderley to recover more than twenty-five tons of gold and silver worth some £300,000 sterling. They were Atlantic men, with Adderley holding property in Jamaica while Davis arrived at the wreck in a Bermudian "Sloope" after visiting Barbados where he "fitted a Small ship of ten gunns to seeke for this wreck." They completed their Bermudian diving contingents in Jamaica and Barbados.[60]

Phipps's methods were informed by an earlier, largely unsuccessful endeavor off New Providence, Bahamas. In 1683, King James II loaned him a ship indifferently called the *Rose of Algier*, *Rose of Algeree*, *Golden Rose*, *Rosebud*, or *Rose*. Captain John Knepp sailed her from London to Boston to obtain a diving bell. In November, "a vessel from the wreck" commanded by Peres Savage arrived in Boston, informing Knepp and Phipps that he and six other captains "consorted together and that they had 30 of as good divers as was ever at that place." They recovered enough wealth for everyone to receive "seven pounds and half of plate [sheets of silver] a man." The expedition proved disastrous for Phipps, Knepp, and New Providence. Mutinous sailors convinced Knepp to remain in Boston. Seven sailors raped the only woman on New Providence in front of her children. King James and Phipps lost money. Still, these events alerted Phipps to the value of enslaved divers.[61]

To salvage the *Concepción*, Phipps purchased two ships in London, the *Henry* and the *Bridgewater*, renaming the latter *James and Mary* after the King and Queen. The ships sailed for Barbados in September 1686 where they were reprovisioned and Francis Rogers boarded the *Henry* as captain, bringing one dugout and John Pasqua, Francis Anderson, and Jonas Abimeleck, who were enslaved divers apparently from Port Royal, Jamaica.[62] On January 20, 1687, Rogers dispatched William Covill, second mate of the *James and Mary*, in the canoe with "Francis & Jonas Abimeleck, ye 2 divers" to look for the *Concepción*. Remarkably, the trio found her "in 2 hours," spotting bronze cannons against the seafloor's white sand in forty feet of water.[63] Numerous other vessels out of Bermuda, Jamaica, the Bahamas, Barbados, and the Turks Islands soon descended on the wreck to pick its bones.[64]

Accounts of the *Concepción* contain discrepancies and focus on recovered wealth, not divers' experiences. Nonetheless, they are revealing. The wreck was worked by upward of sixty aquanauts, most of whom were of African descent. Phipps manned the *James and Mary* with four Mosquito Indians from Cabo Gracias a Dios in what is now Nicaragua. One was named Amataba, another Sancho.[65]

African-descended divers from Bermuda, Jamaica, and Barbados proved central to the operation. Like most slaves in the seventeenth-century English Americas at the time, they were probably African-born. Phipps's diving bell proved cumbersome and was little used. The Mosquito divers, who were seemingly not accustomed to such depths, were often too "ill" from apparently seasickness or pressure-related conditions to work.[66]

African and Indian divers could submerge two to three minutes when performing nonstrenuous work. Dives were shorter when wielding pick-axes, crowbars, and sledgehammers to break open hatches or chisel away coral-entombed wreckage. Divers spent surprisingly little time underwater, roughly forty to sixty minutes per day, usually working during morning and evening when winds and seas were calm and visibility good.[67] Importantly, divers' value, in this and other operations, was not measured by the duration of their labors but by the quantity of goods raised. During brief moments beneath the sea, they could produce tremendous amounts of wealth. For instance, Adderley rented an unnamed "Negroe" diver, who was probably James Locke, from Mary Robinson of Bermuda. He raised 2,358 "pieces of eight," or Spanish dollars. John Pasqua, Francis Anderson, and Jonas Abimeleck similarly recovered much silver.[68] The "ill" Mosquito divers equally harvested considerable wealth.[69]

Word of the success of the *Concepción* rapidly spread along maritime channels of communication. As Phipps departed "towards England" on April 27, 1687, he reported our "Divers haven taken out of y^e Wreck Coyne 1102$^{££}$ w^t. and Bullion 226$^{££}$. Totall 1328$^{££}$ net weight." Simultaneously, wreckers from English, French, and Dutch colonies converged. Experienced Bermudians recovered the most wealth. Adderley and Davis declared three tons of coins and plate worth £27,000. At least thirteen other Bermudian vessels raised more than 16,700 pounds of silver and one ton of gold, worth over £48,000 sterling. The undeclared treasure was much greater. Even Governor Robert Robinson exploited the situation. Claiming King James II granted him rights to one-tenth of what he salvaged, Robinson impressed twenty-four bondmen as divers and mariners.[70]

The wealth that slaves generated changed many Bermudians' fortunes. For example, Adderley's 1690 estate inventory indicates that his home, when compared to other seventeenth-century homes in the English colonies, was filled with a surprising amount and array of luxury items. In addition, he owned fourteen slaves, twenty-five cows, several boats and small ships, and two ship-cannons.[71]

Port Royal, Jamaica, provided a unique training ground for salvage divers. A June 7, 1692, earthquake caused much of Port Royal to liquefy and slide into the sea. Prior to the quake, Port Royal was "one of the world's great harbors" and home to pirates, wreckers, and wrecker-planters who assembled teams of "Diving Negroes." While shipwrecks were ephemeral sites moved by tides and destroyed by storms, this submerged town provided a stable training ground that was leisurely harvested. For the next twenty years, it remained home to more than two hundred enslaved divers who entered still-standing and partially collapsed structures to remove nearly everything inside. There are no known descriptions of this work. John Pasqua, Francis Anderson, Jonas Abimeleck, and other *Concepción* aquanauts undoubtedly dove upon Port Royal. Twentieth-century underwater archaeologists reported that they were "quite thorough and good at their work; missing very little of value," stripping structures so "there was absolutely nothing to be found."[72]

Port Royal divers mobilized to nearby waters. In September 1730, the fifty-four-gun Spanish warship *Genoesa* (probably *Genovese*) wrecked upon Pedro Bank (southwest of Jamaica) carrying a "great Treasure." Jamaica's governor attempted to secure the vessel for Spain. However, Port Royal wreckers sent aquanauts to salvage her and a Captain Ware of the British

Navy, who was sent to secure the vessel, instead "fish's up a great deal of Treasure" in three days and slipped off in the night.[73]

The misadventures of the seemingly delusional Collin Hunter illustrate how divers manipulated white elites. Claiming to possess "Spanish papers" revealing a wreck location, Hunter secured the captaincy of HMS *Dolphin* and financial support from Charles Gerard, Earl of Macclesfield, who appointed William Mills to manage his interests. In February 1699, Hunter departed England for Barbados to obtain divers. Before leaving England, he was accused of conspiring to engage in piracy and was jailed in Barbados on other unrelated piracy charges. After being held for six weeks in the "House of the Provost Marshall," he escaped. Hunter then scoured St. Lucia, Antigua, Nevis, and elsewhere for "Negroe Divers." At Port Royal, he obtained five "Diving Negroes," though slaveholders required "Sufficient Security," for "fear I should run away with them and y[e] kings Ship."[74]

In "very great hopes of sucksess," Hunter sailed to Seal Cays in the Turks Islands and, on April 8, 1700, anchored over a dark mass on the white-sand bottom. A diver soon brought up "Corrall" that "by appearance might a been growing upon wood." "Joyful of this discovery," Hunter commanded that the "Negroe Divers make further progress." After months of dodging about the Caribbean, a skeptical Mills, along with the ship's officers, concluded the silhouette was "nothing but a rock." Knowing divers injured on the "pretended wrack" would produce costs for Gerard, Mills refused to let them work. The following day, Mills consented and "all our divers went down, but they brought up Little Incouragement," concluding, "it is no wrack but a rock." Hunter believed Mills and his "cheating negroes" hid the treasure. In an apparent attempt to save face, Hunter suffered a mysterious attack, causing "y[e] Loss of my Limbs and a violent pain all over my body," allowing Mills to assume command and return to Jamaica.[75]

This search exemplifies white reliance on African skills, white reluctance to injure divers, and aquanauts' ability to negotiate white channels of power. Hunter knew where dive communities were located and his search illustrates how aquanauts from numerous colonies could be drawn together. Hunter and Mills distrusted each other and Mills sought to reduce Gerard's financial exposure by discouraging risks. The captives were keen tricksters who plumbed this abyss of whites' mistrust. Knowing they would not be beaten, they initiated what would become the common slave ploys of feigned ineptitude and work slowdowns. Powerless, Hunter fumed that "they were no sooner down but they were up again soe that they would have no time to search for any thing al tho it was not above 4 & ½ fathoms [25 feet] at yᵉ deepest."[76]

Importantly, divers' ability to manipulate some white people depended on their relationships with other white people. Encounters with unscrupulous shipmasters demonstrated African-descended wreckers' need to maintain connections with white patrons. For example, in 1802 as a free biracial Bermudian boarded a grounded American ship, the desperate captain proclaimed, "name your sum." The wrecker responded: "Five hundred dollars." He refloated the ship, which grounded on an adjacent reef. The captain agreed to pay another $500 to free his vessel. The Bermudian sailed it through "a winding passage, unseen before, being found, just wide enough, and barely deep enough, for the vessel to pass through." In deep waters, the emboldened captain projected American racism onto Bermudian waters, exclaiming that unless the wrecker returned the $1,000 he would take him to America and "as you seem to have a certain touch of black blood in your veins, I may chance to get good interest for my loan of these thousand dollars, by selling you as a slave in the Charleston negro Market!" Using proslavery rhetoric, the captain averred that, just as slave traders allegedly rescued Africans from savagery, he would provide "a great service, by carrying you away from one of the most infamous places in the world, to the finest country imaginable," where slavery might civilize him. Such incidents strengthened bonds to white islanders.[77]

Shipwrecks lured wreckers across the Atlantic. On May 23, 1787, the *Hartwell*, the "finest ships" in the East India Company's (EIC) fleet, sank in forty feet of water off Boa Vista Island (Bonavista in English sources), in the Cape Verde Islands. It contained sixty chests of silver coins valued at £153,642, three more chests belonging to the ship's owner, "several packages of private trade," and one hundred ingots of lead. During the spring and early summer, London newspapers exaggerated her fortunes while describing how enslaved and free Cape Verdians worked the wreck.[78]

William Braithwaite of London and his sons, John and William, secured the sole salvage contract. They had developed a steam engine for pumping air into diving bells. This allowed men to remain submerged for hours, a vast improvement over earlier techniques, which often resulted in men suffocating to death. They worked the *Hartwell* from the summer of 1787 through the fall of 1790. The EIC hired British warships to guard the site before deeming it unnecessary in the summer of 1789. On August 29, 1789, heavily armed wreckers drove the Braithwaites off. Then teams of divers stripped the *Hartwell* faster than the Braithwaites did with their bell.[79]

Wreckers worked unmolested until the HMS *Pomona*, captained by Henry Savage, arrived on October 29, capturing the sloop *Brothers* with its truly Atlantic complement. This vessel was owned by "Robinson & Duffy" from St. Eustatius in the Dutch West Indies and sailed under the Danish flag. Thomas Hammond of New York was the captain and Scotsman Adam Donaldson was mate; together they "procured seven Negroes Men Divers" from St. Thomas in the Danish West Indies. They also "fitted out" a small ship "belonging to St. Thomas" and commanded by "Captain Darby a native of Ireland." These divers recovered some 20,000 silver coins. Donaldson and an enslaved diver named John English reported that aquanauts belonging to other wreckers were equally productive. *Mary*, captained by "a native of Rhode Island," and flying a Dutch flag, recovered "10,000 Dollars" before returning to its homeport in St. Eustatius. The *Swift*, also of St. Eustatius, flew "Swedish Colours" and "got about 8,000 Dollars" but "lost their best diver." Another sloop was stolen "from some English Port" by "an Englishman" and commanded by "Lumbard" of Cape Cod, Massachusetts.[80]

Wreckers lived in maritime colonies. Working as fishermen, sea turtlers, spongers, and interisland sailors, they benefited from others' misfortune, exposing them to charges of piracy. Unsubstantiated tales claimed mooncruisers caused shipwrecks. Among other things, moon-cruisers were accused of hanging false lights at night to lure vessels into dangerous waters. Some allegedly hung lights on oceanside cliffs, shifting the nocturnal horizon up, creating the illusion of a distant port so captains ran aground while sailing toward what appeared to be a harbor.[81] Caymanian legends claim that men walked the windward cliffs of Cayman Brac, on Grand Cayman Island, with torches. Barbadian planter Sam Lord purportedly hung torches from his plantation buildings, trees, and cattle's horns to lure ships onto Cobbler Reef in Long Bay, causing five wrecks between 1826 and 1834. Regardless of why shipwrecks occurred at these locations, bondmen, and probably bondwomen, salvaged them.[82]

Even as white people deemed wreckers piratical, wreckers were respected for saving many lives. As Schoepff reported, "It cannot be denied that these **wreckers** swimming about save the lives of many people who but for them would inevitably be lost."[83] On at least one occasion, wreckers aided a sinking slaver—as was the case of the *Nelly*. En route from Calabar to Jamaica in 1782, the Nelly went down off Grand Cayman, in the Cayman Islands, where wreckers saved 321 of the 429 captives and all but one crewmember.[84]

Reverend Hope Waddell captured conflicting views of wreckers after his ship grounded off Grand Cayman in 1845, listing heavily as it threatened to capsize. At daybreak, "fragments of ships lying on the reef" indicated that these waters had claimed many vessels. Soon a "fleet of canoes" encompassed them and "a host of wild, reckless-looking, coloured men sprang up our sides, like pirates or boarders greedy of prey." With speed and dexterity they stripped the rigging, emptied the hold, and removed all the "doors, fittings, and furnishings." "Swearing shockingly" until "rebuked," they "begged pardon." The best canoe took Waddell's family ashore where "many women," who were presumably the wreckers' wives, "received the children into their arms with tenderness and pity. The head wrecker's house was offered for our use." The passengers' and crew members' personal belongings were carefully stowed in wreckers' homes, described as "fishermen's huts, and hovels of the poorest description." What were initially described as savage, biracial, undiscriminating vultures morphed into caring, discerning men and women. Scraping out a marginal subsistence on the periphery of the British Empire shortly after the abolition of slavery, these mariners could have safely sat ashore waiting for oceanic forces to destroy the ship and possibly drown all aboard. Instead, they rescued, pitied, and sheltered survivors, with Waddell coming to respect them and their multiracial society.[85]

Women and men engaged in other occupations. Natural scientists employed bondpeople to collect marine specimens. During their free time, bondwomen and bondmen in Bermuda, the Bahamas, and the Caribbean harvested shellfish, coral, octopuses, and sponges; consuming and selling their catches.

Conch meat was a regional delicacy among black and white residents. Women carved shells into jewelry and conch could produce pearls.[86] In 1750, natural scientist Griffith Hughes wrote that conch were found "in about five to six Fathoms [thirty-five feet] of Water, in most" Barbadian "Bays." To help counter surface distortions, divers "sprinkle a Spoonful of Oil upon the Surface."[87] Forty years later, an anonymous observer wrote: "We paddled about in a canoe from three to seven fathoms [eighteen to forty-two feet] of water, and wherever he could spy them, the negro threw himself in and brought them up: they are seldom found lying close to each other, but if within a few yards, he would swim from one to the other carrying them along with him: he sometimes brought up four, which will surprise you, when you hear that they are nearly each as big as a man's head, and weighing five or six pounds."[88]

Bahamians were renowned divers, "nick-named Conchs."[89] By the late eighteenth century, the Bahamas served as a health resort. Conch and sponge divers became a source of entertainment for sojourners. Boatmen took whites to reefs, called "sea gardens," where they paid divers to collect shellfish and bits of coral. Wrecking facilitated this branch of tourism, providing "water-glasses," or underwater viewers, which are four-sided wooden boxes with a glass pane on one side, enabling one to view submarine objects unobscured by surface distortions, as described by Johann Schoepff: "Below, on the pure white sand covering the bottom, one can make out every detail, reptilia of a thousand forms, sea-urchins and sea-stars, slugs, shell-fish and parti-colored fish; one floats above whole forests of stately sea-plants, gorgoniae, corals, alcyoniae, flabellae, and many sorts of shrubby spongious growths, their colors not less delighting the eye, and as softly moved by the waves back and forth as a flower-strewn field of the earth." Winslow Homer immortalized black Bahamians in *The Conch Divers* (1885) and *The Sponge Diver* (1898/99).[90]

Slaves dove for lobster, octopuses, and sea urchins. Lobsters are agile swimmers, making them difficult to catch. Divers grabbed many, storing them alive in submerged cages. Others were speared. Slaveholders undoubtedly commanded bondpeople to harvest lobster, which were served to them and their guests. Captives ate and sold others.[91]

Small octopuses, called "sea cats," were caught along the eastern coast of Barbados. Wading and swimming through shallows, bondpeople looked for their whitish undersides contrasted against dark rocks, impaling them with spears. There are no known records of whites consuming octopuses, but they were a favorite among slaves.[92]

Barbadians also dove for white and, to a lesser extent, purple sea urchins, respectively called "sea eggs" and "cobblers." Sea urchins' roe and gonads were a Barbadian delicacy occasionally eaten elsewhere. When John Taylor visited Jamaica in 1687, he reported that they were "full of a yellow substance like the yeolk of an egg, which is very delicious."[93] Women and men waded and swam to sea urchin beds, towing floating baskets called *screelers*. Divers "picked" sea eggs containing male and female reproductive organs, placing them in small hand nets. Upon surfacing, divers deposited

Figure 11. "The Sea Gardens." Water-glasses, or wooden boxes with a glass bottom, were attached to these boats' sides, allowing white tourists to peer through surface distortions to clearly watch black divers as they collected marine specimens for them. This late nineteenth-century image reflects circumstances that similarly occurred under bondage. James H. Stark, *Stark's History of and Guide to the Bahama Islands, Containing a description of Everything on or about the Bahama Islands of which the Visitor or Resident May Desire Information* (Boston: 1891), 231. Author's collection.

them into "screelers."[94] Some canoed to deeper beds.[95] Urchins were broken open and the roe and gonads were packed into clean "half shells," called "husks."[96] In towns, street vendors sang "sea-eggs, sea-eggs" or "Hot Sea-eggs! Hot sea-eggs!" to attract customers.[97]

Americans employed bondpeople to clear fisheries of debris that would snare nets. Some worked for their owners and others for commercial fisheries. Charles Ball documented how he and three other captives established a fishery for their owner on South Carolina's Congaree River. After constructing two African-style dugout canoes (see Chapter 6), the fishery was cleared. They waded and dove in frigid winter-waters to remove logs and "other rubbish." Though cold and grueling, the work was a welcome escape from field labor. Learning of this profitable enterprise, neighbors dis-patched divers to clear waterways.[98]

Commercial fisheries used more dramatic techniques. During the mid-1850s, Frederick Law Olmsted detailed the intercoastal fisheries at Curri-tuck, North Carolina, where the "largest sweep seines in the world" were used. "The shad and herring fisheries" were "an important branch of indus-try, and a source of considerable wealth." Olmsted met the owner of a $50,000 operation, who used a two-mile long seine "manned by a force of forty negroes." Since seines dragged the bottom, it was crucial to remove ensnaring-debris.[99]

Diving was dangerous, requiring the expenditure of "seventy kegs of gunpowder the previous year." In many places, coastal subsidence sub-merged forests, so "stumps of great cypress trees, not in the least decayed, yet protrude from the bottom of the sounds." Divers were key to their extrication. Mooring "two large seine-boats" above a stump, they chained it to a windlass to wrench it free. When a stump would not yield, explosives were used. A diver placed a long, iron-tipped pole on the stump, which sledgehammer-wielding slaves in the boats drove into it. Once a ten-foot cavity was made, the pole was removed and a canister of explosives was inserted into the void. The charge was detonated with the stump still chained to the boats, and the resulting explosion, combined with the upward force of the chains, wrenched the stump free.[100] Equating the prac-tice to "Titanic dentistry," Olmsted said: "The diver has come up, and is drawn into one of the boats—an iron rod is inserted in the mouth of the tube—all hands crouch low, and hold hard—the rod is let go—crack!—whoo—oosch! The sea swells, boils, and breaks upward. If the boats do not rise with it, they must sink; if they rise, and the chain does not break, the stump must rise with them. At the same moment the heart of cypress is riven; its furthest rootlets quiver; the very earth trembles, and loses courage to hold it; "up comes the stump, or down go the niggers!"[101]

"Up comes the stump, or down go the niggers!" This embellished line suggests divers were expendable. Yet, they were not. "The success of the operation," wrote Olmsted, "evidently depends mainly on the discretion and skill of the diver." Some remained "under water, and work there to better advantage than others; but all were admirably skillful."[102] They were deeply valued and, as the next chapter explores, could use their highly skilled labors to negotiate within the system of bondage.

Chapter 5

Undercurrents of Power:
Challenging Racial Hierarchies from Below

Even as bondage was imposed and perpetuated by violence from above the challenges of diving generated strong undercurrents that countered white domination, creating a perplexity of swirling stratified currents that favored divers as they and slaveholders ceaselessly tried to extract concessions from each other. Without divers, water, in some important ways, placed visible wrecks and pearl beds just beyond the reach of covetous white people. Divers parleyed their invaluable expertise, as well as cooperation and resistance, to gain control over their bodies and immediate circumstances. Individually and collectively, they pried concessions from enslavers, exchanging prowess for semi-independent lives of privileged exploitation.[1]

Enslaved divers enjoyed privileges exceeding those reserved for the most expert craftsmen, like sugar boilers, machinists, machine engineers, and shipwrights. Without their wisdom, plantation output would halt and mistakes could ruin thousands of hours of slave labor, causing planters' significant financial loss and "commercial and personal derision." An enslaved boiler could ruin the crystallization of sugar during the final stages of production. An engineer's poor workmanship could cause steam engines used to boil sugarcane juice to break or explode, resulting in injury, death, and the destruction of expensive engines and semi-refined sugar. Coopers' poorly constructed barrels could ooze sugar, molasses, or rum. Slave owners recognized their dependence on craftsmen and granted them privileges to aid "productivity as the enslaved furthered their own interests by accommodating the machine of planters' agenda." One of the most important privileges was elevation into skilled occupations, enabling slaves to evade the drudgery of fieldwork, find dignity in their labor, enhance their self-esteem, become highly regarded by fellow slaves, and sometimes obtain cash payments.[2]

Skilled occupations were privileges that slaves could be stripped of for misconduct or at their owners' whim. While plantation production would quickly cease without craftsmen, bondpeople could be rotated into many positions without disrupting output. White craftsmen could also be hired. Many occupations only required seasonal or part-time labor, resulting in skilled captives spending time in agricultural fields.[3] Ashore, this rotation operated against the formation of a stratum of skilled bondpeople, causing most craftsmen to realize that they were part of the fettered masses. Divers seemingly formed a discrete occupational group, at the same time that bonds of blood and marriage linked them to other captives.[4]

Unlike with enslaved craftsmen and other skilled workers, enslavers did not have the luxury of shifting men in and out of diving positions or of discharging them for minor infractions or in acts of white capriciousness. Divers were highly skilled men who possessed abilities few held. Diving was often seasonal or performed when needed, and slaveholders knew there were few or no replacements. These factors discouraged whites from physically punishing most, knowing injuries could inhibit diving.

The privileges skilled slaves received were not the fruit of benevolence. Whites bestowed favors to extract wealth from slaves' limbs and minds.[5] Diving was arduous and dangerous, taxing one's health and claiming many lives. Yet, aquanauts gained respite from field labor and received material rewards. Although divers lived existences of privileged exploitation as their expertise brought them rewards, they brought substantially more rewards for their owners.

Divers' relationship with white authority remains somewhat nebulous and was subject to numerous variables. Slaveholders employed many divers. Most were apparently hired out. Hired-out bondpeople worked away from their owners and, to varying extents, organized their own time, had fluctuating degrees of control over their work, and received wages. They enjoyed considerable mobility, weaving far-reaching networks of friendship and family as they traveled across the Caribbean and even the Atlantic.[6] Incomes enabled some divers to purchase freedom for themselves and their family members.

Over time, divers were increasingly treated like free white men as the economic importance of salvaging grew. Salvagers generated substantial tax revenues for England while fostering economic opportunities through intra- and inter-imperial seaborne smuggling that benefited most colonists, causing smuggling to shift from the improvised illegal economy of the marginalized to the prosperous pursuit of most ship-owning slaveholders. Divers worked alongside whites who encouraged and rewarded their propensities. Afloat and ashore, aquanauts received roughly the same food, clothing, and shelter as their owners, prompting Governor John Hope to state: "They are Strong well Bodied Fellows and well fed." Many became literate, using this skill to further their opportunities. Some free and enslaved wreckers/salvors became ship captains, commanding white and black mariners.[7]

As essential producers of white incomes in maritime colonies, divers further benefited from the flexibilities of maritime bondage. This convinced whites to cultivate reciprocal relationships that bound slaves to multiracial crews and the islands where their families lived, they owned property, and they received white protection from outsiders. Implicit threats of selling wives and children transformed family members into hostages, compelling wreckers to return home. Simultaneously, enslavers promoted arduousness by avoiding coercive discipline while nurturing a sense of mutual obligation arising from collective responsibilities and extending material rewards. The shared "hardships and dangers" of the sea prompted many whites to judge enslaved shipmates on their abilities and bravery. As the eighteenth century progressed, kinship ties increasingly bolstered shipmate affiliations. In 1824, a New Yorker commented on Bahamian wreckers' intertwined bloodlines, writing: "Most of them have a dash of dark blood in their veins & many are mulattoes." Many whites went to sea with biracial men who they owned. Some recognized divers as relatives, allowing them to use white familial ties to advance their positions. In some important ways, enslaved salvors lived as if they were free so long as they remained enslaved.[8]

Unique opportunities were not confined to maritime colonies. By the 1650s, Barbadian plantation slavery was deep-rooted, allowing sugar to "dominate the Barbadian export sector" in what "was a slave society by at least 1680." From the 1680s into the eighteenth-century, divers received privileges akin to those on maritime colonies. Eighteenth-century Jamaicans and divers from England's other sugar-producing islands received similar treatment. Likewise, sources suggest that those from the seventeenth- and eighteenth-century Danish, Dutch, English, and French islands were equally privileged, though further analysis is required.[9]

Many salvors used incomes and white connections to obtain freedom and become independent wreckers. Hiring out destabilized traditional social relations, permitting bondpeople to construct social and cultural spaces between slavery and freedom where they challenged notions of African inferiority by forming work contracts honored by white employers and government officials. Hiring out was lucrative for slave owners who received a portion of hirelings' incomes. Nonslaveholders benefited from slaves' wisdom, brawn, and skill, giving them entry into the slaveholding ranks, or illusions of this status. Hiring also benefited captives. In many ways, salvage divers were treated like free-wage laborers with varying degrees of control over their lives. Their incomes and control over the production of wealth permitted some to purchase or be awarded their freedom. Yet, as freed people they were forced to maintain bonds with former owners who protected them from outside abuse.[10]

Divers worked largely free of direct white supervision. When not diving, "and, while the other hands are at work, they may lounge, or go to sleep in the boat." They consumed "as much whisky as they want," believing it kept them warm. Displays of "unusual hardihood, skill, or perseverance" were rewarded with "whisky; or . . . money," earning bonuses of a "quarter to half a-dollar" per day. Pride in workmanship, concepts of honor and masculinity, and material rewards drove divers to excel. Olmsted was told, "The harder the work you give them to do, the better they like it." Even though divers frequently suffered from "fevers," they insisted "they were 'well enough to dive.' "[11]

Working free of corporal punishment, enticed by benefits, and not wanting to tarnish their crafted reputations, wage-earning captives worked arduously in a perilous, yet privileged, profession. "What! slaves eager to work, and working cheerfully, earnestly and skillfully?" Olmsted exclaimed, "Being for the time managed as freemen, their ambition stimulated by wages, suddenly they, too, reveal sterling manhood, and honor their Creator."[12]

Whites used incentives rather than coercion to extract incomes from divers' capable minds and bodies. Ship captains and investors equally divided profits with fettered divers, as illustrated by the 1687 affidavit of the *Ann* from Barbados. Praising the five divers who worked the *Concepción*, it read, "Four of ye aforsaid five Divars by name Keazar, Salsbury, Tony & Tom were as good as any that went from Barbados," and "the aforenamed four Divers [received] four single shares," while "the Negro Bamko the other Diver, one share." These shares were in addition to fees paid to their owners.[13]

Some were granted freedom, using their incomes to improve family members' circumstances, as illustrated by James Locke, the diver Mary Robinson hired to Adderley to salvage the *Concepción*. Adderley helped Locke secure his liberty and that of his sister, Betty. On January 27, 1687/88, shortly after Locke's second voyage to the wreck, Robinson "grant[ed] the said James Locke his freedom." Locke now used his income as he chose. On July 22, 1687, "Black James Locke," "with permission [assistance] from Mr. Abraham Adderley," purchased Betty and "a Negroe child called Jethrow," who was probably Betty's son, from Thomas Minors. Perhaps Adderley and Locke colluded to dupe Mary Robinson so that they could salvage other wrecks without her interference.[14]

The *Ann* evidences salvage divers' origins and mobility. Most seventeenth-century Barbadian slaves were African-born, with Bamko and Keazar apparently bearing African names. Divers probably recovered goods that fell overboard in Bridgetown Harbor and were sent to Caribbean wrecks.[15]

Divers seemingly used their expertise to gain white salvors' respect, convincing captains to create two shipboard hierarchies: one in which they beat and berated white and black sailors and another in which enslaved divers escaped corporal punishment while receiving compensation. Phipps purportedly abused white officers and sailors, while treating Indian and black divers well, and there were only two reported deaths among the approximately sixty *Concepción* divers.[16] English planters knew how to work manacled field hands to death. Even as they imposed high mortality rates on field slaves, English salvagers treated divers well.[17] In addition, many were rented from their owners who had to be compensated for injuring or killing their property, providing divers with overlapping protection. They were well fed. Phipps hired "Spanish hunt[rs]" to obtain upward of twenty-nine "wild hoggs" per day. Those suffering from diving disorders and other ailments were granted time off. To reduce injury, diving was only performed in calm seas, often precluding work for several days.[18] Physical and verbal abuse prolonged recovery times, while injured divers were hard to replace. Without divers, salvagers were largely left to gaze at shipwrecks through clear Caribbean waters. Hence, divers were well treated—for slaves.

The examination of enslaved divers expands our understandings of how skilled bondpeople manipulated social and racial hierarchies. While all divers used the same skills, occupational variables shaped experiences just as the cultivation of different crops, such as rice and sugar, informed slaves' lives.[19] Pearl divers were treated comparatively harshly. Pearl beds could be worked seasonally for years, perhaps prompting Spaniards to conclude that injured divers would recover to generate wealth. Shipwrecks were ephemeral places that oceanic forces could destroy, rendering salvaging impossible. Salvagers apparently concluded that injured aquanauts might not recover quickly enough to dive. In addition, pearl operators' ability to replace Indians with Africans perhaps prompted them to conclude that divers were semi-expendable. Still, all divers enjoyed unique privileges in their respective societies.

Captives in an institution that dishonored and disrespected African-descended people, maintained tenuous holds on honor and masculinity. Many surely took pride in the fact that their expertise outperformed Western innovations. Their courage was surely bolstered by understandings that they braved cold waters, sharks, and dive-related dangers. Failure was seemingly not an option as it could diminish their crafted versions of themselves and jeopardize their employment. They were compelled to succeed, enriching slaveholders in the process.

Fishery divers' use of explosives imposed risks while affording benefits. One should not discount the exhilaration of blowing up trees; a rush enhanced by whiskey. All divers gained considerable autonomy. Fishery divers were perhaps the most trusted. They worked away from direct white supervision, and were given alcohol and dynamite—key ingredients of rebellion. Everyone understood that concussions from underwater explosives could kill divers—a risk made palpable when dead and dying fish floated to the surface. These risks permitted divers to sensationally seize honor and masculinity.

Enslavers looted captives' swimming cultures to generate incomes. Divers were highly skilled men who, like other adroit captives, shaped economic growth in ways exceeding what their numbers suggested. Highly skilled carpenters constructed intricate floodgates vital to rice production, helping to make South Carolina the wealthiest colony and state in America up to the Civil War. Throughout the Americas, blacksmiths fabricated and repaired the agricultural tools used to cultivate slave-produced staples. In Brazil and the Caribbean, "sugar cooks" or "boilers" were well versed in sugar production. They knew precisely when sugar cane juice had "tempered," when to pour it from one heating vat to the next, and when to cool it. More than any other sugar-producing slaves, boilers "meant the difference between a profit or a loss on the plantation ledger."[20]

Slaveholders treated aquanauts better than they did most skilled bondpeople. In some important ways, divers resembled enslaved Antebellum industrial workers. Through years of apprenticeship, some became indispensable to iron making. In 1847, the Tredegar Iron Works purchased thirty-two slaves, grooming them for more than a decade. The time and money dedicated to their training suggest that replacements could not be readily obtained and their positions were lifelong appointments. Divers surely began learning during youth. There is no evidence of diving positions passing from father to son. Still, divers would need to become proficient when they were young and they would need to swim regularly to develop the necessary lung capacities, physiques, and composure.[21]

As enslavers pursued never-ending negotiated relationships with divers, they conceded autonomy while tempering claims of absolute authority. Divers knew slaveholders would not exile them to the fields of bondage, giving them leverage for extracting privileges. Slaveholders realized that they were privileged to own men possessing such rare and lucrative abilities.[22]

Divers compelled white people to reassess concepts of race. The inability of whites to dive subsumed assertions that they should occupy skilled positions while slaves performed mindless labor. When terrestrial captives performed skilled work, tensions between members of the white elite and middling white sorts sometimes developed. In the American South, "the elevation of black skilled labor to a par with white work significantly challenged the racialized rubric," causing white men to complain that "their dignity and their pocketbooks suffered from the competition with slaves." White artisans and laborers sometimes engaged in work disruptions and mounted legal challenges to the employment of slave workers, averring that, as white men in societies privileging whiteness, they were entitled to the wages paid to bondmen. The hiring of aquanauts subverted white domination, yet white inabilities precluded claims that diving adversely impacted them, permitting slaveholders to project influence under the water.[23]

The honor that divers obtained and the desire to improve their circumstances made them vulnerable to manipulation. Much of Southern bondpeople's recreational lives were bound to agricultural production, permitting captors to squeeze earnings from their merriment. "Working socials," like corn shucking, hog killing, and wheat threshing, were merry occasions that combined work and recreation. Often, part of festivities required work completed under the illusion of "physical pleasure and emotional release." To enhance the merriment, planters organized shuckers into competing teams.[24]

Whites similarly manipulated divers' sense of honor, masculinity, and yearning for material comfort. Promises of freedom enticed divers to find the *Margarita*. Whites undoubtedly extolled divers' masculinity, fueled competitiveness, and equated failure to femininity. Though the work was arduous, divers welcomed the escape from the monotonies of agricultural labor. Still the fetters of bondage confined divers' advantages to the waters of privileged exploitation.

Expertise and intimate understandings of dominant cultures permitted some divers to capsize belittling attempts. During the 1540s, England's High Court of Admiralty provided a stage for Jacques Francis, John Ik, George Blacke (Black), and five other Africans to challenge Italian notions of race and slavery in England. Venetian salvager Petri Paulo Corsi employed them to salvage the HMS *Mary Rose*, which was Henry VIII's flagship and one of the world's most modern battleships. It sank in about thirty-five feet of water on July 19, 1545 off Portsmouth, England. The Admiralty appointed Corsi in July 1546 and, in July 1547, Corsi was hired by Italian merchants to salvage the merchantman *Sancta Maria and Sanctus Edwardus*, off nearby Southampton.[25]

Francis "was born" on the "Isle of Guinea;" possibly a generic term for a West African island, but probably Arguin or Arguim off Mauritania whose hydrography speaks to the divers' expertise as it is surrounded by "shallows of rocks and sand[bars]" that claimed many ships, providing the team with fertile training grounds. Arguin was deemed the divide between North and Sub-Saharan Africa and "inhabited by black-a-moors," or Sub-Saharan Africans. The Portuguese built a trade castle there in 1448 to divert trade away from Timbuktu, transforming the island into an important port. Whether these divers were members of Arguin's indigenous population or Senegambians who arrived as salvagers, merchants, or slaves remains unknown, though they spoke the same African language, while Francis's name reflects Catholic Portuguese connections and cultural understandings. Word of their expertise possibly floated northward, breaking upon Corsi's ear, convincing him to expand his fortunes by employing them, in 1545, to apparently work other wrecks before the *Mary Rose*.[26]

The Africans completed Corsi's salvage team. Francis became head diver, Ik and Blacke probably served as divers, while the others were apparently assistants or apprentices. Corsi could "dyve under the water," though evidently not as well as Francis. It is improbably that Corsi could have found several African divers in sixteenth-century England, suggesting that they, like future dive teams, arrived together and were free. Regardless, they were treated well with Corsi "payeng for ther meate [a true luxury] and dryncke at the Dolphin" Inn in Hampton.[27]

Salvaging proceeded until the Italian merchants accused Corsi of stealing the *Sancta Maria*'s bell, as well as lead and several blocks of tin bearing the marks of Domenic Erizzo and Bartolome Fortini, prominent Florentine merchants residing in London. Erizzo arrested and sued Corsi in the High Court of Admiralty, prompting Francis to testify in Corsi's defense. The merchants, who had applauded Francis's expertise, turned on him, using Italian concepts of race to preclude his testimony. Attempting to deny Francis's legal personhood, they called him a "slave," "Blacke more," "morisco born where they are not christened," and "gynno [Guinea] born." (These remained imprecise idioms that could aver the inferiority of Muslims, Muslim converts to Christianity, and Africans.) This strategy of exclusion failed. The court valuated Francis's expertise and accepted him as a Christian, as illustrated when he swore upon the Bible to tell the truth.[28]

Relying on these Italian claims and assuming that Africans must have arrived in England as slaves, previous scholars concluded that the divers were enslaved. Yet this seems untrue. Recent scholarship clarifies that while English merchants and privateers profited from slaving in Africa and the Americas, at "home, however, Africans created problems." Before about 1570, "many people were bragging that their island's air was too pure for slavery" while high unemployment rates and suspicion of outsiders discouraged the importation of Africans. Furthermore, Corsi neither claimed the divers were enslaved nor treated them as if they were enslaved, and he seems to have been a member of the middling sorts without the means to purchase several slaves. Even if they had been obtained in Africa as slaves, of which there is no evidence, they were apparently deemed free in England. Regardless, they felt compelled to prove their freedom, with Francis testifying that he was "of his own free will" in Africa and a servant in England. Ik and Blacke stated that they were "servauntes" and "poore laboryng men."[29]

With his legal footing secured, Francis went on the offensive.[30] On February 8, 1547, Francis appropriated the symbols of English civility, appearing in court dressed not as an enslaved African but as a skilled professional and respectable Englishman. Without uttering a word, he defied notions of racial inferiority in the High Court of Admiralty as his athletic, dark-complexioned, well-clad body visually proclaimed "I am black, but comely"—an assertion that would become a familiar mantra for oppressed people of African descent. From the stand, he parried his purported inferiority. In testimony recorded in Latin, Francis identified himself as Corsi's "famulus," meaning "servant" or "attendant," not "servus" meaning "slave," explaining that the two had been in a patron-client relationship for the past "two years." As apparently the best diver in England, Francis provided his expert opinion, explaining he "dyd handell and see under water" the allegedly stolen items that were "takyn and saved" and would have been restored if Erizzo had not "arreste[d]" Corsi. (Fortini abstained from suing after his goods were returned.) Francis then accused Erizzo of inhibiting the salvaging of the king's ship by arresting Corsi in "Maye," "the beste tyme" for diving, as seas were calm.[31]

The court allowed Francis's mastery of the deep to defy English ideas of racial hierarchy, as did everyone else. When Englishmen failed to salvage England's prized battleship, the Admiralty hired Italians. Francis demonstrated that African expertise was more efficient than European techniques, using African aquatics to graduate into his elevated position. He was a skilled professional during his two years upon the wrecks. His testimony, dress, and actions challenged juvenile ideas of race, slavery, and status. The judges agreed, allowing an African to testify against affluent Europeans.

In some important ways, undercurrents of power flowed in divers' favor, providing them with some unique privileges. Freediving enabled bondmen to gain honor, knowing that they mastered skills few possessed and that without their expertise whites were largely precluded from harvesting shipwrecks and pearl beds or removing debris from fisheries. Diving is a gamble over the abyss, permitting divers to push their limits while challenging death. In the depths, every man proved himself during journeys of self-exploration. The divers observed death tolls, knowing skill, luck, and protection from ancestral spirits permitted them to endure.

Studies of Oceanian spear fishermen and Greek sponge divers suggest that precaution was deemed effeminate and childlike, inviting ridicule. Sponge divers used their profession as a rite of passage in which the "ability to face death and to do so purposely is considered the hallmark of manhood." Greek, Oceanian, and enslaved divers knew who the best diver in every team was and which team outproduced others, with desire to be the best motivating them.[32]

Enslaved divers' sense of honor was surely stoked by the realization that they outperformed European technology. Pearl divers harvested more oysters than French and English oyster dredges. Dredges consisted of a rake and trailing net and were dragged across mud-banks or sand bottoms, knocking oysters into the net. They snagged on Pearl Coast reefs, prompting canoe masters to boast that divers were more productive.[33]

Scholars have considered how enslavers promoted plantation production by manipulating slaves' desires while cultivating dependence. The same was true afloat, where whites granted and manipulated privileges to extract wisdom, skills, and wealth. At one level, slaveholders did not care about captives' personal lives, allowing them "by choice or necessity" to "shape some aspects of their lives as laborers." Yet, slave owners twisted African perceptions of honor to meet their own needs. White canoe masters, salvagers, and fishery operators understood bondmen's concepts of honor, manhood, and shame. While whites often did not recognize slaves' concepts of honor and masculinity ashore, they encouraged them afloat; knowing that sulky, cowardly divers were worthless. Audaciousness and masculinity were revenue-generating qualities. Bondmen embraced opportunities to enhance their status. A cruel irony of divers' circumstances is that in the absence of other methods for obtaining honor, they relied on diving to provide their exploited lives with indicators of personal worth.[34]

African-influenced aquatic cultures provided enslaver and enslaved with benefits, locking them in symbiotic relationships. Divers successfully challenged the tenets dictating that all of captives' waking hours belonged to enslavers. Field hands generally toiled from sunup to sundown, sometimes longer. Most aquanauts only dove, working less than two hours each day, even though they could have performed other tasks when not diving. The clock did not measure their value; it was determined by their expertise. Divers' ability to extract unusual privileges made them elites among the enthralled masses. Still, they remained chained to the fettered masses through marriage and friendship.

Slavery stole most of what held meaning and value for Africans. It pirated their lives, their bodies, their time, their humanity. It attempted to pilfer the corporeal sensual pleasures of water and aquatics, bending them to slaveholders' will. Divers used their profession to regain some of their humanity. One cannot diminish the surreal tranquility and solace diving surely afforded. Freediving is an otherworldly experience, allowing one to slide into the deep, becoming almost one with surrounding sea creatures. This serenity provides moments of calm reflection. During the ephemeral moments of a dive, captives could imagine themselves free in home-waters. Freediving is a cathartic experience that is at once soothing and exhilarating. While slaves did not choose this pursuit, they undoubtedly found pleasure in its sensuality. Here, the overseer's whip—the embodiment of terrestrial discipline—could not reach them. True, when their heads broke the water's surface, the quietude vanished and the realities of their circumstances were unavoidable. But for brief moments, they were free and this freedom cannot be discounted.[35]

PART II

Canoe Culture

Chapter 6

African Canoe-Makers:
Constructing Floating Cultures

It is easy to forget water's centrality in societal development throughout Africa and the world. Water connected landmasses and provided an efficient medium for moving commodities and people considerable distances. It was cheaper, easier, and faster to transport goods and people by water than overland, which entailed building and maintaining roads and bridges.[1]

Atlantic African dugout canoes were Africans' versatile solution for navigating the region's diverse waterways. This chapter examines African canoe designs and building techniques to demonstrate that Africans possessed time-tested canoe-making methods and designs. It has been assumed that Amerindians taught enslaved Africans to construct dugouts. This and the next two chapters describe African canoe-making and canoeing and argue that slave-built dugouts reflect African designs and usages.

Atlantic Africa was an aquatic world and Africans developed maritime cultures necessary to traverse and exploit their world. Rivers, streams, lakes, and seas separated landmasses while linking societies through trade and communication.[2] Coastal and interior waters permitted canoemen to rapidly transport goods, people, and information. During the 1580s, André Álvares de Almada observed how Senegambian and Sierra Leonean merchants used rivers and seas to weave vast commercial networks. In 1735, John Atkins elaborated, saying: "Canoos are what are used through the whole Coast for transporting Men and Goods."[3]

Canoemen connected oceanside settlements to interior trade centers.[4] The "Niger-Senegal-Gambia[-Benue] river complex unite[d] a considerable portion of West Africa." Extending for about 2,600 miles, the Niger has a drainage basin of some 817,600 square miles. Its headwaters lay in what is now southeastern Guinea and it flows inland before arching seaward to form the Niger River Bend in Mali. Its waters provided maritime experiences for societies in numerous environmental systems: from the sands of the Sahara to the Sahel, grasslands of savannahs, rainforests, coastal plains, and a delta containing innumerable creeks and streams. Its main tributary, the Benue River, flows about 850 miles through northern Cameroon before merging with the Niger. Several tributaries indirectly link it to Lake Chad. The commercial cities of Bamako, Ségou, Mopti, Djénne, Timbuktu, and Gao were erected along the Great Bend, connecting West Africa to North Africa. With the Sahara functioning as an ocean, these cities served as ports on both the Niger and this sea of sand.[5]

West Africa is framed beneath the Niger's arch and bound together by an array of watercourses, including the calm mangrove swamps of Guinea and Sierra Leone.[6] The lagoon complex of the Bights of Benin and Biafra extends from the Volta River, in what is now Ghana, to the Nigerian–Cameroonian border. This system enabled transport along the Atlantic coast without venturing onto the ocean, as Arthur Wendover expressed in 1682: "These people never goe to sea in their canoes, for the river [coastal lagoon] being so large," facilitated travel.[7] The Senegal and Gambia Rivers give the Senegambia its name and were connected to the Niger River by an overland portage of about 150 miles. The Gambia, like many African rivers, is tidal for about one hundred miles inland, permitting the sea to inform the patterns of interior daily life. The Senegal River is West Africa's second-longest river and during the rainy season can be more than fifteen miles wide.[8]

Similarly, West-Central Africa was "oriented by its rivers, especially the Zaire [Congo] and the Kwanza." The Congo is the heart of a massive hydro system extending 2,900 miles inland, into the East African Rift Valley to be watered by Lake Tanganyika and Lake Mweru. Just below Malebo (Stanley) Pool, some three hundred miles from the Atlantic, the Congo narrows and drops some nine hundred feet within the distance of about two miles while twisting through a series of cataracts known as Livingston Falls. Above Malebo, the Congo is navigable for about one thousand miles. The region is bordered by more than one thousand miles of seas.[9]

Though many coastal urban centers were called "ports," this appellation is typically a misnomer. Atlantic Africa possesses few natural harbors and most "ports" were actually "surf-ports," or landings situated on surf-battered beaches that offered little protection from the sea and possessed no wharves. For instance, at Benguela, Angola, George Tams reported: "The inconvenience of landing in European boats is very great, because, notwithstanding the sheltered situation of the harbour, the breakers never entirely subside; and the wind blows hard from the sea, it is almost impossible to approach ashore."[10]

Surf-ports provided the same functions as harbors; though ships usually anchored one to five miles offshore. Surf-canoemen, serving as lightermen, passed through breakers to load and offload ships. Historian Patrick Manning stressed canoemen's importance to Atlantic commerce, saying: "For the transportation of goods across the surf, some 40,000 tons of goods were carried each way annually in colonial Dahomey at the end of the nineteenth century; slightly smaller amounts were moved in Togo, and larger quantities were moved in Lagos." Some surf-ports were not situated on waterways. Ouidah was some three miles inland from a lagoon inaccessible to ships. Goods were landed through surf, taken across a narrow island, through the lagoon, then overland to Ouidah.[11]

Mastery of waterways required adaptation, not domination. An understanding of oceanic navigations enabled early modern Europeans to exploit the sea. During the "age of sail, shipping routes and even schedules were determined in considerable measure by factors over which ships had little control, but to which they had instead to adapt, such as oceanic currents or prevailing patterns of winds."[12]

Africanists' desire to place the continent into an Atlantic context inspired the study of how waterways shaped African developments, along with a growing interest in precolonial urbanization, and especially "port" communities. Studies of coastal urbanization focus on "the organization of overseas commerce, the relationships between ports and their hinterlands, the effects of their involvement in Atlantic commerce on their political and social structures and demographic growth, and the problems posed for them by the transition from the slave trade to exports of agricultural produce such as palm oil in the nineteenth century."[13] Considerable room for elaboration remains and the examination of canoe production and use is critical for further broadening our intellectual horizons.

Canoemen exploited hydrographic understandings, using knowledge of marine geography and how currents, winds, water depth, and the ocean's tides informed navigation. Atlantic African canoes shared a design and function, informed by cultural valuations, the use of iron tools, and hydrography. Design nuances permitted some to better negotiate particular hydrographies and uses, such as surf, coastal oceans, fishing, and commerce.[14]

The designs of Atlantic African and New World slave canoes are strikingly similar. They were pointed at the bow, and sterns usually came to a rounded point. Bows and sterns rose from the water at about a fifteen- to fifty-degree angle, causing them to project over the water. Most had flat or semi-rounded bottoms, which improved stability, while the sides were considerably worked, giving the hull a v-shape. Even when heavily laden, they had a shallow draft (referring to the water depth required to float), enabling them to pass through shallows, often less than one foot deep. Recognizing canoes' utility, English slave trader William Snelgrave reported: "As the water near the Shore is very shallow, our Boats cannot approach nearer than within two Cables [or 600 feet], so that we are obliged to make use of *Cannoes* which draw much less Water than our Boats, to land our Goods." Their design informed how they handled. Crews in Western rowboats sat backward when rowing. Canoemen faced forward and could rapidly rotate craft on their center axis, a maneuver not easily performed in rowboats.[15]

Dugouts were Atlantic Africans' solution for navigating diverse waterways. Variations affected costs, function, and performance. For instance, cargo and war canoes, sometimes measuring more than one hundred feet long, were designed for calm rivers and lagoons and were too unstable to pass through surf. Surf-canoes were designed to launch and land through breakers. Africans also constructed higher- and lower-quality canoes. Cargo, war, and surf-canoes were expensive and crafted by professionals. Fishermen, merchants, and fishermen-farmer-merchants made more roughly finished and less seaworthy canoes for calm waters. As high quality canoes deteriorated, many were relegated to the calm-water work of lower grade dugouts. Canoe-making was widely deemed a sacred profession with dugouts treated as secular and spiritual items, reflected in the Senegambian proverb: "The blood of kings and the tears of the canoe-maker are sacred things which must not touch the ground." A canoe's value was not solely determined by construction costs; it was also determined by its ability to produce incomes and to return mariners to shore, as well as by social, cultural, and spiritual valuations.[16]

Commercial canoemen paddled great distances. Atlantic Africa contains several of the world's largest rivers, including the continent's second-and third-largest rivers: the Congo and the Niger, respectively. Many rivers permitted European ships to travel well inland; about one hundred miles up the Gambia River and two hundred miles up the Sherbro River (now the Sewa). Canoes traveled farther still. Since canoes were relatively light, they could be portaged around rapids and falls and between noninter-secting watercourses.[17]

Dugouts proved faster and more maneuverable than European row-boats. Surf-canoes used for trade and fishing could catch waves. Rowboats regularly overturned in the surf, prompting W. Jeffrey Bolster to write: "Quicker to respond to short, rapid-fire paddle strokes than were European boats (with their full ends and more cumbersome oars), certain canoes could better negotiate the tumbling surfs that constantly broke over much of the coast." These qualities did not go unnoticed by European merchants and naval officers who regularly replaced rowboats with dugouts, hiring canoemen to crew them to transport goods and people between ship and shore. French botanist Michel Adanson epitomized this practice in 1749: "Our European boats appearing to me too heavy and cumbersome, to make use of them every day in passing that [Senegal] river; I therefore thought to exchange them for a kind of Negro canoo."[18]

Accounts document dugouts' maneuverability. Jean Barbot described rowboats trudging up Liberia's "Rio Sestro," saying the "view, together with the silence of the place, with the cries and vigorous leapings of a multitude of monkeys and apes tumbling about the trees above our heads, with the slow regular dull noise made by our rowers, with our escorting squadron of little canoes manned by blacks wheeling around us to do us honour."[19] Into the twentieth century surf-canoes transported virtually all the goods and people conveyed between ship and shore. During the 1920s, "a keen yachtsman" said Gold Coast fishermen's "canoes were well adapted to their work: they were light but seaworthy, fast when running with the wind, exactly what was needed for working from a steeply shelving sandy beach in heavy surf. The men were wonderfully skillful at handling them in the critical moment when the canoe came flying up the beach on the crest of a wave and took the ground as the wave receded. With their rounded bottom, they settled flat and were easily hauled up the beach."[20]

Their swiftness was equally impressive. Barbot said the "speed with which these people generally make these boats travel is beyond belief."[21] Alvise da Cadamosto noted that Gambian canoes effortlessly overtook Por-tuguese caravels, while Charles Thomas reported on *Kru* mariners' ability to negotiate rough seas: "We were twenty miles from shore, and the sea ran very high; yet these venturers turned and manoevered their light crafts with as much ease and confidence as if they were floating on a lake, and kept close alongside, although we were going at a rate of" nine miles per hour.[22] Canoemen also outpaced small steamers, humiliating Edward Glave while in the Congo Free State when they surrounded his vessel, hurling insults, "corn-cobs, pieces of wood, and stones" at him.[23]

Many white travelers appreciated how canoe-makers' expertise and canoemen's dexterities safeguarded their lives and fortunes. Pieter de Marees felt Grain Coast canoe-makers made "fine canoes," while averring those of the Gold Coast were the best. Rivers of praise flowed into the twentieth century even as travelers evoked Victorian-era racism to cast Africa as a savage continent. For example, in *Among Congo Cannibals*, John Weeks wrote, "They were clever in making canoes, . . . They were also expert in making paddles."[24]

Canoe-making, from felling a tree to finished product, took from several days to a couple of months depending on size. Many tropical trees have large buttress roots flaring off their trunks and extending to more than twenty-five feet up the trunk, requiring them to be cut above these structures. Trunks were hallowed with adzes, chisels, and other tools. Working without calipers, canoe-makers used their hands to calculate hulls' consistent thickness, ensuring balanced craft. Gold Coast professionals used this process to "make the sides only one finger thick, and the bottom two." Burning the interior and exterior sometimes completed the process with the heat creating a tar-like substance that preserved the vessel while killing wood-boring insects. Heating also made canoes pliable, permitting canoe-makers to bend the hull. Canoes designed for lagoons and rivers were expanded while braces prevented the sides from contracting as they cooled. Ocean-going canoes had a more streamlined design.[25] There were variations to this process. Jukun-speaking peoples of north-central Nigeria submerged partially completed dugouts for approximately one month so that they would not split during the finishing process.[26]

Canoe-makers crafted dugouts from tall, strait, trees, with soft, easy-to-work wood that was strong, light, and resistant to bug infestation and sun and water damage. Many were carved from silk-cotton or cottonwood trees (*Ceiba pentandra*) and wawa (*Triplochiton scleroxylon*). Cottonwoods are common in tropical Africa and their properties are ideal for maritime uses. Growing up to 160 feet tall, cottonwoods may have a diameter of six or more feet, contain a toxin rendering it "immune to pests," are "very light and easy to work," and "on account of its very low specific gravity, its buoyancy, and non-liability to absorb, the little loss of buoyancy it suffers even after prolonged immersion being restored by drying." Cottonwoods remain un-branched to a height of approximately eighty feet. This is important as canoes were made from timber located between the top buttress roots to the lowest branch.[27] Bosman described cottonwood timber as "light and porous, and scarce fit for any other use than making Canoes," as it is not suitable for construction and does not produce high heats, rendering it poor firewood.[28]

Triplochiton scleroxylon has several common names, including African white-wood, "obeche" in Nigeria, "wawa" in Ghana, "samba" in Ivory Coast, and "ayous" in Cameroon. It grows up to 160 feet tall, has relatively strong wood, possesses a girth of ten or more feet, and is often unbranched for up to eighty feet. It is easily worked with hand tools. However, it is susceptible to decay and insect infestations.[29] Some canoe-makers used hardwoods commonly known as mahogany, which were more difficult to work. Still, mahogany proved durable. People along the Congo River basin made canoes from cottonwoods, mahogany, and other trees. The Jukun crafted dugouts from *Afzelia africana* and *Khaya senegalensis*, which are types of mahogany.[30]

Historian Walter Rodney explained that in the Senegambia a "large canoe was a valuable piece of property, and was not as common as the thick forest might lead one to believe. Its construction was the work of specialists." These professionals preferred living near timber supplies and constructing dugouts in forests rather than felling and transporting logs to waterside facilities.[31] Villages and families throughout Atlantic Africa tended to specialize in the production of one good, creating generational craft wisdom. Canoe-making villages were home to several canoe-building families, as well as families specializing in other, often related, crafts.[32]

Canoe-making was a widely distributed skill and canoe-makers shipped canoes considerable distances. Craft made for coastal waters were sometimes constructed "sixty or eighty miles from shore." Professionals camped in groves while dugouts were carved. In areas possessing rich timber reserves, semi-permanent and permanent villages were established.[33] Roughly finished dugouts were carved in the forest before shipment to riverside centers for completion. In the Upper Congo, "The tree was felled and roughly shaped in the forest, and then floated to the town of the maker."[34]

Seventeenth-century Gold Coast canoes were primarily made at surf-ports' subordinate villages located approximately one mile inland. Canoe-makers at Takoradi, Axim, and their inland villages produced large, high-quality fishing and transportation canoes, while those from Butri, Ekon, Komenda, Kormanti, and Winneba manufactured smaller craft. The surf-port of Assini served as Asoko's coastal capital. Numerous villages specializing in particular crafts encompassed Assini, including a hinterland canoe-making center. In 1692, a European observer noted that Assini canoe-makers constructed more than forty trade canoes, each exceeding fifty feet in length and five feet in width, with carrying capacities of more than eight tons.[35]

Environmental factors informed where canoe-making occurred. The upsurge of commerce associated with seventeenth-century Atlantic trade precipitated deforestation, depriving many coastal and littoral canoe-makers of timber. Some coastal zones still possessed timber. The Ahanta, who reside along Cape of Three Points on the Gold Coast, maintained several canoe yards around Komenda, Takoradi, Boutri, and other surf-ports that produced sizable seagoing dugouts. In the 1590s, de Marees reported that they manufactured numerous exquisitely crafted canoes from local groves, selling many to other oceanside peoples who had apparently cleared their territories of suitable timber, penning: "Many of these are made at Capo de Trespuntas, as enormously thick and tall Trees grow there, not less than 16, 17, or 18 fathoms in circumference. . . . Many other small ones are made in Anta [Ahanta], because much timber grows there which is good for the making of Canoes and the inhabitants occupy themselves with making and selling them to strangers or their Neighbors." In 1704, Bosman reported that Takoradi's forests still contained many mature trees, writing: "Here and behind *Tocorary*, a Mile *West* of *Zaconde* [Secondi]" is a "large Plain so plentifully and properly adorned with lofty Trees and Woods."[36]

By the mid-seventeenth century, deforestation apparently forced Fetu and Fante mariners to purchase canoes from the Ahanta. During the 1660s, Wilhelm Müller explained: "Few canoes are produced in the Fetu country, because most are made in Antè [Ahanta] and other places on the coast." Barbot observed the Elminans' purchase of Ahanta canoes: "Those who make canoes generally live at Axim, Ackuon, Boutrou, Tackarary and Comendo, since these lands are forested . . . they make them very light and neat. . . . The length of the common canoes is 16–18 feet, and the width is 20 inches, but at Takaorary and Axim they make canoes 35–40 feet long, five feet wide and three feet in depth, and in these can easily carry 6–10 tons of merchandise."[37]

Axim's canoe-building assent resulted from economic calculations and environmental impacts. During the early seventeenth century, this surf-port was largely home to fishermen and merchants; most canoes were imported from Takoradi. As trade expanded, its economic structure changed. Around 1645, its fishing industry collapsed due to overfishing, while canoe-building and salt-making increased.[38] By the late seventeenth century, Axim (more specifically, its canoe-making villages) was regarded as a premier canoe-building center for "very fine, large canoes for crossing bars [surf] and transporting merchandize." On April 2, 1681, Royal Africa Company (RAC) factor Richard Thelwall acknowledged Axim's prowess, noting, "The cheapest and best canoes are to be bought up to windward at Axhim."[39] Axim's later entry into canoe-making probably explains why it possessed desirable trees during the late seventeenth century.

Atlantic commerce flooded Gold Coast markets with cheap European-manufactured goods, resulting in the general decline of artisan manufacturing. The opposite was true of canoe-making. There was increasing pressure for trade canoes to be used to transport slaves and other commodities and, as expanding states competed for resources, there was a rise in warfare and a need for war canoes. Fishermen also needed canoes to feed swelling oceanside and littoral populations comprised of locals, slaves awaiting transshipment, and Western merchants and government officials.[40]

Since transportation costs were relatively fixed and it was more profitable to operate full rather than partially empty dugouts, merchants in the Congo basin increasingly demanded large canoes as long-distance trade expanded during the eighteenth and nineteenth centuries. Initial investments in large canoes were significantly more than smaller ones. However, these costs were quickly recouped as long-distance commerce was more lucrative than short-haul trade.[41]

Deforestation related to canoe production compelled canoe-makers to follow the retreating forest inland.[42] Accra serves as an example of this pattern. As forests receded, professionals moved ever deeper into the interior and coastal peoples, like those at Labadi Beach, lost their ability to make surf-canoes, becoming reliant on landlocked forest peoples to construct "very fine sea-boats." Coastal people took or sent models called "children's canoes" to canoe-makers. Completed canoes were transported along a bed of log rollers to navigable watercourses to be shipped seaward.[43]

The same process occurred at the Ahanta towns of Komenda and Takoradi. During the 1590s Ahanta produced many seaworthy canoes. In 1679, Barbot penned that Takoradi was a major canoe-producing center, crafting dugouts capable of carrying up to eight tons.[44] By the twentieth century, these towns were strictly markets for hinterland-produced canoes.[45]

During the seventeenth and eighteenth centuries, Shama located at the mouth of the Prah River a few miles west of Elmina, was a source of canoes. It is unclear if Shama was ever a manufacturing center or strictly a market.[46] By the early nineteenth century, it was only a market for large oceangoing dugouts crafted along the banks of the Prah, particularly on Supome Island. Supome and the Prah's banks were wooded with mature trees, with the island becoming a contested place for Shamans and Wassas. In 1816, British official Henry Meredith noted: "There is an island on it [Prah] . . . that has been of object jealousy for many years between the Chamahs and Warsaw: the latter are now in possession of it. The banks of the river are lined with an exuberance of timber." Control of Supome enabled Wassa canoe-makers to dominate the market for decades.[47]

Dugouts used on the Niger Delta were purchased from interior peoples, as many riverine communities only had access to spindly mangrove trees. Indeed, the Nembe axioms "Big as the mangrove grows / It makes no canoes" and "The Nembe make no canoes" reflect Eastern Delta realities. Conversely, the Apoi, who are an Ijaw people residing in the Central Delta, supplied dugouts to the Western and Eastern Delta. By the seventeenth century, Ijaw canoe-makers moved to timber-rich regions along the upper Benin River. The oral traditions of Ijaw subgroups, especially the Arogbo and Olodiama, preserved their roles. The Arogbo's name derived from the reality that their capital was originally a canoe-makers' camp that grew into a major manufacturing center: with *aru* roughly meaning canoe and *ogbo* meaning forest. Olodiama sources state that purchasers traveled from as far as the Nembe Kingdom, so the construction of canoes crucial along the "length and breadth of the Niger Delta" remained concentrated along the Delta's western border.[48]

In the 1660s, Müller recorded that the Fetu people purchased many canoes from the Ahanta, while local watermen produced others. "The whole country is full of carpenters; for each native understands how to build his own house and does not need to call a specialist carpenter," wrote Müller. "Yet not all of them know how to make a canoe in which to go out to sea. . . . But there are several among the Fetu people who seek their living in this way."[49]

Canoemen and fishermen routinely made small dugouts to reduce overhead. While most commercial canoes used in the Niger Delta were constructed along the Benin River, the "art was generally known through the delta." Likewise, canoe-making among Jukun peoples was often a reciprocal community activity involving a nonspecialist. "A fisherman who requires a new canoe seeks out some other men who have the same need, and each assists the other." Like barn-raising in early America, individuals helped manufacture numerous canoes. Every man did not need to be an expert to build a barn or canoe; collective wisdom facilitated these endeavors. Since someone probably needed a new dugout every few years, communities continually refreshed and refined their abilities.[50]

Dugouts were made with common tools; adzes and chisels were especially well-suited. Müller watched Fetu canoe-makers produce well-crafted dugouts with minimal tools, stating: "The tools which the carpenters use in their work are machetes, with which they make the wood even, and sharp pieces of iron or pointed nails, with which they hallow it out."[51]

The inland movement of canoe-makers probably weakened canoe-makers' connections to oligarchs who protected them from enslavement, making them more vulnerable to being captured and sold into Atlantic slavery. As canoe-makers moved away from coastal polities, their relationships with coastal patrons became less intimate. Canoe-makers living in camps and small villages were also vulnerable to slave raiders. In addition, many professionals were un-free—bonded, pawns, or slaves—placing them in a precarious status that rendered them vulnerable to sale into Atlantic slavery.[52]

Canoes were the most expensive manufactured commodity in most societies. The Central Congo exemplifies variations in quality. Expensive, finely carved mahogany dugouts lasted up to fifteen years. Cheaper ones made from softer woods rotted in a few years. John Weeks expressed that canoe-makers "were clever in making canoes, which were cut out of solid trees, sometimes from soft wood, but generally from hard timber, such as cedar, mahogany, and even camwood." It was more difficult and time-consuming to work with hardwoods, which was reflected in their prices.[53]

Westerners praised canoe-makers' expertise. In 1929, James Hornell described two types of fishing canoes used in Sierra Leone—"Bonga canoes" and "Kru canoes"—and varying skill levels required to construct them. He felt that thirty-five-foot traditional Bullom dugouts, called "Bonga canoes," were "roughly hewn" with "no particular beauty of line or skillful construction, and obviously ill-fitted for sea work." Still, their sturdy design made them suited for riverine and estuarine fishing.[54]

"*Kru* canoes" were small, sometimes one-man, ocean-going prized possessions. *Kru* dugouts required considerably more craftsmanship than most people possessed and their makers were seemingly trained through apprenticeships. They were hewn from cottonwoods and skillfully "thinned down to a thickness of about half an inch." Fishermen carefully maintained them. At night, canoes were "carried ashore and placed bottom up upon trestle frames." Importantly, *Kru* canoes were used in non-*Kru* communities.[55]

Accounts of canoes belonging to peoples predating the *Kru* identity support Hornell's description. Dugouts made along the Grain Coast, now Liberia, resemble those Hornell described. In 1599, Johan von Lübelfing wrote: "Two Moors came to our ship in a tiny boat, consisting of merely a tree trunk, pointed at both ends and about 2 spans wide, so they had just enough room to sit inside on their knees. . . . They rowed so swiftly that we soon lost sight of them. . . . One would not have thought it possible to travel on the sea in such a tiny boat (which I could easily carry in my hands); [yet] they came so far out to us that we could no longer see the land."[56]

A. P. Brown's 1929 account of the Labadi District east of Accra, Ghana, similarly documents design and quality fluctuations. He identified three types of dugouts: *Ali lele* or *Ahima*, *Tfani lele* or *Anese*, and *Fa lele* or *Bese lele*. *Fa leles* were about nineteen feet long and cost £3–5. Its name means "river canoe," though it was also used for inshore fishing, especially with bottom-dragging nets. Its design was similar to that of the *Ali lele*. They were not originally rigged to sail and were not "considered sufficiently seaworthy for deep-sea fishing."[57]

Tfani leles were about twenty-four feet long, costing £4–5 each. They were primarily used for beach seining and were "more heavily built than the other two types and never sail." Beach seines are large rectangular nets with floats on one of the rectangle's longer sides and weights on the other side, so they hung vertically in the water. One corner of the net was secured ashore while a canoe took the net seaward, then ashore in a sweeping arch. As the seine was hauled ashore, it dragged the bottom, ensnaring everything within its embrace. Whenever possible *Tfani leles* were "launched and beached where there is some natural protection from the waves." They were difficult to launch through surf, but could ride small breakers when landing.[58]

Ali leles were twenty-three to twenty-five feet long, costing £7–8 each, and were the most versatile of the trio. Most fishermen owned one, using it for deep-sea fishing. Brown saved his greatest praise for them, saying: "She is admirably suited to the exacting conditions under which she works, is a fine, buoyant sea-boat, has an easily driven hull and a high speed ratio for her length, yet when loaded she has great stability. She rides the surf well, and when she does capsize is easily righted and baled out. She is strong and stands up to very hard usage and yet is comparatively light."[59]

Africa's heat and humidity took a toll on canoes, while surf and submerged objects battered and frequently staved hulls. Besides being charred, nothing was done to preserve dugouts. The "life of a canoe is largely a matter of hazard." *Ali leles* were the shortest lived because of abuse received during launchings and landings. Ashore, *Ali leles* were "covered with coconut leaves to shade them from the sun and sometimes with prickly pear to prevent people from walking over them." Cracks were caulked and rotten sections and holes removed and mended with pieces cut from discarded canoes. They were relegated to inshore fishing when deemed unfit for deep-sea fishing. As they further deteriorated, they were used as *Tfani*, then patches for other canoes.[60]

Mariners devoted time and resources to maintaining higher quality vessels. Coastal canoemen and fishermen minimized rotting by beaching dugouts at day's end, often placing them in sheds. De Marees explained that Gold Coast canoes were placed "on to four Trestles (specially made for the purpose) to let it dry, in order that it may not rot and may be lighter to use and row." Likewise, Cabindan canoemen at Luanda stowed dugouts under "thatched boat-house[s]."[61] In arid interior regions, canoes were submerged at night to prevent cracking.[62]

These measures, along with removing wood-boring parasites, prolonged dugouts' lives. "The life of a lagoon canoe is reckoned at only some 2–3 years, but the more costly and carefully made canoes for sea fishing, when properly treated and 'patched,' are used for up to 15 years." Canoes seemingly did well in freshwater, with many mahogany dugouts on the Congo River lasting approximately fifteen years.[63]

Dugouts used for crossing surf-zones were called "bar canoes," and later "surf canoes." "Bar canoe" purportedly derived from *barre*, a French term for surf breaking on sandbars formed across river mouths. Surf-canoes were modified dugouts that had to be fast, agile, and durable. They required considerable skill to craft, were built by professionals, and carried virtually all the goods, passengers, and slaves transported between ship and shore. Indeed, "canoemen provided the direct services so essential to the development of internal and external trade and to the enrichment of European and African merchants whose fortunes rose but could also decline. The canoemen and other labor created for some a capitalistic paradise."[64]

Surf-canoes were designed for launching and landing through surf and were capable of riding waves. They varied in size and design. Most ranged from fifteen to forty feet long and carried several tons of cargo, while small *Kru* canoes and those of the previously discussed Cameroonian fishermen were approximately six feet long. When properly loaded, the bows of most other types of canoes were slightly elevated. When landing, surf-canoes were bow-heavy, enabling them to more easily catch waves. When launching, they were slightly stern-heavier, allowing bows to rise above oncoming waves, rather than cut through them.[65]

The Atlantic was both a fishery and a highway that nurtured commerce that predated and complemented European overseas trade. Most mariners did not venture more than about ten miles from shore. Coastal seas connected rivers, facilitating trade and communication between them. Rivers linked coastal societies to each other and interior ones.[66]

Daily wind patterns facilitated the launching of fishing and trade canoes in the morning and afternoon return voyages. In the morning, ocean air warms faster than overland air, causing land-to-sea, or offshore, breezes that reduce the speed and velocity of oncoming surf and assist oceangoing sailing. As the day progresses, the land became hotter than the ocean and rising warm air drew cooler ocean air ashore. In 1669, Nicolas Villault explained how this pattern facilitated Gold Coast canoeing: "They go fishing every morning, yet not so much by design, as by natural impulse, the wind from the hills forcing them as it were to Sea, and altering at night, and blowing hard upon the shore, they are brought home again."[67]

The size and design of surf-canoes evolved as Africans interacted with each other and with Western merchants. Fishermen used surf-canoes prior to European contact. During the first century or so of European-interaction, fishermen began using surf-canoes to transport goods. Portuguese sailors off the Grain Coast during the 1470s reported: "The negroes of all this coast bring pepper for barter to the ships in the canoes in which they go out fishing."[68]

Figure 12. Surf-Canoes. Capturing the difficulty of launching and landing surf-canoes in storm-swept breakers, scenes like this convinced ship captains not to attempt such passages in their slower, less responsive shipboats, or longboats, but to instead hire African canoemen. Wilhelm Sievers, *Afrika; eine allgemeine landeskunde* (Leipzig: 1891), 116. Author's collection.

Gold Coast fishing canoes evolved into cargo vessels. By the late sixteenth century, surf-canoes were crafted to transport cargo, precipitating increases in their length and beam (width). In the 1590s, de Marees noted that Gold Coast surf-canoes were "generally 16 foot long and a half or two foot wide." A century later, most were twenty to forty feet long and five to six feet wide. These modified vessels allowed fishermen to evolve into maritime merchants. Those who performed lightering and short- and long-distance trade, ventured up rivers and across lagoons and coastal seas, creating a group of watermen indispensable to Atlantic commerce.[69]

Fishermen were apparently the first to transform traditional dugouts into surf-canoes and themselves into this new labor group. Hulls were crafted from a single log. Since dugouts' gunwales (the top edge of a boat's sides) were roughly one foot above the water's surface, surf-canoes were

Figure 13. "Small Boats and Cape Coast Castle and Forts William, Victoria, and McCarthy, Gold Coast, mid-19th cent." The "English boat" depicts a Western shipboat, or longboat, while the other three represent Gold Coast, probably Fante, surf-canoes. The larger "Lighter" would have been used for transporting cargo and people between ship and shore and it contains a traditional Akan stool for "high class passengers." The bows of the smaller "surf boat" and "surf canoe" were built up with splashboards to keep water out as these vessels carried people and goods between ship and shore. The two trident-shaped paddles, identified as "oars," were unique to surf-canoes as their shape provided less resistance if they hit surf while canoemen brought them forward between strokes. The image is unsigned and undated. Drawings of Western Africa, University of Virginia Library, Special Collections, MSS 14357, no 7.

modified to keep water out of hulls. Planks called wash strakes, weather-boards, or splashboards were added to elevate their freeboard (vertical distance from the water surface to the top of the gunwale) and increase cargo space by expanding the width. Bows and sterns were further raised. Professional canoe-makers surely assisted early mariners in modifying traditional designs. Later canoe-makers altered surf-canoes before delivering them to customers.[70]

Canoemen in African navies modified dugouts before the arrival of Europeans and in response to it. The Bijago, who lived in the Bijago Archipelago off Guinea-Bissau were feared pirates who altered dugouts to increase dugouts' payloads and protect warriors. In 1619, Manuel Álvares reported that the Bijago "raise[d] (the sides) with two planks we call false-sides, fitted on top, so that the canoes can ride deeper and carry more robbers and loot." During the 1590s, merchant André Álvares de Almada observed how armor was affixed to war canoes to facilitate assaults against European ships: "At the prows they have thick wooden screens which keep off musket balls; hence they can assault boats, and they have captured some ships."[71]

Other alterations were made, like adding decks or thwarts, which are crosswise supports spanning a canoe's width. Most surf-canoes were equipped with these and other features. Some had a forecastle or quarter-deck, which were storage decks respectively located front and aft. While off the Ivory Coast in the 1490s, Duarte Pacheco Pereira observed modified fishing canoes: "The negroes of this coast are great fishermen and their canoes have for'castles." Some had midship cabins.[72]

Canoes used by African elites and those purchased, hired, and rented by Westerners were routinely modified into yachts, complete with midship living quarters and shade canopies located forward, aft, or both. Henry Meredith described these modifications, saying: "Some put a platform in the bottom, and erect an awning with curtain over the for-part of the canoe, where the passengers sit to protect them from the rain or dew at night, and from the heat of the sun by day: others content themselves with an umbrella." In 1864, Hope Waddell observed how Efik rulers on the Calabar River used modified royal canoes as expressions of power. King Eyamba of Old Calabar, or Duke Town, possessed a "great canoe" that was "decked out with several ensigns streaming in the Wind, British ensigns, with the name in large letters. The little house amidships was brightly painted red and yellow. . . . In the bow a large gun pointed forward." Fifteen paddlers manned each side. "A train of inferior canoes, ornamented and arranged in the same style, belonging to the lesser gentry, were in his wake."[73]

Surf-canoemen apparently spearheaded the blending of diverse African, as well as African and European, traditions. As interaction between Europeans and Africans intensified, surf-canoes became increasingly suited for lightering and coastwise commerce. During the 1680s or 1690s, Ahanta canoe-makers, canoemen, and English ship carpenters conspired to modify

surf-canoes, creating hybrids that combined African and European techniques to strengthen dugouts purchased by the English and crewed by
wage-earning canoemen. These mariners used them more frequently and
harshly than their own vessels, completing upward of sixteen ship-to-shore
trips per day through the surf. Describing this usage on March 12, 1681/
1682, a RAC factor at Accra noted that "a tempestuous sea" had "broke
all the canoes att Accra, not one either great or small has escap'd."[74]

Composite craft were created to exploit surf-canoes' speed and maneuverability while adding European-style knees and cross-thwarts to strengthen
their hulls. Prior to European contact, Africans attached cross-thwarts, or
transverse braces, to strengthen hulls, serve as seats, and provide brackets
for securing cargo. Europeans requested cross-thwarts on purchased surf-
canoes. Likewise, knees became common after they were adopted from ship
designs. Knees are curved rib-like braces radiating from the bottom of
canoes and up their interior sides to strengthen the hull by reducing transverse flex created as surf-canoes rode over and punched through breakers.
In 1693, slave-ship captain Thomas Phillips reported that he "set our
canoemen and carpenters to" modify surf-canoes purchased at Winneba
(Gold Coast) for use on the Slave Coast. "The canoos we buy on the Gold
Coast, and strengthen them with knees and weather-boards for and aft, to
keep the sea out, they plunging very deep when they go against a sea."[75] As
English merchants transported canoes and Gold Coast canoemen throughout Africa, they disseminated these modifications to mariners who internalized these alterations.

As late sixteenth-century trade along the Gold and Slave Coasts intensified, the English scrambled to purchase and modify Ahanta surf-canoes.
RAC officials ordered agents at Dixcove in Ahanta to obtain canoes and
knees. On October 1, 1692, Christopher Clarkson reported: "I have endeav-
oured to the utmost of my power in getting the canoes your Worshipps
required, but found them not fitting for service, being old or new burnt
and fitting up, and so amongst them all I have found and bought one large
7 hand canoe and am promised by a Black man that makes them to be
fitted with the rest specified in your letter in three or 4 dayes." On March
23, 1693/1694, Thomas Buckeridge, at Dixcove, reported: "I have sent by
the 13 hand canoe 46 knees according to order." On May 10, 1694, he asked
Cape Coast officials "whether you will please to have Quashee [Kwesi] putt
knees in her here or, when she goes to Cabo Corso." Accounts from elsewhere in Ahanta confirm this practice. These records indicate that by 1691
many Gold Coast peoples routinely reinforced surf-canoes with knees.[76]

Equipping surf-canoes with knees probably developed independently at many surf-ports. It began in Ahanta during the 1680s and apparently informed the process throughout the Gold and Slave Coast as canoemen traveled in hybridized craft. As Fante, Fetu, and other canoemen stopped at different surf-ports, local canoe-makers and canoemen undoubtedly adopted this feature.[77]

Likewise, distinctive-looking Senegalese surf-canoes dubbed *pirogues* resulted from the melding of different African traditions to which were fused European elements. The name *pirogues* is problematic as it derives from an Amerindian term that became the French word for *canoe* and was applied to a range of watercraft, including traditional and modified African dugouts.[78] Niuminka, or Niumi, watermen living on the Djomboss Islands of the Petite Côte (just north of the Gambia River) probably initiated this design. From estuarine communities they exploited rivers and ocean; fishing, harvesting mollusks, producing salt, and engaging in the long-distance coastwise and riverine trade. Merchants and fishermen traveled from the Cape Verde Peninsula to the Casamance River, a distance of some four hundred miles, while riverine networks linked them to trans-Saharan commerce. Niuminka mariners adopted elements from other African peoples and Europeans, perfecting and distributing the pirogue.[79]

Pirogues were probably developed during the late fifteenth or early sixteenth century. Varying in length from eight feet to more than thirty feet, they were reinforced with knees and cross-thwarts, while wash strakes elevated their sides. Bowsprits and aft-sprits extended from the front and back. Below bowsprits were wave breakers, which were wedge-shaped timbers running down the keel to deflect oncoming waves. Africans used sails prior to European contact. The Niuminka apparently adopted European-style square sails, fitting pirogue hulls to accommodate a mast rigged with one or more sails. Larger pirogues were often equipped with European-style tillers and rudders; smaller vessels retained steering paddles. These surf-canoes permitted Africans to rapidly sail out to sea, cross through surf, and travel up rivers, as a Portuguese merchant observed in the 1590s, noting that they "can travel from one river to another along the coast, by raising sails."[80]

During the second half of the nineteenth century, some English surf-boats were exported to Africa. They were fast enough to catch waves. However, they cost far more than surf-canoes, making "the landing" "expensive." In addition, surf-boats did not permit Europeans to sever their reliance on canoemen as the surf-boats were manned by surf-canoemen who "become very expert in handling" these craft.[81]

Figure 14. "Pirogues des Nègres" (mid-to-late 1780s). René Claude Geoffroy de Villeneuve lived in the Senegal region for approximately two years during the mid-to-late 1780s. His engravings were produced from on-the-spot drawings. This image shows two Senegalese-style pirogues with their distinctive bowsprits. The canoe in the foreground is rigged with what was probably a temporary mast and sail. The pirogue in the middle ground is preparing to beach. Ashore are two beached canoes. Note the long bowsprits, stern sprits, and European-style sails and rigging. René Claude Geoffroy de Villeneuve, *L'Afrique, ou Histoire, Moeurs, Usages et Coutumes des Africains: Le Sénégal,* 4 vols. (Paris: 1814), 3; image facing 60. University of Virginia Library, Special Collections.

Canoe-making was not restricted to specific ethnic groups or regions in Africa. Nor was it the exclusive domain of experts. Instead, it was a widely held ability, one that was probably found in the hold of most of the forty thousand slave ships that carried Africans to the Americas. Many possessed carpentry skills sufficient for making sound canoes, although, as we will see in Chapter 8, their contributions have been all but ignored.

Chapter 7

Mountains Divide and Rivers Unite:
Atlantic African Canoemen

We cannot regard enslaved Africans as land people. As previous chapters have described, many came from societies where understandings of swimming, diving, waterscapes, canoe-making, and canoeing were ingrained into the collective memory. Many were as comfortable in dugouts as European colonists were on land. Theirs was a world afloat, and the Middle Passage did not strip them of their aquatic heritage.

Canoes were central to Atlantic Africa's social, cultural, political, and economic development, serving three interrelated primary purposes: trade, fishing, and warfare. There were no sharp boundaries between terrestrial and maritime lives, as even those who worked in land-based occupations used dugouts to fish, visit family and friends, and complete market voyages.[1] Waterways facilitated canoe-borne trade between interior markets and coast entrepôts. Polities created navies to maintain sovereignty and expand their commercial and political spheres of influence. The Atlantic slave trade was a phenomenon of waterscapes, and canoeing was both a mode of transporting slaves to market and, in the geopolitical context, a method of resistance to human commerce. Being such a central facet of so many aspects of Atlantic African culture, widespread canoeing knowledge provided many captives shipped to the Americas with maritime acumen.

Trade canoes were mobile marketplaces of goods and ideas while canoemen were cultural brokers who helped weave discrete societies into a community of communities, bound together by commercial and cultural exchanges. While transporting goods, canoemen circulated traditions, as the "buying and selling of commodities is almost always accompanied by the contact of cultures, the exchange of ideas, the mingling of peoples, and has led not infrequently to political complications and wars." Pidgin languages developed, while some languages, like Wolof, Bobangi, Fulani, KiKongo, Lingala, Hausa, Arabic, and European languages, became lingua francas.[2]

It can be argued that farmers and manufacturers generated much of Africa's wealth. If not for them, canoemen would not have had to ship goods to market. If not for canoemen and canoewomen, who were often also farmers and manufacturers, much of producers' energies would have been useless because goods would not have reached market. Maritime trade was not disconnected from shoreside events; they were intertwined.[3]

Without canoes, travel in most of tropical Africa would have been exceedingly difficult as tsetse flies spread the often-fatal *nagana* disease to draft animals. Consequently, human head-porters and canoemen were the primary modes of transport. Analysis of canoemen and head-porters in the Bight of Benin indicates that canoemen transported more goods twice as fast and much farther in a day than porters. In six to eight hours, four to six mariners could convey upward of five tons, or seventy people, about twenty-one miles. It took about 125 porters two or three days to accomplish the same task.[4]

Large bulky commodities did not lend themselves to portage. Elephant tusks measured up to ten feet long and can weigh over two hundred pounds. The casks needed to transport grains, gunpowder, and liquids comprised much of the weight a porter could carry. A forty-hand canoe could transport "around 12 puncheons (weighing 9 tons)" of palm oil, or between 840 and 1,200 gallons. Some 240 men were required to porter the same amount.[5]

With Europeans' arrival, dugouts were integrated into overseas commerce. Hence, "canoe-born trade began to complement that of European deep-sea ships, securing much of western Africa in the web of Atlantic commercial capitalism."[6] European rowboats were too slow to catch waves, making it difficult to land on the African coast. From the fifteenth through the early twentieth century, then, Westerners employed surf-canoemen to transport most goods and people between ship and shore.[7] Surf-canoes carried approximately the same weight as European longboats, with the advantage of being able to traverse breakers.[8]

Nearly every traveler was impressed by surf-canoemen's dexterities and surf-canoes' speed and maneuverability. In 1827, Augustus Adee described how U.S. Navy sailors relied on Liberian canoemen, writing: "As we approached to shore, we saw that a landing thro' the surf was impracticable with our boat and made a signal to the natives. . . . A canoe came off to us, in which we were paddled thro' the surf, and landed without being much wet."[9]

The British and American navies published hydrographic guides of the African coast in which they repeatedly warned shipmasters not to attempt the surf in rowboats but to employ canoemen. For example, in 1856, the British Navy extolled canoemen, saying: "The surf is so high, and it requires so much skill as well as local experience to pass through it with success, that no ship's boats should ever attempt to land; but the natives in their canoes have from long practice acquired the habit of landing and embarking with ease and safety."[10]

Canoemen regularly paddled out to sell goods to passing ships. When Duarte Pacheco Pereira sailed down the Grain or Pepper Coast in the 1490s, he traded with local fishermen. "The negroes of all this coast bring pepper for barter to the ships in the canoes in which they go out fishing." They often sold the highly coveted melegueta pepper (*Aframomum melegueta*), glorified as the "grains of paradise." As William Bosman cruised the Ivory Coast during the 1680s, "*Negroes* in three Canoa's laden with Elephant's Teeth came on Board." These activities permitted fishermen to increase their incomes while attracting European merchants to their surf-ports.[11]

With waterways so central to commerce and trade, many men and women gained canoeing experience throughout their lives. Canoemen comprised a significant portion of most waterside communities. During the seventeenth century, Gold Coast canoemen constituted between 5 and 25 percent of the coastal population, while canoe-borne fishermen constituted an additional 30 to 60 percent. Inland waterside demographics were probably comparable. These estimations do not include those who transitioned between maritime and terrestrial occupations.[12]

Many land-based producers possessed maritime abilities. Merchants often faced shortages of paddlers, compelling them to recruit farmers, laborers, porters, and others as paddlers. The canoes plying the Congo River Basin were routinely more than sixty feet long, with each requiring thirty to seventy paddlers. Trading voyages could last up to five months. Large-scale merchants impressed dependent family members and slaves or called for volunteers who wanted to engage in small-scale trading but lacked transport. Since a single canoe invited attack, members of one village or neighboring villages formed flotillas. A fleet of ten canoes required between three hundred and seven hundred paddlers, providing many with months of maritime experience.[13]

To consolidate wealth and protect commerce, maritime merchants formed corporations that scholars call "canoe houses." Historian G. I. Jones described their structure in the Niger Delta as "a compact and well organized trading and fighting corporation, capable of manning and maintaining a war canoe." Traditionally consolidated along bloodlines and headed by the oldest male family member, they evolved to meet the demands of overseas trade, becoming corporations of related and unrelated merchants, paddlers, warriors, and slaves, bound together by fictive kinship and market capitalism. As Atlantic trade expanded, leadership shifted to the wealthiest member, reflected in the titles the Efik of the Nigeria Delta bestowed upon the heads of their trading houses: *Ete Ufok*, "father of the house," replaced by *Etubom*, "father of the canoe."[14] Canoe house chiefs organized paddlers from their dependents, including teenagers seeking to become maritime merchants. Adolescents refined their dexterities during voyages, learning to detect shallows and snags by observing how water heaved and plunged over rocks, sandbars, and hippopotami. Youthful lessons enabled some to accumulate enough wealth to establish their own independent or satellite canoe houses during adulthood. Additionally, rulers and canoe house leaders could impress citizens, slaves, canoemen, and canoes, compelling many people to become proficient mariners.[15]

While scholarship on canoe houses focuses on the Niger Delta Region, sources indicate that similar processes occurred throughout Atlantic Africa. In 1668, the ruler of the Kingdom of Benin, located in southwestern Nigeria, drafted canoemen to facilitate trade with Portuguese merchants. When ships arrived at Ughoton (or Gwato), a riverine port located on the banks of the Benin River some thirty miles from its mouth, the king, accompanied by "twenty or thirty" merchants, went "forthwith and travel[ed] posthaste overland to Gotton [Ughoton], commandeering on their way many canoes and oarsmen as they require." Similarly, as Ndobo, a chief on the upper Congo River, prepared for a long-distance commercial voyage, he impressed 125 of "the hardiest men of the land" to crew "five large canoes."[16]

Canoeing was learned during childhood. Girls and boys on the upper Congo learned to handle dugouts "from the days of their babyhood," so by adulthood "they are all experts at the job and know instinctively how to guide canoes along the waters of the vast rivers of the Congo Basin."

Likewise, Gold Coast "fathers bring their children up to it from the age of nine or ten" to fish from canoes.[17] "Children's canoes," or models used by canoe-makers, became toys for youth who wove small fishing seines, attached them to their canoes, and waded into the shallows to pretend to seine and catch waves.[18]

Canoeing was often learned as an essential means of locomotion. In the Central Congo Basin, rains deluged floodplains twice a year, making hunting less dangerous and more productive. Swimming animals were unable to attack canoe-borne hunters who surrounded "a small herd that happens to be swimming together." Poles were thrown into the water "to hamper their progress and exhaust them," making buffalo easy to kill. "It is not unusual to see an elephant swimming across the river; and this monster is as helpless as any when away from terra firma. He has very little power when in deep water, as in order to breath, he must keep his trunk raised above the surface of the water, and is deprived of a formidable weapon."[19]

Many Slave Coast peoples who were nonmariners similarly possessed canoeing skills. Most communities engaged in nonagricultural activities, like fishing, salt making, and European trade, all of which required dugouts. Canoes were essential to the survival and prosperity of the island state of Lagos, linking it through trade and commerce to the mainland, defending it from naval assaults and waging warfare against neighbors.[20]

While long-haul commerce was a male occupation, women conducted short-distance trade. On Lake Nokoué, in present-day Benin, Tofin tradewomen fished and conducted commerce in "mosquito boats," which were under fifteen feet in length. When slave raiders became especially problematic, women could be prohibited from canoeing—to prevent them from being kidnapped. For this reason, on June 1, 1785, Antera Duke, an Efik merchant at Old Calabar noted that women were prohibited from paddling to market.[21] Unfortunately, accounts of canoewomen are sparse and lack substance, yet they reveal that many women were adroit mariners.

Canoemen were armed against piracy, which was the greatest danger they faced in the Congo River Basin. Rather than participate in trade, some riparian villages, like Inganda, Wagata, and Monnsolle, plundered canoes.[22] At times, piracy disrupted waterborne commerce in the Slave Coast's lagoon system.[23] In other instances, waterside villages engaged in privateering, with trade rivalries, geopolitical disputes, and reprisals for past offenses precipitating predation.[24]

In places without canoe house traditions, canoemen organized themselves into labor groups that developed an artisanal-conscious mentality and often acted collectively to wield political and economic force. Affiliated war canoes protected and extended commercial networks, carried goods downriver, and were brought under state control during times of war.[25] Knowing their importance to trade, canoemen's collective actions permitted them to resist European attempts to organize and regulate them for several hundred years while demanding favorable work conditions and wages.[26] Meredith recognized the need to respect canoemen, advising employers that canoemen "perform their duty with cheerfulness; and if encouraged, will go through a vast deal of labour: but they must be treated with exactness and punctuality. When they call for any customary allowances, or for payment, they do not like to be put off; they expect that their labour should meet with its instant reward." Explaining that canoemen used work slowdowns to counter offenses, he wrote: "If they be not punctually attended to they become neglectful and inattentive to the interest of their employer."[27]

Europeans were compelled to honor their spiritual beliefs. Many Gold Coast canoemen refused to work on Tuesday, "which is the Sabbath they celebrate." In 1887, Alfred Ellis elaborated, writing: "Tuesday was the day sacred to the god of the sea, for it is now the day commonly sacred to the majority of the existing gods of the sea. Any fisherman who violated this rule was fined, and his fish cast into the sea."[28]

Canoemen often refused to work in heavy seas. Gold Coast mariners were reportedly some of the best and most intrepid surfboat-men in the world. Yet many abstained from passing through high surf to avoid liability for perishables that got wet or fell overboard and to prevent damaging their vessels.[29]

Ship captains commonly employed sailors to work and physically punished transgressions. Attempts to suck canoemen into captains' spheres of control were countered, forcing most to abandon this tactic.[30] Canoemen responded to abuse by breaking goods and allowing perishables to get wet. They could avenge serious breaches by permitting canoes to capsize, which could result in the loss of goods and offending white lives. Since overturned canoes were an accepted risk, canoemen escaped reprisal by claiming it was an accident.[31] Some apparently killed especially contemptuous merchants. In 1897, Mary Kingsley cautioned: "It is highly advisable to have your conscience clear, at any rate regarding your past treatment of your Kru or Accra boat-boys, before you trust yourself to them to take you through a surf." She relayed how a "bad man" on the Gold Coast "ill-used his men and when they took him out through the surf to go aboard the ship that would carry him home, there was the usual catastrophe, which no one thought much of." When his body washed ashore, "three iron shark hooks, with lots of line attached" were found embedded in his clothes, which the abused canoemen used to "play him like a fish, until the surf beat the life out of him."[32]

Canoeists also engaged in work disruptions akin to those of white sailors. Scholars have posited that the term *strike* derived from the collective work stoppage of London seamen in May 1768 who struck work in the same manner they would strike, or lower, sails to halt a ship's progress. In 1685, Gold Coast canoemen responded to physical abuse by refusing to unload the *Mavis*, which arrived from London with soldiers, provisions, and building materials to establish an English settlement at Sekondi. They were pressuring Captain Henry Nurse to either compensate them for Dutch abuses or persuade Dutch officials to right their wrongs. Canoemen also used slowdowns to protest abuses. In 1910, Slave Coast mariners protested the construction of roads that would divert goods they transported by prolonging six- to seven-hour voyages for upward of six days.[33]

Some stole goods to breach voids in remuneration. Others set fire to European supplies and storage facilities. Such actions caused many Westerners to regard canoemen as "rogues."[34] Regardless, Westerners were forced to treat them well.

Centrality in overseas shipping permitted canoemen to transcend occupational identities to buttress wider relationships, such as lineage, ethnicity, and perhaps race. Some struck to support caboceers and chiefs who were denied trade gifts or rents from Europeans. Occasionally they struck in support of fellow workers who were mistreated, held as political pawns, or panyared, meaning they were held against someone else's debt.[35] Many organized into corporate work groups that successfully negotiated for desired wages and working conditions.[36]

Canoemen often restricted themselves to a single coastal stretch and radiating rivers. Some pursued medium- and long-distance trade to connect coastal markets to riverine markets located considerable distances upriver. Senegambians transported kola nuts down the Gambia, into the ocean, and along the coast to "the neighborhood of Great and Little Scarcies rivers, [in Sierra Leone] a distance of three hundred miles." Likewise, salt was carried along the coast and up the Gambia.[37]

Others paddled and sailed hundreds of miles. Barbot explained that Gold Coast mariners navigated "cargo canoes," using "them to transport their cattle and merchandise from one place to another, taking them over the breakers loaded as they are. This sort can be found at Juda [Ouidah] and Ardra [Allada], and at many places on the Gold Coast. Such canoes are so safe that they travel from Gold Coast to all parts of the Gulf of Ethiopia [Guinea], and beyond that to Angola."[38]

Canoemen of Guinea-Bissau, a region embraced by the Gambia and Scarcies Rivers, completed coastal voyages that took them up rivers. Lacking iron ore reserves, canoemen imported and disseminated it and other goods throughout the area. In the 1580s, André Álvares de Almada observed in Biafada that canoes carried "more than one hundred people, as well as cows and other goods." Canoemen connected small states situated along the Rio Grande, Rio Corubal, and upper Rio Geba to Atlantic markets, using seasonal winds to sail north along the coast. At the Bissau islands, they traded with Papel mariners. Papel canoemen wove through estuaries dispersing goods throughout upper Guinea-Bissau. They headed up Rio Geba past the Bissau islands to trade with farming and salt-producing riparian settlements.[39]

Accounts indicate that some surf-canoemen, especially the *Kru* and Fante, worked hundreds of miles of coastline. Canoemen, along with their dugouts, were routinely loaded aboard ships to serve as lightermen before paddling home. Bridge documented how Western commerce depended on them, writing: "The Kroomen are indispensable in carrying on the commerce and maritime business of the African coast. When a Kroo-boat comes alongside, you may buy the canoe, hire the men at a moment's warning, and retain them in your service for months."[40]

Gold Coast canoemen were regularly employed on the Slave Coast, where skilled canoemen traditionally plied the calm lagoons paralleling the coast and did not venture through the surf into coastal waters.[41] In the mid-1640s, a Dutch slave trader at Little Popo described this practice: "If you wish to trade here, you must bring a new strong canoe with you from the Gold Coast with oarsmen, because here one cannot get through the surf in any [row]boat." Robert Norris similarly observed Fante canoemen at Ouidah: "Landing is always difficult and dangerous, and . . . can only be effected in canoes, which the ships take with them from the *Gold Coast*: they are manned with fifteen or seventeen *Fantees* each, hired from *Cape Coast* or *El Mina*; hardy, active men, who undertake this business, and return in their canoe to their own country, when the captain . . . has finished his trade." Other Gold Coast peoples were similarly employed. Meredith reported that Portuguese and "French ships bound to Whidah and other parts of the Slave-coast, were supplied here [Shama] with canoes and canoe-men."[42]

Surf-canoemen repatriated their earnings, bolstering local economies. European reliance on canoemen enabled them to demand favorable wages, which were routinely paid in gold and goods, while crews were provided a canoe for homeward voyages.[43] Thomas Phillips related how he paid seven Cape Coast canoemen: "Their pay is certain and stated, half of which we pay in Gold at Cape Corce; and the rest in goods when we have done with them at Whidaw [Ouidah]; 'tis also customary to give them a canoo to carry them back." Komenda's economy became largely based on selling surf-canoes and providing crews to "Portuguese vessels from Brazil" bound for the Slave Coast. Komenda surf-boats were usually "seventeen, nineteen, or twenty-one men" canoes. "The success of a voyage much depends on the exertions of these people; they are therefore well paid, and treated with kindness and liberty: each person clears about ten pounds by his trip; but before he returns to his native town. . . . The canoe is given them to return home, and they dispose of it for eight or ten pound."[44]

Some Gold Coast canoemen established permanent Slave Coast residences. In the mid-seventeenth century, Elminans immigrated to what European sources called "Little-Popo" (now Ancho or Aného). When the Akwamu conquered the Kingdom of Accra in 1681, refugees migrated to the town of Gliji, adjacent to Little Popo, establishing the Gen, or Ge, state.[45] Equally, Ouidah remains home to the Kocou, Cotia, Agbessikpé, and Gbeti families, which descend from Gold Coast canoemen. Gold Coast canoemen and their dependents generally lived in ethnic enclaves, providing maritime services for Western merchant and naval ships.[46]

Littoral Africa possesses networks of lagoons, bays, rivers, and creeks, enabling canoes to parallel the coast in calm, sheltered waters without venturing into the Atlantic. Perhaps the most important lagoon system extends from Lagos eastward some eighty miles, linking Badagry (or Agbadarigi), Porto-Novo, Contonou, Ouidah, and Grand-Popo, Little Popo, Keta Lagoon, and the Volta River. Canoemen could similarly travel westward from Lagos, through the Niger Delta, and across the Bight of Benin. The Slave Coast's great lagoon facilitated fishing, commerce, and state building, providing a livelihood for thousands of water people. Dugouts were indispensable for navigating the lagoon, which varied in depths from several feet to one-foot.[47]

Since most interior waterways were calm, people used dugouts measuring upward of one hundred feet in length and capable of transporting loads in excess of ten tons or more than one hundred forty people.[48] During the 1490s, Duarte Pereira described the size of trade canoes navigating estuaries around Bonny: "The bigger canoes here, made from a single trunk, are the largest in the Ethiopias of Guinea [Gulf of Guinea]; some of them are large enough to hold eighty men."[49]

Waterscapes connected coastal and littoral peoples to the interior. During the late seventeenth century, a Dutch official reported how coastal waters connected him to interior waterways around the Volta River, saying he "sometimes sent boats there which brought him slaves and clothes, which the natives buy from Abyssinians and Nubians, whose neighbours they are, the river coming down to the sea from very far in the interior country." While the Volta does not flow through Abyssinia and Nubia (Ethiopia and the Sudan), the statement reflects vast commercial networks.[50]

Overland travel in the Niger Delta was nearly impossible, yet trade canoes bound littoral and coastal markets to hinterlands some 2,600 miles up the Niger Valley while linking the Bights of Benin and Biafra. In 1867, William Reade described the Delta as the "Venice of West Africa" and, in 1888, Harry Johnston explained how canoes tied the coast to the interior: "The [Palm] Oil Rivers are chiefly remarkable among our West African possessions for the exceptional facilities which they offer for penetrating the interior by means of large and navigable streams and by a wonderful system of natural canalization which connects all the branches of the lower Niger by means of deep creeks. There are hardly any roads existing in the Delta; the most trivial distance that a native requires to go, he generally achieves in a canoe."[51]

The Ijo Kingdom of Bonny was advantageously located on a coastal island at the mouth of the Bonny River in the eastern Delta, enabling it to control trade between the interior and the sea. Bonny's location, coupled with canoemen's skill, made it the primary port of embarkation for approximately 1.2 million slaves exported from the Bight of Biafra during the eighteenth century.[52] Goods originating several hundred miles upriver passed through Bonny's geopolitical waters. Consequently, large numbers of slaves were warehoused in the capital, Bonny. Its merchants purchased most captives on credit from newly arrived slave-ship captains, sending fleets of thirty or more canoes to interior markets. John Adams observed this operation in 1832, reporting that Bonny was a "wholesale market for slaves, as not fewer than 20,000 are annually sold here; . . . Fairs . . . are held every five or six weeks at several villages, which are situated on the banks of the rivers and creeks in the interior, and to which the traders of Bonny resort to purchase them. . . . Large canoes, capable of carrying 120 persons, are launched and stored for the voyage." Slavers returned from the interior bearing "1,500 or 2,000 slaves, who are sold to Europeans."[53]

Canoes similarly helped propel the Efik Kingdom of Old Calabar into the second most important slave-trading center in the Bight of Biafra. Located in the Cross River estuary, Efik canoes had easy entrée into hinterland markets and source populations that could be raided for slaves. "Given their skill as traders, their trade networks to the interior, and their fleets of canoes capable of ferrying large numbers of people, the Efik were well positioned to capitalize on the arrival of European merchants." Likewise, merchants along the eastern Niger Delta used canoes to expand and consolidate their economic and political power.[54] English slave traders extended credit to Efik canoe houses and trade families who dispatched fleets inland to purchase humans or raid small Ibo and Ibibio riparian villages.[55]

In West-Central Africa, a steady stream of trade and fishing canoes filled with slaves, ivory, wax, wood, dyestuffs, and other goods flowed across rivers and coastal waters, linking producers to Portuguese trade settlements.[56] Barbot noted the commercial currents along the Sierra Leone River, saying it "is done by the natives coming down-river in canoes, in order to do trade with the English and French who land there." Employed on the Gold Coast from 1739 to 1749, Ludewig Rømer learned how "Mountain Negroes" came from the interior in dugouts to purchase fish at the Keta Lagoon.[57] As previously discussed, Biafada and Papel canoemen traversed the rivers and littoral waters of Guinea-Bissau.[58]

Polities established checkpoints to tax and regulate canoe-borne traffic.[59] In 1847, King Eyo of Old Calabar dispatched enslaved canoemen to establish riverside villages that would extend his commercial control, giving "him command of the rivers and channels."[60] In the 1640s, a Dutch slave trader documented the purchase of captives along the New Calabar River, writing: "For a man one generally gives 120 bracelets, and in a customs duty 2 to the Foufera [village officials], 2 to the oarsmen [canoemen] and one to the brokers; for a woman 100 bracelets and the same customs duty as above, and for a boy or girl correspondingly."[61]

Duties on water-borne trade were about 10 percent of cargo's value plus "trade dashes" (payments or tips in goods at a standardized amount) and other commercial concessions. In 1861, Francicso Valdez documented the duties in Guinea-Bissau, writing: "The inhabitants of Cachen [Cacheu] come in their canoes to Bolor, where they enter the Lala, by which they process up to Zinquichor [a Casamance River port]; but in their progress they are obliged to pay a tax or tribute, called daxa, to the King of Guinguim. Through this channel, a considerable trade is carried on between Cachen and Zinquichor, principally in waxes, hides, ivory, and gum."[62] In the Calabar and Cross River estuary, duties were routinely called "comey" a term perhaps deriving from "customs."[63]

The selling of enslaved water people comprised a significant portion of Africa's export trade. Zamba, who was raised about a five days' paddle up "the river Congo" before being kidnapped into South Carolinian bondage in 1800, recalled that his slave-trading father employed over thirty "well armed" canoemen to deliver hundreds of people down the Congo. "Sometimes my father carried down his people, as he called them, to the slavers in large canoes." Voyages presented opportunities to raid riverside villages, which, in one instance, yielded "a hundred and thirty" water people.[64]

Western accounts similarly illustrate canoemen's slave-trading involvements. By the 1490s, fishermen in the eastern Niger Delta were conducting a brisk trade with the Portuguese, as they transformed fishing communities into slave-trading states. While Duarte Pacheco Pereira traded along the New Calabar and Bonny Rivers, he reported that the "bigger canoes" were capable of holding "eighty men, and they come from a hundred leagues [about three hundred miles] or more up" the New Calabar River, bearing "many slaves, cows, goats and sheep." In 1699, Jean Barbot observed Bonny's expanding slave-trading function, writing: "Large canoos, some sixty foot long and seven broad" carried "European goods and fish to the upland Blacks; and bring down to their respective towns, in exchange, a vast number of slaves, of all ages and sexes, and some large elephant teeth." Canoemen from the river-port of New Calabar frequented inland slave markets where they "got fifteen slaves." On July 26th, "above forty great canoos parted from Calabar up the river, to purchase slaves inland." Two days later, "the canoos return'd with a great number of slaves." Barbot concluded that New Calabar's canoemen completed round-trip slaving voyages in "two or three days." Those from Bonny took "eight or ten days."[65]

Crass at it sounds, humans were perishable commodities, occupied more space than other goods, and required fast shipment to market. They needed food and water, and food costs and mortality rates increased the longer the

Figure 15. "A Slaver's Canoe." While in the Congo during the 1880s and 1890s, Edward James Glave wrote numerous articles and a book detailing his experiences and produced many of the accompanying illustrations. During a ten-day stint on the Ikelemba River, Glave encountered "dozens of canoes" transporting slaves, as this was faster than overland treks and often kept captives healthier, allowing merchants to demand higher prices for them. E. J. Glave, "The Slave-Trade in the Congo Basin. By one of Stanley's Pioneer Officers. Illustrated After Sketches from life by the Author," in *The Century Illustrated Monthly Magazine* 39 (1889–1890), 832–833; image is on 832; quote is on 832. Author's collection.

journey. In addition, slaves could fight back, thus more canoemen were employed to prevent rebellion. Dugouts used to cargo slaves to Lagos could be eighty feet long, requiring crews of thirteen to transport up to one hundred captives, figures conceivably reflecting interior circumstances.[66]

It was typically more profitable to ship slaves to the coast than to march them overland. It could take weeks to walk to the coast, and journeys were made more onerous by heavy headloads. Voyages were faster and less strenuous, reducing deaths and enabling merchants to sell healthier humans at higher prices than those trekked overland.[67]

Canoemen were also employed to prevent slaves from escaping from slave ships. When slavers anchored in rivers and coastal waters, sailors used numerous techniques to prevent captives from jumping overboard to either drown themselves or regain shore. Captains routinely employed canoemen to recapture those who leapt overboard, as described by an anonymous Dutch slave trader in the mid-1640s: "At night they [canoemen] lie on board your ship with their canoes, in order to fish the slaves out if they jump into the water."[68]

Extended interaction with slave traders placed many canoeists themselves in vulnerable positions that resulted in enslavement and shipment to the Americas. Occupations for slaves in Africa were limitless, and many found themselves paddling canoes. Faced with continual shortages of paddlers, Western merchants and government officials employed canoemen to train slaves. For example, in 1686 the RAC at Ouidah trained "20 or 30 stout slaves" to serve aboard surf-canoes. Many enslaved canoemen worked on the coast for years before being shipped to the Americas.[69]

Coastal and littoral oligarchs and canoe house heads also employed enslaved canoemen. While Hope Waddell was at Old Calabar in 1847, he reported: "Those employed in canoes are fed, and are in crews of six to ten each canoe, under a captain or supercargo." These captives occupied a central role in overseas commerce. "King Eyo had many thousand slaves, and four hundred canoes, his son said, with a captain and crew for every one."[70]

Some canoemen were bonded (meaning un-free, though not enslaved) as either political pawns or panyars, who were kidnapped or otherwise held against someone else's debt. Others were kidnapped into bondage as a slave-ship surgeon observed when an African trader invited an "unsuspicious countryman" to visit him aboard a slaver. When he came alongside, "some black traders on board, . . . leaped into the canoe, seized the unfortunate man, and dragging him into the ship, immediately sold him." Captain Samuell Starland documented how a canoeman he hired at Kormatin, now Abanze, became a pawn. On March 27, 1682, Starland and his canoeman spent the night at Winneba, a Gold Coast surf-port, which the Akron attacked, capturing and holding the man until the English ransomed him. As un-free people, pawns and panyars were vulnerable to being sold into the Atlantic slave trade, while many free and bonded paddlers were enslaved during conflicts. For example, Gold Coast canoemen employed by the English were reluctant to paddle past Dutch, Portuguese, or French trade settlements, and vice versa, for fear of being enslaved.[71]

Some lost their freedom in other ways. Canoemen endeavoring to become merchants, yet lacking the capital to do so, sometimes pawned themselves to European or African merchants in exchange for goods. If unable to repay the loan, they could be sold. Some slave-ship captains punished theft and desertion with enslavement. False accusations were probably used to transform many nonsellable people into commodities. In addition, many free surf-canoemen were shipped to the Americas as slaves when slave-ship captains seized them to top off nearly complete cargoes.[72]

Once enslaved, most captives began their Atlantic crossings in surf-canoes. Venture Smith was born in the Gold Coast and was probably shipped through the surf at Anamabu. Recalling this boyhood journey to New England, he wrote: "All of us were then put into the castle, and kept for market. On a certain time I and other prisoners were put on board a canoe, under our master, and rowed away to a vessel belonging to Rhode-Island." Olaudah Equiano was similarly transported through the Niger Delta in a canoe, saying, "I was put into one of these canoes, and we began to paddle and move along the river."[73] Slave traders recognized their reliance on surf-canoemen, with John Atkins explaining that African waves were "a natural Prohibition to Strangers, and whence it follows in respect to Trade, that Ships are obliged to send their Boats with Goods near Shore, where the Natives meet them, and barter for Slaves, Gold, and Ivory."[74]

Canoemen leveraged their expertise to inflate wages and command respect, as evidenced by Charles Thomas, a Long Island proslavery ideologue. He believed American "darkeys" were happier and better off enslaved than living as "Guinea niggers" and "savage Africans," while disparaging dugouts as "shapeless hulks." Still, he was forced to laud Cape Coast surf-canoemen and surf-canoes, saying, "Uncle Sam's boats are not built for beaching, we have to trust ourselves again to a big dug-out and a dozen noisy paddlers to bear us through the surf; for which we pay an English shilling, or an American quarter, each."[75]

Canoemen knew whites were weak swimmers who were terrified of surf and sharks. Danish merchant Ludewig Rømer was impressed by canoemen's ability to negotiate Accra's waves, which inflated to spectacular heights in the white mind to terrify white voyagers. "It looks dangerous when you are sitting or lying in these Negro vessels among those breakers. These waves come rolling as high as bell towers. You can see when the wave will break, and the black boatmen (*remadorer*) must then see to it that the canoes ride on top of the wave before it breaks, or, in all haste, row their vessels back, letting the wave break first."[76] Many made their fears palpable. As Michel Adanson passed through surf breaking across the mouth of the

Figure 16. "Slaves Being Transported to Slave Ships." Slave ships were forced to anchor at least a mile offshore and employ canoemen to carry goods and people through the surf, as this image documents. Based on accounts of Jean Barbot, *A Description of the Coasts of North and South Guinea and William Smith, A New Voyage to Guinea* (1744), in Thomas Astley, ed., *A New General Collection of Voyages and Travels* (London: 1745–47), 2: plate 61, facing 589. University of Virginia Library, Special Collections.

Senegal River with other Europeans, "Some hid themselves through fear of being drowned; and some through apprehension of being wet."[77]

Some canoemen had fun at whites' expense. Paul Isert, described how Accra's canoemen used a nautical game of chicken to inflate their incomes:

> The Blacks now started to prepare themselves to breast the breakers. The captain of the canoe made a short address to the sea, after which he sprinkled a few drops of brandy as an offering. At the same time he struck both sides of the canoe several times with his clenched fist. He warned us Europeans to hold fast. The whole performance was carried out with such gravity that we felt almost as if we were preparing for death. An additional cause for alarm is that, having

Figure 17. "Surf-Boat Capsized." English traveler Verney Lovett Cameron captured European fears of surf rather than African realities. Judging by the size of the canoe and the canoemen, this conjured wave would have been more than twenty feet high, far larger than surf typically breaking along the Atlantic African coast. Verney Lovett Cameron, *In Savage Africa or, The Adventures of Frank Baldwin from the Gold Coast to Zanzibar* (London: 1887); opening vignette. Author's collection.

started to go through the breakers, they must often paddle back again because they had not timed it to the right moment. They are said to do this often deliberately in order to torment the Whites in the breakers for a long time, so that in acknowledgement of their great struggle they would be given a larger bottle of brandy. In a few minutes, however, we were safely across and our boat was on the sand.[78]

This "performance" was done seemingly to exacerbate white fears, which were undoubtedly woven into embroidered accounts that canoemen told and retold amid beached canoes. Canoemen seemingly belabored landings to terrify white passengers, demonstrate their control over whites' lives, and inflate their tips. Adanson experienced this while negotiating surf breaking across the mouth of the Senegal. They were in "this dangerous passage" for at least ten minutes, during which time they were "lifted up by the billows which bended under us; and now tossed by others which dashed against the sides of the vessel, and covered it all over with water." Once out of the surf-zone, "it is customary on this occasion to make a handsome present to the negroes of the bar; each passenger behaved generously towards them, and they were very well satisfied."[79]

That canoemen protracted their time in the surf-zone is evidenced by their acute familiarity with surf patterns. Waves break in sets with several-minute intervals between sets. Knowing how surf patterns facilitated launching and landing, with John Atkins explaining, "They count the Seas [waves], and know when to paddle safely on or off." As canoemen prepared to land Pierre Mary at Jakin on the Slave Coast, they let the first two pass, catching the third and larger wave whose energy drove them ashore to avoid becoming stranded in shallows.[80]

Having demonstrated control over passengers' lives and fortunes, canoemen demanded white respect at the same time whites racialized Africans. Whether intentionally or accidentally, canoes manned by the best watermen could overset in the surf and offended canoemen could swim away from rather than toward drowning Westerners. Prudent white people realized their lives could depend on canoemen and refrained from offending them. In 1693, English slave-ship captain Thomas Phillips advised Europeans to shelve racial beliefs, saying, "We venture drowning every time we go ashore and come off again, the canoos frequently over-setting, but the canoo-men are such excellent divers and swimmers, that they preserve the lives of those they have any kindness for, but such as they have any displeasure to they will let shift for themselves," and can "impute all to accident."[81]

Warfare, as well as trade, transformed many civilians and combatants into commodities bound for the Americas.[82] European travelers, as well as scholars, have generally treated land- and water-based warfare as two discrete methods of fighting, waged by soldiers and sailors, suggesting canoes were troop transports. Yet just as many Africans were farming-fishermen, many combatants were mariner-soldiers who were perhaps more accurately *marines*, capable of crewing canoes and fighting on land and water. Many states used navies to cut off food supplies, bombard land forces, and launch amphibious assaults. In many areas, marines, not soldiers, waged war. In addition, piracy compelled maritime merchants to become trained in naval warfare.[83]

Relatively few canoes were built exclusively for war. Larger polities maintained fleets, while smaller states seemingly did not. During peacetime, larger war canoes regulated commerce. During conflicts, polities pressed trade and fishing dugouts and crewmembers into service.[84] In times of conflict, many African navies were capable of defending territorial waters against European encroachment. As Europeans headed along the African coast during the fifteenth and sixteenth centuries, memories of the conquest of the Canary Islands, Morocco, Caribbean, and Aztec Empire caused many to conclude that they could similarly subjugate Atlantic Africans. Initially, the Portuguese experienced some success by raiding unsuspecting coastal and riverside settlements. Africans quickly responded to this new sea-borne threat.[85]

To meet growing demands for European goods, coastal and littoral peoples supplied slave traders with increasing numbers of captives. Many were interior peoples sold to oceanside middlemen. Yet, coastal and littoral societies understood they could produce slaves by preying on neighbors, harvesting canoe-makers and male and female canoeists in the process.[86]

Coastal states seemingly preferred to wage naval battles on estuaries and tidal rivers, as illustrated when André Álvares de Almada wrote: "Neither the Jalofs nor Barbacins [or Serer people] make war by sea." Instead, they "travel from one river to another along the coast" in dugouts that "can carry more than one hundred warriors."[87] It would have been impossible to launch large canoes through surf; suggesting that they accessed the sea from river mouths.

Most slaves exported from Guinea-Bissau from the fifteenth through the early eighteenth centuries were products of maritime warfare. Captives were drawn from and produced by Papel, Bijago, Baïnuk, Joola, Balante, Nalu, Landuma, Baga, Biafada, Bussis, and other coastal and littoral societies of fishing farmers, a point Álvares made when reporting that people there "are employed in farming and fishing." These societies sacrificed many men and women canoeists to the Atlantic slave trade.[88]

Piracy enslaved numerous canoemen. Pirates from Guinea-Bissau seized passing trade canoes, selling passengers and crews.[89] The Bijago lived in decentralized, stateless societies on coastal islands called the Bijago, or

Bissagos, Archipelago located "in the delta of Jeba [Géba], Rio Grande or Bolola and Cassini rivers." They pursued small-scale farming, fishing, and maritime commerce until canoe-borne slave raiding became the cornerstone of the Bijago economy, exemplifying how piracy was used to enslave other maritime peoples, as well as pirates' vulnerability to enslavement.[90]

Bijago canoes were about seventy feet long and lightly crewed by twenty to thirty men to provide room for plunder, of which slaves and cattle were the most coveted items. The Bijago were apparently the dominant force plying this sheltered sea, enabling them to launch largely unchallenged raids. Europeans were amazed by their speed, as expressed by Gaspard Théo-dore Comte de Mollien in 1820: "It is difficult to conceive the rapidity with which their canoes glide through the water." Likewise, Almada testified: "They frequently travel more than ten leagues [about thirty miles] when making war, since they carry their attack into the Rio Grande, into the land of the Beafares [Biafadas], where they spread destruction and capture many people; and into the São Domingos River as far as Cacheu, where they do the same." (Cacheu was a Papel town and home to a Portuguese commercial settlement and slave-trading fort. It is more than ten miles up the Caheu River and about thirty miles north of the Bijago Archipelago.) The Bijago crept along coastal waters and rivers, timing landings to occur under the cover of darkness. The Biafada were among the principal victims, as were Baïnuk, Joola, Balante, Nalu, Landuma, Baga, Papel, and other maritime peoples.[91] The Bijago also plunder fortified Portuguese commercial settlements, with Álvares reporting their attack on the Biafada town of Guinala where they "burnt the house of Our Lady of Guinela in 1610, and they have made large-scale assaults on Biguda." The Bijago continued to successfully assault European settlements into the early nineteenth century and did not shy away from attacking and capturing European ships.[92]

Afloat, the Bijago rarely hesitated to battle anyone they encountered, prompting Álvares to write: "Those not aboard the Bijagos fleet cannot escape their claws. . . . If they encounter two or three canoes from other points on the coast they do not avoid them, even if they are war-canoes, unless they are stronger. Hence they say that all the other nations on the sea are their chickens."[93] The Bijago formed a loose, decentralized confederation that applied ashore, with members often attacking and enslaving each other at sea.[94]

For decades, neighboring Africans and Portuguese settlers were unable to contest Bijago domination.[95] The Biafada and Portuguese eventually challenged the Bijago by building forts and launching counter raids, which, by the 1630s, diminished Bijago assaults.[96] Likewise, by the 1570s, the Bussis successfully defended against Bijago incursions by transforming their egalitarian society into a militarized state. They lived on a coastal island, situated between Rio Cacheu and Rio Geba ("Bussis" in historical sources; now named Ilha de Pecixe). The king could "field nearly 2,000 men." Day and night, soldiers kept such a vigilant watch against the "inhabitants of the Bijago Islands" that it was said "a bird cannot appear out at sea or cross the land without it being generally known." Through slave trading, the king obtained cannons, muskets, and "no shortage of gunpowder." Instead of waiting for Bijago assaults, he dispatched defensive and offensive fleets of "fine war canoes." The "Bijago dared not touch his island because the king has promulgated a law to the effect that any of his subjects who yields ground in battle will be sold" into slavery and any who failed in naval warfare must "throw themselves overboard with a stone tied to their necks."[97]

By the early seventeenth century, the Bijago Islands were a major slave-producing center frequented by Portuguese, Dutch, English, French, and Spanish, merchants. The Bijago also took captives and other commodities to Bissau, a Portuguese commercial center on the Papel island Bissau.[98] For some two hundred years, the Bijago used mastery of the sea to harvest slaves, making themselves one of Guinea-Bissau's most important slave-producers. Yet they were not the only producers of slaves in Guinea-Bissau. The Biafada, Papel, Baïnuk, Joola, Nalu, Balante, Landuma, Baga, and Bussis peoples they preyed on enslaved them and each other.[99] Prior to the early eighteenth century, Europeans were unwilling to purchase Bijago slaves, believing they were suicidal.[100] By the mid-eighteenth century, Portuguese slave traders' insatiable demand for captives, predation by neighbors, and interisland fighting resulted in a devastating population decline as mounting numbers of Bijago men, women, and children crossed the Atlantic.[101]

War canoes built for lagoon and river conflicts were large enough to be fitted with fixed and swivel guns. African naval arms races suggest many believed the side with the most naval guns (fixed or swivel cannons, as well as muskets and blunderbusses) would prevail. Africans seemingly equipped a small but significant number of canoes with cannons, concentrating them to provide decisive advantages.[102]

Lagos built a powerful navy to protect and extend its economic influences. It launched a series of naval and amphibious assaults against Badagry, a sometimes-independent sometimes-tributary state to its west. Dalzel

Figure 18. "King Eyo's State Canoe." King Eyo Honesty of Creek Town on the Calabar River was the "largest trader in the country," according to Hope Waddell. He commanded a fleet of trade canoes armed with fixed and swivel cannons. The large-caliber gun on this dugout had to be fired forward, allowing the canoe and water to absorb its recoil. Hope Masterton Waddell, *Twenty-Nine Years in the West Indies and Central Africa: A Review of Missionary Work and Adventure, 1829–1858* (London: 1863); image on title page, quote on 242, 249. Yale Divinity School Library.

noted that Ologun Kuture, the Lagosian *ọba*, or ruler, "equipped thirty-two large canoes, and stationed them three miles to the eastward of Badagry, to cut off communication" and food supplies and to carry slaves back to Lagos. French sources claimed that when Lagos and its allies invaded Badagry in 1788 they used a flotilla of some 2,000 canoes to transport approximately 40,000 marines. On October 10, 1793, Kuture "threatened to destroy the Badagrees in toto and to effect it has armed 600 canoes." His amphibious force succeeded.[103] Warfare between the two states continued into the mid-nineteenth century.[104]

Bonny, advantageously located on an island at the mouth of the Bonny River, also used flotillas. War canoes affiliated with its canoe houses protected and extended trade networks and were brought under state control during wars. Most canoe houses had ten or more "war-canoe chiefs," providing it with a formidable navy. In 1823, John Adams recorded that the "power" of Bonny's king "is absolute; and the surrounding country, to a considerable distance, is subject to his dominion. His war canoes are capable of carrying one hundred and forty persons each, and have often a gun of large calibre

Figure 19. "One of the Great Naval Battles Between the Waganda and the Wavuma." While this battle occurred in Central Africa on Lake Nyanza, now Lake Victoria, those of similar scale and tactical complexity were waged on Atlantic African waters. Note the figureheads adorning most of the war canoes and shields that are seemingly mounted to their sides. "One of the Great Naval Battles Between the Waganda and the Wavuma, in the Channel Between Ingira Island and Cape Nakaranga," Henry M. Stanley, *Through the Dark Continent, or The Source of the Nile Around the Great Lakes of Equatorial Africa and Down the Livingston River to the Atlantic,* 2 vols. (New York: 1878), 1; opposite 260. Author's collection.

mounted on the bow. He destroyed the town of Calabar twice," making it a tributary.[105]

During the eighteenth century, the Kingdom of Warri, situated in the western Niger Delta, transformed itself into the region's most powerful state. One traveler believed its naval and marine forces numbered 60,000 strong. Warri rarely fought on land, using its navy to subjugate neighbors by cutting off food supplies.[106] In West-Central Africa, oligarchs' political and economic strategies produced great numbers of slaves.[107] Similar circumstances unfolded on coastal, littoral, and interior waters.[108]

Limited sources reflect that many interior polities possessed large flotillas, with some launching more than five hundred war canoes during naval battles. Henry Stanley typically viewed Africans through a racist lens, yet was impressed by their sophisticated naval warfare. He observed a series of battles between the Waganda and Wavuma on Lake Nyanza, now Lake Victoria. As a guest in Waganda, Stanley watched the battles, "safe from harm or danger, on the slope of Nakaranga mountain." Drums were used to issue commands as considerable coordination was required to maneuver the fleets, each containing some two hundred canoes and more than fifteen thousand crewmen.[109]

Many of the prisoners of war sold into Atlantic slavery were undoubtedly mariners. Naval warfare and saltwater and freshwater piracy produced many prisoners and captured male and female noncombatants from waterside communities. Approximately 10 percent of the eleven to twelve million captives exported from Africa were shipped from the Slave Coast. Regional warfare undoubtedly produced tens of thousands of naval prisoners, as well as civilians who possessed maritime skills.[110]

Canoemen moved large quantities of European imports inland and carried African products seaward. Many states used war canoes to expand and protect their commercial networks and geopolitical boundaries while guarding their citizens from enslavement. In the process, they enslaved numerous water people and lost many maritime members. Into the belly of slavers were poured hundreds of thousands of maritime captives—fishing-farmers, canoe-makers, pirates, maritime merchants, canoemen and canoe-women, marines, paddlers, and naval crewmembers. Their wisdom and abilities were reconstituted and reimagined upon the waterscapes the Western Hemisphere.

Chapter 8

Maritime Continuities:
African Canoes on New World Waters

During the early stages of colonization, planters throughout the Americas huddled along coastlines, where they could consolidate resources and power while maintaining links to Atlantic economies. Since they concluded that water was an unnatural space for humans, they did not culturally colonize waterscapes. This allowed African-born slaves to physically and intellectually colonize these spaces. Incessant waves of saltwater canoe-makers, canoemen, and canoewomen broke upon the shores of the Western Hemisphere, forming cultural beachheads where they recreated and reimagined maritime traditions. Enslaved water people imposed African meanings on waters they populated with African deities, using dugouts as cultural markers and conduits for connecting with African spiritual worlds. African-inspired aquatics were born inland upon the floodtides of bondage.

Canoeing and canoe-making were enshrouded in secular and sacred cultural meanings that were not washed away by the waters of the Middle Passage or beaten from slaves by the taskmaster's whip. When captives of the same ethnicity were clustered together they could recreate specific ethnic traditions. Sources suggest that those from different ethnic groups merged traditions, providing cultural anchors to past societies while forging new identities with members of their bonded communities. Dugouts and New World waterscapes became cultural spaces, as Chapters 10 and 11 will show, evoking memories of home, helping to bridge ethnocultural differences while providing numerous benefits, like ephemeral escape from white authority and the ability to rapidly travel considerable distances to socialize and sell goods.

Slaves' worlds of wood and water formed vibrant floating culturescapes that scholars have largely ignored. This chapter considers how saltwater captives recreated and reimagined African cultures by fabricating canoes with designs that mirrored those of Africans. Captives did not need canoe-making instruction, and sources suggest that Amerindians and Westerners were not the primary sources of their maritime architecture. The design of unmodified dugouts crafted throughout Atlantic Africa was very similar and seemingly allowed enslaved canoe-makers and canoemen of diverse backgrounds to conclude that shared dugouts embodied enough of their ethnic valuations to remain culturally viable.

Dugouts suffer from a problem of identity that confuses their origins. Scholars generally assume dugouts used by white and black settlers were based on Amerindian prototypes. None compared the design or manufacturing techniques of those used by people of African and Indian descent. To further complicate matters, Europeans applied an array of overlapping names to canoes. The most common were "canoe" and "pirogue" (and variants of this term), derived from Arawak and Carib Indians, respectively. The English term "canoe" and French "canot" apparently descend from the Spanish "canoa," which was adopted from Taíno Indians, an Arawakan people.[1] In 1535, it was recorded that "Caribs call them Piraguas." The French usually called dugouts "pirogues" (reserving "canau," "canot," and "canoë," for Indian bark canoes) as Michel Adanson noted while in Senegal, saying the "Negroe canoo, which the French call 'pirogue.' "[2] Early Portuguese travelers called canoes "almadias," a term rooted in Arabic.[3]

Colonists applied "canoe," "pirogue," and, to a lesser extent, "barge" to dugouts to distinguish their size and shape.[4] Europeans increasingly affixed "canoe" to smaller dugouts and "pirogue" to larger craft, as Jean Baptiste Du Tertre explained in 1667. "We call their biggest boats, Pirogues, & the Savage word is *Canoüia*." In 1774, Edward Long said canoes "of largest size are called *petiaguas*."[5] *Pirogue* was also given to other watercraft.[6] By the nineteenth century, *pirogue* often referenced specific types of watercraft. Sometimes it was used to denote vessels' shapes, as James Hungerford delineated: "A long periagua (a canoe with a square stern)." In southern Louisiana, pirogues were flat-bottomed skiffs often associated with Cajuns. French travelers also gave this name to distinctive-looking Senegambian surf-canoes.[7]

"Barge" was occasionally assigned to large dugouts, as Pieter de Marees expressed: "The Barges with which they sail on the sea and which they make use in their Towns are cut out of one Tree," noting that Africans in the

Cape Coast–Elmina area "call such a barge *Ehem*; by the Portuguese it is called *Almadie* and by us the Dutch *Cano*." Many Europeans called both pleasure craft and large flat-bottomed rowboats used for lading and discharging ships *barges*. Planters called pleasure yachts, which were usually modified dugouts, "plantation barges" and "tentboats." In Dutch Guiana and Suriname, they were routinely called "barges," while "*grand canot*" was the Dutch term, with John Stedman saying the "elegant barges or tentboats, adorned with flags, and attended by small bands of music."[8]

Many chroniclers used "row" and "paddle" interchangeably, confusing the type of watercraft being used. Many mistakenly said Africans and slaves rowed canoes. By the late eighteenth century, some planters fitted canoes with oarlocks, compelling canoemen to row dugouts in a European manner.[9]

In addition to confusion around nomenclature, scholars confront a dearth of detail and description, as few chroniclers provided meticulous, comparative descriptions of Amerindian, African, and slave dugouts. De Marees explained that those constructed on the Gold Coast "are made different from the Iangados [jangandas, or log rafts] which are used in Brazil and S. Thome [Colombia?] and also from the Phragios in the East Indies." His comparisons indicate design differences and were based on travelogues and possible firsthand observation.[10]

Chroniclers deduced that dugouts used throughout the Americas were based on indigenous designs, and they passed down this conclusion to scholars, who seemingly concluded that bondpeople's canoes were of an Amerindian design. Historian W. Jeffrey Bolster cautioned against such postulations, writing: "Without knowledge of African canoe-builders, contemporary chroniclers simply assumed that canoes and pirogues were of Indian origin." Thus, "Africans have rarely been given credit for their contributions."[11]

The tools, construction techniques, and designs of Amerindian dugouts differed from those of African-descended peoples, with North American, Caribbean, and South American Indian canoes sharing similar architecture. Tools seemingly informed canoe designs. Africans and slaves used *iron* tools. The bows and sterns had considerable overhang, meaning they rose from the water at about a fifteen- to fifty-degree angle, causing them to project over the water. They had flat or semi-rounded bottoms and the exterior was considerably worked, giving hulls, which were one to four inches thick, a v-shape.

Figure 20. Caribbean Amerindian Canoes. This is probably the first European-produced image of an Indian canoe. Note its square, barge-like shape and bow- and aft-sprits, features distinguishing Amerindian dugouts from those made by African-descended peoples. Gonzalo Fernández de Oviedo y Valdés, *Coronica de las Indias: La hystoria general de las Indias agora nueuamente impressa corregida y emendada* (1535; Salamanca: 1547), book 6, chap. 4, 50, lxi, Yale University, Beinecke Rare Books and Manuscripts Library.

Amerindian dugouts, in contrast, were made with fire, and, to a lesser extent, *stone* axes and *stone* and *shell* scrapers. They were "scow- (or punt-) shaped," with broad, square bows that projected slightly forward. The stern either mirrored the bow or rose almost vertically from the water. Bottoms were planed flat, while sides retained trees' roundness, giving them a u-shape, while hulls remained much thicker than dugouts made by African-descended peoples. Some had bow- and aft-sprits, which were seemingly used for overland portage.[12]

A handful of sixteenth- and seventeenth-century images depict Amerindian dugouts before they were subjected to European influences. Gonzalo Fernández de Oviedo y Valdés, Jacques Le Moyne de Morgues, and John White were early travelers who intimately engaged with native peoples. Most scholars agree that their drawings, paintings, and writings accurately depict Amerindian culture.[13]

Residing on San Domingo from 1514 through 1523, Oviedo traversed the Caribbean cultivating an appreciation for Amerindian customs. He recorded one of the few accounts of Arawak and Island Carib culture. His voluminous accounts include descriptions and apparently the first European-produced image of an Indian dugout.[14]

Figure 21. "Storing Their Crops in the Public Granary," Jacques Le Moyne de Morgues (c. 1564). Jacques Le Moyne de Morgues rendered forty-three water paintings of Timucua Indians, who are now extinct, in what is now Florida. The paintings document Timucua dugouts' square prow and how hulls retained trees' roundness. Although the paintings have been lost, scholars believe that Theodore de Bry reproduced Le Moyne's paintings as engravings. A granary is in the background. *Indorvm Floridam provinciam inhabitantium eicones, primum ibidemad vivinn expressae a Iacobo Le Moyne cui cognomen de Morgves* (*Narrative of Le Moyne, an Artist who Accompanied the French Expedition to Florida Under Laudonnière*) (Frankfurt: 1591). Yale University, Beinecke Rare Books and Manuscripts Library.

Jacques Le Moyne de Morgues was a member of the ill-fated 1564–1565 French expedition to establish a colony north of St. Augustine, Florida. His water paintings and descriptions of Timucua peoples have been lost. However, scholars believe Theodore de Bry faithfully reproduced forty-three of Le Moyne's images as engravings, five of which include dugouts.[15]

John White was an English artist and governor of Roanoke Colony. He traveled the region from 1585 to 1586, producing water paintings of

Croatan society. De Bry reproduced White's images as etchings in Thomas Harriot's *A Briefe and True Report of the new found land of Virginia* (1590, second edition). Nine pictures and one map depict canoes in the background. One image includes a fishing canoe in the foreground while another illustrates five stages of canoe manufacturing.[16]

Robert Beverley was a Virginia planter and government official. His account includes a description of canoe-making and two slightly altered versions of White's and de Bry's images. Beverley's illustration "A Woman and a Boy Running after Her" (adapted from White's and De Bry's "Their manner of careyng their Children") includes a birch-bark canoe to contrast these watercraft.[17]

The tools used by Indians apparently informed canoes' shape and every aspect of canoe-making. Controlled fires were used to fell trees, remove limbs, shorten logs, and hollow trunks, as reported by Swedish botanist Pehr Kalm: "When the *Indians* intend to fell a thick strong tree, they could not make use of their hatchets, but for want of proper instruments employed fire." Stone axes were used to splinter wood, making it easier to burn, with Oviedo explaining that Caribbean peoples "cut and hammer the wood digging it out. And they burn what has been hammered and cut a little at a time."[18]

Beverley documented this process in the Chesapeake Region: "They bring down a great tree by making a small fire round the root, and keeping the flame from running upward, until they burn away so much of the basis, that the least puff of wind throws it down." Trunks were burned to the desired length and hallowed, while scrapers were used to "rake the trunk, and turn away the fire from one place to another, till they have deepened the belly of it to their desire. Thus they also shape the ends, till they have made it a fit vessel for crossing the water, and this they call a canoe, one of which I have seen thirty feet long."[19]

Canoe-makers along North America's Atlantic seaboard adhered to this method. Harriot reported that "only with the help of fire, hatchets of stone, and shels" are dugouts made. John Smith similarly noted that the Powhatan of Virginia crafted canoes "of one tree by burning and scratching away the coals with stones and shels."[20] First Peoples of the Caribbean used similar techniques.[21]

This was a time-consuming process that could take up to one year to complete. In 1667, Jean Baptiste Du Tertre reported that Island Carib canoe-builders "spent entire years making their boats."[22] It is improbable

Figure 22. "Their Manner of Fishynge in Virginia." This canoe's blunt prow and stern and rounded sides is representative of Indian dugouts. Thomas Harriot, *A Briefe and True Report of the New Found Land of Virginia* (London: 1588), plate XII, 55. Yale University, Beinecke Rare Books and Manuscripts Library.

Figure 23. "The Manner of Making Their Boats." This image documents the numerous stages of Indian canoe-making. It shows how dugouts were crafted with fire and stone and shell tools, while depicting their relatively blunt bows and sterns and hulls' round, tree-like shape. Thomas Harriot, *A Briefe and True Report of the New Found Land of Virginia* (London: 1588), plate XII, 55. Yale University, Beinecke Rare Books and Manuscripts Library.

that slaves, who were forced to give most of their time to slaveholders, adopted this laborious process.

The building techniques of African-descended peoples were fundamentally different from Amerindians. Using iron tools, they crafted dugouts within a few days. Jean Baptiste Labat reported that two Martinician canoemakers completed a substantial dugout in a "forthnight." Charles Ball of South Carolina made two pine dugouts, "together with five other hands," in "less than a week." Likewise, two African-born and one country-born slave completed a fifteen-foot dugout in six consecutive Sundays for Thomas Thistlewood.[23] African peoples reserved fire for preserving wood during the final construction stage. Indeed, a taboo prohibited some captives from using fire to hallow trunks as it offended the tree's spirits.[24]

Stone and fire had limited capabilities, which seemingly informed Indians' design. Amerindian canoe-makers probably left hulls comparatively thick because they did not want to risk compromising the strength of canoes that took so long to craft. These tools probably influenced the shape of canoes' prows and sterns. It was undoubtedly faster and easier to use one fire to make a flat bow possessing one angle than several fires to form pointed prows.[25]

Few detailed descriptions of Amerindian dugouts exist. Some compared them to European serving dishes. In 1492, Christopher Columbus reported that Taíno dugouts of the Bahamas were "hollowed like a tray from the trunk." Many Europeans said they resembled animal feeding troughs, with the Spanish word *canoa* meaning trough. Oviedo said Taíno and Island Carib canoes look like "kneading or water troughs," which his drawings depict. After arriving in Virginia in 1609, Henry Spelman lived with native peoples, becoming the colony's most skilled interpreter, stating the Patomecke "canoes" are "made in form of a Hoggs trowgh."[26] Surviving dugouts illustrate this design.[27]

These descriptions are revealing. Their broad bows prompted many to compare them to European barges and feeding troughs, while reinforcing European beliefs that Indians were uncivilized. Descriptions were used to aver that Indians were incapable of making boats more sophisticated than pig troughs. In 1612, Virginia's secretary William Strachey claimed that Indian dugouts were heathen craft. Likewise, Ebenezer Cook used disparaging inferences when writing *The Sot-Weed Factor*. Parodying pamphlets promoting colonization, he asserted that Maryland was a savage land, using dugouts to punctuate his point, he wrote: "Canoo, a Vessel none can brag on; / And fashion'd like a trough fro Swine."[28]

Scholars have incorrectly assumed that captives adopted Indian canoes. In 1997, Bolster recognized that "the style of construction" seen throughout the Caribbean was the same as in West Africa. Still, no study has considered the African influences imprinted onto slave canoes.[29]

Scholars routinely dismiss the technologies and advantages of traditional watercraft; implicitly treating them as novelties unworthy of serious deliberation. Erik Gilbert, a historian of East Africa and the Indian Ocean, explained that many historians blindly wedded themselves to the "tacit belief in the triumph of modernity over tradition," assuming Western vessels were superior to those of non-Westerners. Many scholars seem unaware of Africans' maritime cultures, are dismissive of their accomplishments, or did not consider the possibility of slaves recreating African canoeing customs. One seminal scholar categorized African maritime traditions as "subsistence" before asserting that "both the French and Island Caribs served as teachers," informing generations of scholarly interpretation. Otherwise praiseworthy studies have constructed narratives of maritime slave societies in which captives were conspicuously absent.[30] Much of the scholarship on traditional watercraft disregards Sub-Saharan Africans or dismisses their canoes as primitive.[31] Even when some recognize that bondpeople maintained African maritime practices, they are reluctant to relinquish notions that Indians influenced slaves' traditions.

Understandings of slave culture have long been inhibited by attempts to minimize African-descended people's accomplishments.[32] Scholars who cut across this grain have encountered stiff opposition.[33] It was equally difficult for many to accept that Africans designed the ubiquitous dugouts that became crucial commercial vehicles in many Atlantic economies.[34]

European colonists were initially reluctant to crew Amerindian dugouts, suggesting white people were not the authors of a new canoe design.[35] Whites regarded Indian dugouts as "flimsy little boats"; they were unnerved that gunwales were only a few inches above the water and that they sat at water level. In addition, passengers usually got wet from spray and waves lapping over dugouts' sides, which whites found disagreeable and life threatening. Most sixteenth- and seventeenth-century colonists' greatest concern was dugouts' limited lateral stability, making them prone to rollover.[36]

It may be difficult to conjure the fear of dugouts that gripped poor-swimming colonists. Oviedo tried, saying: "It is not fun for a man to move along in the water while holding on to a canoe, especially if he doesn't know how to swim, which has happened many times to Christians who have drowned." In 1665, Raymond Breton, a French missionary and linguist among the Garifuna, or Black Caribs, expressed the reluctance of French Caribbean settlers to use Carib dugouts as "they did not learn from them to row them, steer them, or jump overboard to right them when they overturned: the Savages are not afraid of overturning, wetting their clothes, losing anything, or drowning, but the French fear all these things." In 1736, English colonists remained reluctant to canoe with one man, describing them as "small and dangerous . . . , liable to be overturn'd by the least Motion of the Sitters in it. The Negroes manage them very dexterously, with a paddle."[37]

Ethnocentrism and xenophobia caused settlers to reject Amerindian dugouts as un-European. Brewington captured colonial Virginian and early twentieth-century American views, saying: "Let it not be thought that the adoption was a matter of choice, for surely few of the dominant race ever admit that some poor savage's implement is better than their own." Rather than purchase canoes from Indians, colonists initially requested that the Virginia Company send English shipwrights. When the Company refused, the "purses of private Adventurers" funded the transport of "about 20 men and boys." However, "theis Shipwright[s]" died shortly after landing in about 1620. In 1622, some "boatwright[s]" arrived and constructed a few vessels, but shortages continued. Starving in the midst of the Chesapeake's marine reserves, some colonists purchased canoes from Indians to harvest oysters.[38]

Colonists' rebuff of dugouts conforms to larger patterns of cultural rejection in which they concluded that the Americas were a savage place that needed to be civilized and Europeanized. Settlers surely knew they would be more comfortable in the tropical and semitropical Americas if they divested themselves of layers of European clothing. Most clung to English modes of housing, dress, and diet, feeling threatened by the "alien characteristics" of their new surroundings, fearing the adoption of new customs would erode their English identities. They civilized the land by planting crosses, "houses, gardens, and fences," transforming wildernesses into English pastures and fields, and they introduced familiar creatures, like English honeybees, sparrows, starlings, and red foxes to recreate the English countryside's bucolic sights and sounds.[39] Many believed that Amerindian canoes would make them less sophisticated, less English, less godly. Strachey blasted "Indian Canoas," exclaiming that they would cause moral decay: "Who, when we should labour a wane and diminution of the most imposture, the most false, and yet eye-pleasing objects of our carnal sences, not soe much as making out (after the least of them in poor Indian canoes), how their godlike representations beguile use that we neglect all good things and (like English lords) pursue these on the same streeme of delight, in swift barges [large canoes]?"[40]

Many early colonists believed that Indian dugouts remained too close to nature to be civilized. Nature creates few sharp edges and ninety-degree angles, preferring roundness. Colonists needed to transform trees so that they no longer resembled their natural shape, replacing the roundness of nature—of wigwams and dugouts—with squares, rectangles, and triangles that articulated civilization's domination of savage wildernesses. Virginians' stripped nature from the wood used to erect their homes. "The tree was chopped, drawn, hewn, sawed, chiseled, shaved, pierced with nails, and hidden with paint. Nature was made to submit utterly to the ideas of man." Indians and Africans did not erase nature from their watercraft, allowing them to retain natural curves. Colonists believed that those dressed in European attire while seated in dugouts were the incongruent mix of the civilized and savage.[41] Seventeenth-century colonists did not revolutionize canoe designs, which retain their indigenous curves. Instead, colonists replaced Indians with Africans, which seemingly allowed African dugouts to replace Indian ones.[42]

Another flaw in the assertion of Europeanization is the claim that Virginia planter Robert Rose invented the twin-hull canoe by lashing two dugouts together to increase stability. Twin-hull canoes, sometimes called "tobacco canoes," could carry more weight than single-hull dugouts but were less maneuverable.[43] In 1756, prominent Virginia educator James Maury averred that the "ingenious Mr. Rose" made this "great improvement of inland navigation." Future writers drew upon Maury, with scholars accepting their conclusions. In 1800, William Tatham proclaimed: "The practice of fastening two canoes together to transport tobacco . . . was supposedly begun by the Reverend Robert Rose of Albemarle County, Virginia, around 1740. This method became known as the 'Rose Method.'" Such claims exalted white Virginians' ability to allegedly exploit nature better than Indians could. Indeed, Maury dismissed canoes as "tottering vehicles," unworthy of white-use until Rose civilized them.[44] If we peer beneath this river of praise we find it choked with snags ready to rip the hull off this theory.

The first problem with the "Rose Method" was that it was at least two hundred years old when Rose "invented" it. Oviedo observed sixteenth-century Indians using the "Rose Method," recording the practice in picture and print. Others similarly documented this practice.[45]

Europeans did not have a tradition of multihull watercraft. Africans, Amerindians, and Oceanians did. They secured two or more canoes together side-by-side or made catamarans by securing platforms between two vessels.[46] Rose was a Scottish landsman with little or no maritime experience and never claimed to invent this method. He purchased a plantation abutting the James River and several slaves capable of making dugouts. His canoe-makers produced several each year. They probably introduced this technique to facilitate shipping tobacco-laden barrels weighing in excess of one thousand pounds.[47] Rose could also have learned of this method from accounts of Oceanians and Amerindians.

The persistence of African canoe-making expertise is consistent with the experiences of other groups. Amerindians maintained conventional designs even after adopting iron tools. In 1667, Jean Baptiste Du Tertre explained that many surviving Island Carib canoe-makers used iron "axes, adzes, and other tools" they "bought from Europeans" to rapidly craft dugouts. Yet, Breton reported that Carib canoes kept their scow-shape.[48] Elsewhere, Indians rejected Western tools. One can still find First Peoples making bark and dugout canoes.[49]

Chinese fishermen who migrated to nineteenth-century California built traditional watercraft.[50] In the San Diego and San Francisco areas, they constructed *hong xian tuo, cao chaun,* and *fanchuan,* commonly called "junks." While the redwood (*Sequoioideae*) used to create these craft and its related smell were new to Chinese mariners, these ships provided familiar social and cultural spaces, connecting them to family members, friends, and home communities.[51]

Zanzibari dhows survived British imperialism and the introduction of steamships, permitting local entrepreneurs to thrive. Dhows are distinctive-looking wind-powered ships used to transport goods throughout the Indian Ocean. Nineteenth-century British officials denounced dhows as premodern threats to the modernization of Zanzibar's colonial economy. Despite concerted British efforts to submerge the dhow trade beneath steamer's modernizing effects and the economic and political forces of capitalism and colonialism, dhows maintained their traditional form and function. The "dhow economy represented more than an anachronism"; it was part of the broader social fabric that rigorously resisted subversion.[52]

Like these and other peoples, enslaved Africans apparently maintain their traditions. The large-scale importation of Africans undoubtedly precipitated the introduction of African-style dugouts. Previous Chesapeake Bay scholarship concludes that the prevalence of dugouts with pointed bows began after 1650 as the result of European influence. This claim ignores the fact that the second half of the seventeenth century witnessed a sharp increase in slave imports, which probably accounts for this change. During the first half of the seventeenth century, Virginia's slave population grew slowly, increasing from twenty-three in 1625 to three hundred in 1650. From 1650 to 1670, the slave population doubled every ten years and did so again between 1680 and 1700. In 1708, Virginia was home to roughly 120,156 Africans.[53]

Seventeenth-century Chesapeake slaveholders purchased slaves primarily from the Senegambia, the Bight of Biafra, and West-Central Africa—regions where water was a signifying feature.[54] Records indicate that many Tidewater Virginia captives were from the Senegambia as it is narrowly defined, meaning Senegal and The Gambia.[55] Captives from the Bight of Biafra, specifically those broadly denoted as Ibo, comprised the majority of imports.[56]

Many of these captives were water people from regions where water dominated the land more completely than in the Chesapeake. Assemblages of slaves from these three regions surely recognized cultural similarities, facilitating amalgamations.[57] Many were probably capable of maintaining discrete ethnic traditions. Others blended similar Biafran traditions.[58]

Most captives did not need tutoring in canoe manufacturing. Here, as elsewhere, African maritime culture thrived as bondpeople wielded iron tools to craft dugouts. John Thornton delineated the process of cultural transmission: "African culture was not surviving: It was arriving. Whatever the brutalities of the Middle Passage or slave life, it was not going to cause the African-born to forget their mother language or change their ideas about beauty in design or music; nor would it cause them to abandon the ideological underpinnings of religion or ethics—not on arrival in America, not even in their lives." The continuous influx of captives facilitated African cultural continuity by reinvigorating communities' cultural memories.[59]

Slaveholders' prejudices facilitated cultural retention in slave populations. Many preferred Africans from specific ethnic groups and regions, believing they were better workers or possessed desirable skills. Thus, captives from the same ethnic group or African region were routinely concentrated in small geographic areas. Slave traders typically made the bulk of their purchases at one African port, gathering many from given ethnic, cultural, and language groups, and selling most at a single New World port. Michael Gomez explained how "North American discriminatory tendencies resulted in distinct patterns of ethnic distribution throughout the colonies/ states," laying the foundations for subsequent slave cultures. This promoted the creation of "African ethnic enclaves," so, for instance, "Virginia and Maryland were the preserve of the Igbo," Senegambians were clustered in South Carolina and Georgia, while Akan "were universally acclaimed and sought." During the seventeenth- and early eighteenth-centuries, North American slave communities were "for all practical purposes African."[60]

Other scholars consider how slaves sharing similar cultural understandings gravitated toward each other, finding ways to construct common cultural terrains. James Sweet contends that "Africans were not unlike migrants in any other diaspora who sought to maintain social and cultural relations within ethnic boundaries." Choices to bond with those sharing ethnic similarities facilitated maritime retentions while the adoption of Western traditions did not remove African underpinnings. The "essentially African perspective" continued to permeate captives' "social and cultural fabric."[61]

Planters' decision to establish waterside estates and concentrate slaves from the same ethnic group along with captives' decision to bond with those of the same ethnicity created nuclei for recreating and reimagining African maritime traditions. "Indeed, the foundations of the relationship between African-descended people and the land had been pioneered by the original communities of enslaved Africans concentrated along the densely settled courses of the Ashley, Cooper, and Stono Rivers" of South Carolina.[62]

Ibo traditions were recreated in Tidewater Virginia, the Carolinas, the Caribbean, and Latin America. Virginian slaveholder Richard Brook posted a December 24, 1772, newspaper advertisement regarding an escaped Ibo canoeman who plied his skills on Chesapeake waters. It read, "A new Negro Fellow of small Stature, and pitted with the Smallpox; he calls himself BONNA, and says he comes from a place of that Name [Bonny] in the *Ibo* Country, in *Africa*, where he served in the Capacity of a Canoe Man." Thomas Thistlewood employed Ibo canoemen while an eighteenth-century Jamaican overseer and slave owner. Olaudah Equiano served as a plantation overseer on Central America's Mosquito Coast. Employing his Ibo language and cultural skills to help select and manage Ibo slaves, he said, "I chose them all my own countrymen." They arrived with canoeing skills, which they promptly used to flee.[63]

Enslaved water people imaginatively blended Atlantic African traditions. Gwendolyn Midlo Hall cautioned that "creolization was not the process of Africans melting into a European pot." It routinely entailed the coalescing of different ethnic traditions. Gomez elaborated, saying that "acculturation" occurred in two overlapping spheres. "First, there was the world of the slaves, in which intra-African and African-African American cultural factors were at play." There were also communications between slaves and people of European and Amerindian descent.[64]

The merging of dugout-making traditions seemingly entailed two types of coalescences: first, exchanges between saltwater slaves of discrete ethnicities and, to a lesser extent, exchanges between slaves and Indians while adopting Western customs. Scholars have documented slaves' rejection of Western culture, preferring to maintain ethnic or blended African traditions. In societies where displaced Africans were the majority, bonded communities closely resembled African societies.[65] Even when comprising a small proportion of the society, as in the American North, captives fiercely sought to retain African traditions.[66]

Amerindians probably helped early saltwater bondpeople adapt African technical skills to New World environments by indicating what types of trees were best suited for constructing dugouts.[67] Cottonwoods grew in much of the tropical Americas, permitting many to work with familiar timber. Those from regions devoid of cottonwoods did not find recognizable trees, while North America and arid Caribbean islands were bereft of cottonwoods. Africans could identify trees with tall, straight trunks but would not necessarily know if their timber was bug- and rot-resistant. They probably relied on Amerindian advice while, perchance, showing Indians how to use iron tools.

Contentions that enslaved Africans adopted Amerindian canoe designs rest on five assumptions. The first two are that Indians had the opportunity and the inclination to tutor slaves. The others are that Africans' maritime traditions were both inconsequential and inferior to those of Amerindians, that slaves were willing to adopt Amerindian techniques, and that slave-built dugouts were based on Native American prototypes. Space precludes detailed analysis of these assertions, in part, because cultural retentions were informed by discrete developments throughout the New World. Still, an overview strongly suggests that Amerindians did not teach enslaved Africans to make dugouts.

Jean Baptiste Labat illustrates the problems with these assumptions. When in Martinique during the 1690s, he "rented two mulatto canoe carpenters who were slaves on a plantation near Rivièr Capot" to build a dugout. It is unlikely that Caribs were in the Rivièr Capot region. As the French began colonizing Martinique in 1635, they sought to rid the island of its original inhabitants. By about 1665, they had decimated the indigenous population, forcing the few survivors onto Caravelle Peninsula, on the island's opposite side. It is improbable that embattled Caribs paused to tutor slaves. In addition, there was considerable "antipathy between" Martinique's Caribs and

"Negroes," with members from both groups regarding each other as "Savages" and refusing to cooperate with each other. More important, the design reflects African influences. Labat recognized differences in African and Amerindian canoes. He used the term "dug-out" when referring to sharp-bowed African-style craft and "canoe" when referring to blunt-prowed Indian vessels. Describing this vessel, Labat said, "the dug-out differs from a canoe in that it is sharp and raised at both ends," while the punt-shaped Indian "canoe has only the front raised and its rear edge is cut squarely." He also indicated that the canoe-makers were specialists, calling them "charpentiers de canots," or "canoe carpenters." While surely not full-time canoe-makers, they used iron tools to complete the dugout in "a fortnight."[68]

Even if Amerindians had the opportunity and desire to teach Africans, we cannot assume Africans were willing students. Africans snubbed Western traditions and plausibly rejected Indian canoe designs. They surely recognized that Indians' Neolithic canoe-making techniques took far longer than African ones. Fettered by the temporal constraints of bondage, the adoption of Indian techniques seems counterintuitive.

Indians and Africans did not universally enjoy amicable relations necessary to facilitate cultural cross-fertilization. Numerous factors, including negative perceptions that Amerindians and Africans held of each other, narrowed the possibilities for cultural brokerage.[69] Labat documented tensions, saying Carib "arrogance leads them to believe themselves far superior to the Negroes, & the Negroes, at least as arrogant as they, regard them with even greater scorn, especially when they are Christians, & never call them anything but Savages." Du Tertre similarly reported that Brazilian Indians regarded Africans as savages and refused to associate with them, believing "they would be considered slaves if they were seen talking with them."[70]

Assertions that Amerindians informed slaves' maritime traditions also rest on the assumption that members of stable Amerindian societies had the opportunity do so. At first glance, it seems like for about 140 years (from 1500 to the 1640s) Indians and Africans coexisted. In most colonies, Indian societies were quickly destabilized by disease and warfare. Hence, the period when stable indigenous populations existed and significant numbers of slaves were present was brief or nonexistent.[71]

Colonization entailed genocide—the conquest and elimination of indigenous Americans who were replaced by Africans. While First People and cultures persevered, the Atlantic slave trade largely rose out of the collapse of Amerindian populations under the onslaught of European colonization. Enslaved Africans were not routinely imported into a region in large numbers until after this devastation was complete.[72] Hence, African "slaves were comparatively unimportant" to colonization from "roughly 1450–1650."[73]

Some colonies, like Barbados, Bermuda, and the Cayman Islands were uninhabited when Europeans arrived.[74] Elsewhere, indigenous populations were destroyed by warfare, disease, and forced migration before plantation economies ushered in floodtides of African humanity. The Spanish did not establish plantation economies until the nineteenth century. They reduced or annihilated Amerindians on their Caribbean islands during the sixteenth century. During the sixteenth and seventeenth centuries, European powers battled each other and Indians for control of the West Indies, devastating Amerindian populations. The establishment of plantation slavery forever altered the landscape and people; ripping up native vegetation and planting cash crops and captive Africans in fields fertilized by the ashes of Indian civilizations.[75]

Scholars continue to debate how colonialism exacerbated Amerindians' vulnerabilities to Old World diseases and the numbers killed by disease. Regardless, colonialism "created conditions in which many new diseases could spread and in which those diseases produced extremely high fatality rates. Biological catastrophes certainly resulted from the arrival of infected Europeans and Africans in the Americas, but the dissemination of those germs to Natives and their impact on indigenous bodies also depended on nonbiological processes of colonialism." Some have surmised that sixteenth-century Amerindian populations plummeted by upward of 95 percent.[76]

Caribbean colonization and slavery precipitated perhaps the greatest population collapse in history, almost eliminating Arawak and Island Caribs from every island except Dominica and St. Vincent by 1660. In the Bahamas, the process was more rapid. Christopher Columbus made landfall there in 1492. Within twenty-five years, the Lucayan, the archipelago's Arawakan peoples, had been eradicated or shipped to Hispaniola as slaves.[77]

The English Leeward Islands of Antigua, Montserrat, Nevins, and St. Kitts "lacked settled indigenous communities at the onset of European settlement." Only St. Kitts possessed a Carib population in the early seventeenth century, and it was destroyed before the large-scale import of Africans. In 1625, the English and French launched a nocturnal massacre, exterminating most; "survivors fled to the Carib stronghold of Dominica."

Its slave population rapidly grew during the mid-seventeenth century so that by 1678 there were 1,897 whites and 1,436 Africans on the English portion of the island. By 1707, there was a slave majority.[78] Similar circumstances destroyed Tobago's Carib population,[79] while the Danish West Indies (St. Thomas, St. Croix, and St. John) were dispossessed of Amerindians well before Africans arrived.[80]

Jamaica's Arawaks were largely eradicated before England took Jamaica from Spain in 1655. A 1611 census listed 1,510 inhabitants, including 696 Spaniards, 558 African slaves, 107 free blacks, 75 foreigners, and 74 Arawaks living in Spanish settlements. Rumors claimed some Arawaks lived in the interior. It is unclear what Jamaica's demography was when England appropriated the island. By 1673, there were 7,768 white people, 9,504 slaves, and apparently no discrete Arawaks, though individuals and groups possibly integrated themselves into maroon communities.[81] Some scholars argue that no Arawaks remained in 1655.[82] Regardless, it seems improbable that Arawaks provided the archetype for dugouts crafted by generations of African- and country-born captives.

In North and South America, the process was uneven and incomplete. Amerindians could flee advancing colonists while many became members of multiracial communities containing African-descended peoples. Still colonization uprooted and devastated many societies. As bondage spread inland, its bow wave thrust Amerindians back, while dragging captives inland in its wake.[83]

The Indian slave trade helped depopulate North America, forcibly transporting Amerindians across colonial and environmental borders, selling many into Bahamian, Bermudian, and Caribbean bondage, while moving Caribbean Indians to North America. This inhumane trade continued into at least the 1720s. Still, there is no evidence that displaced Indians were the source of Africans' canoe-making expertise.[84]

Indigenous societies were similarly destabilized in northeastern Brazil, where most slaves were concentrated. The Portuguese reached Brazil in 1500. During the 1560s, a smallpox outbreak decimated Tupi-Guarani peoples. African slaves began arriving en masse during the 1570s. In 1600, some fifty thousand Africans comprised roughly half the enslaved population and by 1620 few Amerindians remained on Brazil's sugar estates. During "the 1570–1620 transition period" from Indian to African labor, colonists minimized slaves' ability to rebel by pitting the two groups against each other, employing Indians to pursue runaways. "Throughout the colonial era,"

Indians remained "both the best potential allies and the most effective opponents of slave fugitives." When Amerindians and Africans were enslaved on the same estates, planters stratified labor forces along racial lines, which surely diminished cultural bartering.[85]

In the Amazonian states of Pará and Maranhão, the Tupinambá-, Tabajara-, and Caeté Tupi-Guarani–speaking groups and Jê speakers were equally decimated before large numbers of Africans began to be imported after 1751. From 1751 to 1842, about 143,360 slaves were imported, mostly from littoral Guinea-Bissau.[86] More important, Tupi peoples constructed bark canoes, not dugouts.[87] If Amerindians taught captives to construct dugouts, we should expect them to have taught Africans to craft bark canoes. Bark canoes were fabricated in the American northeast, Chile, Guiana, and northern Brazil. There is no evidence that slaves in these regions made bark canoes.[88]

The ebb and flow of colonial expansion (c.1500–1700) killed off and displaced many native peoples before most could influence slaves' maritime cultures. The design of slave canoes remained the same despite the presence, absence, or vibrancy of the Amerindian populations. African-style dugouts were the common denominator despite Amerindian variables.[89]

Comparatively few captives were imported into the Americas prior to the proliferation of plantation slavery during the mid-seventeenth century. Between 1630 and 1780, more than two-and-one-half times as many Africans as Europeans left their homelands for the English Americas. By 1820, eleven to twelve million Africans arrived in the Americas, compared to 2.4 million Europeans. Most entered societies largely stripped of their original inhabitants and were clustered in ethnic communities, facilitating the recreation or reimagining of ethnic traditions.[90]

African traditions were continually imported into the Americas as slavery gorged upon humans.[91] From the sixteenth to the nineteenth century, canoe-making skills were carried to the New World in some forty thousand slave ships required to transport roughly 12.5 million Africans to the Americas.[92] Some canoe-makers were professionals; many were watermen. All carried mental mockups of dugouts.

It is illogical to conclude that saltwater captives replaced their canoe-making customs with Indian practices. If this occurred, why stop here? We should expect to find Africans making Indian-style bark canoes, constructing Indian-style houses, and adopting numerous other Amerindian customs. Enslaved members of different ethnic groups recreated and reimagined distinct traditions, some of which were merged into synthesized arrangements. These practices resembled African traditions, providing captives with a sense of cultural stability. Early enslavers "sequestered" themselves and their two-legged property along waterscapes where bondpeople used familiar iron tools to craft African-influenced dugouts that encapsulated recognizable African meanings.[93]

Cultural exchanges seem to have primarily resulted from the blending of African traditions. The ubiquitous design found throughout Atlantic Africa probably permitted diverse captives to construct dugouts with a shape that embodied and expressed their cultural values. Hence, dugouts seemingly provided diverse peoples with a cultural plane to intertwine similar traditions and beliefs, permitting them to form customs that retained resonances of home, while becoming members of multiethnic slave communities.

As the next chapter describes, dugouts quickly became central modes of transportation in New World slave societies, and enslaved canoemen were crucial to European colonization and slavery's expansion. Transporting slave-produced cash crops to river-ports and seaports and from wharves to ships at anchor, canoemen connected plantations to overseas markets and colonies to the metropolis. Captives equally used canoes to construct their own far-reaching informal economies.

Chapter 9

The Floating Economies of Slaves
and Slaveholders

Canoe-making, colonization, and the establishment of plantations routinely went hand-in-hand. Timber was produced as fields were cleared for agricultural production. It was used to build houses, barns, and fences, as well as to cook and heat. Some was allocated for the construction of transportation vehicles, like wagons and boats. Travel by boat was more efficient than by land vehicles because it was difficult and expensive to build and maintain road systems, whereas water travel was cheaper and easier than going overland. Canoes linked coastal settlements to each other and to hinterlands, transporting goods from plantations downstream directly to ships.

Unfortunately, settlement-period documents do not extensively detail how enslavers exploited Africans' canoe-making and canoeing dexterities. Yet, later accounts of would-be planters, like the account of Thomas Thistlewood, probably mirror the endeavors of earlier slavers. Arriving in Jamaica in 1750, Thistlewood sought to integrate himself into the colony's plantation system by, among other things, exploiting African maritime expertise. While managing William Dorrill's Egypt Estate, Thistlewood established an estate that produced provisions for Jamaica's sugar economy. Over the years, he bought several bondpeople and, in 1766, purchased 160 acres of coastal morass along the Cabarita River, called Breadnut Island to establish Paradise Pen Estate, or "the Pen." This estate, located on Bluefields Bay, produced crab, freshwater and saltwater fish, waterfowl, livestock, fruit, vegetables, timber, and flowers that were sold to neighboring planters and at the port of Savanna-la-Mar.[1]

Thistlewood's bondmen illustrate how saltwater and creole slaves collaborated during their free time to construct and sell dugouts. Bondpeople participated in what have been called "working socials," which were "public work environments where bondpeople labored to complete a task" during free time. (These social events hint at how captives spent their private lives. Many fused diverse maritime skills to earn money). In March 1767, Thistlewood commanded slaves to clear land, which included the felling of cotton-woods. An Egypt creole named Mulatto Davie determined to turn a profit by contracting with Thistlewood to make a dugout for the agreed upon price of 50s (Jamaican currency). On March 8, 1767, Davie began making "a small fishing canoe of the biggest of the young cotton trees cut down in my garden He has hired Job and Flanders to help." Flanders was Egypt's carpenter/cooper and Job his assistant. Both were Akan. On April 19, 1767, the trio "finished the canoe" they worked on for "six Sundays." Flanders apparently made several canoes, including one belonging to fellow Akan bondman Cubbenna, or Kubenna, who was Egypt's driver. Perhaps Davie helped make previous dugouts; at the least, he owned one. Thistlewood's dugout measured 14 feet, 7½ inches long; 27½ inches wide; and 15½inches deep. He had not specified the canoe's dimensions beforehand and thought "she is scarce worth a fourth part" of what he paid. Lacking another boat, he paid full price.[2] One year later, on August 25, 1768, he acquired another, larger canoe, measuring "about 26 feet long, near 4 wide & 3 deep." This "very leaky" canoe was abandoned by planter John Parkinson, and Thistlewood's slaves restored its seaworthiness.[3]

Other slaveholders similarly benefited from slaves' canoe-making abilities. While in the Georgia Low Country during the 1840s, Charles Lyell observed how rice plantation bondmen "employ their spare time in making canoes out of large cypress trees, leave being readily granted them to remove such timber, as it aids the land owner to clear the swamps," selling them for about four dollars. Likewise, in the late eighteenth century, Charles Ball's owner established a plantation along South Carolina's Congaree River, exploiting Ball's dexterities to advance this endeavor. The fabrication of dugouts augmented plantation production. Trees were felled to clear fields and the timber used to make dugouts, which became essential to plantation production. Canoes transported bondpeople and overseers to and from fields and carried slave-produced crops to the plantation for processing and to market. They were also used for fishing with catches being sold to whites, fed to field slaves, and used as fertilizer.[4]

Importantly, cottonwood timber was largely only used for dugouts as it is a weak construction material and produces insufficient heat to be used as fuel. While residing in Jamaica during the early nineteenth century, James Kelly decried "the uselessness of the timber." Likewise, Jamaican planter Matthew Lewis noted that the cottonwoods "answers no purpose," except "to furnish the negroes with canoes." Hence, slaves' ability to exploit this otherwise worthless timber uniquely advanced colonialism and slavery.[5]

As slavery pushed inland, dugouts linked estates to seaports, with Robert Rose illustrating how canoe-makers facilitated the establishment and expansion of interior plantations. Rose migrated from Scotland to Essex County, Virginia, in 1724. Large planters already controlled the desirable Tidewater real estate, compelling later arrivals to move into the Piedmont region. Caught in this migration, Rose established several riverside plantations. During the 1740s, his canoe-makers manufactured numerous dugouts, which he and his neighbors used to ship slave-produced tobacco to market. On March 14, 1748, he explained: "My people were making a Canoe, being the 3d, for carrying Down Tobo [tobacco]." On March 15, 1749, Rose noted, "Our people busie in Making canoes." He did not provide canoe-makers' names, ethnicities, or birthplaces. Like most other captives at the time, they were probably African-born. The number of canoes made is unknown. Rose owned some prior to 1748, when bondmen made at least three, and in 1749 they crafted several more, suggesting that they made between six and ten. Rose's 1751 inventory listed 101 slaves and they surely did not produce enough tobacco to require this many canoes, so his canoe-makers were probably producing surpluses for sale.[6]

These canoe-builders and canoemen served Rose well: they produced dugouts at minimal labor cost. The dugouts permitted Rose to rapidly ship hogsheads of tobacco to market. (Hogsheads were large barrels weighing roughly 1,000 pounds each.) Shipping neighbors' tobacco probably enlarged Rose's profits. The large number of manufactured canoes suggests he sold some—apparently favoring short-term gains over the potential long-term profits from transporting neighbors' tobacco. Or, perhaps Rose sold these dugouts to neighbors before they purchased them elsewhere or had their slaves craft them. Another possibility is that hogsheads were shipping to market in double-hull canoes. There, the canoes were unlashed, one was sold, and the other paddled home.

Reimert Haagensen provides a tantalizing glimpse at how canoemen facilitated St. Croix's plantation system during its settlement. Haagensen arrived at St. Croix in 1739, just six years after Denmark purchased the uninhabited island from France in 1733. Haagensen rapidly educated himself in the business of plantation slavery and by the early 1740s he was a leading planter and administrative official. His description of the production of lime used to make mortar and plaster for construction illustrates how canoe-making and canoeing were crucial to the establishment of colonies and plantations. Slaves cut coral, called "seastone," from "reefs surrounding nearly the entire islands; this makes things much easier for the plantations located near the beach." Lime "produced from seastones is considered much better for use than that which is produced from stones on land. For this reason, the [Danish West India] Company has used only lime burned from seastones in their various buildings, namely the fort, the battery, the windmills, the cookhouses and cisterns." It was also used in sugar production. Sugarcane was ground to extract the juice. As the juice was boiled, lime was added to "Temper," or crystallize, it. Describing how coral was harvested, Haagensen wrote: "Two slaves row a boat from shore to the reef, or as it is called canoe, where 5 or 6 other slaves are standing, breaking off the stones with thick wooden sticks. When the boat arrives, they fill it with stones. While the boat is returning to shore with those stones, the slaves loosen other ones until the boat returns."[7]

In this manner, captives harvested the ocean's resources to lay the foundations and erect the edifices of bondage. Canoes were hewn from trees cleared for agricultural production. Coral was used to construct planters' homes, windmills used to grind sugarcane into profits, government buildings where officials regulated St. Croix's expanding sugar economy, and fortifications that protected this plantation enterprise.

Slavery voraciously devoured all in its path. It destroyed indigenous societies; tore living reefs from their fastnesses; ripped up native vegetation; and watered the fields with displaced Africans' blood, sweat, and tears. Like captives described by Thistlewood and Lyell, those in the Danish West Indies advanced the plantation system through labors often completed during their free time.[8] Slaveholders cunningly twisted slaves' desire for minimal comforts to expand their own interests. These practices were surely replicated throughout the Americas, helping plantation slavery take root.

Just as the waters of the Cabarita River converged with those of Bluefields Bay, so too did the canoe-making traditions of Thistlewood's Akan and "Ebo" watermen. In 1761, while Thistlewood was the Egypt overseer, he purchased an "Ebo" man he renamed Dick, branding him with his mark. Dick was "5 ft. 7$^{3}/_{10}$ ins. tall, about 22 yrs. old, Country name Sawnoo, alias Dowotronny."

A jack-of-all-trades, he served as field hand, slave driver, carpenter, and fisherman. He also demonstrated Biafran canoe-making abilities. In 1767, he brought down a "great old Cotton Tree" that was "between 80 to 90 feet high & 40 feet around, including its irregularities [buttress roots]."[9]

Like sixteenth-century saltwater captives, Davie, Flanders, Job, and Dick used canoe-making skills to their advantage. Job, Flanders, and Dick arrived in Jamaica seemingly with carpentry skills, which conceivably precipitated their elevation to carpenters. Davie, Job, and Flanders knew they could sell Thistlewood a much-needed dugout. Perhaps lacking the skills to make a canoe, Davie subcontracted carpenters, permitting all three to gain perquisites.

These less-than-ideal canoes helped Thistlewood establish himself. Like settlement-era colonists elsewhere, he needed boats. Unable or unwilling to purchase better canoes, he made do with a small dugout and refurbished canoe.

Thistlewood's decision to amass canoes meshes with other slaveholders' decisions. He chose not to build wheeled vehicles or European-style framed boats that required specialized tools to construct. Canoes were less expensive and easier to construct and maintain than framed boats. Boatbuilders needed numerous, often specialized, tools, which most slaveholders did not own. Canoe-makers used common axes and adzes.[10]

Early New World settlers generally lacked access to roads, concluding that waterborne travel was cheaper and easier than clearing and maintaining roads. Thistlewood's Paradise Pen was bisected by the King's Highway, which encircled the island, providing, at least in theory, direct overland access to the seaport of Savanna-la-Mar and most of Jamaica's other urban centers. Poor road conditions, though, convinced Thistlewood and others that it was cheaper and easier to use dugouts. Thistlewood raised draft animals, using them for agricultural production and for sale. Many planters made the same decision, using livestock primarily for agricultural production while manning dugouts with enslaved watermen as expressed by a Virginian in 1687: "As their houses are at most a hundred or fifty feet distance from these creeks, at ebb-tide they not only visit in their small boats, but carry their traffic through this channel, so horses & oxen do not work, except when they take a fancy to work them."[11]

Thistlewood used canoes to relocate to Paradise Pen. In June and July of 1767, bondwomen transported seed yams, plantains, and "many things" to Thistlewood's fields and slaves' provision grounds. On July 3, the first large shipment of goods arrived at Paradise Pen. On "September 1st 1767," slaves "carried my Book-case, in the battoe, to the Pen, and the books in baskets upon Negroes' heads, &c. . . . Had my desk carried to the Pen in the battoe." On the third, an Ibo man named Lincoln "carried in the battoe to the Pen: cask of muscavado sugar, 196 lb net; cask of rum, 28 galls net of strong proof; manchioneal table, 3 old chairs; pisspot; 8 empty bottles, &c." That afternoon, Flanders helped Thistlewood transport fruit trees. Thistlewood came to appreciate his canoemen's ability to ship expensive commodities that could be destroyed if a canoe overturned.[12]

Thistlewood's canoes exemplify the life cycle of many African dugouts, conceivably enabling bondmen to perpetuate familiar practices. As previously discussed, coastal Africans used high quality canoes fabricated by professionals for deepwater fishing and coastwise trade. As oceangoing canoes became less seaworthy, they were retired to the calmer waters. Parkinson's slaves launched and landed the twenty-six-foot, seemingly high quality canoe through the surf before discarding it. Thistlewood's captives restored it to calm-water use.

Years of working as an overseer permitted Thistlewood to comprehend how canoemen, fishermen, crabbers, and African-inspired dugouts could further his economic interests. As a reward, slaves laboring in other capacities were also rotated into these positions. Plantation authorities routinely preferred using watermen to transport goods rather than sending them over bad roads that damaged wagons, draft animals, and commodities. Numerous diary entries detail how watermen transported news, white people, goods related to plantation production, and slave-produced cash crops. After becoming Egypt's overseer, Thistlewood set about making repairs caused by a hurricane. Canoes transported wood, lime, thatching, and other building materials. On November 19, 1752, he "sent Nero, Will, Hector and George to the seaside to load the canoe and back with thatch. Received canoe-load of thatch soon after noon. Sent the canoe away again loaded with 86 bundles." By November 22, at least 509 bundles of thatch were used to repair the "Millhouse" and other buildings.[13]

Participation in formal economies was surely a familiar process for many African-born canoemen. Before being enslaved, they completed short-haul voyages while working for themselves or others. For them, New World bondage probably retained strong echoes of home.

After Egypt's lackluster 1752 sugar harvest, the owner, William Dorrill, converted it to the production of goods to supply sugar plantations. He hired out many slaves to Richard Bowen's Salt River Estate where Thistle-wood was temporarily reassigned, using a dugout to facilitate the move. On October 24, he received "by the canoe, a dozen of bills [machetes], 3 barrels of mackerel, and one of flour—and a letter from Mr. Fookes. Wrote to Mr. Fooks, sent back in the canoe, stones, old gun, 3 new iron staples, 36 pieces of old iron, under the care of Pompey who came in canoe." Canoes also conveyed white visitors, laborers, and letters. On March 23, 1754, "received a letter from Billy [William Mould, who was Dorrill's store clerk, book-keeper, and driver] by Philip Gudgeon, who came with the canoe. Received 3 sugar tierces."[14]

Thistlewood seemingly used maritime positions to reward good behav-ior, enabling those with maritime skills to temporarily escape agricultural production. An Egypt slave named Sancho seems to have been somewhat of an exception. Sancho was a skilled fisherman who provided Thistlewood with "very fine" snook, making him a favorite. In February 1752, he and Thistlewood got into a wrestling match when Thistlewood tried to punish him. Sancho was stripped of this position and sent to the fields. In March 1752, Sancho discovered his wife, Quasheba, having an affair with fellow slave Morris. Apparently feeling sorry for Sancho, and craving seafood, Thistlewood elevated him back into his maritime occupation.[15]

Thistlewood rotated skilled bondmen into canoeing positions during lulls in their primary occupations. In this way, he kept them working with-out subjecting them to the perceived insult of being a field laborer. For example, Quashe, or Kwesi, a deeply trusted Akan slave driver, sometimes worked as a canoeman. Quashe had apparently been given an old dugout by John Filton, who Thistlewood replaced as Egypt's overseer on September 11, 1751. Quashe used it to travel both on his own and on his owners' accord, allowing both to benefit from Quashe's property. Likewise, the above-mentioned Pompey sometimes functioned as a canoeman but was primarily a cooper.[16] On November 18 and 19, 1751, Cudjoe, a semiskilled Akan carpenter, and four other captives transported the previously men-tioned thatching. Thistlewood wrote: "Before day in the morning sent away the canoes. Cudjoe steers her, Morris, Dover, London, and Adam are the oarsmen." Apparently, Cudjoe's status as the most skilled landsman trans-ferred to water, where he held the senior position and exerted himself the least.[17]

Canoeing could also extract labor from those unfit for other rigors. On December 28, 1751, Morris "cut himself badly with an axe in the leg." To keep this field hand and semiskilled carpenter working, Morris was temporarily assigned as steersman.[18]

These experiences provided Thistlewood with lessons familiar to seasoned slaveholders. Even on an island dominated by sugar production, captives could be profitably employed in maritime pursuits. He understood that maritime slavery and agricultural production were symbiotically interlocked in a relationship that made both more profitable. When establishing his own estate, Thistlewood freighted goods along canals to the Cabarita River, and into Bluefields Bay. From there, it was an easy jog to Savannala-Mar.[19] He adhered to the somewhat common practice of rotating slaves into skilled and semiskilled positions as a reward. To maximize production and maintain morale, captives were typically placed in positions they were proficient in rather than in unfamiliar occupations.[20]

Thistlewood surely knew the folly of rotating landsmen into maritime positions. Greenhorns could possibly negotiate an empty canoe along calm waters. However, properly loading and balancing a heavily laden dugout and successfully navigating it would prove exceedingly difficult. Bringing one through surf breaking across the Cabarita's mouth into Bluefields Bay would have been nearly impossible.[21] Canoe-makers and canoemen did not wield as much influence over their work and lives as divers did, in part because they were more fungible. Still, their expertise could confer grounds for negotiation within the system of bondage, enabling them to gain more limited privileges.

Thistlewood illustrates the relationship between establishing slave-producing estates and canoeing. Fields were cleared for cultivation. Settlers used felled trees to build shelter and advance their economic interests. During settlement periods, colonists often experimented with commodities they hoped would produce wealth. Likewise, Thistlewood used dugouts while experimenting with agriculture, timber, and livestock production. Canoes helped maximize slave-produced outputs by providing a cheap, efficient, reliable source of transportation that did not deprive his fields of draft animals or many transportation slaves.

For these reasons, it is not surprising that, as documents show, most waterside slaveholders owned at least one dugout and seemingly favored dugouts over wagons and European-style framed watercraft. Dugouts were considerably less expensive than other watercraft or land-craft. For one thing, boatbuilders used specialized tools, which most slaveholders did not own, and framed boats took longer to construct. Variables, like types of wood and usage, make it difficult to compare the life expectancy of canoes to framed boats. Most New World dugouts were made from cottonwood and cypress and apparently remained seaworthy longer than rowboats. In 1709, John Lawson explained that cypress "is very lasting, and free of Rot. A Canoe of it will outlast four Boats, and seldom wants repair."[22]

Canoes were cheaper to acquire and maintain than wagons.[23] One draft animal cost more than most dugouts. The 1745 inventory for James Winright of Carteret County, North Carolina, listed five horses valued at £40, £20, £30, £25, £17, while his "Large Cannoe" was valued at £8. Thomas Thistlewood recorded the prices of horses and canoes. In 1760, he purchased a horse for £35 and a saddle and spurs for £13. In 1772, he witnessed a sale in which Vine, an Akan bondwoman, sold a horse to a white man for £17. In 1778, Thistlewood purchased a horse from one of his slaves named Franke, "for which I paid her £12 cash down."[24] Likewise, eighteenth-century York County, Virginia, estate inventories indicate that yokes, harnesses, carts, and wagons cost significantly more than dugouts.[25] Dugouts were cheaper than comparable wooden-framed boats, while sails and rigging could cost more than canoes.[26]

Maintenance costs also favored canoes. Some slaveholders prolonged dugouts' lives by painting them. Many did nothing.[27] It could be expensive to feed horses on Caribbean islands that devoted most of their arable land to cash crops, with Edward Long reporting that some "grass-planters have made upwards of 1500*l. per annum* by this commodity." Thistlewood produced scotch grass, employing canoemen to deliver it to Savanna-la-Mar's stables, noting that "horse keeping in Savanna la Mar stands in between 45 and 50 pounds per ann. in grass and corn; 3 bitts worth or more per day." In addition, livestock needed to be housed and cared for.[28]

Canoes' low cost was seemingly reflected in rates charged for traveling in them. Northern and European travelers often concluded that canoes provided the cheapest method of traversing slave regions. As British traveler Basil Hall toured the American Southeast in 1827–1828, he and his companions found canoes more favorable for traveling than carriages or steamboats. They paid "12 dollars, or about £2. 16 [shillings]" per day for a private carriage with an additional "three quarters of a dollar a-day, or about three shillings" for the "baggage-wagon." They also paid for the empty carriage's return trip. Frequently choosing canoes, they traveled for free as planters routinely loaned them dugouts and canoemen, which afforded intimate views of the region in a novel un-European method.[29]

Canoes also outpaced wagons and carts. Sources on American westward migration indicate freight and passenger wagons averaged ten to fifteen miles per day.[30] Travel through the tropical and semitropical American South, Caribbean, and Latin America was not as direct and was often inhibited by waterways and marshy ground.

Dugouts' slender shape, shallow draft, and responsive design made them suitable for negotiating New World waters. They were energy efficient in an age with few sources of energy, enabling a few slaves to rapidly transport several tons of goods. Sailing vessels could travel faster, but keels necessary for sailing into the wind precluded them from shallows. Edmund Ruffin, who sought to enhance nineteenth-century Southern agricultural production, applauded the versatility of cypress dugouts, capable of passing through "four inches of water," concluding they were ideally suited for shipping goods through North Carolina's swamplands. In addition, since canoes did not depend on wind, lulls did not impact travel. Canoes were sometimes rigged with temporary or permanent sails. However, paddlers usually propelled them, providing a relatively fast, predictable source of transport that could be measured in minutes and hours even when traveling considerable distances.[31]

By the early eighteenth century, many slaveholders had acquired canoes. Just as white prejudices facilitated the retention of African traditions by concentrating slaves of the same ethnicity in small geographic areas, white desires for dugouts probably furthered captives' ability to recreate maritime traditions. This means that even if slaves did not want to maintain African canoe-building techniques, some were compelled to do that.

There has been no sustained scholarly deliberation of slaveholders' exploitation of African woodworking and carpentry skills. To exploit these African dexterities, enslavers merely had to employ slaves as carpenters, and not in a particular African form of carpentry (like mask-making), which seems to be the case with canoe-makers. Canoe-making was a task performed by many carpenters, coopers, and shipbuilders, and sources suggest that into the early nineteenth century many Low Country and Caribbean canoe-makers were African-born. The carpenters and coopers working for Thistlewood and Rose were skilled canoe-makers. A cooper named Cudjoe resided on one of Charles Manigault's Low Country Georgia plantations. Like Thistlewood's Cudjoe, Manigault's Cudjoe and carpenters seemingly made dugouts. Perhaps the construction of dugouts alerted slaveholders to African-born captives' woodworking skills, precipitating their employment in an array of carpentry occupations, like shipbuilding, house building, and rough and finished carpentry.[32]

Canoe-making skills were seemingly preserved in several ways. African- and country-born woodworkers laboring under their owners' direction surely took on apprentices. Others probably learned from African-born fathers, uncles, or community members. Orphaned by his parents' sale, Charles Ball was raised by his paternal grandfather, who "was brought from Africa," and maintained numerous African traditions. When sold into South Carolinian bondage, Ball was a "rough carpenter," possibly learning carpentry from his grandfather. Equally, groups of bondmen born in the Old and New Worlds and possessing different dexterities collaborated in "working socials" to construct dugouts, with each contributing labor and skills while learning from others. This was a common practice in agricultural societies, evidenced in home construction and repair in Atlantic African and slave communities.[33]

Few, if any, planters employed full-time canoe-builders. Many captives made dugouts during their free time. Enslaved carpenters, coopers, and shipbuilders were required to craft many. The Manigaults, a wealthy nineteenth-century Georgia rice-planting family, owned several carpenters and coopers who constructed and maintained boats for their plantations, which were located on Argyle Island and could only be accessed by boat.[34]

Pierce Butler's plantations (1744–1822) were similarly situated on Butler's and St. Simons Islands, in Georgia's Altahama River Estuary. His six shipbuilders, York, Yankey, Bungy, Sauney, Caesar, and Lynas[?], built two deepwater ships. With great pride, he boasted: "My carpenters require no White man to enable them to erect as good a House as I would desire. . . . My ship carpenters built me two Sea vessels without any White person directing them." These ships were crucial to Butler's economic enterprise, carrying cotton, rice, and sugar to Charleston, Savannah, and other Atlantic ports. Returning, they brought slaves, tools, news, provisions, and visitors.[35]

Butler's carpenters also built and maintained smaller, equally important, vessels, including canoes. His dugouts plied estuaries and coastal waters, transporting slaves, seeds, tools, and provisions between his plantations and markets. Some dugouts were more than thirty-five feet long and manned by ten paddlers and a helmsman. Smaller ones were built for Fish Harry and Crab Quash, who kept Butler's table stocked with seafood. When Frances Kemble spent four months on Butler and St. Simons Islands in the winter of 1838–1839 after marrying Butler's grandson, Pierce Butler II, she observed that carpenters remained hard at work, noting the numerous plantation canoes, flats, and other boats.[36]

Slaves found benefits in canoe-making as surely as slaveholders did. Sources suggest that bondpeople of diverse ethnicities blended their knowledge in ways that strengthened new group identities. Canoe-makers regularly sold dugouts to slaveholders, overseers, other white people, and slaves. On June 26, 1765, Henry Ravenel of South Carolina paid Pearoe 5£ "for a Canoe." Captives also sold dugouts at urban markets. Edward Long reported that Jamaican bondmen sold large dugouts to white people for "50£. to 60£." and smaller ones for "10£. to 30£., Jamaica money." Analogously, Charles Lyell noted that Low Country Georgia slaves made dugouts in their free time and "sell the canoes for about four dollars, for their profit."[37]

Davie, Flanders, and Job did not generate large incomes from their endeavor, but the rewards were not purely monetary. Canoe-making was surely a source of pride, permitting them to showcase expertise while preserving ethnic traditions. As Flanders and Job constructed dugouts, they engaged in Akan forms of carpentry that undoubtedly evoked memories of home, like fathers teaching them this skill. They may not have been from the same ethnic group. As members of the Akan-language group, they spoke mutually intelligible languages, using African vocabularies and meanings uncorrupted by English translation while discussing the shape and meanings of the canoe. For them and for Dick, canoe-making certainly contained spiritual meaning, which may have been especially true for Job and Flanders, the Myals who possibly used the dugouts and waters of Westmoreland to communicate with ancestral spirits.

Canoe-making enabled captives to subvert white authority while simultaneously promoting white interests, as Charles Ball illustrates. He was raised in Calvert County, Maryland, where he possibly learned to craft dugouts from his African-born grandfather. As a young adult, he was sold to a South Carolina planter, whose estate was situated along the Congaree River. Early one February, Ball found a good fishing stream, catching half a bushel of fish. Ball's owner determined to exploit this skill, appointing him the "head of a fishing party," comprised of himself and three other slaves, "for the purpose of trying to take a supply of fish for his hands" and to sell at market. Ball welcomed the opportunity, knowing he would work free from direct white supervision. His owner bought materials for weaving a net and the owner's son purchased two old leaky framed boats. Knowing the boats "would not have supported the weight of a seine and the men necessary to lay it out," Ball declared them "totally unfit." He then "*advised* the building of two good canoes from some of the large yellow pines in the woods. My *advice* was accepted, and together with five other hands, I went to work at the canoes, which we completed in less than a week."[38]

Ball's ability to *advise* his owner was surely a momentous event in his oppressed life. Ball proclaimed that his owner and his son did not know what they were doing and needed to take directions from a slave who, according to racial stereotypes, was purportedly stupid. True, Ball could only advise his owner. Still, his owner concurred, rewarding Ball's expertise by placing him in charge of the fishery. Explaining how this served as a source of self-respect, Ball wrote: "Things went pretty well, and I flattered myself that I should become the head man at this new fishery, and have the command of the other hands." Ball's wisdom and dexterities were further lauded when neighboring planters gathered to examine the fishery and congratulate "themselves upon a discovery so useful and valuable to the planting interest; and all determined to provide, as soon as possible, a proper supply of fresh river fish for their hands." The captives who witnessed these praises surely retold the event, making Ball the lion of the hour.[39]

Dugouts afforded mobile social spaces, permitting slaves to pursue commercial activities that subverted the authority of slaveholders and government officials who sought to control terrestrial places. Slave quarters, woods, and swamps provided privacy from white authority, but remained vulnerable to furtive whites. At illicit gatherings, bondpeople often posted watchmen to warn against approaching patrollers. When antebellum Southern captives congregated to sing or pray for freedom, many placed pots upside-down on the ground to "take up the noise."[40]

Waterways offered secure, secluded spaces away from Argus-eyed and keen-eared slave regimes. At work and during off times, canoes were beyond the eyes and ears of the most observant whites. The stealthiest overseer would find it nearly impossible to catch canoemen engaged in forbidden conversations, while dugouts permitted captives to travel with greater freedom than previously supposed.

Dugouts enhanced women's and men's ability to participate in what scholars call slaves' internal or informal economies. Internal economies were secondary institutions within the system of bondage that informed family and community structures, allowing captives to "create a more comfortable environment for themselves." Women "discovered ways to further utilize their skills . . . by raising chickens, cultivating corn, churning butter, and producing honey and other items" sold to fellow captives, to their owners, and at urban markets. Commercial networks created a community of communities, linking producers and street vendors who catered to white and black consumers. Considerable deliberation has been devoted to understanding these informal economies. Little scholarly attention is given to comprehending how captives traveled to and from market and how these journeys shaped familial and communal dynamics. Trips to weekend markets could be upward of twenty miles each way. Canoes permitted bondpeople to quickly complete a market journey. Voyages were not insular events. Canoes converged to form fleets, facilitating communication within their holds and among voyagers in surrounding vessels.[41]

"Gender played a prominent role in the accessibility to these markets." Bondmen, especially semiskilled and skilled workers, enjoyed the most geographic mobility and opportunities to engage in informal economies during work hours. During the week, women were frequently relegated to fields; inhibiting market activities. Still, women dominated many Sunday markets, using dugouts to transport several hundred pounds of goods and their children to market; returning home with cash and purchases.[42]

Timber was generally an abundant resource, enabling most bondwomen and bondmen to obtain a dugout. Indeed, canoes were routinely sold through the informal economy. Roswell King Jr., manager of the Butler Island Estate in Low Country Georgia, noted that a "certain number [of slaves] are allowed to go to town on Sundays to dispose of eggs, poultry, coppers' ware, *canoes* &c." Men and women used family canoes to hunt, fish, harvest shellfish, and gather wild fruit and nuts. Canoes' speed was crucial, as white authority could restrict bondpeople's time at market. King punished marketers who did not return "by 12 o'clock." Despite temporal constraints, dugouts' enabled captives to provide many urban and rural whites with nearly all of their fresh produce, dairy, and seafood. Staples produced during slaves' free time were typically the only foodstuffs Antiguans ate as they "raise pigs, goats, and fowls, and it is by their attention to these articles, that the whites are prevented from starving, during such times of the year as vessels cannot come to these coasts with safety."[43]

Two important developments occurred in eighteenth- and nineteenth-century Low Country South Carolina and Georgia. First, just as waterways connected plantations to overseas economies, they bound informal economies to the urban markets. Second, free and enslaved black people "virtually monopolized the transportation of goods in and around" urban areas.[44]

Dugouts were crucial for rapidly shipping goods, including heavy and bulky items, enabling captives to dominate markets despite shopkeepers' opposition. Many Low Country captives used dugouts to transport rice. Planter Thomas Akins of South Carolina permitted Ammon to cultivate and sell rice. In December 1748, Ammon sold "a Barrel of Rice" to "his Brother Joe" who lived some fifteen miles away. Joe "came for it" in a canoe with three fellow slaves and stayed the weekend. Others transported stolen rice. Bob, one of Charles Manigault's captives, was caught in Savannah with a canoe and "8 or 9 bushels of Rough Rice," an amount too heavy to shoulder.[45]

Canoes' ability to outpace other watercraft meant they regularly transported perishables. James Wetherell documented how "canoes come with fish and the more delicate kinds of fruit, requiring a quicker mode of conveyance than the barcas [barges] afford, occasionally a monkey, some stands of parrots, or some curios 'bicho' [small beast]."[46] Hence, dugouts supplied markets with legitimate and illegitimate goods.[47]

Retailers elsewhere used dugouts. When George Gardner traveled throughout northern Brazil, he documented slaves transporting goods on Rio São Francisco in single- and double-hull canoes, saying that a "market, or fair," was held "every Saturday" at the waterside village of Propiá, drawing buyers and sellers from up and down the river. The "whole of the previous day, particularly towards evening, canoes continued to arrive from all quarters with articles for sale." Accounts indicate that most of those who transported foodstuffs throughout northern Brazil were African-born slaves who traded during their free time. Others worked for their owners or were hired out as wage-earning slaves.[48] Women traveling to market often transformed dugouts into bumboats, selling goods to shipboard passengers.[49]

Importantly, dugouts allowed mothers to take children to markets, transforming voyages into family affairs, extending the time shared with children. When Johann Rugendas traveled to Brazil in 1821, he observed canoe-borne women carrying goods to market, rendering a watercolor of them preparing to board canoes with children and goods. Gardner witnessed a similar scene at Propiá. Having slept in a canoe on Friday night, he "awoke early on the morning of the fair, by the noise of a motley multitude of men, women, and children of all colours, from the deep black African, to the scarcely white inhabitants of Brazil."[50]

Figure 24. "Mompox [Columbia] Marketplace." Slaves sold goods from their beached dugouts, which were used to quickly transport perishables, including fresh fish, meat, poultry, fruit, and vegetables, as described by Dessalines d'Orbigny. One captive is selling live turtles, which were a delicacy. A husband and wife apparently crewed the canoe in the foreground, allowing them to extend the precious little time they had together while they made money selling goods produced during their free time. Alcide Dessalines d'Orbigny, *Voyage Pittoresque dans les deux Amériques* (Paris: 1836); image is opposite 59; text describing image is on 80–81. University of Virginia Library, Special Collections.

Revenues made family members' exploited lives more bearable and, at times, enjoyable with purchasing patterns falling "into five broad, and to some degree overlapping categories: food, clothing, 'luxuries,' recreation, and religion." Hans West reported that after Danish West Indian marketers sold "their wares, they purchased for themselves other necessities like fish, meat, pork, rum, candles, head scarves, cloth for jackets for their wives, and other similar items."[51] As canoemen carried Charles Lyell along Georgia's waters in 1846, he "met a great number of negroes paddling their canoes on their way back from Darien, for it was Saturday, when they are generally allowed a half holiday, and they had gone to sell on their own account their poultry, eggs, and fish, and were bringing back tobacco, clothes, and other articles of use or luxury."[52]

Dugouts were not merely vehicles of commercial exchange. They linked marketers to multiple social spaces that lined fresh and salt waterscapes—including slave quarters, gardens, churches, and markets—and transformed what would have otherwise been discrete communities into communities of belonging. Rivers, swamps, and coastal and interisland waters were woven into long tapestries of cultural environments. Canoes allowed families to travel broadly, exchanging traditions and maintaining connections with family members and friends scattered by forced sale. If permitted to arrange their living spaces, bondpeople often replicated African spatial organizations, so slave villages resembled African compounds in terms of layout and architecture. When "the slave family was together in its home, gathered around the fireplace, the master and his power were shut out for the moment," allowing them to socialize and recreate and reimagine African traditions.[53] Slaveholders usually exerted little control over the built environments and cultural contours of slave villages; even less over family canoes and waterscapes.

Slaves did not confine the intimate social and cultural elements of their lives to terrestrial settings. Plantation surveys indicate that waterscapes often separated slave quarters from provision gardens. Canoes quickly traveled to and from gardens while transporting tools, produce, and children, enabling parents to maximize their free time while bonding with children.[54]

Canoeing, canoe-making, gardening, hunting, fishing, and marketing influenced how bonded families organized their time and passed down customs. These intertwined activities conformed to traditional African gender roles, enabling families to knowingly and unknowingly retain traditional familial relationships. Households were the primary means of production in many African and slave economies and tasks were usually gender specific. Canoe-manufacturing was a male craft, marketing was often monopolized by women, and men and women performed agricultural work. Men and women, young and old, all had designated obligations. Typically, bondmen and bondwomen worked in gardens, with women shouldering more of the burden when men hunted and fished.[55]

Dugouts, like homes and provision grounds, were intimate spaces for family members. Families were the basis of community life, and fishing, gardening, and commuting provided members with time to express love.

Fathers and sons surely bonded while carving canoes that mothers, daughters, and sisters paddled to market. As fathers imparted generational wisdom upon sons, some, perhaps, used the same tools their fathers held while instructing them. When carving family canoes, they surely understood that family members' safety rested on their craftsmanship, compelling them to carefully fabricate balanced vessels that were less likely to deposit loved ones and their material production into the water.

Dugouts were used to move goods and people in patterns that disregarded white authority. Captives' ability to sell commodities and the mobility necessary to do so contradicted their fettered status. Legal codes defined bondpeople as property incapable of owning property. Yet societies' social and economic stability rested upon slaves' ability to own and sell goods, especially foodstuffs. Maritime commerce permitted them to travel in ways that undercut white authority.[56] With and without white consent, and often in violation of the law, slaves carved family canoes. Many fathers probably made them and, in the process, instructed sons. Hence, garden production and commerce necessitated familial interactions, permitting African skills to be inherited by generations of country-born slaves.[57] Mothers and daughters paddling to and from gardens and markets extended valuable time together, knowing they were responsible for enhancing their family's material comfort. While traveling, mothers taught children to handle canoes, provided life lessons, and gave instructions on commercial negotiation and how to navigate white authority.[58]

Some vendors traveled considerable distances on planter-merchants' boats, often called "plantain boats," which were usually large modified canoes. Manned by slaves working for their owners, these vessels transported cash crops to market and returned laden with the accoutrements of plantation bondage. Planters often permitted marketers to voyage aboard these vessels upward of two hundred miles round-trip. Since St. John Island in the Danish West Indies did not have a regular market, marketers sailed aboard plantation boats to the adjacent island of St. Thomas. In Jamaica, some traveled to distant seaports. Whether owned by planters, free black men, or others, these vessels were crewed by a mix of free and enslaved mariners and white men.[59]

Alexander Barclay observed hucksters' autonomy aboard plantain boats, noting they were permitted to sail to Kingston, "a distance coastwise of sixty to seventy miles" to sell "plantains, yams, edoes, and corn." These voyages lasted several days. "A return was brought in Irish salt-pork, butter, mackerel, cod-fish, linens, printed cottons, muslins, handkerchiefs, and crockery-ware,—articles regularly retailed in the plantation village." The boat was registered to a "free person" and plantation slaves voyaged unsupervised.[60] For vendors, the passage was surely as rewarding as their commercial transactions, allowing them to enter multiracial milieus that suspended terrestrial notions of race and slavery, while extending their economic spheres and networks of friends and associates.

Studies of the internal economy expand our understandings of slave experiences and how they manipulated slaveholders' economic systems to extract benefits. The market could be a liberating space where "bondwomen and bondmen escaped the rigors of agricultural and nonagricultural production." It allowed them to slip between slavery and freedom to challenge traditional cultures of power. While they could be swindled, the "law of the market" often empowered sellers. During the bargaining process, they sold property on their terms, slipping into "de facto equality" with white purchasers that allowed them to set prices. Here normal hierarchies of power were suspended. Whites continually sought to restrain female vendors who they felt had too much autonomy, dominated the market by marginalizing white traders, charged exorbitant prices, and collectively defied white supremacy. Since many marketers paid their owners for the privilege of trading and provided white residents with most of their foodstuffs, slaveholders and legislatures refused to constrain them.[61]

While informed by local geographies and community dynamics, market voyages could serve as "working socials." Drawn together like flocks of migratory birds, canoewomen remained in fleets, disbanding along the waterfront, and re-forming during homeward passages. Voyagers interacted with members of waterside communities, engaging networks of family, friends, customers, and producers. Markets connected Jamaican "slaves with the world outside their plantations; it created contacts with neighboring plantations, established linkages between the coast and interior, and spread news, not only of family and plantation disputes but of political events with the island and even in England." Canoe-borne commerce enhanced this process, permitting women to fulfill social obligations. Flotillas comprised of people from numerous slaveholdings transformed waterways into social and cultural tides. For instance, ships approaching Rio de Janeiro slipped "through a fleet of gracefully shaped canoes and market-boats." Rural slaves near Bahia similarly formed a massive flotilla. "Around the landing-places cluster hundreds of canoes, launches, and various other small craft discharging their loads of fruit and produce. On one part of the praya [beach] is a wide opening, which is used as a market-place."[62]

Fleets were mobile marketplaces of information. As they drew together and disbanded they absorbed and radiated news and gossip. Captives living on different plantations from spouses, children, and friends linked up with loved ones in these convoys. When distance or opportunity precluded such reunions, greetings were surely passed along watery grapevines of communication.

Markets equally provided opportunities for reconnecting. For instance, when the previously discussed South Carolina slave named Joe traveled to Irishtown plantation to purchase rice from his brother Ammon, they spent the weekend together. Joe and the three slaves who helped crew the canoe, socialized with Irishtown captives, spending "all Saturday night playing and dancing having a Fiddle with them."[63]

Many white urban residents accused slaves of extortion. Voyages certainly afforded the privacy and time necessary for conspiring. Captives undoubtedly discussed business, exchanging market information, like price enumerations, what was in demand, what was scarce, and what was abundant.[64]

Dugouts were simultaneously mobile spaces of illicit exchange. While Charles Ball served as a fisherman, he traded fish stolen from his owner to a white "keel-boat" captain for bacon. As Ball stood in the canoe and the captain upon deck, they negotiated the trade. A canoe transported the fish to the captain and "the bacon was received into our craft." When Ball and a slave named Nero pushed off, the captain said that "he should be down the river again in about two weeks, when he should be very glad to buy any produce that I had for sale," especially cotton. Nero stole "two bags of cotton" and sold it to the captain for "thirty or forty dollars." Toiling at night for their owner, the fishermen knew their actions went unseen and unheard, emboldening them to steal fish and cotton.[65]

Rural and seaport bondpeople often congregated along waterfronts to sell crafts, dairy, produce, seafood, game, poultry, building materials, and an assortment of other commodities directly from their dugouts. Jamaican wharfinger James Kelly explained that bondpeople congregated on his dock, selling sailors "provisions" from their gardens "or exchanging salt beef for them." Waterfront positions permitted some to use dugouts as bumboats, paddling out to ships to conduct floating trade as James Wetherell witnessed in Bahia: "Upon a barca reaching the city, a scene of confusion ensues, boats put off with market women to besiege the new arrival, large cartes of fowls are borne off by the fortunate purchasers, [b]ananas and oranges are piled in golden heaps, the shore boats are quickly laden with cabbages, yams, sugar cane, pumpkins, or melons."[66]

"Bumboat" apparently derives from "boomschuit," the Dutch word for dugout, with "boom" meaning "tree" and "schuit" meaning "boat." Bumboats were floating huckster stalls that extended commercial activities as women and men laundered passengers and crewmembers' clothing and sold produce, seafood, and curios, affording many whites with their first glimpse, smell, and taste of the tropics. At Port Royal, Jamaica, ships were greeted by "bom-boats, coming alongside the ship with coffee, fruit, and vegetables." Some further augmented their profits by ferrying passengers and crewmembers ashore.[67]

Bumboat-men and -women regularly sold exotic animals, such as turtles, snakes, monkeys, and parrots, to neophytes in the land of bondage. While Wetherell resided in Brazil, he watched canoemen transport monkeys and parrots to markets and to recently arrived ships. When Massachusetts botanist Moses Ashley Curtis arrived in Wilmington, North Carolina, he made a novel purchase, writing, "A boat came along side with three negroes who offered an alligator for sale. I hade never seen one before & my curiosity stimulated me to a purchase," which was probably added to his herbarium of dried specimens.[68]

Bondpeople also conducted floating trade with passing vessels. They paddled out to sell firewood to ships anchored in the Cape Fear River. One former slave delineated how maritime commerce met captives' material needs neglected by their owners, saying, "Slaves on this plantation, being near Wilmington, procured themselves extra clothing by working Sundays and moonlit nights, cutting cord-wood in the swamps, . . . they would then get a permit from their master, and taking the wood in their canoes, carry it to Wilmington, and sell it to the vessels, . . . and with the money buy an old jacket of the sailors, some course cloth for a shirt, &c."[69]

Bumboats permitted captives to work as semi-independent entrepreneurs who paid their owners a monthly stipend for this privilege. Bumboat-women and -men spent most of their time afloat and along the waterfront as part of largely black communities. They navigated waterscapes away from slaveowners' view.[70]

Bumboat-women and -men were also cultural brokers, providing many Westerners with their first sights, sounds, tastes, and textures of bondage.

They brought passengers and crew members news from Europe and the colonies. Updates on tropical diseases were of special importance, and white people were glad to hear that ports-of-call were free of exotic forms of death.[71]

Some women forewarned of premature white deaths, as Robert Renny grimly observed while arriving at Jamaica. A "canoe, carrying three or four black females, came along side ship, for the purpose of selling oranges, and other fruits." As the canoe departed, one took the lead in a call-and-response dirge; the others provided the chorus:

New-come buckra [white person],
He get sick,
He tak fever,
He be die,
He be die,
New come, &c.

Like Sirens, the bumboat-women lured ship-weary voyagers shoreward; enticing them with tropical fruit. They warned whites not to get too close as contagions earned Jamaica its dubious reputation of the "grave of Europeans." Slavery afforded white people pleasures and dangers. These women articulated the realities of tropical life.[72]

Bumboat-captives provided examples of slavery's cruel realities. While Charles Campbell served aboard a Jamaican coastal trader, a bondman came aboard "to dispose of some fruit. A quarrel ensued between the Negro and one sailor about the price of the article which was the subject of barter." The mate became "so enraged" that "he took up a piece of wood, and began to beat him unmercifully," prompting the man to jump "overboard, and was immediately drowned."[73]

This incident underscores how bumboat-slaves could be sucked into the whirlpool of maritime violence churned by shipmasters and officers. As slave owners' property, bondpeople were not permitted to be abused by ship officers. Still, some officers mistreated bondpeople. When whites injured or killed someone else's slave, they faced civil and criminal charges and slaveholders' extralegal wrath. The mate's race and status permitted him to avoid "legal inquiry" and the "captain of the ship paid the master of the Negro a sum of eighty pounds as an equivalent for the loss of the

slave and the matter was hushed." Ships' officers could escape legal culpability, as slaves could not testify against white people. Yet, planters could
employ economic and political influences to preclude trade and, thus,
advance their interests. These were not slaveholders' only weapons. Years
of labor made captives strong and some were skilled in Western and African
forms of martial arts. Planters sometimes used bondmen as "coercive
toughs" and enforcers who extended their will and avenged wrongs. Ship
captains knew of bondmen's fighting abilities, for they sometimes disci-
plined sailors ashore, returning those who deserted with battered faces.[74]

Slave women monopolized most urban markets. By the early eighteenth
century, Kingston was Jamaica's largest market, yielding the most varied
and specialized array of goods. Female marketers influenced trade throughout the island. In Bahia, women insinuated control over the sale of fresh
whale meat, fish, and fruit. During whaling seasons, they enjoyed a brisk
business in cooked and uncooked whale meat. In 1845, Daniel Kidder
observed: "Vast quantities of this flesh are cooked in the streets, and sold
by" bondwomen. Fifteen years later, whale meat was "brought to market
wrapped in banana leaves ready to cook." In Bermuda, whale meat, or "sea
beef," was often the only fresh meat available to slaves and poor whites.
When whalers hauled catches ashore, slave men and women "assist in cutting off the blubber" and, for their efforts, were free to take "all the fleshy
parts."[75] Bondpeople profited from the exploitation of the ocean's resources
with captives in the Danish West Indies producing surpluses of finned fish
and shellfish, as well as fruit, firewood, wild fowl, iguanas, and livestock,
which they sold to whites. Columbian slaves similarly supplied markets
with crafts; live turtles; and fresh fish, meat, poultry, and produce.[76]

Marketing and distribution systems were conducted through overlapping formal and informal spheres. White merchants organized formal networks and often tried to manipulate captives' economies by employing
female slaves as retailers. Simultaneously, informal markets permitted
bondwomen, working in their accord, to defy traditional white perceptions,
definitions, and parameters of gendered labor.[77]

Slaves' ability to manipulate some urban markets suggests that, to an
extent, they reimagined "canoe houses." In Atlantic Africa, to recall, canoe
houses were militarized maritime corporate trading firms comprised of
related and unrelated merchants, warriors, paddlers, and others bound by
fictive kinship and market capitalism. Bondpeople were obviously unable

to fully recreate these institutions, yet they seemingly reconstructed components of them or, at least, constructed commercial networks that mirrored them in significant ways. Shipmate relationships formed aboard slavers, and canoes provided networks of fictive kin, while bonds of real and imagined kinship constructed within slave quarters extended these linkages. These ties were crucial for producing, distributing, and selling goods, and stringing together conglomerates that functioned as one organism or, perhaps, as corporate societies. They seemingly worked in concert; permitting discrete associations to operate with concerted will to insinuate considerable control over availability and pricing.

Canoes became contested spaces as whites claimed marketers used them to manipulate prices and smuggle goods, prompting many to try to prohibit their use. While John Luffman was in Antigua in 1788, he observed "the smuggling of the produce of this island to the slave markets" with whites also fearing goods were shipped to Saint Eustatius, a Dutch island. In 1772, an irate observer complained that bondwomen's virtual monopoly of Charleston's seafood market rendered whites victims of their capriciousness, blasting that captives were able, "at their pleasure, to supply the town, with fish, or not; and of course to exact whatever price they think proper." He claimed women dominated markets by colluding with rural bondpeople to funnel the most desirable "poultry, fruit, eggs, &c" brought in "from the country" to enslaved vendors so they, and not white shopkeepers, sold the best goods. Averring that canoes were used to conceal superior products from white retailers, he railed:

> These women have such a connection with, and influence on, the country negroes who come to that market, that they generally find means to obtain whatever they may chuse, in preference to any white person; and thus they *forestall* and *engross* many articles, which some few hours afterwards you must buy from them at 100 or 150 percent advance. I have known those black women to be so insolent, as even to *wrest* things out of the hands of white people, pretending they had been bought before, for their masters or mistresses, yet expose the same for sale again within an hour after, for their own benefit. I have seen the country negroes take great pains, after having been first spoke to by those women, to *reserve* whatever they chose to sell to them only, either by keeping the particular

articles in their canows, or by sending them away, and pretending they were not for sale.[78]

The same legislation designed to prevent fugitives from paddling to freedom (discussed in Chapter 11) was unsuccessfully used to thwart commerce. An Antiguan law passed in 1669 ordered boat owners to secure vessels ashore. A 1773 law prohibited commerce between "any Boat, Vessel, or Canoe" and ships in St. John Harbor and a "Penalty of ten Pounds" levied against offenders because "divers Felonies and Frauds have been committed, by Means of Boats, commonly called Bum Boats, being permitted to trade with Ships and Vessels in the Harbour and Road of St. John; which, under a Pretence of supplying such Ships and Vessels with Provisions and Vegetables, have received and conveyed away great Quantities of stolen Goods."[79] By 1696, South Carolina law severely punished bondpeople who took dugouts without permission. In 1737 and 1744, the Grand Jury prohibited captives from conducting floating trade, claiming they sold alcohol and stolen goods.[80]

Some slaveholders demanded strict regulation of dugouts owned by themselves and their captives. South Carolina planter P. C. Weston commanded: "Every boat must be locked up every evening and the keys taken by the Overseer. No negro will be allowed to keep a boat." Pierce Butler fumed that slaves were stealing and selling his rice to Darien's duplicitous shopkeepers. In 1799, he ordered overseer William Page to halt the use of canoes without permission and threatened to "make an example of" any offenders by burning "the canoe, whether it belongs to me or one of the Negroes, in order to prove to them you're fixed determination." Vendors used dugouts regardless of laws and slaveholders' locks, hatchets, and threats, probably knowing enslavers were dependent on them and their canoes for transportation.[81]

Almost any slave who wanted a canoe could obtain one. Waterways were typically lined with dense vegetation that shielded furtive passages. Unsanctioned canoes were hidden in canebrakes or shrubbery or were weighted down and submerged.[82]

Whites hoped maritime accidents would deter bondpeople. In 1852, Charles Manigault's overseer reported that a bondwoman belonging to a neighboring planter drowned while canoeing to market, scoffing: "Mr. John Williamson lost a negro woman by drowning. So much for their excessive canoeing to Town."[83] In 1808, Roswell King, who was now Butler's overseer, hoped the drowning deaths of five slaves would discourage canoeing. On December 25, they slipped away from Butler Island "in a small canoe" and headed for his Hampton Plantation on St. Simons Island, setting off "against the incoming tide, with a strong N.W. wind," making conditions dangerous. The canoe overturned and the youth apparently succumbed to hypothermia and drowned. They were "your favorite Sawyer Jack, . . . Carter Moses of ab$^{\circ}$ 18 y^{rs} of age, Harry's boy Jacob ab$^{\circ}$ 16 y^{rs}, Woster's Tipee of ab$^{\circ}$ 16, & Deanna's Judy of ab$^{\circ}$ 14 years of age." King was furious that they violated "his Master's & my orders" and determined to make an example of them, saying: "All the reply I made after hearing of this unfortunate accident was that there friends might find the bodies and bury them like dogs, for not one should have a coffin." He swore "the next got Drowned in violation of your Orders or mine I would sell the bodies to be Cut to Pieces by the Doctors." The slaves on Butler's plantations surely learned of the deaths and desecration and were probably appalled by King's callousness. However, maritime accidents did not stop voyages into the internal economy. As King forewarned, "They do not care a least about your orders or mine, out of sight—for the Danger of *fire & water* I am always telling of them."[84]

Likewise, Manigault's slaves habitually took canoes on illicit voyages made more egregious when selling rice stolen from him. In 1852, "Bob was apprehended in Town with a boat and 8 or 9 bushels of Rough Rice and lodged in jail by one of the constables" for selling rice without written permission. Bob was a repeat offender who angered Manigault in life and death. Approximately one year after the woman belonging to the neighboring planter drowned, Bob "drowned in the River in returning from Town . . . where he had been to trade."[85]

Most slaveholders apparently accepted that they were powerless to stop these commercial tides, while knowing they benefited from bondpeople's informal economies as they differed costs associated with provisioning captives.[86] Many slave owners also capitalized on slaves' dugouts, as exemplified by Thomas Thistlewood. He became overseer of Egypt Estate on September 16, 1751, when the previous overseer left, creating a power vacuum compounded by a hurricane. On September 27, "Messrs Jemmison and Mason," an attorney and plantation manager, used the turmoil to try to seize a canoe and other property belonging to Thistlewood's slaves. Thistlewood penned: "They pretended to bring an order from John Filton for the fishing dory, old canoe, he gave to Negro driver (Quashie), old seine [fishing net] he gave Phibbah," his mistress and cook. Having no legal means to protect their property, they beseeched Thistlewood. He drove the men away; knowing the canoe would facilitate Egypt's rebuilding while wanting to prohibit outside interference that could undermine his authority and disrupt productivity.[87]

Knowing that canoes furthered white interests; captives used them to gain privileges mirrored in self-hiring practices. Bondpeople's ability to hire themselves out placed them on "shaky legal ground." Since captives were not recognized persons, hiring arrangements were tacit rather than legal contracts with state and colonial legislatures often outlawing the practice. Yet, slaveholders, legislators, and employers ignored their illegality to benefit from these arrangements. While slaves were similarly not permitted to own property, slaveholders encouraged the practice as it bound them to slave societies, while reducing provisioning costs.[88]

Slaves surely negotiated for concession when *permitting* whites to use their dugouts. They gained respites from field labor and captained their own vessels, which enhanced their self-esteem and status. Canoe owners probably parlayed restrictions that white authority sought to impose on them, gaining permission for them and their family members to more freely canoe. They surely felt some sense of satisfaction knowing whites were reliant on them; perhaps providing saltwater captives with a sense of ethnic pride.

On weekends, streams of market-going canoes passed waterside slave quarters, fishing grounds, gardens, and swimming holes. Whites caught fleeting glimpses into slaves' otherwise hidden world. One Saturday afternoon, Frances Kemble, wife of Pierce Butler II, observed how canoes and the Darien and Altahama Rivers provided communal space. With her enslaved canoeman, Jack, they passed captives "in parties of three and four rowing boats of their own build, laden with their purchases, singing, laughing, talking, and apparently enjoying their holiday to the utmost." Except for ephemeral encounters, bondpeople enjoyed privacy to interact and partake in African-influenced expressions.[89]

Chapter 10

Sacred Vessels, Sacred Waters:
The Cultural Meanings of Dugout Canoes

Canoes were vital to informal slave economies, as well as to formal slave-holder economies. Still, like other traditional watercraft the world over, canoes represented more than modes of transport, commerce, and economy. They were "a social map" articulating cultural understandings, spiritual beliefs, aesthetic values, and personal and collective identities, causing mariners to remain reticent of adopting other societies' watercraft.[1] African canoes had a soul and gender. Their timber and the waters they plied connected water people to ancestral spirits and water deities. Canoes could serve as cultural markers that expressed societal values and aesthetics. Ralph Waldo Emerson captured how humans embody and reflect societal and cultural values, penning, "[There] is nothing but is related to us, nothing that does not interest us,—kingdom, college, tree, horse, or iron shoe,—the root of all things are in man." Dugouts were intrinsic fibers in African material cultures. The "true poem is the poet's mind; the true *ship* is the *ship-builder*," and the true *canoe* is the *canoe-maker*. Canoes connected societies to waterscapes, while water people the world over were hesitant to alter their vessels' design and cultural meanings. Canoe designs probably remained engrained in slaves' cultural understanding even as, and perhaps because, they were subjugated.[2]

Boats, in any context, are more than assemblages of wood, iron, rope, and sail. They are "complex cultural artifacts," indelibly stamped with collective symbolisms. Mariners develop intimate relationships with their watercraft. People routinely name and adorn vessels with secular and sacred symbols. Maritime architecture embodied societal aesthetics, values, and traditions. Most mariners are reluctant to abandon generational, time-tested watercraft, routinely rejecting outside boat designs even when technological advances afforded benefits. We still find an array of traditional vessels—African, Amerindian, and Oceanian canoes; Zanzibari Dhows; and Chinese junks—even though these societies have endured centuries of Western contact. The abandonment of traditional craft meant the discarding of ancestral spirits and deities.[3]

Mariners entrusted their lives and fortunes to watercraft that became existential extensions of their bodies. To alter their craft was to alter themselves, their way of life, their belief systems, and their social and cultural institutions. Facing pressure to adopt Western watercraft, most societies refused to fundamentally change their existences. Instead, their boats took on new meaning: one of resistance to colonialism, imperialism, and capitalism. The Enata of the Marquesas Islands exemplify this refusal to make Western-style boats. Europeans felt "a boat was sturdier, more useful, safer than a canoe. But a canoe to Enata was more than a mode of transportation. No one man owned it. In its parts it was a social map of their different skills, different wealth. A canoe was invested with both labour and *tapu* [sacredness]. A boat was nothing."[4]

Canoes conjoined the sacred and the earthly, making them secular workplaces and spiritual objects hewn from revered trees capable of serving as conduits to the watery spirit world. As for most Africans, spirituality was integral in canoe-builders' everyday lives. Sources indicate that most Atlantic African societies maintained reverence for trees and bodies of water.[5]

More specifically, mature cottonwoods were generally regarded as the dwelling places of spirits. In 1871, Joseph Skertchly crassly recorded Fon/Dahomean beliefs, penning: "The worship of Atin-bodum consists in faith in its power of averting and curing disease, . . . Any tall tree is considered to be inhabited by this deity, but those especially sacred to it are the Hun, or silk-cotton tree."[6] Others shared similar beliefs. The Bullom/Sherbro, a maritime people residing on Sierra Leone's coastal islands and littoral zone, believed that "certain spiritual beings, often called *bloms*" lived in cottonwoods. Many peoples, including the Bullom, believed spirits resided in "the soil, waters, flora, and fauna. . . . Their assistance or noninterference in human affairs may be invoked by prayers and offerings and by the meditating influences of ancestor spirits. Trees are the favorite abode of spirits, the most powerful of which are thought to reside in an area's tallest trees. Villagers shelter under large trees for the protection afforded by resident spirits. Stones commemorating ancestors placed at the base of the trunks synergistically bond the community, the living, and the resident spirits."[7]

Many believed that groves of old cottonwoods were especially sacred, as Thomas Winterbottom explained: "In these gloomy retreats, where the sublime beauties of nature are heightened by imposing silence, and rendered still more awful by the impenetrable shades with which they are veiled, the imagination is powerfully acted upon, . . . These groves, therefore, or trees, distinguished from others by their stately and venerable appearance, were the most ancient of temples; and this custom is followed in Africa at present day, where under the shade of the wild cotton or pullom tree, they assemble to perform their solomn sacrifices and other rites."[8]

Anthropologist Carol MacCormack's description of Bullom/Sherbro village life is representative of Atlantic African spirituality. She wrote:

> It is in the protective shadow of two groves of virgin forest, each containing several towering cotton trees. . . . The swept space of the village ends abruptly at the edge of the forest. During an initiation season this margin is marked by a screen of palm fronds, and a portal through which the candidates for initiation, and members of society, pass. The sacred grove functions as a burial ground, as a site for communication with ancestral spirits, and as sacred space for rites of passage and other congregations. The cotton trees act as a focus for communication with extraordinary powers. They form a vertical axis, between the sky of an ultimate creator, and the deep earth/ground water of ancestral abode.[9]

Cottonwoods housed the souls of future generations—connecting the here and now to the spirit world. Chinua Achebe, in his fictional representation of Ibo life, explained, "The spirit of good children waiting to be born lived in a big ancient and sacred silk-cotton tree located in the village square. So women who desire children go to sit under its shadow so as to be blessed with children." Dahomeans performed spiritual ceremonies beneath their boughs, pouring libations into "perforated calabashes placed around their roots" to honor spirits residing inside them. The Asante conducted waterside rituals beneath "silk-cotton tree[s]." Cottonwoods and canoes figured prominently in initiation ceremonies that transitioned children into adulthood at the Bullom/Sherbro village of Thoma. During rites of passage, spirits ate children's souls and the spirit of the sacred grove gave birth to new adults. An infusion of cottonwood leaves was used to produce a gelatinous substance simulating afterbirth, which was rubbed on initiates. As the forest birthed inductees, community members "beat on the 'belly' of the forest spirit (beat on buttress roots of the cotton tree or an up-turned canoe), announcing its labour has begun."[10]

Reverence for cottonwoods was commonly based on beliefs that the trees interlaced the living, ancestral spirits, and deities by connecting earth, sky, and water. Cottonwood canoes seemingly retained hallowedness. That reverence may also have been based on the cottonwoods' canoe-making suitability and the prosperity and honor they afforded fishermen, canoe-men, and maritime warriors.[11]

Mahogany dugouts were equally revered. Jukun peoples of northeastern Nigeria crafted dugouts from *Afzelia africana* and *Khaya senegalensis*. When selecting trees, "each man goes forth into the forest armed with a white cloth, and when he sees a tree of dimensions suitable for the making of a canoe he binds the cloth round that tenant tree. It may be noted that in expeditions of this character there are two leaders among the party, one charged with religious duties, and one the person considered most expert in the practical work of canoe-making."[12] The first duty was to appease spirits living in groves where timber was harvested. This was done through offerings and prayer. Before a single axe stroke was made, the canoe-maker sought divine permission, saying: "Great Ones, permit us."[13]

Spirituality was thus an integral part of canoe-building, including the selection of timber. Canoe-makers along the upper Congo River did not drink water while constructing dugouts, believing that "otherwise it would leak." Charms were used to prevent cracking, to "ward off evil influences from spoiling it," and to guard against theft.[14]

Like mariners throughout the world, canoemen personified their vessels. Canoes were named and their souls honored. Gold Coast peoples believed canoes could be male or female, and their gender determined how they moved across the water. Fante watermen performed welcoming ceremonies for newly purchased canoes that included placing food offerings on them. Jukun-speaking peoples called newly purchased canoes their "bride, and before entering it deposits a little flour on the prow as an offering to the soul of the canoe." The Ga from modern-day Ghana and Togo similarly made sacrifices.[15]

Honors continued throughout a canoe's life. Canoemen regularly "fed" dugouts, placing sacrificial food on them so that their spirit would protect them. Ga fishermen recognized that canoes were indispensable means of production that safeguarded their lives, regarding them as companions and collaborators. On Tuesdays, which were sacred, Ga fishermen gave dugouts gin or other beverages to "drink" and "fed" them by placing food on their prows. Well-treated canoes guided owners to schools of fish, telling them when to cast nets.[16]

Canoes forged bonds with ancestral spirits and deities. Coastal and littoral peoples believed that the spirit world lay on the other side of or beneath the ocean; hence, the ocean was revered as the residence of the dead.[17] Members of some of the ethnic groups within the Kingdom of Dahomey believed that the Land of the Dead, called Kutomen, lay across a great river, which souls crossed in a canoe. Kutomen was said to be beneath the ground; though it was sometimes identified as actual rivers. Others believed it was the lagoon situated between Dahomey and the ocean. Indeed, the lagoon-side port of Contonou, or Kuntonun, means "At the mouth of the river of the dead."[18]

Dugouts promoted communication with aquatic spirits. Residents of the lagoon-side city of Ouidah paid respect to Hu, god of the sea. Temples honoring Hu and other deities were built on beaches "where canoe-men offer donations of food to induce the deity to give them a smooth sea" and he was represented as "small canoes stuck over with shells." Residents of Ouidah also paid tribute to Dohen, "whose special province it was to call [Western] vessels to that port."[19] Religious taboos prohibited rulers of Dahomey and neighboring polities from looking upon the sea. According to Thomas Winterbottom, the ocean was the "national feteesh of the Eyeo [Oyo] nation, . . . bordering upon the kingdom of Dahomey to the northwest, and they are fully persuaded that immediate death would be the consequence if they looked upon it."[20]

Canoes provided mariners and their communities with important connections to the spiritual world. In rough seas, mariners evoked ancestors' protection. As Charles Thomas explained, the *Kru* held that they were divinely safeguarded while on the water. Likewise, in 1863, Richard Burton recorded a *Kru* belief pertaining to a spirit residing in or around a large rock that Europeans disparagingly called "Grand Devil," located a few miles from the mouth of the Cavalla River. *Kru* and other peoples believed that if one did not respect this oracle they could not voyage along the coast.[21] Thus, spirituality was associated with traversing waterways during work and warfare.

Dugouts' ornamentation articulated cultural, spiritual, and political understandings of wood and water, while reflecting personal and collective identities. The extent to which hulls were painted is unclear, though, gunwales were routinely adorned with pictograms, iconographic symbols, and motifs carved in high and low relief. Some had figureheads. In the mid-1660s, Nicolas Villault documented the spiritual meanings of Gold Coast ornamentations, penning, "*Canoes* are very neat and beautiful, painted and adorned with all possible care; they fasten *Fetishes* to them, to preserve them from storms & disasters."[22]

Canoes were steeped in social and cultural meaning, as their ornamentation further reveals. Beached dugouts were meeting places where goods were sold and "fish taxes" paid and where women discussed market prices, men told tales of the sea and discussed maritime techniques, and kids played with "children's canoes," observing and mimicking future professions. Art historian Michael Coronel stressed: "A canoe is not only a boat but a concept permeating practically every facet of community life; it serves broad and varied functions, including aesthetic and the sacred." Anthropologist Jojada Verrips elaborated, stating: "Fishermen are no exception to the 'rule' which says that human beings tend to treat crucial means of production not as sheer objects but instead are inclined to transform them into specific kinds of subjects, 'companions' or 'collaborators', for instance, by decorating them abundantly and giving them 'names' and sometimes even food."[23]

Charms were hidden inside hulls to protect against danger and increase fishermen's catches.[24] Motifs enabled owners to conspicuously demonstrate status and group affiliation. Canoe owners showcased wealth by elaborately adorning vessels. Canoes' soul; gender; and Christian, Muslim, or animist affiliations were reflected in their iconography. Some ethnic groups used specific color and character combinations to distinguish themselves. Today, the gunwales of Ga canoes are typically painted white with a blue rectangle in the middle.[25]

Adornments also expressed other group identities. Members of the Akuapem, Akyem, Asante, Baoulé, Anyi, Brong, Fante, and Nzema ethnicities comprising the Akan ethnolinguistic group in Ghana and the Ivory Coast organized themselves into *asafo* companies, which were political-military institutions that served as local militias and philanthropic social-cultural groups. Pictograms and numbers identified particular *asafos* while artistic expression further emphasized group identities.[26] The "competitive nature of these companies is expressed in the gunwale carvings on many canoes." At Cape Coast, *Asafo* Number 1, which is red, beached its canoes next to *Asafo* Number 4, which is yellow. Since sea snakes were deemed good luck, guiding fishermen to prey, their motifs were carved onto canoes belonging to Number 1 were "altered into a bravado challenge," depicting a red-headed sea snake ingesting a yellow-headed one.[27]

Early modern travelogues indicated the presence of motifs, but they did not describe them.[28] Today, the Fante have a reputation for creating some of the most ornate and skillfully decorated canoes.[29] Unfortunately, we cannot track changes in designs or elaborateness over time.[30]

Bows were sometimes fitted with beakheads or figureheads, which travelers, unfortunately, did not describe in detail. For instance, in 1564 John Hawkins said dugouts had "a beake head, and a sterne very proportionably made and on the outside artificially carved."[31] While this tradition predated European contact, canoe-makers seemingly engaged in artistic mimicry, adopting elements from European shipbuilders. Western ships were often garnished with figureheads, bowsprits, beakheads, and trailboards. Figureheads, often of women, nationalistic symbols, saints, or mythical characters, were typically the most intricately carved adornment. This was especially true during the seventeenth century when ornamentation was a "riot of extraneous decoration."[32] The size and flamboyance of African figureheads seemingly grew in lockstep with European practices; a process informed by salvaging figureheads from European shipwrecks and mounting them to large canoes. In New Calabar, figureheads representing Catholic saints that once adorned Portuguese vessels were mounted onto war canoes.[33] Unfortunately, we do not know the meanings Africans gave to them.

Traditional African prow ornamentations included African animals and motifs affording spiritual protection. Many figureheads were not permanent, with de Marees explaining that Gold Coast canoemen "do not forget to drape them with some Fetisso [fetish] of Sanctos: they often paint and colour them with Fetisso and drape them with ears of Millie and Corn, so that the Fetisso may protect them well and not let them die of hunger."[34]

Others were permanent. In 1889, Edward Stallibrass noted the Bijago use of figureheads: "The bow of the canoe is ornamented with a figurehead, generally representing either a cow or a hippopotamus, while the stern is carved to represent the tail of a rattlesnake." The hippopotamuses were surely intended to channel the power of these aggressive and dangerous creatures into Bijago warriors. Cows possessed spiritual and economic

Figure 25. "Canoe on the Bonny River." This photograph details the size and intricacies of figureheads mounted on some riverine dugouts. Joseph H. Reading, *Voyage Along the Western Coast or Newest Africa: A Description of Newest Africa, or the To-day and the Immediate Future* (Philadelphia: 1901); opposite 70. Author's collection.

value. The resemblance to a rattlesnake was probably coincidental, as the Bijago surely did not have the familiarity with this New World viper for it to express cultural meaning.[35]

In the tropical Americas, many slaves constructed dugouts from silk cottonwoods. If we take the Americas in their entirety, sources suggest most slave-built canoes were hewn from cottonwoods. Different genera are found throughout the tropics. All are ideal for canoe construction.[36]

Amerindians probably told some African-born captives which New World trees possessed desirable qualities. Others learned through trial and error, undoubtedly applying their botanical knowledge to the process. Cedar was used on arid Caribbean islands, as it is decay- and insect-resistant, lightweight, and strong. Dugouts in the Danish West Indies were "constructed from cedar, which are subject to neither worms nor rot."[37]

Bald cypress (*Taxodium distichum*) was commonly used in the American South. Its easily worked timber is called "the wood eternal" and is ideal

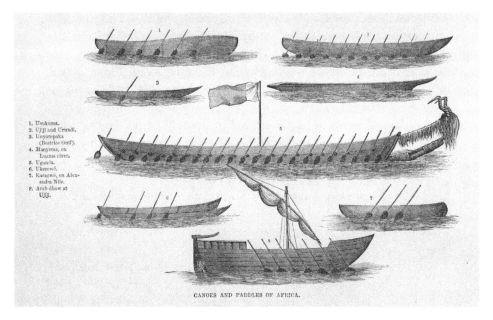

1. Usukuma.
2. Ujiji and Urundi.
3. Unyampaka
     (Beatrice Gulf).
4. Manyema, on
     Luama river.
5. Uganda.
6. Ukerewé.
7. Karagwé, on Alex-
     andra Nile.
8. Arab dhow at
     Ujiji.

CANOES AND PADDLES OF AFRICA.

Figure 26. "Canoes and Paddles of Africa." This image documents late nineteenth-century canoe designs in the interior West-Central and Central Africa. The bows and sterns of most canoes project forward and back, providing them with considerable overhang and a streamlined appearance. Canoe 6 looks similar to Senegalese pirogues. Canoe 5 has the same figurehead as those in Figure 19 in this book. The war canoe also has a long ram projecting from its bow that could be used to push and possibly tip enemy canoes. Author's collection.

for construction where resistance to water, decay, and insects is needed.[38] The *Liriodendron tulipifera* of the American Southeast is commonly dubbed the tulip tree or yellow poplar but was also "called Canoe-wood."[39]

Pine, which is soft and easily worked, was used to quickly construct canoes; however, those canoes probably rotted relatively quickly. Charles Ball's decision to build two pine dugouts was informed by the fast-approaching fishing season. The choice to rapidly construct softwood dugouts paralleled African customs. Congo River peoples used mahogany to craft high-quality, expensive canoes, with life expectancies of some fifteen years. Softwoods were used to hastily make small, inexpensive craft to meet short-term demands.[40]

African spiritual beliefs about trees, especially about cottonwoods, were inherited by subsequent generations during slavery and even after slavery was abolished. Many believed that cottonwoods were dwelling places for deities and were portals to the spirit world, facilitating transcendental communication across the Kalunga. While John Stedman was in Suriname during the 1770s, he "enquired of an old negro" why saltwater captives "paid such particular reverence and veneration" to cottonwoods, "bringing their offerings to the wild cotton-tree." The slave responded that "having no church nor places built for public worship (as you have) on the Coast of Guinea, and this tree being the largest and most beautiful growing there, our people, assembling under its branches when they are going to be instructed, are defended by it from heavy rains and scorching sun. Under this tree our gadoman, or priest, delivers his lectures."[41]

Enslaved members of the same ethnicity often retained spiritual beliefs about silk cottonwoods. Akan captives in Jamaica maintained the name for cottonwood, as well as its spiritual characteristics.[42] When Flemish painter Pierre Jacque Benoit traveled to Suriname during the 1830s, he recorded slaves' reverence for cottonwoods in print and in painting. The spirits residing in cottonwoods were not hewn from these trees as they were carved into dugouts, nor did they cease to be conduits to the spirit world. Trunks transformed into canoes became the enduring legacy of once-living objects. Reborn for a new purpose, dugouts retained many of their original spiritual properties. As in Africa, canoes were sacred and secular vessels.[43]

Missionaries attempted to persuade free and enslaved people born in Africa and the Americas to renounce such convictions. For example, beginning in 1784 Baptist missionary George Liele attempted to convert Jamaican slaves to Christianity. Liele had been a slave in Georgia and assisted his protégé, Andrew Bryan, in establishing the First African Baptist Church of Savannah, which will be discussed in Chapter 11. Liele moved to Jamaica in 1783, establishing the First African Baptist Church of Kingston. He urged saltwater slaves to abandon beliefs regarding cottonwoods while discouraging converts from holding spiritual meetings beneath their canopies.[44] Still, black Jamaicans retained these spiritual beliefs even after white people lynched black people from them, which could have transformed them into symbols of oppression (and was probably one of the intentions.)[45]

Members of the diaspora believed spirits residing in cottonwoods must be venerated before trees were hewn. In 1871, some forty years after Jamaica abolished slavery, Charles Kingsley learned of the trees' spirits. He noted that if people "intend to cut one down, they first pour rum at the root as a propitiatory offering."[46]

Ideologies concerning cottonwoods persevered into the late twentieth century. Throughout the New World, planters refrained from removing some large cottonwoods from agricultural fields to avoid offending African-descended people's spiritual convictions. In Jamaica, Kingsley observed that "here as in Demerara [British Guyana], the trees are left standing about in cane-pieces [sugar cane fields] and pastures." Monica Schuler documented the retention of African values in 1971 when interviewing Imogene Kennedy whose African-born maternal grandparents were from Dalvey, Jamaica. Kennedy described how cotton trees housed spirits in Africa and the Caribbean and that the graves of many "old-time Africans" were scattered around its buttressed feet. Beneath one tree, Kennedy fasted for twenty-one days, communicating with ancestral spirits who taught her the "African" language, as well as songs and prayers.[47]

Spiritual beliefs concerning water and water deities also survived the diaspora. Many African- and country-born slaves and their free descendants, believed spirits resided in bodies of water and that cottonwood dug-outs facilitated communications with them and other spirits. Acts of suicide reflect the retention of African-influenced convictions concerning wood and water.[48]

Despite many African prohibitions on suicide, a number of saltwater slaves took their own lives, believing in death they would return to ancestral homelands. To facilitate this transmigration, many incorporated wood or water into these final acts. Africans did not believe death marked the end of life; rather, it was the transition to a new phase of existence. In many societies, it was believed the dead were reborn within their homelands. During the late seventeenth century, the first governor of St. Thomas in the Danish West Indies complained that Akan slaves "believe that at their death they return to their fatherland, or as they express it: '*mij dodte mij loppe in myn land*," prompting many to commit suicide. The translation of this Dutch Creole adage is "When I die, I shall go to my own land." Misunderstanding transmigration, some Jamaican slave owners "hanged up" corpses to demonstrate they remained in Jamaica. After several captives belonging to one planter "hanged themselves," he threatened to "hang himself, also, and to transmigrate, with them, carrying the whip in his hand, into their own country; where he would punish them ten times more severely than he had hitherto done."[49] Beliefs pertaining to the cyclical nature of life persevered with many ending their physical beings to regain freedom in the spirit world.[50]

Figure 27. "Old Cudjoe Making Peace." Cudjoe, or Kodwo, was a member of the Akan people of modern-day Ghana. He was the leader of the Leeward Maroons, which was one of the groups of rebellious slaves with which Britain signed peace treaties. On March 1, 1738, Cudjoe signed a treaty with the British beneath the canopy of a cottonwood tree, suggesting the spiritual value Jamaican slaves affixed to these trees. Planter Robert Dallas wrote, "All the solemnities attending it were executed under a large cotton-tree growing in the middle of" Maroon, or Cudjoe's, Town. "The tree was ever after called Cudjoe's tree, and held in great veneration." Indeed, Cudjoe probably believed that signing the treaty under a cottonwood made it a sacred binding contract, comparable to swearing an oath on the Bible. Robert C. Dallas, *The History of the Maroons, from Their Origin to the Establishment of Their Chief Tribe at Sierra Leone: Including the Expedition to Cuba for the Purpose of Procuring Spanish Chasseurs and the State of the Island of Jamaica for the Last Ten Years with a Succinct History of the Island Previous to That Period,* 2 vols. (London: 1803), 1: image is on frontispiece; quote is on 57. Author's collection.

African cosmology provided a foundation for transmigration beliefs as people routinely integrated elements believed to facilitate this process into suicidal acts. Many Atlantic Africans believed water and wood linked the living to the world of the spirits, which was located either in or across a real or imagined body of water. The soul formed an intimate relationship with water as it journeyed to the spirit world where it waited to be born anew. This was evidenced when one drowned or hanged oneself from wood beams in the home or tree branches. Seemingly the most common methods of suicide, they oriented souls toward the spirit world.[51] Charles Ball came to this understanding while helping an African-born father and American-born mother bury their young son. The father made "a miniature canoe, about a foot long, and a little paddle, (with which he said it would cross the ocean to his own country)."[52]

Ideologies regarding wood and water layered sacred meanings onto otherwise secular spaces. Many connected with African spirits and water deities through canoeing. Benoit observed how slaves used cottonwood dugouts as votives. While negotiating the Commewijne River, he encountered a drifting dugout containing numerous articles, including scissors, a mirror, jars of wine and gin, seashells, beads, vegetables, and a carved calabash containing herbs and fruit. He believed a sick leader floated the offering to "Mama Sneki" in hopes of being cured. The seashells may have been especially important for establishing good relations with deities, as many African-descended peoples associated them with the spirit world.[53]

Many Africans carried mental blueprints for canoes to the Americas. Slaveholders' purchasing patterns helped those of the same ethnicity retain traditions, while compelling diverse workforces to blend their customs. The coalescences of maritime traditions were familiar processes for African-born slaves as cultural blending regularly transpired throughout Atlantic Africa for generations. Canoe-building and canoeing facilitated the retention of spiritual and cultural beliefs by providing slaves with sacred items. Religious traditions were embedded in canoe-making, rendering the customs as palpable as the grains of wood in the hulls. Spiritual beliefs about trees and water could not be untangled without destroying the cultural meanings of both. Hence, dugouts probably served as cultural anchors, enabling captives to creatively reimagine traditions that provided connections to homelands even while forging new collective identities with members of their bonded communities.

Chapter 11

A World Afloat: Mobile Slave Communities

Plantations were international institutions, containing white and black households comprised of captives, overseers, managers, bookkeepers, and slaveholders. The Atlantic slave trade created a watershed, channeling diverse Atlantic African maritime traditions into New World aquatic crossroads. Struggling to make sense of New World bondage, members of different ethnicities gravitated toward cultural similarities. Dugouts undoubtedly transformed New World waterscapes into culturescapes reminiscent of home.

Along riverbanks and freshwater and saltwater shores, bonded community members used African muscle memory to craft dugouts. Shoving off from shore, they projected African customs across waterscapes. Bearing ritualized scars and paddling seminude, canoemen coordinated their strokes to the rhythms of African paddling songs while populating waters with African deities. In the process, they layered African meanings onto waterscapes that once possessed Amerindian cultural values.

Canoes were cultural confluences and mobile cultural spaces away from slaveholders' purview. Indeed, many became mobile communities, even if they were ephemeral. Within the crucible of dugout hulls, captives became *shipmates* akin to those bonds formed between sailors and saltwater slaves during the Middle Passage. Sailors fashioned familial-like bonds that transformed collections of men into close-knit, hybrid communities while sharing cramped quarters during months at sea. Together shipmates endured privations, storms, harsh discipline, and scant privacy while performing dangerous collective labor essential to the safety of each other and the ship. Terrestrial valuations were redefined as sailors were judged more by skills, strength, and endurance, than by race and socioeconomic status.[1]

Ships were part of shipmate identities that were personified and integrated into fictive families, making them more than collections of wood, nails, cord, and canvas. A ship was, as the hands of the *Mercury* described, their "father, mother, brother and sister, in fact [their] very life." Vessels were mariners' source of income and means of salvation that returned them home. The ship and all therein were part of an itinerant social and cultural sphere that defined shipmates and their relationship to each other and to the rest of humanity.[2]

Upon the waters of the Middle Passage, saltwater captives internalized shipmate affinities to form lifelong social organizations with their fellow voyagers. Shipmates forged bonds based on shared suffering to facilitate the formation of new group identities, using "shipmate" to express sibling-like relationships created while weaving networks of fictive kinship that replaced family members lost during forced migration. Thomas Winterbottom reported that those "who have gone to the West Indies in the same vessel, ever after retain for each other a strong and tender affection: with them the term ship-mate is equivalent to that of brother and sister, and it is rarely that matrimonial connections take place between them."[3]

The waterscapes of the Western Hemisphere provided fertile expanses for cultivating shipmate relationships, while canoes afforded unwilling colonists recognizable cultural and community spaces. The ties that transformed canoemen into shipmates were not merely woven from the threads of oppression. Many were spun from similar traditions, permitting them to speak the same maritime language even if they were members of different language groups. The communities formed within canoes could be enduring. Crews could remain intact for years. Operating as a single organism, crewmembers could anticipate shipmates' actions.[4]

Members of different ethnicities found accord in collaboratively crafted dugouts, permitting them to become shipmates. It would not be unimaginable to find a band of water people from the Bight of Biafra, the Senegambia, and Angola working together along the shores of the Western Hemisphere to construct dugouts that provided this diverse collective with echoes of home. Canoes necessitated cooperation from construction to use, articulating New World social cohesions. Together, captives selected trees and agreed on the canoe's dimensions. Perchance, canoe-makers borrowed a whipsaw from their owner, using it to cut logs to the appropriate length. As a Biafran and Senegambian stood on opposite sides of the whipsaw, pushing and pulling in concerted effort, they better understood their similarities. Forming a whipsaw equality, they made their enslaved lives more bearable by minimizing cultural differences while emphasizing commonalities. Together they shaped the canoe's hull. Pairing down a log, they chiseled away dissimilarities to merge their social and cultural understandings. When the dugout was completed, the trio paddled in unison, hauled fishing nets, and shared their limited cultural space.[5]

Dugouts provided a cohesive sense of spirituality that could transcend ethnic, linguistic, and religious differences. Captives did not have to be from the same ethnic group, speak the same language, or practice the same religion to share similar beliefs about dugouts and waterscapes. As dugouts bound Angolans, Senegambians, and Biafrans together, canoemen possibly felt their canoes materially linked them to the realm of their ancestral spirits, allowing them to embark on voyages that transcendentally connected them to past lives. They conceivably believed their canoe was a vortex for communicating across the Atlantic, across the Kalunga, with deities and ancestral spirits.[6]

These emblematic canoemen were not simply theoretical. They are found in runaway slave advertisements. The 1738 flight of an "Angola Negro, named Levi" and an "Ebo Negro named Kent" from Elliot's Bridge, South Carolina, speaks to slaves' ability to reimagine themselves as community members. Their owner, William Martin, recognized their maritime skills, setting them to work on a "Pettiauger"—a modified canoe. In the South Carolina Low Country, the duo found themselves in a boat that surely reminded them of dugouts manned on home waters. They were from African societies separated by one thousand miles of coastline and would not have recognized each other in past lives where they went by different names, spoke different languages, and worshiped different deities. In South Carolina, however, they seemingly found commonality in their boat, waterscape, and bondage. Levi and Kent spent much time together in their canoe's confined cultural space, sharing the same labors, sorrows, and privileges. They paddled under the same summer sun and through the same winter rains, and, perhaps, seated in their African-style dugout, they experienced their first snowfall together. After hours of paddling under a hot sun, they surely plunged overboard to cool off. Drifting with rising and falling tides, they shared stories of past lives. They spoke of fishing, commercial voyages, and perhaps naval battles that precipitated their enslavement. They ruminated about the parents, wives, and children they were torn from and pondered the new lives they were creating together.[7]

This canoe became an African cultural prism through which Kent and Levi perceived and experienced their new world. Canoes permitted slaves to understand the Americas much differently than most white people did. Sitting in canoes, Kent and Levi observed water, land, and sky from the same perspective they had viewed Africa. Both probably believed the wood of their vessel and the waters they traversed connected them to ancestral spirits. Initially their relationship was based on shared bondage. A maritime accord facilitated a growing friendship in which they eventually trusted each other enough to risk running away together.

Other advertisements indicate that analogous groupings similarly coalesced. On June 25, 1738, two country-born bondmen named Basil and Glocester stole a canoe and headed from Coggins Point, Virginia, with Sam, "a Tawny, well made, Madagascar Negro."[8] In April 1745, two North Carolina slaves stole a canoe. One was an unnamed country-born slave. The other was "a tall yellow Fellow, named Emanuel" who "calls himself a Portugueze," suggesting connections to a Portuguese settlement on the African coast. His "yellow" complexion indicates that he was a Luso-African, the child of a Portuguese father and an African mother.[9]

In Brazil, many "Congo" communities, which were comprised of diverse West-Central African peoples, elected kings to construct "ritual memory" that "symbolically link Afro-Brazilians to African political structures and to their African ancestors."[10] "Congo Negroes" on the island of Itamaracá, Brazil, layered meanings onto elections by using canoes to stage mock naval battles during a ceremony called "the christening of the king of Moors." White and black spectators gathered to watch mock warfare between several hundred canoemen. This ritualized event included the construction of an offshore platform representing "a Moorish fortress." On shore, "two high thrones" were erected where the "Christian king" and "Moorish king" sat. "On this day all the *jangadas* and canoes were put on requisition; the owners of them and others of the inhabitants of the neighborhood were divided into two parties, Christians and Moors." The "Christian king" demanded that his counterpart "undergo the ceremony of baptism, which he refused." War was declared and the "Christian" navy stormed the fort. The Moors paddled shoreward with the Christians in pursuit as the navies battled each other. Ashore, they "fought hand to hand for a considerable time, but in the end the Moorish king was taken prisoner, hurled from his thrown, and forcibly baptized."[11]

The ceremony adhered to the ritualized "Iberian" tradition of "*Moros e Christianos* dances that enacted a Christian discourse of triumph over heathenry honed in the *Reconquista*" while mirroring West-Central African military reviews. During military reviews, rulers observed soldiers sparring in martial arts that came to be called "*capoeiragem or capoeirs Angola*" in Brazil. West-Central African captives living throughout Latin America performed terrestrial versions of "*Moros e Christianos*" that symbolized "battle against heathenry" in which Catholic Kongolese forces prevailed, often as a result of the "miraculous intercession of Saint James," a "warrior saint." "*Moros e Christianos*" allowed Itamaracá's "King of the Congo nation" to review marines, articulating group identities informed by Old and New World circumstances. This ritual illustrates that many of the island's predominantly African-born population was capable of performing coordinated maneuvers, standing while swinging mock weapons, and disembarking and embarking at the fort and beach. Landsmen probably would have been incapable of such actions; precipitating mass baptisms as canoes capsized.[12]

Canoes surely connected captives to communities in Africa and the Americas while ritualized battles provided cultural spaces. "Christian" naval supremacy surely enhanced the king's authority. Like swimming competitions and blood sports, these events undoubtedly strengthened community bonds, affording participants dignity and self-respect, while offering "Congo" slaves a source of pride. They conceivably represented great "Congolese" achievements as fictitious memories blurred into historical myths that allowed warriors to bask in past glories.[13]

Other militaristic rituals were performed. Canoemen at Olinda, Brazil, constructed hierarchical rankings "corresponding to military titles. Certain individuals, by suffrage of the body, are elected severally to the rank of sergeant, ensign, lieutenant, captain, major, and colonel." These ranks carried weight. "When commissioned officers are met by inferiors or privates, they are entitled to a salute of one, two, three, or four strokes upon the water, with the vara setting-pole. An omission thus to salute is regarded as a crime in this aquatic community, and is subject to punishment." It is unknown if these practices had an African equivalent.[14]

Slaves near Rio de Janeiro articulated other traditions. In 1816, amateur naturalist John Luccock took a boat excursion up Guanabara Bay with a Portuguese sailor and "four stout negroes" from West-Central Africa. On an islet, Luccock found the skeletal remains of a "porpoise." He precipitated a work stoppage by tossing the skull, which possessed spiritual meaning for the captives, into the boat, dismissing their convictions as "superstitious dread." The boatmen were already uneasy about plying Guanabara's sacred waters and voyaging past the burning of "spiral" seashells used to produce lime. Many Africans believed seashells, especially spiral-shaped ones, possessed spiritual meaning as they represented the circular travels of one's soul. The slaves were deeply aggrieved when their entreaties to jettison the skull were ignored and the sailor escalated the situation by tossing "it into the lap of one of them." This proved the breaking point and the bondmen went on strike until the skull was "thrown overboard." Luccock contemplated the "alternative[s], either compel them to proceed by severity, or give up the obnoxious skull. The latter was decided on." Tossing the skull overboard, Luccock accepted that he caused the mutiny and felt coercion would exacerbate the situation. Furthermore, he possibly recognized that the canoemen could cast him, the sailor, and skull overboard and claim their drowning deaths resulted from an accident.[15]

Canoemen articulated African beliefs concerning the dignified beauty of their nude bodies. Many whites were shocked by what they regarded as canoemen's shameful displays of nudity. Arriving at Rio, Parisian traveler Adèle Tousaint-Samson was paddled shoreward by semiclad men bearing ritual scars upon their faces. While in the Brazilian state of Maranhão in 1811, Henry Koster similarly observed: "These fellows are mostly dark-colored mulattos and blacks, and are entirely naked excepting the hats which they wear upon their heads; but when they come on shore, they partially cloth themselves."[16] Such accounts suggest that captives perceived New World waterscapes through African lenses that embraced beliefs regarding the aestheticism of human bodies. Denied most sources of self-respect, many were proud of their muscular, sweat-glistening physiques that were gifts from their creator and toned by their toils. Canoemen seemingly knew their seminude bodies offended Westerners and delighted in effortlessly tormenting them by wearing little clothing. In 1854, Maturin Ballou recognized how country- and African-born bondmen in Cuba found pride in their bodies, saying that they "wear only a short pair of pantaloons, without any other covering to the body, thus displaying their brawny muscles at every moment. This causes rather a shock to the ideas of propriety entertained by an American; but it is thought nothing of by the 'natives.'"[17]

If formal attire could challenge white systems of power, so could nudity. Scholars have documented slaves' understanding of Western fashion, considering how they used clothing to reflect individual and group identities while challenging their status. White people accused captives of appropriating European formalwear to partake in vainglorious displays that countered their debased status. Slavery was a labor institution and whites felt bondpeople should wear clothing that indexed their debased status. Coarse clothing, like blackness, symbolized savagery and oppression. Many whites concluded that dress clothing allowed captives to defy their debased status and assume privileges reserved for whites.[18] African mores transformed enslaved bodies into expressions of individuality, skill, and strength, while country marks articulated ethnicities. Canoemen's dearth of clothing was seemingly a form of cultural resilience, perhaps even resistance against white valuations.

Some planters appropriated, rather than challenged, African valuations to articulate their wealth. Slaveholders often conspicuously demonstrated their prestige by elegantly dressing domestic slaves. Pleasure canoes were similarly manned by muscular, elaborately, though semiclad, canoemen, permitting whites to observe their athletic physiques, as John Stedman learned. When Stedman's ship entered the Suriname River, canoemen paddled "a number of gentlemen" out to "welcome our arrival in the colony." The canoes were manned by "negroes, who were entirely without cloaths, except a small stripe of check or other linen [loin]cloth." Slaveholders selected "their handsomest slaves for this office, and . . . the rowers who were healthy, young, and vigorous, looked extremely well and their being naked gave us full opportunity of observing their skin, which was shining and nearly black as ebony."[19]

When dugouts overturned, canoemen swam to right them, recover goods, and save drowning white passengers, reflecting scenes that transpired on African waters. Pinckard appreciated and respected canoemen's swimming, saying: "Let them have a boat, or a canoe, and it is almost impossible they can be drowned. Even if they are upset, and the boat turned keel upwards, they rise at her sides, and there continue to swim and paddle until they again *right* her, then bailing out the water resume their seats and proceed as if nothing had happened." They also swam to cool off, relax, and cleanse their bodies. Pinckard observed this practice in Dutch Guiana where five canoemen propelled him "from half-past eight in the morning until seven in the evening. That even negroes could support so many hours of heavy and incessant labour in such a climate was past our conjecture." Despite Pinckard's relative cultural sensitivities, he racialized Africans' canoeing and swimming abilities, as discussed in Chapter 3. Assuming Africans' animal-like endurance allowed the canoemen to paddle for some ten hours, Pinckard concluded that a few brief dips rejuvenated their limbs, saying when the bondmen became "extremely heated, and bathed in perspiration" they plunged "into the river, and swam about in order to cool themselves, and drive away fatigue."[20]

Reconstructed and reimagined African traditions could subvert white domination by permitting bondpeople to fabricate realities ashore and afloat that remained distinct from those slaveholders sought to impose. Even as canoemen labored for their owners' interests, most worked beyond the eyesight and earshot of white authority, finding opportunities to form their own traditions. Canoemen did not own their own bodies, but they culturally transformed the Americas as they infused waterscapes with the sights and sounds of maritime Africa.

Not content to merely insinuate their cultural understandings onto New World waterscapes, some captives used these waters and their maritime skills to pursue freedom. Some formed multiethnic crews and used dugouts to pursue routes to liberty, imbuing water with the double meanings of hardship and hope. Canoe-borne escape offered possibilities that swimming, one's feet, and horses did not. They allowed entire families to flee to isolated places and travel to distant colonies, and they inspired transatlantic passages.

Runaway-slave advertisements indicate that many of the males and females who crewed dugouts were of different ethnicities, suggesting captives' willingness to trust their lives and aspirations to different, yet similar, traditions that were probably synthesized. Many had scarcely stepped off slave ships when slaveholders sat them in canoes and handed them paddles. In 1727, Virginia planter-merchant Robert "King" Carter reported that "7 of my new Negros" stole a canoe and freedom. Unfortunately, the ethnicity of these fugitives, who were attempting to return to their homeland(s), went unreported.[21] They were hardly the only ones to paddle eastward, into the rising sun. On January 19, 1775, "FOUR NEW NEGRO MEN and A WOMAN" departed Governor James Wrights' "plantations at Ogeechee," Georgia, "in a small paddling canoe," intending to "go look for their own country." In February 1734, James Paine reported "3 Negroe Men named Hector, Peter and Dublin, all of Angola" stole a neighbor's "Canoe" while fleeing his Wando River, South Carolina, estate. Hector and Peter were brothers and Peter had "Country-marks cut in the shape of a Diamond on each of his Temples." The trio, who "speak but very little English," were recent imports attempting to regain "Angola." A September 12, 1771, *Virginia Gazette* advertisement reported the flight of "two new Negroes" named Step, who had "Country Marks on his Temples," and "Lucy." They departed with "several others, being persuaded that they could find their way back to their own Country."[22] Some made it far from shore before being intercepted.[23]

Runaways placed tremendous faith in their seamanship and the strength of their arms. Or perhaps they were not embarking on physical crossings but on metaphysical passages across the Kalunga on voyages that were more of faith than of brawn. North American dugouts were not constructed of cottonwood. Surely they hoped deities would not begrudge them this shortcoming and would assist on physical or spiritual journeys to rejoin loved ones. Even if they died en route, the mediums of wood and water would channel their souls to ancestral realms.

Like Oceanians, many Caribbean captives understood that they lived in a "sea of islands" that expanded their horizons far beyond the dry spaces enslavers sought to chain them to. Many, including those bound to terrestrial labor, were tuned into the whisperings of the Atlantic world that spoke of opportunities, inspiring some to strike out in dugouts for freedom or less severe forms of bondage on adjacent islands. Slaves were informed of regional and global circumstances through engagements with interisland trade and smuggling that routinely transcended imperial boundaries and, as discussed in Chapter 9, they traversed coastal and, at times, interisland waters to reach markets where they sold goods produced during time off. Simultaneously, ports were marketplaces for news where enslaved ship pilots, sailors, sea turtlers, fishermen, salvage divers, and other free and enslaved, black and white mariners funneled intelligence among mariners, passengers, and shoreside communities. Serving as the overseas eyes and ears of urban and rural slave communities, maritime slaves broadened field hands' understanding of the Greater Caribbean.[24] These networks of communications and the skills necessary to crew African-style dugouts could transform islands from grains of sand and chunks of coral thrust up from the depths, into concentric links of opportunity, creating constellations of hope and freedom. For those willing to take the voyage, their "universe comprised not only land surfaces but the surrounding ocean as far as they could traverse and exploit it."[25]

During the eighteenth century, members of the Danish West Indies' largely African-born population paddled to the Spanish colonies of Puerto Rico and Vieques. After Britain abolished slavery in 1834, Denmark's now largely island-born population chose the British Virgin Islands. Fugitives departed in such numbers that they precipitated some planters' financial ruin while threatening the archipelago's economic stability. One St. Croix planter reported, "The heirs of Bondwyn lost everything, when all their slaves ran away to that island [Puerto Rico] in the course of a single night; the plantation had to be sold because of it."[26]

During the late 1830s and through the1840s, French bondpeople similarly sought the post-abolition British Caribbean. Vessels passing "Guadaloupe, were obliged to keep at least a league's distance from the land" so that fugitives could not reach them. Officials stationed "small vessels, called *guarda costas*," offshore to intercept those who "venture out in skiffs, canoes," and "make for Dominica, Montserrat, or Antigua." These expert mariners negotiated currents pulling them toward the barren waters south of Puerto Rico as they paddled about twenty-five miles to Dominica, thirty-five miles to Montserrat, and forty miles to Antigua.[27]

Captives equally fled the British Caribbean and Bahamas. Many eighteenth-century Jamaican bondpeople absconded to Cuba, where plantation slavery had not yet developed and conditions were less brutal. In 1789, planters from "the North Coast of Jamaica" informed King George III that "many of the Slaves inhabiting that district" paddled 100 miles to the "Southern Shore of Cuba," beseeching him to dissuade Cuban officials from encouraging their property to flee there and return those who had. This was a difficult voyage, as prevailing currents and winds pulled canoes northwestward into the empty expanse of the Gulf of Mexico. Many completed this crossing, for "several planters" went to "Cuba in search of the fugitives whom they have found," but they were prohibited from retaking them. On December14, 1809, Jamaica's legislature decreed that bondpeople who "attempted to go off this Island, in any sort of ship, boat, canoe, or other vessel . . . shall suffer death, or such other punishment as the court shall think proper to direct." After 1793, Saint-Domingue (Haiti) became a popular destination.[28]

English slaveholders elsewhere faced similar challenges. Hundreds of seventeenth-century Barbadians fled to St. Vincent and French-held islands.[29] In 1796, Bahamian officials proclaimed that if "any negro or other slave" was captured fleeing "these Islands in any ship, boat, canoe, or other vessel" they faced corporal punishment or transportation out of the colony. Many were attempting to reach Cuba or East Florida, which remained in Spanish hands until 1821. Some possibly sought freedom in Haiti.[30]

Many eighteenth-century South Carolinian and Georgian fugitives paddled to Spanish Florida. In 1769, "three NEW NEGROES, of the Guinea country" fled from John's Island, taking "a canoe belonging to Mr. John Holmes." Boston, the alleged instigator, "speaks very good English, Spanish, and Portuguese," while "Toney and Marcellus cannot speak any English." Likewise, some twenty years prior, "two *Angle* [Angolan] Negro-Men, one named *Moses*, middle siz'd, his country name *Monvige*," the "other a lusty and elderly Fellow, named *Sampson*, his Country Name *Goma*," escaped "in a Canow to the Southward."[31]

Spanish officials enticed South Carolinian and Georgian slaves with promises of freedom, expedited by Catholic conversion. Facing a shortage of white settlers, Spain sought to use black proxies to populate and protect the colony. In 1738, a number of Carolina fugitives were settled approximately two miles north of St. Augustine to establish the town of Gracia Real de Santa Teresa de Mose, or Mose, which became a beacon of freedom.[32]

Eighteenth-century slaves fled to Florida on foot, on horseback, and in canoes. In November 1738, the South Carolina legislature decried that "19 Slaves belonging to the said Davis, and 50 other Slaves belonging to other Persons inhabiting Port Royal ran away to the Castle of St. Augustine." In 1741, it was similarly reported that "Numbers of Slaves did from Time to Time by Land and Water desert to St. Augustine; and to better facilitate their Escape carried off their Master's Horses, Boats, &c." Overland journeys, especially when passing through marshy regions with children and the elderly, would have been tedious.[33]

Florida largely ceased being a sanctuary when an 1821 treaty ceded it to the United States, prompting many Black Seminoles to flee to the Bahamas. Black Seminoles are the descendants of fugitive slaves who intermarried with Seminoles. They began arriving in the Bahamas by canoe in 1819, seeking refuge with their former British allies.[34]

Elsewhere, captives canoed into secluded swampy areas. Maroons in Dutch Guiana famously used dugouts to retain independence while living deep within swamplands.[35] These, and others, paddled to geographic freedom, residing in remote waterside communities situated beyond slavery's grasp.

White people responded by transforming dugouts into contested cultural spaces. Legislatures prohibited slaves from using and owning canoes. From 1669 through 1722, legislatures on the English Leeward Islands, comprised of St. Kitts, Antigua, Nevis, and Montserrat passed a series of laws designed to keep Africans chained to their islands. An October 28, 1669, Antiguan law commanded residents "upon this Island, or hither trading, shall keep any Boat or Boats, Canoe, Piriagoe, or any Vessel whatsoever" secure and the "Masts, Oars, Sails, Rudder, and Paddels" must be separately stored "on Shore." If "Servants or Slaves" fled in the vessels of noncompliant slaveholders or shipmasters, "the Owner or Master shall make good double Damages, to the Owner of such Servants or Slaves."[36] The Nevis "Act against running away with Boats and Canoes" (1700) condemned fugitives to "suffer the Pains of Death, without Benefit of the Clergy." Subsequent acts strengthened this law, while a 1638(?) abridgement sought to keep canoe-borne fugitives from importing overseas news and gossip by publicly whipping then jailing "any Negro coming to the Island in any Barklog, Boat, or Canoe, without a credible white Person."[37]

Similar laws were passed in the Danish West Indies, where primeval forests supplied timber for clandestinely hewn dugouts. On October 2, 1706, St. Thomas's Privy Council ordered the destruction of all trees large enough to carve into dugouts. A December 30 proclamation offered a reward for the return of any slave, dead or alive, who fled to Puerto Rico. Unable to stem this flow to freedom, the legislation limited the size of white-owned canoes. Later, the governor prohibited vessels from venturing "outside the harbor with only slaves aboard."[38]

South Carolinians passed a 1696 act that anticipated Caribbean laws. Just twenty-five years after the colony was founded, captives fled in such numbers that legislators ordered slaves who stole canoes be whipped thirty-nine times for the first offense and have an ear cut off for the second.[39] Yet, sixteenth- and seventeenth-century laws, naval patrols, and threats did not stop these human tides.

These were not the voyages of greenhorns. Whether they had been farmers, artisans, or merchants in Africa, most probably arrived in the Americas with sound maritime skills. Many relied on the same communication networks that informed them of foreign opportunities to determine the most promising bearing before paddling upward of a hundred miles across or against prevailing wind and in water currents made trickier as currents bounced off and swirled between islands. Multiethnic crews seemingly merged traditions while forging shipmate affinities strong enough to inspire daring freedom-seeking voyages.

In addition to configuring themselves as shipmates, bondpeople used canoes to fulfill other social roles and obligations, such as maintaining familial bonds that could run them afoul of slaveholders' desires. Charles Ball reported how Nero, a fellow slave, paddled to see "his wife, on a planta-tion a few miles down the river." Pierce Butler's slaves routinely voyaged to family members, with and without permission. In 1763, Savannah River planter Patrick MacKay blasted that he was "disturbed by negroes, who come there by land and water in the night-time, and not only rob, steal, and carry off hogs, poultry, sheep, corn, and his potatoes, but create very great disorders amongst his slaves; by debauching his wenches, who have husbands, the property of the subscriber, and some are so audacious as to debauch his very house wenches." MacKay threatened to shoot trespassers, hiring "a white man properly armed for that purpose."[40]

Throughout the American South, waterways stood between slave quar-ters and many churches, compelling captives to travel to Christian services in African-inspired dugouts. In Georgia, flotillas carried parishioners to the preaching of Reverend Andrew Bryan. In 1773, Bryan, a former slave, founded the Bryan African Baptist Church (the first permanent black Bap-tist church in America), which, in 1788, became the First African Baptist Church of Savannah. Late eighteenth-century bondpeople from "rice and indigo plantations along the Savannah River" were permitted to "attend these preachings" and came in "numbers of cypress log dugouts, . . . pad-dling down and up the river on the Sabbath mornings and evenings." Some sixty years later, Frances Kemble reported that slaves from her husband's outlying estates similarly arrived at the main plantation for services.[41]

Canoes that possibly still possessed African spiritual meanings were cen-tral in many conversion experiences, as many captives needed them to reach services. Bryan founded his church during the Great Awakening, which inspired many saltwater captives to add Christianity to their spiritual beliefs. In 1790, he had approximately five hundred followers, most enslaved. On Sundays, Low Country waterscapes were thick with churchgo-ing dugouts. Converts generally did not abandon traditional beliefs but instead layered Christianity onto African understandings. While evidence is lacking, canoes and waterscapes possibly retained African cultural and spiritual meanings for some.[42]

The Great Awakening attempted to define social landscapes according to Christian traditions. Yet Christianity could not necessarily convert waterscapes and churchgoing dugouts, nor should these fleets be used to quantify slaves' religious fervor. Into the early nineteenth century, conversions did not demarcate the abandonment of African beliefs. As fleets of bondwomen and bondmen traveled to services, they paddled to the African rhythms of canoemen's songs. After the service, many probably ate African-informed dishes, filling their nostrils with the aromas of Africa and their mouths with the flavors and textures of past lives. After communal meals, many conceivably partook in a communal swim, allowing them to enjoy their bodies while reaffirming communal bonds. For many, canoeing to and from church possibly arranged waterways into culturescapes that retained the sights, sounds, smells, feelings, and flavors of Africa.[43]

Conversion routinely merged beliefs. The Protestantism introduced to American slaves "tended to be rigid and inflexible, hostile to the kind of association between African deities and Christian saints found in a number of Catholic societies elsewhere in the New World." Beyond whites' gaze, slaves were "free to Africanize the religion, thus engaging in reinterpretation and true synthesis simultaneously." For many, canoe-making, canoeing, and perceptions of waterways probably informed this process of "reinterpretation and true synthesis." Even as canoes bore Africans toward Christianity, conversion probably did not erase Africans' spiritual beliefs but instead expanded their cultural horizons.[44]

Churchgoing voyages also permitted many to conjoin spiritual and material needs. The "fact that the public market and many retail stores remained open until 9:00 A.M." on Sundays "offered an opportunity to trade as well as to worship." For many, church passes concealed market expeditions. Leastways, Savannah's white retailers vehemently defended their right to conduct business on the Sabbath as trade with bondpeople was considerable.[45]

Scholars have argued that shipboard dynamics and collective work allowed African-descended sailors to defy shoreside realities while being evaluated more on their skill and courage than on their race.[46] Likewise, some acceptable canoe-borne behavior was impermissible ashore, allowing some bondmen to redefine their social relationships with white women so that in some important ways they more closely resembled shipmate affinities than relationships between slave mistresses and enslaved men. Elite white women typically did not travel overland with bondmen unless accompanied by a white male chaperone. Frances Kemble routinely violated the mores with canoemen. In 1839, she embarked on a fifteen-mile voyage with nine canoemen. As the trip concluded, the "men were in great spirits" with one saying "something which elicited an exclamation of general assent." The helmsman explained "there was not another planter's lady in all Georgia who would have" traveled "all alone with them in the boat; i.e., without the protecting presence of a white man."[47]

Ashore, bondmen were generally prohibited from touching white women. Afloat, touching between white women and bondmen occurred regularly. As Jack taught Kemble to paddle a small canoe called the *Dolphin*, the two touched and he possibly encircled her body with his arms while providing instruction. Jack surely held Kemble's hands, arms, and probably torso while helping her into and out of the canoe and surely carried her through shallows.

African traditions of seminudity induced greater levels of intimacy—intimacies white people embraced. Tousaint-Samson recounted her experience with seminude canoemen at Rio de Janeiro. She was paddled shoreward by shirtless "robust negroes," "naked to the waist" as "the perspiration" ran "down their bodies." In the shallows, the "negroes step into the water and carry me off in their strong arms to land." They silently proclaimed their masculinity and Tousaint-Sampson welcomed their muscular embrace as black and white flesh pressed together and their sweat mingled. In 1939, when it was even more forbidden for black men to touch Southern white women than under slavery, apologist Caroline Lovell remembered canoemen's reassuring embrace: "The children were always carried to and from the boat in the brawny arms of the oarsmen, and with their little arms around the men's necks they felt safe and contented as possible." During low tide, which prevented beaching, "The family had to be carried ashore, and two Negroes would form what was called a 'chair' with their hands, and carry" adults ashore. Lovell, Tousaint-Samson, and other white females found safety in African arms.[48]

Kemble's reliance on Jack thrust the duo into a relationship that seems largely unimaginable ashore. Their relationship quickly developed, with Kemble going so far as to call Jack "my friend." They formed a rare bond between an enslaved man and a plantation mistress; a topic lacking scholarly deliberation. This relationship afforded both Jack and Kemble considerable benefits.[49]

Kemble trusted Jack with her life and was appreciative of the skills he imparted. After learning to "row tolerably well," an overconfident Kemble placed her daughter, Sally, in the *Dolphin* "with the intention of paddling myself a little way down the river." She "clumsily and slowly" paddled, tiring herself. She quickly "became nervous, and paddled all on one side," spinning the canoe in circles, alarming Sally who began to "fidget" and stood up, "terrifying me with her unsteady motions and the rocking of the canoe." Kemble laid Sally down and, with renewed determination, negotiated to shore, where she deposited her "precious freight." This was a valuable lesson. Ashore, Jack was a trusted personal slave with no sway over Kemble's life. Afloat, he held her life in his hands. Kemble accepted her subservient role as student and resolved not to go canoeing again without Jack until refining her skills, writing: "I have taken no more paddling lessons without my slave and *master*, Jack."[50]

Jack formed an intimate teacher/student friendship with a powerful and worldly woman. Kemble became committed to him. Kemble's husband respected the bond between the two, enabling Kemble to formalize Jack's privileged status when she exclaimed "'my boy Jack,' . . . will never be degraded to the rank of field hand or common laborer."[51]

Jack was the son of the "head driver" and benefited from dispensations his father received. Intelligent and inquisitive, Jack possessed an inexhaustible "curiosity about all things beyond this island, the prison of his existence." Kemble expanded his worldly knowledge, taking him on Low Country excursions during which Jack bombarded her with questions concerning her travels through Europe and the American North.[52]

Jack's status enabled him to obtain privileges for his compatriots. Butler banned the keeping of pigs because of their "filth and foul smells." Jack cunningly asked Kemble to reverse this policy. To deflect "his torrent of inquiries about places and things," Kemble "suddenly asked him if he would like to be free." Jack became instantly befuddled, the "fear of offending by uttering that forbidden whish—the dread of admitting, by its expression, the slightest discontent with his present situation." He parried: "Free, missis! what for me wish to be free? Oh no, missis, me no wish to be free, if massa only let we keep pig!" Feeling horrible for tantalizing Jack with "that forbidden wish," and knowing the savory pleasures "pork and bacon" would bring to slaves' "farinaceous diet," Kemble "preferred poor Jack's request" to Butler.[53]

Kemble returned to Butler's Philadelphia home in April 1838. Soon after, Jack's "health failed so completely" that he was sent to Philadelphia for medical treatment. Kemble was true to her word; Jack was never "degraded to the rank of field hand or common laborer." He died enslaved in a free state.[54]

Captives taught planters' sons how to construct dugouts used by white and black playmates, providing them with intimate understandings of slave culture. Joseph LeConte, a renowned geologist and paleontologist who helped establish the University of California, cultivated a love for nature while interacting with his father's captives. The waters encompassing his Liberty County, Georgia, plantation formed an immense playground. Documenting the construction of their mobile play structure, LeConte penned: "When I was about ten years old, the three younger boys, John, Lewis, and I undertook, with the help of an intelligent and ingenious negro man, Primus, and with the permission of father to use Primus for the purpose, to make a fine dugout canoe out of a large cypress log three feet in diameter." Teaching the boys to craft a canoe was surely light work for Primus, who probably received some perquisites. Unfortunately, LeConte provided no information on Primus.[55]

The boys surely bonded while constructing the dugout, creating another kind of intimacy among playmates. While in his late seventies, LeConte fondly recalled the pleasures of canoeing. "During the times of high water by winter freshets, the rice-fields, at that time bare of rice, formed a splendid sheet of water two miles long and half a mile wide. We sometimes rigged a mast and sail, but the canoe was not suited to this kind of propulsion, we often suffered shipwreck in water two or three feet deep. But to a boy this only gave zest to the enjoyment." LeConte also respected the culture of his father's saltwater captives, saying they taught him more than eight of his nine white teachers.[56]

The LeContes surely shared empty winter rice fields with enslaved boys who manned family dugouts. These saturated fields were playgrounds and the canoes play structures, permitting white and black youth to interact with their surroundings while hunting waterfowl and small alligators and racing. Glory was surely not reserved for the winners, as races precipitated spectacular wrecks that afforded bragging rights for audacity and bravery.[57]

Flooded fields and canoes took on diverging meanings. Enslaved children enjoyed wintry waters. Come spring, their mothers and fathers waded knee-deep in the muddy waters as mosquitoes encircled their bodies. As the boys matured, they took up their places in the field. Encapsulated within levees raised by enslaved hands, these places of joy became places of subjugation.

Sources suggest that dugouts and New World waterscapes provided salt-water slaves with natural and built culturescapes reminiscent of home, facilitating the retention of ethnic-specific traditions while concurrently blending Atlantic African customs. As enslaved canoe-makers and canoe-men were compelled to work with people from different ethnic groups, they cultivated shipmate relationships, fostering cross-cultural affiliations and exchanges that transformed canoes into creolizing constructs. The privacy that dugouts afforded facilitated the cultural process. Unlike in terrestrial spaces, authority figures could not sneak up on those engaged in illicit conversations on the water, allowing captives to express yearnings for freedom or derive price-fixing strategies. Canoes enabled bondpeople to extend family resources, while maintaining and expanding social networks. For some, canoes provided passages to freedom.

Chapter 12

The Watermen's Song:
Canoemen's Aural Waterscapes

The cultural winds of the African diaspora blow westward to the Americas, with most scholars following this trajectory. Paddling's songs provide an example of when it is prudent to reverse course. White Northern and European travelers to the slaveholding Americas demonstrated considerable interest in these songs, perhaps because they were routinely sung in European languages while their African structures, rhythms, and meanings provided an exotic yet understandable experience. Travelers to Africa provided comparatively little documentation of songs that few understood.[1] Hence, this chapter examines slaves' paddling songs before briefly considering their African precursors.

African-descended canoeists used songs to regulate paddling rhythms while constructing aquatic soundscapes. They were the dominant soundmarkers reverberating across Atlantic African and New World waterscapes. They were one of the last African sounds captives heard as African canoemen paddled them toward slave ships. They were one of the first sounds heard as enslaved canoemen transported them shoreward to New World bondage. Songs were an essential component of African maritime cultures. Enslaved canoemen paddled across freshwater and saltwater to these rhythms just as they and their antecedents had in Africa. Saltwater slaves consciously preserved this tradition, while its African origins remained a subconscious tradition for country-born captives.[2]

African-descended people found it appropriate to sing while working. African musicologist, Nicholas Ballanta explained: "Music in Africa is not cultivated for its own sake. It is always used in connection with dances or to accompany workmen." Music created a sense of cohesion among collections of canoemen, helping to transform them into shipmates.[3]

Songs completed the sensory experience of African-informed aquatic cultures, while allowing captives to challenge white control over their lives. Songs dominated waterscapes, superimposing African soundmarkers upon spaces claimed by enslavers. Concurrently, paddling songs regulated the pace of labor, setting it to manageable African rhythms rather than faster slaveholder-preferred regimens. Thus, they can be regarded as a form of resistance to both forced labor and acculturation.

Paddling songs were a form of socializing. They recreated ethnic traditions while serving as aquatic crossroads that facilitated cultural coalescences. Songs permitted people to creatively reimagine themselves and their communities, by allowing "people to chart histories, to cast and recast recollections, to remember (as well as forget) the past; it helps anchor daily emotions from the simplest to the most anguishing and complex; it helps broker fears, anxieties, and notions of loss and threat just as it facilitates aspirations, hopes, dreams, and fantasies; it helps human beings mourn worlds gone by, probe worlds that trap, anticipate worlds not yet born."[4]

As Africans navigated trade, fishing, and war canoes, they did so to the steady cadence of paddling songs. The lyrics could be unintelligible to those from different ethnic and language groups, but their rhythms were recognizable. It was the cultural pulse of life, of community, of work, of productivity.

The pounding of rice in mortars with pestles to remove uneatable husks provided some African and enslaved communities with "the heartbeat of daily life, the echo of cultural identity." It was the aural representation of food preparation, of productivity, of domesticity.[5] Paddling songs afforded similar meanings. Westerners became voracious consumers of slave-produced commodities, which, in turn, imposed vigorous labor regimes upon captives. Enslavers wanted canoemen to rapidly ship slave-produced wealth to market. Paddling songs permitted them to reclaim manageable work tempos by introducing African labor ethos. They simultaneously remained the sound of profits, informing slaveholders that canoemen's broad shoulders, muscular torsos, and strong arms were enhancing their wealth. They indicated that canoemen were carrying newly imported slaves inland with the rising tide. They indexed the hardships endured by agricultural bondpeople laboring in rice, sugar, tobacco, indigo, cotton, coffee, and cocoa fields. Paddling songs signified that canoemen were transporting slave-produced commodities to merchant ships that would carry them to consumers oblivious to bondpeople's sufferings.

Canoemen sang antiphonal, or call-and-response, songs. Ballanta described them as "mainly rhythmic—short phrases mostly of two bars; solo and chorus follow each other instantly." Some were sung in African languages or Arabic. Entwined African and European languages provided the lyrics of others. Eventually, most were sung in European languages that adhered to African rhythmic traditions and perhaps contained some African words. Any song with a proper rhythm could serve as a paddling song and, like field songs, they were often popular sacred or secular songs. Many were spontaneously created.[6]

Paddling songs provided a slow, steady rate of work. The solo, or verse, was sung by the helmsman and was a few words in length, followed by a short chorus sung by mariners who paddled one stroke before or while repeating the chorus, which typically remained unchanged throughout the song. The rhythmic pull of paddles could enhance the beat. Songs' cohesive pulse promoted efficiency while reinforcing new group identities. One descendant of Low Country Georgia planters noted that the "sweep" of sea island paddlers "synchronized with the rhythm of the song."[7] As John Lambert traversed the South Carolina–Georgia Low Country, he observed how canoemen "rowed lustily to a boat-song of their own composing. The words were given out by one of them, and the rest joined chorus at the end of every line." Providing the lyrics to the first verse, he recorded:

	CHORUS:
"We are going down to Georgia, boys,	Aye, Aye.
To see the pretty girls, boys;	Yoe, Yoe.
We'll give 'em a pint of brandy, boys,	Aye, Aye.
And a hearty kiss, besides, boys.	Yoe, Yoe.
&c. &c. &c."	

Delineating the song's pragmatic function, Lambert said it "had a pleasing effect, as they kept time with it at every stroke of their oars."[8]

Canoemen frequently composed extemporaneous lyrics, covering topics like marine animals, passing scenery, canoemen, and passengers. Reflecting on the subjects woven into lyrics, William Grayson of Beaufort, South Carolina, penned: "The singer worked into his rude strain any incident that came in his way relating to the place of destination, the passengers on board, or the sweetheart at home, his work or amusements by field or flood."[9] Rarely did they mention maritime functions. While the popular spiritual "Michael Row the Boat Ashore" describes rowing, it does so metaphorically and was originally sung by field laborers. During the mid-nineteenth century, Low Country canoemen sang it "when the load was heavy or the tide was against us."[10] During the Civil War, liberated Hilton Head mariners extemporized the following lines, which were added to the end of the song:

> Michael haul the boat ashore
> Then you'll hear the horn they blow.
> Then you'll hear the trumpet sound.
> Trumpet sound the world around.
> Trumpet sound for rich and poor.
> Trumpet sound the jubilee.
> Trumpet sound for you and me.[11]

The lyrics to cadences created as paddling songs were rarely recorded. In August 1842, Bartholomew Carroll Jr., editor of the South Carolina magazine *The Chicora; or Messenger of the South*, published the lyrics to three paddling songs.[12] As the canoe departed Charleston, head-canoeman, "Big-mouth Joe," initiated the song:

> Now we gwine leab Charleston city,
> Pull boys, pull!—
> The gals we leab it is a pity,
> *Pull boys, pull!*—
> Mass Ralh, 'e take a big strong toddy [mixed alcoholic drink],
> *Pull boys, pull!*—
> Mass Ralph, e aint gwine let us noddy,
> *Pull boys, pull!*—
> The sun, 'e is up, da creeping,
> *Pull boys, pull!*—
> You Jim, you rascal, you's da sleeping.

In a song about their voyage, the canoemen discussed their labors and social arrangement in their world afloat:

Massa Ralph, mass Ralph, 'e is a good man,
Oh mah Riley, oh!
Mass Ralph, mass Ralph, e'e sit at the boat starn [stern],
Oh mah Riley, oh!
Mass Ralph, mass Ralph, him boat 'ecan row,
Oh mah Riley, oh!
Come boys, come boys come, pull, let me pull oh,
Oh mah Riley, oh!

The last song emphasized group cohesion by mocking a laggard who imposed more work upon his shipmates. Importantly, it also illustrated how the chorus could be altered.

One time upon dis ribber,
Long time ago—
Mass Ralph 'e had a nigger,
Long time ago—
Da nigger had not merit,
Long time ago—
De nigger couldn't row wid spirit,
Long time ago—
And now dere is in dis boat, ah,
A nigger dat I see—
Wha' is a good for nuthing shoat, ah,
Ha, ha, ha, he—
Da nigger's weak ike water,
Ha, ha, ha, he—
'E can't row a half quarter,
Ha, ha, ha, he—
Cuss de nigger—cuss 'e libber,
Ha, ha, ha, he—
'E nebber shall come on dis ribber,
Ha, ha, ha, he—[13]

Work songs' flexibility dictated the pace of labor. Agricultural songs, often called "corn songs," had a faster tempo, with overseers often preventing unhurried cadences. Watermen slowed their tempo, often appending improvised verses to maintain control over labor. The authors of *Slave*

Songs of the United States (1867) described how watermen slowed the popular "Rain Fall and Wet Becca Lawton." "One noticeable thing about their boat-songs was they seemed often to be sung just a trifle behind time; in 'Rain Fall,' for instance, 'Believe cry holy' would seem to occupy more than its share of the stroke, the 'holy' being prolonged till the very beginning of the next stroke; indeed, I think Jerry often hung on his oar a little just there before dipping it again." In addition, a "long hold on 'Oh,' in 'Rain Fall,' was only used in rowing." Another observer reported that when "Rain Fall" was utilized during paddling, "at the words 'Rack Back holy!' one rower reaches back and slaps the man behind him, who in turn does the same, and so on." Some have speculated that this was an African retention, though no African antecedents are known.[14]

James Hungerford documented how Maryland canoemen sang an unhurried and improvised version of "Round' de Corn, Sally," a field song. When a white passenger asked a slave named Charley to sing this accord, he replied, "Dat's a corn song; un we'll hab ter sing it slow ter row by." When pressed, Charley used the opportunity to slyly improvise five verses that lampooned each white voyager, causing "much amusement at the expense of each of us."[15]

Musical instruments were occasionally used when captives were not working. At Smithville, North Carolina, Moses Ashley Curtis watched watermen transform the popular song "Sally Was a Fine Girl" into a paddling song. As his ship lay at anchor, "a boat full of blacks came rowing by us in time to 'Sally was a fine girl, ho! Sally, ho!' ad infinitum & accompanied with a trumpet obligato by the helmsman."[16]

Some were sung in African languages before being translated into European ones. When members of the same ethnicity were thrust into dugouts' narrow culturescapes, they could perpetuate aural traditions. In the 1790s, George Pinckard recorded Akan lyrics while traveling up Guyana's Demarara River. Paddling over ten hours per day for several days in a row, "they showed strong signs of fatigue" as the day progressed. The helmsman rallied "his comrades with song." He "invented extempore lines for a favorite African tune, finishing each verse with '*gnyaam gnyaam row*,' '*gnyaam gnyaam* row,' in which all were to join by way of chorus; and we found that *gnyaam gnyaam row*,' never failed to give additional force to the oar—and consequent headway to the boat." *Gnyaam*, or perhaps *Gye Nyame*, indicates membership in the Akan cultural group, for it means "Except God (I fear none)." In this instance, it seemingly translated to "for God [or the

"Try it, at any rate," said the major.

"Sartinly, sah, ef de marsters un mistisses wants it."

Charley was evidently somewhat vexed at the disparaging remarks made by the petitioners on his previous performance. Nevertheless, there came a quiet smile to his face as he began the following song:

ROUN' DE CORN, SALLY.

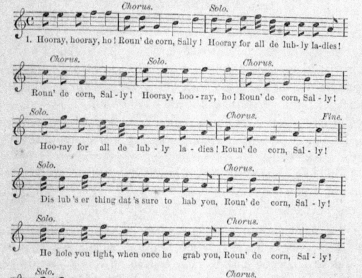

Chorus. *Solo.*

1. Hooray, hooray, ho! Roun' de corn, Sally! Hooray for all de lub-ly la-dies!

Chorus. *Solo.* *Chorus.*

Roun' de corn, Sal-ly! Hooray, hoo-ray, ho! Roun' de corn, Sal-ly!

Solo. *Chorus.* *Fine.*

Hoo-ray for all de lub-ly la-dies! Roun' de corn, Sal-ly!

Solo. *Chorus.*

Dis lub's er thing dat's sure to hab you, Roun' de corn, Sal-ly!

Solo. *Chorus.*

He hole you tight, when once he grab you, Roun' de corn, Sal-ly!

Solo. *Chorus.*

Un ole un ug-ly, young un prit-ty, Roun' de corn, Sal-ly!

Solo. *Chorus.* *D. C.*

You need-en try when once he git you, Roun' de corn, Sal-ly!

2. Dere's Mr. Travers lub Miss Jinny;
   He thinks she is us good us any.
   He comes from church wid her er Sunday,
   Un don't go back ter town till Monday.

   Hooray, hooray, ho! etc.

3. Dere's Mr. Lucas lub Miss T'reser,
   Un ebery thing he does ter please her;

Dey say dat 'way out in Ohio,
She's got er plenty uv de rhino.
　　　　　　Hooray, hooray, ho! etc.

4. Dere's Marster Charley lub Miss Bettie;
I tell you what—he thinks her pretty;
Un den dey mean ter lib so lordly,
All at de Monner House at Audley.
　　　　　　Hooray, hooray, ho! etc.

5. Dere's Marster Wat, he lub Miss Susan;
He thinks she is de pick un choosin';
Un when dey gains de married station,
He'll take her to de ole plantation.
　　　　　　Hooray, hooray, ho! etc.

6. Dere's Marster Clarence lub Miss Lizzy;
Dressing nice, it keeps him busy;
Un where she goes den he gallants her,
Er riding on his sorrel prancer.
　　　　　　Hooray, hooray, ho! etc.

Figure 28. Charley's Version of "Roun' De Corn, Sally." In his autobiographical novel, James Hungerford provided one of the few known recordings of an extemporaneous paddling song. It illustrates how canoemen slowed and improvised field songs to provide themselves with an appropriate paddling tempo. It equally documents how lyrics cunningly mocked members of the slave-holding ranks resulting in punishment. James Hungerford, *The Old Plantation, and What I Gathered There in an Autumn Month* (New York: 1859), 191–192. Author's collection.

creator] I row" and possibly served as a spiritual mantra motivating the canoemen while they reflected upon their Akan past.[17]

Other customs may have been retained. Bahian canoemen slapped their paddles to enhance songs' beat by "every now and then raising the paddles completely out of the water, and striking the flat part of them with their hands, keeping time with the chorus." Likewise, as fatigue crept over Surinamese captives, *"fumming wattra"* encouraged shipmates. It entailed "beating the water with" each stroke "in such a manner that it sounds different from the rest, to which the others' sing a chorus."[18] While these customs seem African, they may have been created in the Americas.

Songs articulating African realities enabled saltwater paddlers (as well as bondpeople toiling in the fields they passed) to reflect upon Africa. Some lyrics sung in European languages reiterated African themes. When Prince Ferdinand Maximilian of Austria visited Bahia in 1860, he noted that songs were "mingled sometimes with laments for the free home on the other side of the broad terrible ocean." Country-born canoemen expressed New World realities, hopes, desires, and tribulations. African paddling songs and those containing African phrases were sung well into the nineteenth century, even after African meanings were forgotten.[19]

Cultural blending could alter the types of songs watermen preferred. As America's nineteenth-century slave population increasingly became Christian, work songs followed this trajectory, so by 1853 most boat songs were hymns. In the Caribbean and in Latin America many African-descended people maintained African religious beliefs into the twentieth century, suggesting that their songs did not undergo a similar process. There, creolization was primarily the blending of African traditions. For instance, some nineteenth-century Brazilian ports became home to sizable Muslim populations. At Salvador, Muslims of different ethnicities became shipmates, sharing beliefs, blending ethnic traditions, and altering the cadence of Islamic hymns.[20]

Paddling songs helped forge collective identities, as diverse peoples were forced to crew canoes. Within dugouts, captives composed new lyrics. Many songs were extemporaneous and increasingly sung in European languages. Creolization possibly began by singing in African lingua francas, like Mande, Kimbundu, Kikongo, Hausa, Wolof, Efik, and Duala; or in creoles, like *fala de Guiné*, or "Guinea speech"; and Arabic. When Henry Koster arrived in Brazil in 1809, he disparagingly alluded to how African lyrics were fused to enslavers' Portuguese vernacular, saying that bondmen sang "some ditty in their own language, or some distich of vulgar Portuguese rhyme." Ultimately captives sang in their enslaver's tongue.[21]

Paddles and oars were used as rhythmic accompaniments. The steady cadence of paddles striking the water or oars thumping against oarlocks could provide or augment the beat. Canoemen also manipulated paddles and oars in non-work-related methods to enhance or alter rhythms. One canoeman could slap his paddle on the water to set the rhythm or provide an alternate beat. While Albert Von Sack was in Suriname, he observed how paddles set the rhythm, saying: "Sometimes one negro sings a line, and beats the water with his oar in a particular manner, which gives a signal for marking the time, whilst the other rowers repeat the line in a chorus." As noted above, Bahians sometimes slapped paddle blades.[22] The stomping of heels or slapping of body parts were sometimes rhythmic devices but threatened to throw paddlers off beat and seem to have been infrequently used.[23]

Slaves seldom narrated lyrics for white people to record. Former captive Welcome "Bees" Beese provides a rare exception. Beese was a waterman, a master carpenter, and a fixture in the Gullah community surrounding Murrells Inlet, South Carolina. When he was approximately 104 years old, he recounted how he would "sing when we rowin' Cap'n White to [George-]town on the Waccamaw [River]!," documenting how canoemen used oars as a rhythmic source, singing:

> Caesar boy—Caesar!
> Poor Caesar gone kill the Mauser fattenin' hog!
> (A r-r-r-r-r-Rap!) (A noise made with the oar)
> He condemn to hang!
> Caesar boy—Caesar!
> Poor Caesar boy condemn to hang!
> Caesar boy—Caesar!
> Caesar kill poor Mause fattenin' hog

Beese then provided the lyrics to a more reverent paddling song.

> Oh, where Mausser William?
> Sing "Glory in my soul!"
> One day gone—another come!
> Sing "Glory in my soul!"

We'll broke bread together!
Sing "Glory in my soul!"
Pender Meddlsome—Meddle everybody!
Sing "Glory in my soul!"

Oh, where Danny Blue-jay?
Sing "Glory in my soul!"
Pender Meddlsome—Meddle everybody!
Sing "Glory in my soul!"[24]

Songs helped transform members of various ethnicities into shipmates. As Pinckard traversed the Demarara River, he observed the above-mentioned helmsman motivating his fellow African-born canoemen while reconfirming their collective identity. Their improvised song mirrored their metamorphosis from discrete ethnic identities to synthesized group identities. The coxswain cared for and respected his crew, surrendering the steering paddle to the weariest paddler and placing "himself amidst the crew in the centre of the boat," while retaining his role as head lyricist. The canoemen first sang the Akan chorus of "*gnyaam gnyaamm row*." The coxswain's improvised verses enunciated Guyanese themes and were probably sung in Dutch. "The names of the slaves, their wives, their food, drink, and all their pleasures were introduced in song," illustrating the shipmates' intimate relationships. The head canoeman cunningly reminded white passengers of "the compensation each might expect as the reward of his exertions were all adroitly included." Cohesion was audibly and physically expressed through call-and-response and the synchronized paddling it facilitated. The verses' lyrics denoted camaraderie, permitting the crew members to temporarily suspend their fatigue and paddle with a renewed collective sense of urgency that benefited all. The canoemen did not forget ancestral lands. Songs retained their African structure, even as European vernaculars obscured their origins. The verse was sung in Dutch and spoke of the lives Africans were forced to create and endure in Guyana. At the end of each verse, the African chorus—the African heartbeat—burst upon the soundscape as all joined together in the familiar lyrics of "*gnyaam gnyaam row*."[25]

Captives took pride in their creativity. Many apparently refused to use the cadences of mariners enthralled on other estates, while songs enabled them to internalize the institution of slavery and in the process enhance their feelings of self-worth. Many field hands used their pecuniary value to enhance their self-esteem. Frederick Douglass explained that captives believed "the greatness of their masters was transferable to themselves. It was considered as being bad enough to be a slave; but to be a poor man's slave was deemed a disgrace indeed!"[26]

Likewise, songs articulated plantation pride, which were scenes both of subjugation and of home. Georgia sea island canoemen "seemed to feel that the reputation of their masters depended on their skill in rowing and singing, for they invariably sang as they rowed. Just as there was a spirit of rivalry among the planters to have the best boat, there was also a desire on the part of the slaves to sing the best songs. The oarsmen of one plantation would never sing the songs belonging to another plantation, but would try to compose a song that would be finer than that sung by the neighboring oarsmen." There was probably considerable competition among bondmen to compose the most creative lyrics. One can imagine them singing taunts while passing the canoes and wharves of neighboring plantations.[27]

Songs increased group cohesion, projecting community affiliations across waterscapes and landscapes, announcing their unseen presence even when fog, darkness, and vegetation veiled canoemen. Indeed, the daughter of a Georgia planter recalled: "So well did these songs become known on the plantations that, when a boat had passed in the night, one would know the plantation to which it belonged by the songs that were being sung." Field hands surely prided themselves on beliefs that canoemen from their estate composed the funniest or most melodious tunes.[28] Paddling songs' affiliations to specific plantations projected the approach of returning planters, calling wives, children, and field slaves to gather at the landing to greet their return. In 1852, Louis Manigault recorded how canoemen heralded his return: "The singing in the boat attracted the attention of the little Negroes at the landing, who immediately spread the report around the settlement that the boat was coming, so by the time we reached the steps the whole crowd was close by."[29]

Songs subtly and, at times, explicitly expressed sentiments that could not be spoken. While canoemen bore John Lambert through the Georgia–South Carolina Low Country, "brandy was frequently mentioned, and it was understood as a frequent hint to the passengers to give them a dram [shot]. We had supplied ourselves with this article at Purrysburg, and were not sparing of it to the negroes, in order to encourage them to row quickly." Upon reaching Savannah, the canoemen were so intoxicated by the "libations" that they "nearly upset the canoe."[30]

Paddling songs permitted mariners to cunningly mock whites without retribution—putting sentiments to lyrics that were impermissible in spoken word. In 1819, English traveler William Faux observed that songs were "abounding either in praise or satire, intended for a kind or unkind master." James Hungerford explained how passengers asked a slave named Charley to sing "Roun' de Corn, Sally," as noted above. Charley initially declined, but his owner, Major Sullivan, insisted. At the end of the song, Charley improvised five verses that teased the white passengers. The last one satirized Hungerford and Miss Lizzy Dalton, who he was courting, singing:

> Dere's Master Clarence [Hungerford] lub Miss Lizzy;
> Dressing nice, it keeps him busy;
> Un where she goes den he gallants her,
> Er riding on his sorrel prancer.

The passengers laughed as friends were spoofed, becoming uncomfortable when Charley sang about them. "The hit at Lizzie and me was the hardest, as we were both present, and was, therefore, I suppose, introduced at the end. Several laughing efforts were made by the ladies to interrupt the singing, when the words began to have reference to those who were present; but the old major insisted on 'having it out.'" Sullivan undoubtedly knew Charley would chide the passengers, taking pleasure in their torment, as the enslaver temporarily abandoned the racial bonds shared with fellow voyagers to conspire with the enslaved. His "laughter rang out loud and far through the clear air."[31]

Boatmen similarly lampooned Caroline Gilman during a moonlit cruise with Lewis Barnwell, the son of a neighboring planter she was courting. Cruising South Carolina's Ashley River, with her brother as chaperone in a boat named *Miss Neely* (Gilman's nickname), Lewis asked Juba "to sing us a song." The first two verses praised the boat and her speed while the third mocked Lewis. Finishing the second verse, "a sly expression passed over his face" before singing:

> Maybe Maus Lewis take de oar for Neely
> Berry handsome boat Miss Neely!
> Maus Lewis nice captain for Neely,
> [Chorus] Ho yoi!

The meanings of this verse remain unknown. Perhaps Juba was intimating that Barnwell was not masculine enough to man the oars. Perhaps the first line was a sexual innuendo, suggesting Barnwell was incapable of using his "oar" to ride *Neely*, meaning Gilman. Yet in the last line, Juba implied that Barnwell was the "nice captain," suitably matched for Gilman. If insult or sexual connotation was implied, the passengers remained unaware; or pretended to be.[32]

Others openly criticized slaveholders. Prince Maximilian recorded the following Bahian song:

Men Senhor me da paneadas	My Master gives me beatings [punches]
Isto não esta na sua razão	He's not in his right mind:
Com gosto he beijaria a mão	I would happily kiss his hand
Se só me disse bofetadas.	If he would only give me slaps.

Slave owners apparently did nothing to censure slaves, or did not record incidents that embarrassed them enough to provoke punishment. Leastways, Maximilian said slaveholders are "impervious to shame; and to them the language of the blacks is only that of beasts, possessing nothing intelligible to their ears."[33]

Assuming paddling songs were sung for their benefit, whites became intoxicated with romanticized affinities. Songs were a novel entertainment for those originating outside the realms of bondage. For most whites, everything about maritime slavery was exotic, probably explaining why canoemen's songs were the most commonly reported-on work songs.[34]

Slaveholders routinely invited travelers to embark on canoe-borne sightseeing excursions while being serenaded by canoemen. In February 1734, an anonymous "young gentleman" departed Georgetown, South Carolina, "in a large canoe . . . with the intent to take a view of the lands on Waccuma River." Likewise, when Matthew Lewis arrived in Jamaica in 1816, he employed canoemen to visit "the ruins of Port Royal, which, last year, was destroyed by fire."[35] Gazing at waterscapes from canoemen's perspective, white people stared up at the world while beholding submarine environments. Song enriched the experience. In 1829, English traveler Basil Hall jaunted down the Alatamaha River in a thirty-foot cypress dugout. "The oars were pulled by five smart negroes, merry fellows, and very happy looking, as indeed are most of their race, in spite of all their bondage. They accompanied their labour by a wild sort of song." Enthralled by his plea-sures, Hall almost forgot the canoemen were enslaved and hard at work.[36]

Likewise, in October 1837 John Anderson, a magistrate in St. Vincent, together with his "wife & children" traveled from Kingston, St. Vincent, to La Soufrière Volcano "in a six oared canoe." Expressing the thrill of the voyages, he penned:

> There is something positively luxurious in sitting at one's ease in a large sized Canoe under a Tropical sky, (of which the heat is coun-teracted by the grateful influence of the bright blue waves, —) shooting past cliffs, and vallies, of the loveliest hues, and over coral reefs that glimmer in the transparent water, — changing its etherial shade to green, — whilst the boatmen raise their cheerful chorus of wild African, or Negro song. "Pull mi pretty braves, – Yo– Yo– Yo." And then the long grateful quaff of some cooling beverage as they rest on their oars! — a West Indian sun must be felt, to appreciate its welcomed offer!

While Anderson regarded this twenty-mile journey as "luxurious," the canoemen surely had a different impression. Scorched by the "West Indian sun" Anderson found inviting, they strained to propel Anderson, his wife, six children, and their luggage.[37]

British traveler Trelawney Wentworth indicates why some Westerners had a self-centered perception of paddling songs. In 1822, he traveled from Tortola in the British Virgin Islands to St. Thomas in the Danish West Indies. While canoemen made the twelve-mile crossing, Wentworth enjoyed the seascape as "a light breeze now and then came down from the mountains loaded with odours emitted from the aromatic plants and shrubs in the woodlands." One paddler whose "countenance bore the stamp of much covert humour and sagacity, and who appeared to be a sort of *improvisatore* among them, commenced a lively strain." Wentworth penned the lyrics of this improvised song that eulogized his travels:

> Hur-ra, my jol-ly boys, *Fine time o' day.*
> We pull for San Tha-mas boys, *Fine time o' day.*
>   San Thamas hab de fine girl,
>   *Fine time o' day.*
>   Nancy Gibbs and Betsy Braid,
>   *Fine time o' day.*

Massa cum from London town,
>   *Fine time o' day.*
Massa is a handsome man,
>   *Fine time o' day.*
Massa is a dandy-man,
>   *Fine time o' day.*
Him hab de dollar, plenty too,
>   *Fine time o' day.*
Massa lub a pretty girl,
>   *Fine time o' day.*
Him lub 'em much, him lub 'em true,
>   *Fine time o' day.*
Him hunt 'em round de guaba [peanut] bush,
>   *Fine time o' day.*
Him catch 'em in de piece,
>   *Fine time o' day.*[38]

Everything about this experience was alluring. Bondmen's labors allowed Wentworth to bask in Caribbean pleasantries. The lyrics praised his features and dress, while claiming beautiful women would pleasure him. Such songs surely inflated white egos.

Songs evoked melancholy nostalgia for some white people who embarked on transcendental voyages to different places and times. African-informed songs were so ubiquitous that they provided whites with a sense of familiarity in new places. For example, during the winter of 1828, Massachusetts clergyman Abiel Abbot spent three months on John's Island, South Carolina, before heading to Cuba, where the songs of coffee bean sorters evoked Low Country memories. "Most were singing in a low tone; one leading, and several responding in chorus, as in the water-song of Carolina," wrote Abbot. For some, songs were a catalyst for mental voyages. Roughly seventy years after American slavery was abolished, Caroline Lovell lamented that the paddling songs of her childhood "haunts the memories of all who were that time and place"; they were "strange songs that were wild and melancholy and ineffably sweet." This imagery was equally woven into inland watercourses. "Negro rowing songs rose like barbaric chants on the watery highways of the West. Plantation owners on the Mississippi had crews of black oarsmen who sang as they rowed and improvised good-natured verses to match the occasions of the day," penned scholar Constance Rourke in 1931.[39]

The memoirs of former slaveholders and Southern apologists transformed paddling songs into affirmations of bondage. In 1899, Edward McCrady sought to reimpose a system of racial subjugation, painting serene depictions of slavery in which anxious wives waited for canoemen to transport husbands back to moonlit plantations. "The patroon [head canoeman] had charge of the boat hands, and the winding of his horn upon the river told the family of his master's coming. He, too, trained the boat hands to the oar and taught them the plaintive, humorous, happy catches which they sang as they bent to the stroke, and for which the mother of the family often strained her ears to catch the first sound which told of the safe return of her dear ones." McCrady enabled whites to imagine themselves back in the era of slavery, transforming canoemen into symbols of white security. Canoemen became part of the visual and audio backdrop in which whites sipped mint juleps while enjoying magnolias' sweet fragrance. This illusion imposed a hierarchy of power—transforming planters into mythical masters of all that was seen and heard. In a similar vein, Louis Manigault returned, in 1867, to the ashes of his Gowrie Plantation, which his father had built into a rice-producing juggernaut. Ingesting the devastation caused by General Sherman's army during the Civil War, canoemen's songs played in his head, enabling him to mentally resurrect familial glory. In embroidered memory, he recalled strolling along the riverfront as the liberating sound of Union artillery played in the distance. Yet, "to the very last moment our Negroes behaved well and I left the entire Gang unloading the flat of rice, still pleased to see me, and singing as they bore the heavy loads on their heads." In the midst of burnt and looted buildings, Manigault imagined happy, valuable watermen offloading wealth while their song drowned out the misery of financial destruction, permitting him to envision the prosperity enjoyed by the ownership of human bodies.[40]

Some whites went so far as to eulogize paddling songs. In 1833, Caroline Gilman, the wife of a South Carolina planter, published a ballad titled "The Plantation":

> Yon skiff is darting from the cove;
> And list to the negro's song,
> The theme, his owner and his boat.
> While glide the crew along.

And when the leading voice is lost,
Recording from the shore,
His brother boatmen swell the strain,
In chorus with the oar.[41]

Some believed slave songs were the New World's only original form of folk music. In 1854, J. Kinnard argued that enslaved canoemen and field hands were America's "ONLY TRULY NATIONAL POETS," a conclusion reached after assuming a slave had no "foreign influences, receives the narrowest education, travels the shortest distance from home, has the least amount of spare cash, and mixes least with any other class." When Fredrika Bremer, a Swedish writer, toured the United States in 1850, she similarly deduced that slaves developed "a really new and refreshing" culture "illustrated in their own songs—the only original folk-songs that the New World possess." Such claims incorrectly concluded that culturally devoid Africans produce "original folk-songs" free of "foreign influences."[42]

Many whites believed that paddling was so easy that songs soothed muscles, while proslavery ideologues averred canoemen's ability to sing meant their labor was light. William Grayson, a planter and defender of bondage, countered Harriet Beecher Stowe's *Uncle Tom's Cabin* in *The Hireling and the Slave, Chicora, and Other Poems* (1856). He used canoemen's songs to aver: "Light is the rower's toil that song relieves."[43]

Even those who disliked bondage indulged in canoemen's songs. The sights and sounds of Latin American and Caribbean slavery revolted James Alexander. Regardless, he took pleasure from its benefits. In British Guiana, a planter "was so kind as to man a canoe with some of his people" for a sightseeing cruise. Ignoring the heat, humidity, and canoemen's unrequited toils, he noted the "negroes merrily plied the paddles, and we brushed past the overhanging trees to their favorite song of 'Velly well, yankee, velly well oh!"[44]

Historian Mark Smith explained that rural bondage offered slaveholders and white travelers a quietude produced by nature's gentle sounds. They did not want landscapes absent of sound, preferring resonances "deemed pleasant and distinctively rural and, as such, they were considered quite in an abstract sense." Sounds associated with urbanization and manufacturing represented modernization, progress, the spread of democracy, and the accumulation of wealth. Many white Northern and European urbanites longed for sweet, melodious pastoral quietude—the calming soundscapes of lowing cows, bleating sheep, babbling brooks, and faint train whistles, mixing with birds' chorus.[45] Travelers disliked the rattling of shackles, cracking of whips, slaves' anguished screams, and cries of auctioneers selling human flesh. Still, slave societies' waterscapes and landscapes afforded a pleasing quietude.[46]

Travelers concluded that aquatic sounds occupied the same niche as bucolic ones. When Englishman William Malet visited South Carolina, he observed "the hollow bark of the crocodile; the bellowing of the bull-frog, and night long—the note of summer, just as the cuckoo's is in England." The pleasant reverberations of bondage played over these soundmarkers.[47] In the Caribbean the blowing of conch shells regimented bondpeople's work patterns, while in the American South bells called slaves to work. The work songs of watermen and field hands permitted travelers to transport themselves back to simpler, idyllic times.[48]

Canoemen were central figures in aurally triggered transmigrations, allowing white travelers to sublimely ignore the cruelties of bondage while enjoying exotic soundscapes and waterscapes. Enthralled by their experiences, most passengers concluded that paddling songs were expressions of joy and contentment.[49] Canoemen bore them through an aquatic paradise, gliding over underwater gardens filled with red and white coral reefs, purple sea anemones, orange sea stars, purple and white sea urchins, and fish of every hue and shade, while porpoise, dolphins, and seals leapt about, flying fish glided by, and seabirds circled overhead. Snacking on tropical fruit, they were cooled by offshore breezes that wafted the sugary scents of tropical flowers into their nostrils. Canoemen's call-and-response songs completed this sensory excursion, filling their ears with sweet accords.

One did not need to set foot in a canoe to enjoy this serenity. While nursing her sick mother in the Bahamas (1823–1824), "Miss Hart" became ensnared by the romantic tapestry of the canoemen's song. Gazing off the veranda, she yearningly "watched several little boats as they passed to and fro in the moonlight, and occasionally I caught a note of a boat song, as sung by a fisherman, or the sailors as they rowed homeward; and once, I heard, as it appeared to me, music coming over the waters, mingled with sounds of mirth, as of revelers returning from a feast; and I heard the shrill sound of the conch shell, blown, as I thought, to announce the approach of a friend or a lover." The songs vicariously transport Hart across waters, seating her among enslaved canoemen and white celebrators.[50]

Most white observers incorrectly concluded that paddling songs were expressions of joyful contentment. Bondmen were probably glad to escape the rigors of agricultural labor. Still, paddling remained strenuous work. For African-born watermen, these songs had recognizable rhythms. Their African vernacular surely reminded many of African waterscapes, sparking memories of the loved ones and homelands they were torn from. In Africa, they could be expressions of one's income-generating labor. In the New World, they became songs of oppression, articulating slaves' unrequited toils.[51]

Paddling songs were also a source of security for slaveholders. Silence, Mark Smith explained: "Rubbed nerves raw simply because silence was the unheard note that might precede rebellion." Slaveholders created acoustic constructs of race that asserted Africans were inherently noisy. Singing simultaneously bolstered claims that black people made noise when content and fell silent when brooding, as Douglass explained: "Slaves are generally expected to sing as well as to work. A silent slave is not liked by masters or overseers. *'Make a noise,' 'make a noise,'* and *'bear a hand,'* are the words usually addressed to the slaves when there is silence amongst them." Toiling in the midst of cash crops, captives were often out of sight. Singing enabled authority to follow unseen movements, knowing the captives were not discussing illicit activities.[52]

Paddling songs provided the same security. Songs indicated that canoemen were not discussing flight or rebellion. Singing canoemen were not scheming canoemen.

Even as song provided illusions of blissful content, captives knew better. Douglass was surprised by this misperception, writing: "I have often been utterly astonished, since I came to the north, to find persons who could speak of the singing, among slaves, as evidence of their contentment and happiness. It is impossible to conceive of a greater mistake." Songs were coping mechanisms and lamentations, articulating the realities of cruelly exploited lives. "The songs of the slave represent the sorrows of his heart; and he is relieved by them, only as an aching heart is relieved by its tears. At least, such is my experience," wrote Douglass. "I have often sung to drown my sorrow, but seldom to express my happiness. Crying for joy, and singing for joy, were alike uncommon to me while in the jaws of slavery."[53] Likewise, canoemen's songs were not joyful expressions.

For many African-descended peoples, singing while working was a cultural imperative. Songs were linked to physical activities. They did not measure contentment; rather, they gauged labor. The more the captives worked, the more they sang. Ballanta delineated that the "rhythmic interest of the songs impels them to work and takes away the feeling of drudgery."[54]

Some whites believed that because the paddling songs did not conform to Western standards, they were inferior. Perhaps the most common criticism was that they were simplistic and needed lengthy narratives, like sailors' work songs, known as sea shanties, or chanteys. John Lambert dismissed South Carolinian lyrics as "mere nonsense; any thing in fact, which came into their heads." Actress Frances Kemble found merit in canoemen's singing abilities, expressing: "Their voices seem oftener tenor than any other quality, and the tune and time they keep, something quite wonderful; such intonation and accent would make almost any music agreeable." However, she complained that the lyrics were monotonous "barbaric chants."[55]

Most critics misunderstood these songs. As in Africa, lyrics were constrained by the rhythm, so "words are sung not only with respect to accent but also with respect to quantity but in English, except with the best composers, only accent is observed."[56] Hence, canoemen adhered to aural aesthetics that went unrecognized by many whites while they rejected Western songs because they did not provide the cadence necessary for paddling.

Most whites seemingly failed to comprehend extemporaneous songs' veiled double meanings. For example, Kemble derided an impromptu song, charging it was "astonishingly primitive" and a "very transparent plagiarism" from the children's song "Coming Through the Rye." As canoemen bore her husband Pierce Butler II, "headed down the Altamaha" river, Kemble "stood at the steps to see him off" while they sang:

Jenny shake her toe at me,
Jenny gone away;
Jenny shake her toe at me;
Jenny gone away;
Hurrah! Miss Susy, oh!
Jenny gone away.

We, like Kemble, do not know this song's meaning. Perhaps it recalled some recent mischief around a communal fire. It could have lampooned an unwitting Kemble. Slaves theatrically satirized white culture in dance, dress, and song. The cakewalk originated in Southern slave quarters as a parody of planters' ballroom dances. Kemble may have come close to the song's meaning when she said: "What the obnoxious Jenny meant by shaking her toe, whether defiance or mere *departure*, I never could ascertain."

The canoemen seemingly substituted "Jenny" for "Frances" to mock how she waved to her departing husband, allowing them to laugh at both the lyrics and an unknowing Kemble as she ridiculed a song about herself. Regardless, whites were not privy to songs' true meanings, or lack thereof.[57]

It can be argued that cultural resilience is the most forceful form of resistance. Paddling songs were expressions of cultural endurance, permitting captives to insinuate African soundscapes onto waterscapes claimed by enslavers. African lyrics and rhythms floated above rural and urban settings' often overwhelming white soundscapes, forcing white people, in many ways, to accept African valuations of quietude and labor. During the American Revolution, Elkanah Watson witnessed four saltwater canoemen reconstitute an African experience on the waters of Winyah Bay, South Carolina. "The evening was serene, the stars shone brightly, and the poor fellows amused us the whole way by singing their plaintive African songs, in cadence with the oars." Patriots and Loyalists battling for control of these waters believed European-descended people would define this space. Future planters invariably sat on Winyah Bay's banks, watching canoemen paddle past, believing they were lord and master of all that was seen and heard. Yet, canoemen enveloped this waterscape with African traditions. Watson and his companions traveled like Africans. Seated on the bottom of the canoe, they felt water pulsating against the hull as it skipped over waves. Someone owned the canoemen's bodies, but their voices set the tempo of their labors as call-and-response songs and the splashing of paddles dominated the soundscape. As the canoemen pulled across the bay, they could imagine themselves upon the Gambia, Sassandra, or Congo Rivers. These unknowing white voyagers were at the center of an African experience and could not similarly envision themselves on the Thames, Seine, or Hudson.[58]

Others more forcefully resisted Westernization. In 1805, Anglican missionary Henry Martyn traveled to Salvadore, Brazil, where he clambered into a dugout's contested cultural space. He wore a "black cassock," the ankle-length robe of Anglican clerics; spoke several European languages; and sought to spread Anglicanism. The "Mahomedan rowers" were "dressed in white." Paddling Martyn toward an awaiting ship, they sang Arabic "hymns all the way to the honour of Mohomet." Perhaps, the canoeists were not members of the same ethnic group but used Arabic as a lingua franca, while their faith, which was expressed by their beards, dress, and songs, permitted them to visually and acoustically reject Christianity. Martyn understood their message, penning: "I went away in no small dejection, that the Gospel should have so little effect, or rather none at all." So great was this "abomination" that Martyn equated his exodus to the "Hegira [Hijra]," or Mohammad's flight from Mecca to Medina to escape persecution. Conceivably, the Guyanese captives who sang "*gnyaam gnyaam row*," or, "for the Creator I row," similarly proclaimed their Akan faith and rejection of Christianity.[59]

Paddling songs were eventually consumed and coopted by dominant white cultures, perchance redefining how slaves perceived them. Their value as expressions of cultural resistance was possibly blunted, as they increasingly became part of societies' broader cultural fabric. Still, they continued to allow captives to dictate the pace of their labors.

African work songs received surprisingly little attention from white chroniclers. Travelers did not take regular interest in them until the mid-nineteenth century, perhaps because they were almost always sung in African languages. Most accounts are terse and exclude consideration of social, cultural, and political meanings.[60]

The paddling songs of African-descended peoples on both sides of the Atlantic are strikingly similar in structure, use, and meaning, suggesting that slave accords were the product of cultural transmission. Accounts indicate that African songs, used to synchronize paddling, were call-and-response and were frequently improvised. Unfortunately, sources are separated by considerable time and space, inhibiting sustained ethnic analysis.

Descriptions reflect African influences upon enslaved canoeists. In 1803, Thomas Winterbottom documented the use of impromptu harmonies, saying paddlers "generally sing during the whole time, and one of the passengers accompanies the song with a small drum. One rower sings a couplet, in a somewhat recitative voice, which is closed by a chorus in which they all join. When there are several rowers, the couplet is repeated by a second person, and concluded by a chorus." They often described familiar topics. "The subject of the song is either a description of some love intrigue, the praise of some woman celebrated for her beauty, &c. or it is of a satirical cast, lashing the vice of the neighboring *head men*, or lampooning the females in general. They are commonly impromptu, seldom the result of much study, and frequently describe the passengers in a strain of either praise or of the most pointed ridicule."[61]

Call-and-response songs provided paddling rhythms.[62] Percussions played by passengers and helmsmen frequently augmented oral cadences. John Weeks, a late nineteenth-century missionary on the upper Congo explained: "When paddling their canoes, either a small drum was beaten or a stick struck rhythmically on the edge of the canoe to give time to the stroke of their paddles, and to the rhythm of their songs, solos, and choruses. As a rule one sang a solo, and others took up the chorus." Paddlers' piston-like rhythm permitted many to work long hours. Canoemen also used body parts to produce rhythms. Describing how Ndobo, an oligarch on the upper Congo, commanded merchant-warriors manning his fleet to commence their voyage, Edward Glave wrote: " 'Cooma!' (beat time), shouted Ndobo, and one man in each canoe raised a foot to the gunwale of the dug-out, and hammered out the time for the paddlers' strokes."[63]

Songs' flexibility promoted multiethnic, cultural, and racial synthesis. At the Portuguese town of Luanda, George Tams observed the coalescing of African and European languages. As four "Cabindian" canoemen bore him shoreward, their song "opens with: *A bu-bu-bu-bu-bu*, to which the chorus reply, *A bia*. The leader then articulates in Portuguese, *Quem viro o Mundo* [Who in the world]? to which the others reply, *Maria Segunda* [Marria II, Portugal's queen]. They conclude in the Cabinda language, which is evidently a dialect of the Lingua Bunda." The Bakongo paddlers were from the nearby port of Cabinda and slaves belonging to a Spanish physician whom Tams was visiting. They negotiated the patriarchal relations the Portuguese imposed upon Luanda, using the Portuguese language to vocalize ties to social superiors while articulating their right for respect and privileges. The captain "asserted that he was by birth a prince, and was the son of the king of Cabinda, and in confirmation of this statement, he exhibited three iron rings on his left arm, none but a royal personage, being allowed to wear more than two." Bonds to African royalty entitled him to deference, for even "in a state of slavery, the negroes attach great importance to alliance with the royal blood, it is a subject of great personal pride, and the claim is recognized by all other negroes;" a claim that may have elevated his position. They also beseeched benevolence through their patriarchal (if you will) relationship with Queen Maria, known as "the Good Mother."[64]

Improvised lyrics transformed waterscapes into arteries of communication, conveying news along commercial networks. "The songs were generally topical, and as they paddled up or down river they gave all the latest information of interest to the villages as they pass them," Weeks reported. "I have often been amazed at the rapidity and accuracy with which news was spread in this way." Canoemen conveyed "up or down the river all the gossip about the doings and sayings of the white men of the station, accounts of punitive expeditions, judgments passed on captives and prisoners, their treatment of the native who had taken the taxes there, what new white folk were expected and who was leaving for Europe."[65] Just as maritime trade situated waterside communities at the center of commerce, paddling songs placed them at the vortex of communication.

Songs remembered a plethora of occurrences. Weeks divided African songs into three categories: "topical," like those "sung in canoes while distributing news"; "local," in which daily events were "temporarily recorded, as the bravery, cowardice, unsociability, generosity, meanness, thievishness, etc. of all the men and women of the village or town"; and those of "funeral festivities, when the praises of the dead are sung."[66]

Paddling songs provided waterscapes with human soundmarkers, as F. Harrison Rankin indicated while in Sierra Leone, penning: "No Negro spins his canoe through the water without a melody." Michel Adanson described how watermen's songs played across waterscapes: "They sung a kind of song, the burden of which I heard at a great distance, and it is not disagreeable."[67] As Ijo women of the Niger Delta paddled to and from their farms, they sang the following song, vocalizing how the environment influenced their culture and worldview:

Paddle, paddle
Oh! Paddle
The carp was paddling
A canoe underwater
But the paddle
Broke in his Hand
Paddle, paddle
Oh! Paddle[68]

Songs were so integral to paddling that silence aroused suspicion. They announced the approach of merchants on the upper Congo, giving "warning to the village that a canoe was approaching, and that the folk in it were friendly. A canoe of any size that approached a town without singing and drumming was regarded as an enemy's canoe, and was treated as such, i.e. spears, stones, etc. would be thrown at the occupants."[69]

Praise songs reaffirmed society members' honor, masculinity, and femininity. Impromptu songs sometimes provided superficial compliments to women and men with Winterbottom noting that surf-canoemen's songs are "either a description of some love intrigue, the praise of some woman celebrated for her beauty." More often, they proclaimed superiors' vertical honor. While Anna Maria Falconbridge was at Bance Island, Sierra Leone, during the 1790s, "King Naimbana" visited the English settlement in an elegant canoe. Requesting a translation of the canoemen's song, Falconbridge wrote: "The song I am told was expressive of praises to their Chief, and of their satisfaction for the treatment they received from us." Perhaps mariners were expected to eulogize superiors. When John Atkins was in Liberia during the 1730s, he said, "If they carry a Cabiceer [trade official], always sing; a Mark of Respect." Praise songs subtly requested respect by extoling employers' fair treatment. While they surely would not have ridiculed African superiors, the absence of complimentary lyrics could enunciate discontent.[70] Canoemen also recognized masculinity and horizontal honor, articulating compatriots' accomplishments. When masqueraders depicting water spirits were transported in canoes during ceremonies, their virtues were similarly extolled.[71]

Songs gently mocked, even ridiculed, individuals. They could be "of a satirical cast, lashing the vice of the neighboring *head men*, or lampooning the females in general. They are commonly impromptu, seldom the result of much study, and frequently describe the passengers in a strain of either praise or of the most pointed ridicule." Sierra Leonean canoemen derided vain women with so much humor they could disrupt paddling, with Rankin saying: "Several of their effusions amused themselves highly; and, as the extempore verse concluded with some pungent and unexpected idea, shouts of laughter delayed their chorus."[72]

Standards of social decorum were articulated, informing perceptive white passengers of proper behavior. Oblivious voyagers violated African customs, as Francisco Valdez did when he was paddled ashore in Angola during the 1850s. The canoemen countered with a work slowdown, using song to voice their desires while informing him of their laggardly progress. Valdez became "annoyed at their tardy movements" dictated by the song's beat and "expressed my impatience at the delay, and also at their monotonous song, always ending with the words, '*Oh! angana matta bicho*' (master kill the worm for me); the meaning of which is, that the master must give them to drink a *petit coup*, to drown the worm which is supposed to be gnawing them, and the craving of which, if not satisfied, would eventually devour the entrails of the poor Cabinda!" The Cabindan canoemen clearly informed Valdez that, as their "master," he should reward their labors. Yet, Valdez missed the song's meaning, fuming: "As it appeared that this song would never end, my impatience increased to the *ne plus ultra*; for it seemed to me that, contrary to the generally received opinion, the more they sang the slower went the canoe." Exasperated, he asked the helmsman why they were so unhurried. Using a story to illustrate his point, he indicated that they wanted fair compensation for their labors. Failing to perceive the tale's meaning, the protracted voyage proceeded.[73]

No one is known to have recorded the lyrics to an entire African paddling song. At best, Africans transliterated, provided summarized interpretation, or translated portions of songs. While New World slaves refrained from using the songs of those belonging to other plantations, Africans were not bound to such prohibitions. Along the upper Congo, cultural exchanges were common as canoemen "borrowed tunes freely from other tribes, and soon learn[ed] to sing all the European tunes we cared to teach them." Adhering to Victorian concepts of race, Weeks assumed Africans, who he deemed "Congo Cannibals," were simplistic, and could be easily distracted by primitive music, saying, "I do not think that any sounds affected them like the rhythmic beat of their drums. To that beat they would paddle for hours beneath the tropical sun." Weeks's superficial analysis missed the point that European songs did not offer the tempo necessary.[74]

White opinions diverged, with some concluding that paddling songs were uncivilized; others appreciated their subtle complex artistic expressions. Manuel Álvares held an unfavorable opinion of Bijago mariners, using paddling songs to portray them as piratical savages. "The captain stands at the prow, flourishing his shield and spear, and chanting (war-songs); and this soldiery of hell row to the rhythm of his chant." During the 1830s, Peter Leonard praised surf-canoemen's dexterities and ability to foster commerce, while using their songs to express racialized opinions. Describing the *Kru,* he wrote: "In rowing they have always a song of some sort or other at command, to which they keep time with the oar, sometimes melodious, but usually harsh and untuneful." His view of Accra's surf-canoemen was similar.[75]

Some were more appreciative. Rankin fondly wrote: "All sing; and on the rivers of these glowing climes, where all is genial and laughing, as the song breaks upon his ear, the traveller forgets to be a *critic*." Yet he could not provide a compliment without being a *critic*, saying: "The voices may be harsh when near, the words uncouth, the artist terrible to look upon, the music startling from contempt of all artificial rule."[76]

Mary Kingsley offers perhaps the most balanced analysis; comprehending songs' complexities and sophistication. Traveling along Atlantic Africa's coastline and up its rivers, she appreciated canoemen's songs. While on Gabon's Ogooué River, Kingsley valued the "elaborate songs" of the Fang "canoe crew." Describing another voyage, she penned: "The men are standing up swinging in rhythmic motion their long red wood paddles in perfect time to their elaborate melancholy, minor key boat song."[77]

Kingsley understood the structure and meanings of paddling songs used throughout Atlantic Africa, recognizing overarching similarities. Comparing songs of the Igalwa who lived near the Niger River's confluence with the Benue and the Mpongwe of Libreville Gabon, she penned:

> M'pongwe and Igalwa boat songs are all very pretty, and I have heard elaborate tunes in a minor key. I do not believe there are any old words to them; I have tried hard to find out about them, but believe the tunes, which are of a limited number and quite distinct from each other, are very old. The words are put in by the singer on the spur of the moment, and only catalogue—whatever its component details might be—sung to the fixed tune, the trade information sung to another and so on. . . . I have elsewhere mentioned pretty much the same state of things among the Ga's and Krumen and Bubi.

Kingsley was a widely traveled, perceptive ethnographer who recognized similarities in canoeing songs, especially those of the Ga-Adaŋbé in Togo and Ghana, Bubi of Bioko Island (or Fernando Pó), West-Central Africans, and *Kru* of Liberia. She reported that water people throughout Atlantic Africa similarly used rhythms while extemporaneous lyrics described immediate circumstances.[78]

Paddling refrains provided waterscapes with their dominant human-made soundmarker. Songs were an essential component of maritime culture that enhanced the sensual pleasures of water while alleviating canoemen's labors. They were an intrinsic component of slaves' maritime cultures, underscoring the meanings and values Africans placed on maritime traditions. Captives of the same ethnicity surely sang lyrics, allowing them to reflect on their African lives. Songs' pliability facilitated cultural blendings as members of different ethnicities sang together on both sides of the Atlantic. African rhythms remained the foundation for lyrics sung in African, European, or blended languages. Songs reinforced and articulated the cohesiveness of canoemen's multiethnic *shipmate* relationships.

African-informed paddling songs echoed across slave quarters, over the fields where agricultural hands toiled, and into the Big House where planters and their guests enjoyed the wealth of plantation slavery. Their resonances provided slaveholdings and their bonded communities with distinct soundmarkers. They carried over the swamps of Suriname, Brazil, Louisiana, and the South Carolina and Georgia Low Country. They echoed across sluggish rivers, like the Mississippi, Potomac, and Ogeechee in the American South; the Cabarita, Milk, and Black Rivers of Jamaica; the Demerara, Berbice, and Saramaca Rivers in Suriname, and the Amazon and São Francisco Rivers in Brazil. Along the coastlines of the Americas they were heard above the sound of crashing surf. They played across the calm waters of the Baía de Guanabara, Chesapeake Bay, and Baie de Port-au-Prince. Paddling songs penetrated the milieu of river ports and seaports, floating up the deck and rigging of wooden ships and into the ears of white sailors and passengers. They drifted out to approaching slave ships and into their holds, conceivably causing some captives to conclude that they had come full circle. They glided across wharves and wafted down narrow streets where they mingled with the dirge of enslaved porters transporting the freight and white passengers that canoemen offloaded.[79]

A Sea Change in Atlantic History

Even as Atlantic history opens vistas of scholarly inquiry, our intellectual strides remain hobbled by previous interpretations. We assume the cultural process was terrestrial while many hold African cultural transmissions to higher standards of proof than those of European and Asian migrants.[1] Sources do not neatly diagram the African roots and Atlantic routes of slaves' maritime cultures. They do reveal that African-descended peoples shared strikingly similar customs. Situating canoeing and swimming beneath a broad arc of time and space while examining them through an Atlantic lens, we can logically conclude that slaves recreated and reimagined African traditions in New World waterscapes.

We must move beyond landlocked paradigms. Water was an experiential place: a youthful playground, a medium for market-bound women to socialize during voyages, a space for males to express honor and masculinity. African maritime cultures were sensory, visceral experiences. Swimmers enjoyed the weightlessness of gliding through the blue—of warm waters, cool breezes, and the taste of saltwater or freshwater upon their lips. Dugouts remained one dimensional without the sights, sounds, and feelings inherent in swimming, singing paddling songs, and engaging in other traditions. Saltwater captives used African valuations and maritime traditions to chart an "aqueous continent," binding themselves to home-waters, while creating cultural understandings with members of new diverse waterside communities.[2]

African-born canoemen and canoe-makers resurrected canoe designs, manufacturing techniques, paddling methods, and other cultural components, imbuing New World waterscapes with resonances of home. Canoes and waterscapes were often sacred, connecting mariners to ancestral spirits. Paddling songs enveloped waterscapes with African soundscapes while articulating shipmate affinities. Perceptions of the human body permitted water people to proudly display their muscular physiques.

Equal creativity was used while reimagining immersionary cultures. Swimming afforded corporeal pleasures as water soothed taxed muscles, allowing captives to temporarily enjoy their brutalized bodies. It transformed waterscapes into childhood playgrounds. Aquatics offered moments of surreal liberty as captives parted the waters of bondage. Contests and aquatic blood sports could enhance communal bonds and participants' sense of self-worth.

Slave-trading patterns created ethnic enclaves while slaveholders' prejudices and desire to exploit African-derived aquatics promoted, even forced, cultural retentions. Enslavers sought to appropriate aquatic expertise, encouraging and coercing captives to dive and craft dugouts. Still, divers cloistered their wisdom, maintaining considerable control over the deep and their lives.

Ironically, Atlanticists largely remain "continental" scholars, as the Oceania scholar Epeli Hau'ofa would say, approaching the Atlantic world with our collective back to the sea.[3] We erect boundaries between land and sea, forgetting that many humans were farming-fishermen and fishing-farmers. Historian Daniel Vickers stressed that all "the North American colonies were originally maritime colonies" with most scholars historicizing the ocean as "an obstacle over which settlers had to pass in order to play their historical roles as conquerors, planters, or Christians. Once ashore, we are usually told the planters turned their backs to the water" while founding "agricultural villages where the sea played no further role in their lives." Yet most colonists maintained maritime bonds, using "freshwater channels of trade to the interior," completing "routine voyages," and working in seafaring-related professions. The maritime experiences of men evolved over their lifetime and many shifted between maritime and shoreside occupations. Seaport wives, mothers, daughters, and widows understood oceanic rhythms, often working in maritime-related professions.[4]

Connections to water were not uniquely coastal. Many people residing in the heart of West-Central Africa and the American heartland were freshwater mariners. Abraham Lincoln—the "Rail Splitter," a decidedly terrestrial moniker—gained maritime skills while plying the Mississippi (1828–1831), which became his culturescape for understanding bondage.[5]

Perceptions of the sea swing from sublime bliss to that of a tumultuous abyss. Water is neither and both. Waterscapes were spaces of hope, of unique opportunities for those capable of negotiating them. Still, we cannot forget that the Middle Passage consumed Africans' aspirations. Nor can we forget that maritime bondage confined Africans to the narrow channels of slavery, excluding them from the deep broad seas of freedom. Maritime slavery was a cruel master. Captives incurred high rates of suffering for their unusual privileges, while chroniclers stripped slaves of their names and ethnicities, diminishing them to "negroes," "slaves," and "niggers," denying them of their humanity and personhood.

This is more than a story of human tragedy pockmarked by the scars of subjugation. It is one of human endurance. Even as colonization physically and conceptually altered landscapes, captives insinuated African valuations onto waterscapes. Their center of gravity shifted as the waters of the Middle Passage imposed new circumstances upon them, raising existential questions of identity, home, and belonging. Yet the liquid that facilitated shipment into bondage also provided a sense of familiarity and purpose as captives forged new multiethnic group identities. Beachhead cultures were established, cultural anchors cast, and pluralistic connections linked saltwater slaves to home waters and new communities of meaning and practice. Waterscapes were places of shifting horizons and prospects. Maritime slavery offered unique opportunities for negotiating benefits, enabling captives to challenge the supremacy of the dominant class by exchanging wisdom and expertise for lives of privileged exploitation.

Water can provide sensual pleasures and heartbreaking miseries. Facing two ways—toward water and toward land—we can consider the visceral waterscapes many captives intimately knew. It is time to take the deep intellectual dive. Hopefully, *Undercurrents of Power* will be the breath before the plunge as we embark on a concerted sea change that plumbs the depths of African-descended people's aquatic cultures.

Epilogue

Our story does not end with the abolition of slavery. Aquatic implications intertwine with current social issues, matters of cultural identity, and American concepts of race. The early swimming abilities of African- and European-descended peoples raise provocative issues concerning today's American society. Since many early black people were adroit, why are there relatively few dominant African American competitive swimmers today?

While perceptions and practices are changing, today many African Americans do not hold swimming in high regard, considering it a "white" or "un-black" practice. During the June 30, 1990, Los Angeles Memorial Coliseum stop in Nelson Mandela's Freedom Tour, comedian Nell Carter joked with the seventy thousand, mostly black, spectators that if black people knew how to swim there would be no African Americans to greet Mandela because their ancestors would have swum back to Africa. The audience that had come to hear Mandela speak, including me, understood the joke and laughed.[1]

My awareness of black-held beliefs made historical accounts of aquatics intriguing. Many white Americans believe blacks are less capable than whites because, among other reasons, some believe blacks' bones are denser, making them less buoyant than whites. The news media reported on white and black perception that blacks cannot swim. Most infamously, Los Angeles Dodgers' vice president Al Campanis was fired in 1987 after telling Ted Koppel on the TV show *Nightline* that blacks were not "good swimmers" because they lack "buoyancy."[2]

Today African Americans remain less likely to be proficient swimmers than white people, with tragic consequences. Myths purportedly explain why African Americans are relatively poor swimmers. They claim that slaveholders instilled pervasive fears by using water tortures and by circulat-ing stories of aquatic monsters while the Atlantic slave trade inflicted psy-chological scars, causing captives and their descendants to fear water. These historical memories were probably created during the 1960s as African Americans began taking a concerted interest in their history as it related to the Civil Rights Movement. Sustained deliberation is required to under-stand why twentieth-century African Americans largely abandoned their inherited aquatic African tradition. Segregation and cities' unwillingness to build expensive recreational facilities in black neighborhoods, as had been built in white neighborhoods, deprived black communities of pools. In 1940, for example, Washington, DC, had "three inadequate indoor and two outdoor pools for Negroes, whereas there were nearly fifty pools for other swimmers." In addition, most African Americans lacked the resources to pay for swim lessons or gain access to pools.[3]

Concurrently, Jim Crow–era racial violence transformed waterscapes from places of leisure to foreboding scenes of subjugation. Early twentieth-century race riots drove black Americans from coastal and inland beaches. For instance, the 1919 Chicago Race Riot began on July 27 when white men threw rocks and bricks at Eugene Williams, a black teenager who inadver-tently drifted into a white swimming area, resulting in his drowning death. Waterscapes also became the final resting place for numerous murdered black bodies, who were the victims of racial violence. Perhaps the most infamous example was the lynching of fourteen-year-old Emmett Till on August 28, 1955, who was beaten to death and dumped into Mississippi's Tallahatchie River. Hence, natural waterscapes came to possess dubious meanings, transforming many into undesirable swim places.[4]

African Americans' inadequate swimming abilities precipitated a high rate of drowning deaths. Regionally specific statistics indicate that African Americans are far more likely to drown than whites. In 2008, the *Boston Globe* reported: "Nearly 60 percent of African-American children can't swim, almost twice the figure for white children," while the Centers for Disease Control and Prevention estimated that African American children are 5.5 times more likely to drown to death than are white children, repeat-edly labeling this drowning death rate an "epidemic."[5]

While definitive conclusions concerning contemporary swimming prac-tices must await sustained deliberation, until fairly recently African Ameri-cans were usually more proficient swimmers than whites. The abolition of slavery placed black and white swimmers on divergent trajectories. Despite the recent national and international successes of African American competitive swimmers, aquatics remain on the periphery of acceptability within the African American community. Like the banjo (another African transmission), swimming was abandoned and posthumously deemed a "white" activity.[6]

Notes

Introduction

1. J. G. Beaglehole, ed., *The Journals of Captain James Cook on His Voyages of Discovery: The Voyage of the Resolution and Discovery, 1776–1780, 5 vols.* Cambridge: 1967), 3:2, 1164–1165. Also see Beaglehole, *James Cook*, 3:1, 628; John Hawkesworth, ed., *An Account of the Voyages Undertaken by the Order of His Present Majesty for Making Discoveries in the Southern Hemisphere*, 2 vols. (London: 1775), 1:475; Patrick Moser, ed., *Pacific Passages: An Anthology of Surf Writing* (Honolulu: 2008), 1.

2. William Bradford, *History of Plymouth Plantation, 1620–1647*, 2 vols. (1912; New York: 1968), 155 (italics added).

3. John Gillis, *The Human Shore: Seacoasts in History* (Chicago: 2012), esp. 7; *King James Bible*, Genesis 1:1–2:3, 2:4–25; Eric Leed, *The Mind of the Traveler: From Gilgamesh to Global Tourism* (New York: 1991), esp. 19; Alain Corbin, *Lure of the Sea* (1988; New York: 1994), 1–18; Christopher Connery, "There Was No More Sea: The Suppression of the Oceans, from the Bible to Cyberspace," *Journal of Historical Geography* 32 (2006): 494–511; Max Oelschlaeger, *The Idea of the Wilderness: From History to the Age of Ecology* (New Haven: 1991), 44–46; Rachel L. Carson, *The Sea Around Us* (Oxford: 1951), esp. 14–15; Rachel L. Carson, *The Edge of the Sea* (Boston: 1998), 1–37. Chapter 1 elaborates on Christian perceptions of the sea.

4. For "Atlantic Africa," see John K. Thornton, *Warfare in Atlantic Africa, 1500–1800* (London: 1999), 12–16; Toyin Falola and Matt D. Childs, eds., *The Changing Worlds of Atlantic Africa: Essays in Honor of Robin Law* (Durham: 2009); Akinwumi Ogundiran and Toyin Falola, eds., *Archaeology of Atlantic Africa and the African Diaspora* (Bloomington: 2010), 5; Jane I. Guyer, *Marginal Gains: Monetary Transactions in Atlantic Africa* (Chicago: 2004), 22; Alison Games, "Atlantic History," in Philip D. Morgan and Jack P. Greene, eds., *Atlantic History: A Critical Appraisal* (Oxford: 2009), 742.

5. "Water people," "shore-folk," "sea people," and "river people" are idioms describing societal connections to marine environments. Robert W. Harms, *River of Wealth, River of Sorrow: The Central Zaire Basin in the Era of the Slave and Ivory Trade, 1500–1891* (New Haven: 1981); Robert Harms, *Games Against Nature: An Eco-Cultural History of the Nunu of Equatorial Africa* (New Haven: 1987), 12, 15, 16, 19; Joseph C. Miller, *Way of Death: Merchant Capitalism and the Angolan Slave Trade, 1730–1830* (Madison: 1988), 54.

6. Daniel Vickers with Vince Walsh, *Young Men and the Sea: Yankee Seafarers in the Age of Sail* (New Haven: 2005); Michael N. Pearson, "Littoral Society: The Concept and the

Problems," *Journal of World History* 17, no. 4 (December 2006): 353–373; John Gillis, *Islands of the Mind: How the Human Imagination Created the Atlantic World* (New York: 2009); Jerry H. Bentley, Renate Bridenthal, and Karen Wiggen, *Seascapes: Maritime Histories, Littoral Cultures, and Transoceanic Exchanges* (Honolulu: 2003), 21–37; Bernhard Klein and Gesa Mackenthun, eds., *Sea Changes: Historicizing the Ocean* (London: 2004); Christer Westerdahl, "The Maritime Cultural Landscape," *International Journal of Nautical Archaeology* 21, no. 1 (1991), 5–14; A. H. J. Prins, *Sailing from Lamu: A Study of Maritime Culture in Islamic East Africa* (Assen: 1965), 3–4; Philip E. Steinberg, *The Social Construction of the Ocean* (Cambridge: 2001); "Oceans of History Forum," *American Historical Review* 3, no. 3 (June 2006): 717–780; Kevin Dawson, "Enslaved Swimmers and Divers in the Atlantic World," *Journal of American History* 92, no. 4 (March 2006): 1327–1355; Kevin Dawson, "Enslaved Ship Pilots in the Age of Revolutions: Challenging Perceptions of Race and Slavery Between the Boundaries of Maritime and Terrestrial Bondage," *Journal of Social History* 47, no. 1 (Fall 2013): 71–100; Kevin Dawson, "Swimming, Surfing, and Underwater Diving in Early Modern Atlantic Africa and the African Diaspora," in Carina E. Ray and Jeremy Rich, eds., *Navigating African Maritime History* (St. John's: 2009), 81–116. For interconnected maritime and terrestrial cultures, see Harms, *River of Wealth*; Harms, *Games Against Nature*; W. Jeffrey Bolster, "Putting the Ocean in Atlantic History: Maritime Communities and Marine Ecology in the Northwest Atlantic, 1500–1800," *American Historical Review* 113 (February 2008): 19–47; Miller, *Way of Death*; Sandra E. Greene, *Gender, Ethnicity, and Social Change on the Upper Slave Coast: A History of the Anlo Ewe* (London: 1996); Emmanuel Kwaku Akyeampong, *Between the Sea and the Lagoon: An Eco-Social History of the Anlo of Southeastern Ghana c.1850 to Recent Times* (Oxford: 2002); Robin Law, *Ouidah: The Social History of a West African Slaving "Port," 1727–1892* (Oxford: 2004); Kristin Mann, *Slavery and the Birth of an African City: Lagos, 1760–1900* (Bloomington: 2007); James F. Searing, *West African Slavery and Atlantic Commerce: The Senegal River Valley, 1700–1860* (Cambridge: 1993); Ralph A. Austen and Jonathan Derrick, *Middlemen of the Cameroon Rivers: The Duala and Their Hinterland, c.1600–c.1900* (Cambridge: 1999); Carina Ray and Jeremy Rich, eds., *Navigating African Maritime History* (St. John's: 2009); Walter Hawthorne, *Planting Rice and Harvesting Slaves: Transformations Along the Guinea-Bissau Coast, 1400–1900* (Portsmouth: 2003); Walter Hawthorne, *From Africa to Brazil: Culture, Identity, and an Atlantic Slave Trade, 1600–1830* (Cambridge: 2010); W. Jeffrey Bolster, *Black Jacks: African American Seamen in the Age of Sail* (Cambridge: 1997); Lisa Norling, *Captain Ahab Had a Wife: New England Women and the Whalefishery, 1720–1870* (Chapel Hill: 2000); Margaret S. Creighton and Lisa Norling, eds., *Iron Men, Wooden Women: Gender and Seafaring in the Atlantic World, 1700–1920* (Baltimore: 1996); Marcus Rediker, *Between the Devil and the Deep Blue Sea: Merchant Seamen, Pirates and the Anglo-American Maritime World, 1700–1750* (Cambridge: 1987); Peter Linebaugh and Marcus Rediker, *The Many-Headed Hydra, Sailors, Slaves, Commoners, and the Hidden History of the Revolutionary Atlantic* (Boston: 2000).

7. For cultural construction, see note 20.

8. Rhys Isaac, *Transformation of Virginia, 1740–1790* (New York: 1982), 52–57, esp. 52, 53.

9. Also see Bolster, "Putting the Ocean," 19.

10. Daniel Vickers, *Farmers and Fishermen: Two Centuries of Work in Essex County Massachusetts, 1680–1850* (Chapel Hill: 1994), esp. 1, 13–30; William Cronon, *Changes in the*

Land: Indians, Colonists, and the Ecology of New England (New York: 1983); S. Max Edelson, *Plantation Enterprise in Colonial South Carolina* (Cambridge: 2006), 33–52; Larry Gragg, *Englishmen Transplanted: The English Colonization of Barbados, 1627–1660* (Oxford: 2003), esp. 58–87; Richard S. Dunn, *Sugar and Slaves: The Rise of the Planter Class in the English West Indies, 1624–1713* (Chapel Hill: 1972), 263–299; Jorge Cañizares-Esguerra, *Puritan Conquistadors: Iberianizing the Atlantic, 1550–1700* (Stanford: 2006).

11. Michael A. Gomez, *Exchanging Our Country Marks: The Transformation of African Identities in the Colonial and Antebellum South* (Chapel Hill: 1998), 177; Nicholas Thomas, *Islanders*, 1–28; Bushnell, "Indigenous America"; Ras Michael Brown, *African-Atlantic Cultures and the South Carolina Lowcountry* (Cambridge: 2013).12. John Mack, *The Sea: A Cultural History* (London: 2013), esp. 21–23; Jerry H. Wigen, "Introduction," in Jerry H. Bentley, Renate Bridenthal, and Kären Wigen, eds., *Seascapes: Maritime Histories, Littoral Cultures, and Transoceanic Exchanges* (Honolulu: 2007), 1–17.

13. W. Jeffrey Bolster, *The Mortal Sea: Fishing the Atlantic in the Age of Sail* (Cambridge: 2012), 3.

14. For African connections to freshwater and saltwater, see Law, *Ouidah*; Walter Rodney, *A History of the Upper Guinea Coast, 1545–1800* (New York: 1970); Miller, *Way of Death*; Harms, *River of Wealth*; Harms, *Games Against Nature*; George E. Brooks, *Landlords and Strangers: Ecology, Society, and Trade in Western Africa, 1000–1630* (Boulder: 1993); Greene, *Gender, Ethnicity, and Social Change*; Boubacar Barry, *Senegambia and the Atlantic Slave Trade* (Cambridge: 1998); Akyeampong, *Between the Sea*; Mann, *Birth of an African City*; Searing, *West African Slavery*; Robert S. Smith, "To the Palaver Islands: War and Diplomacy on the Lagos Lagoon in 1852–1854," *Journal of the Historical Society of Nigeria* 5, no. 1 (December 1969): 3–25; Robert S. Smith, "Canoe in West African History," *Journal of African History* 11, no. 4 (1970): 515–533; Austen and Derrick, *Middlemen of the Cameroon Rivers*; Hawthorne, *Planting Rice and Harvesting Slaves*; Ray and Rich, *Navigating African Maritime History*.

15. Leed, *Mind of the Traveler*, 19. The historiography of Atlantic history is too broad to compile a comprehensive bibliography. The following provide examples of its contours: Bernard Bailyn, "The Idea of Atlantic History," *Itinero* 20, no. 1 (1996): 19–44; Paul Gilroy, *The Black Atlantic: Modernity and Double Consciousness* (Cambridge: 1993); Nicholas Canny, "Writing Atlantic History; Or, Reconfiguring the History of Colonial British America," *Journal of American History* 86, no. 3 (1999): 1093–1114; Peter A. Coclanis, "Atlantic World or Atlantic/World," *William and Mary Quarterly* 63, no. 4(2006): 725–742; Bernard Bailyn, *Atlantic History: Concept and Contours* (Cambridge: 2005); Bernard Bailyn and Patricia L. Denault, eds., *Soundings in Atlantic History: Latent Structures and Intellectual Currents, 1500–1830* (Cambridge: 2009); Alison Games, "Atlantic History: Definitions, Challenges and Opportunities," *American Historical Review* 3, no. 3 (June 2006): 741–757; Jorge Cañizares-Esguerra, Matt D. Childs, and James Sidbury, eds., *The Black Urban Atlantic in the Age of the Slave Trade* (Philadelphia: 2013).

16. Bolster, *Mortal Sea*, 13; Bolster, "Putting the Ocean;" Greg Dening, "Deep Time, Deep Spaces: Civilizing the Sea," in Bernhard Klein and Gesa Mackenthun, eds., *Sea Changes: Historicizing the Ocean* (London: 2004), 13–36, esp. 13; Jerry H. Bentley, "Sea and Ocean Basins as Frameworks of Historical Analysis," *Geographic Review*, 89 (1999), 215–224.

17. James Sidbury and Jorge Cañizares-Esguerra, "Mapping Ethnogenesis in the Early Modern Atlantic," *William and Mary Quarterly* 68, no. 2 (April 2011): 181–208, esp. 208.

Also see John Thornton, *Cultural History of the Atlantic World, 1250–1820* (Cambridge: 2012), esp. xi, 3; Roquinaldo Ferreira, *Cross-Cultural Exchange in the Atlantic World: Angola and Brazil During the Era of the Slave Trade* (Cambridge: 2012), 243; Amy Turner Bushnell, "Indigenous America and the Limits of the Atlantic World, 1493–1825," in Philip D. Morgan and Jack P. Greene, eds., *Atlantic History: A Critical Appraisal* (Oxford: 2009), 191–212.

18. Epeli Hau'ofa, "Our Sea of Islands," in Epeli Hau'ofa, *We Are the Ocean: Selected Works* (1993; Honolulu: 2008), 31–32, 39; Nicholas Thomas, *Islanders: The Pacific in the Age of Empire* (New Haven: 2010), 20; Eric Waddell and Vijay Naidu, eds., *A New Oceania: Rediscovering Our Sea of Islands* (Suva, Fiji: 1993); Greg Fry, "Framing the Islands: Knowledge and Power in Changing Australian Images of the 'South Pacific,'" *Contemporary Pacific*, 9 (1997): 305–344; Albert Wendt, "Towards a New Oceania," *Mana Review* 1 (1976): 49–60. For "Historical jigsaw puzzle," see Barry, *Senegambia*, xvi. For additional scholarship on Oceania, see Alice Te Punga Somerville, *Once Were Pacific: Maori Connections to Oceania* (Minneapolis: 2012); David Igler, *The Great Ocean: Pacific Worlds from Captain Cook to the Gold Rush* (Oxford: 2013); Robert Borofsky, ed., *Remembrance of Pacific Pasts: An Invitation to Remake History* (Honolulu: 2000); John Gillis, "Islands in the Making of an Atlantic Oceania," in Bentley, Bridenthal, and Wiggen, eds., *Seascapes*, 21; Matt K. Matsuda, "The Pacific," *American Historical Review* 3, no. 3 (June 2006): 758–780; Dening, "Deep Time," 13–36. For "jigsaw puzzle," see Barry, *Senegambia*, xvi. Also see John Thornton, *Africa and Africans in the Making of the Atlantic World* (Cambridge: 1992), xiv, 187–191.

19. Jason R. Young, *Rituals of Resistance: African Atlantic Religion in Kongo and the Low-country South in the Era of Slavery* (Baton Rouge: 2007), 1–20, esp. 3, 9–10; Michael A. Gomez, *Reversing Sail: A History of the African Diaspora* (Cambridge: 2005), 1–2; James H. Sweet, *Recreating Africa: African-Portuguese World, 1441–1770* (Chapel Hill: 2003), esp. 116, 123; Thornton, *Africa and Africans*, 320; Gwendolyn Midlo Hall, *Slavery and African Ethnicities in the Americas: Restoring the Links* (Chapel Hill: 2005), esp. 164–172. For scholarship situating the African diaspora in Atlantic paradigms, see Ferreira, *Cross-Cultural Exchange*, 242; Thornton, *Cultural History*, 3; Matthew Restall, *The Black Middle: Africans, Mayas, and the Spaniards in Colonial Yucatan* (Stanford: 2009), 1–5; Sidbury and Cañizares-Esguerra, "Mapping Ethnogenesis," 181–208; James Sidbury, *Becoming African in America: Race and Nation in the Early Black Atlantic* (New York: 2007); Gomez, *Exchanging Our Country Marks*; Vincent Brown, *The Reaper's Garden: Death and Power in the World of Atlantic Slavery* (Cambridge: 2008), esp. 1–12; Andrew Sluyter, *Black Ranching Frontiers: African Cattle Herders of the Atlantic World, 1500–1900* (New Haven: 2012); Linda M. Heywood, ed., *Central Africans and the Cultural Transformations in the American Diaspora* (Cambridge: 2002); Maureen Warner-Lewis, *Central Africa in the Caribbean: Transcending Time, Transforming Culture* (Kingston: 2003). For Atlantic history, see note 16.

20. For example, Paul E. Lovejoy, *Transformations in Slavery: A History of Slavery in Africa* (1983; Cambridge: 2011); Paul Lovejoy, "The African Diaspora: Revisionist Interpretations of Ethnicity, Culture and Religion Under Slavery," *Studies in the World History of Slavery, Abolition and Emancipation* 2, no. 1 (1997); Thornton, *Africa and Africans*; Miller, *Way of Death*; Gomez, *Country Marks*; Michael A. Gomez, "African Identity and Slavery in the Americas," *Radical History Review* 75 (1999): 111–120; Sweet, *Recreating Africa*; James H. Sweet, *Domingos Álvares, African Healing, and the Intellectual History of the Atlantic World* (Chapel Hill: 2011); Ben Vinson, "African (Black) Diaspora History, Latin American History—A Comment," *The Americas* 63, no. 1 (July 2006): 1–18; Gomez, "African Identity," 111–120.

21. Toyin Falola and Matt D. Childs, eds., *The Yoruba in the Atlantic World* (Bloomington: 2004); Sweet, *Recreating Africa*; Sweet, *Domingos Álvares*; Ferreira, *Cross-Cultural Exchange*; Young, *Rituals of Resistance*; Midlo Hall, *Slavery and African Ethnicities*; Heywood, ed., *Central Africans*; Kristin Mann and Edna G. Bay, eds., *Rethinking the African Diaspora: The Making of the Black Atlantic World in the Bight of Benin and Brazil* (London: 2001); Kwasi Konadu, *The Akan Diaspora in the Americas* (Oxford: 2010); Hawthorne, *Africa to Brazil*.

22. Herman L. Bennet, *Colonial Blackness: A History of Afro-Mexico* (Bloomington: 2009), 20, 29; Matt D. Childs, *The 1812 Aponte Rebellion in Cuba and the Struggle Against Atlantic Slavery* (Chapel Hill: 2006); Sweet, *Domingos Álvares*, esp. 4; Vincent Brown, *Reaper's Garden*; Young, *Rituals of Resistance*; Edda L. Fields-Black, *Deep Roots: Rice Farmers in West Africa and the African Diaspora* (Bloomington: 2008); Ferreira, *Cross-Cultural Exchange*, 242–248.

23. For cultural resistance, see Sweet, *Recreating Africa*, 7, 161–188, 229; Sweet, *Domingos Álvares*, esp. 6; Young; *Rituals of Resistance*; Gomez, *Country Marks*; Ferreira, *Cross-Cultural Exchange*, 242; Sharla M. Fett, *Working Cures: Healing, Health, and Power on Southern Slave Plantations* (Chapel Hill: 2002); Walter C. Rucker, *The River Flows On: Black Resistance, Culture, and Identity Formation in Early America* (Baton Rouge: 2006); Jennifer L. Morgan, *Laboring Women: Reproduction and Gender in New World Slavery* (Philadelphia: 2004); Karol K. Weaver, *Medical Revolutionaries: The Enslaved Healers of Eighteenth-Century Saint Domingue* (Urbana: 2006).

24. Walter Johnson, *Soul by Soul: Life Inside the Antebellum Slave Market* (Cambridge: 1999), esp. 9, 11; Kevin Dawson, "Slave Culture," in Robert Paquette and Mark M. Smith, eds., *The Oxford Handbook of Slavery in the Americas* (Oxford: 2010), 467–470.

Chapter 1

1. Gomes Eannes de Azurara, *The Chronicle of Discovery and Conquest of Guinea*, 2 vols. (London: 1899), 2:226–228.

2. Nicholas Orme, *Early British Swimming, 55 BC–AD 1719: With the First Swimming Treatise in English, 1595* (Exeter: 1983); Richard Mandell, *Sport: A Cultural History* (New York: 1984), 179–180; J. Frost, *The Art of Swimming: A Series of Practical Instructions on an Original and Progressive Plan* (New York: 1818); Anonymous, "Swimming," *Sailor's Magazine* 11 (January1839): 152; Theodorus Bailey Myers Mason, *The Preservation of Life at Sea: A Paper Read Before the American Geographical Society* (New York: 1879), 2–3; Davis Dalton, *How to Swim: A Practical Treatise Upon the Art of Natation, Together with Instruction as to the Best Methods of Saving Persons Imperilled in the Water* (London: 1899), esp. 1, 130–133; Thomas Tegg, *The Art of Swimming* (London: c. 1805–1824), 5–6; Richard McAllister Smith, *The Confederate First Reader: Containing Selections in Prose and Poetry* (Richmond: 1864), 20–21; William Percey, *The Compleat Swimmer: Or, The Art of Swimming* (London: 1658), v; Archibald Sinclair and William Henry, *Swimming* (London: 1893), 27, 186–280; Everard Digby, *De arte Natandi Libri duo Quorum Prior Regulas Ipsius Artis, Posterior Verò Praxin Demonstrationemque Continet* (Londini: 1587); Everard Digby, *A Short Introduction for to Learne to Swimme: Gathered out of Master Digbies Booke of the Art of Swimming* (1587; London: 1595), 3–4; Richard Nelligan, *The Art of Swimming: A Practical, Working Manual* (Boston: 1906); Melchisédec Thévenot, *L'Art de Nager (The Art of Swimming)* (London: 1699), i–viii, 1, 4–5; Rediker, *Devil and the Deep Blue Sea*, 93, 258.

3. Corbin, *Lure of the Sea*, 1–18, esp. 2, 7; Cañizares-Esguerra, *Puritan Conquistador*, 35–55, 123–125, esp. 123; William Straton Bruce, *Commentary on the Gospel According to St. Matthew* (Boston: 1867), 79–81, 85, 227, 462–463; Orme, *British Swimming*, esp. 24–25; Piero Camporesi, *Fear of Hell: Images of Damnation and Salvation in Early Modern Europe* (University Park: 1987), esp. 15–22, 38, 57, 82, 140; John Winthrop, "Model of Christian Charity" in *The Journal of John Winthrop, 1630–1649* (Cambridge: 1996), 9.

4. Orme, *Swimming*; Mandell, *Sport*, 18–24, 60–62, 112–113, 179–181; Sinclair and Henry, *Swimming*, 1–20.

5. Georges Vigarello, *Concepts of Cleanliness: Changing Attitudes in France Since the Middle Ages* (Cambridge: 1988); David Eveleigh, *Bogs, Baths and Basin* (Gloucestershire: 2002).

6. Mandell, *Sport*, 179–181; Dunn, *Sugar and Slaves*, 307; William Bosman, *A New and Accurate Description of the Coast of Guinea, Divided into the Gold, the Slave, and the Ivory Coasts* (New York: 1705), 283; Percey, *Compleat Swimmer*, 11–12; Thomas Wentworth Higginson, *Army Life in a Black Regiment: Adventures of the First Slave Regiment Mustered into the Service of the United States During the Civil War* (1869; Toronto: 1962), 156; J. G. Stedman, *Narrative of a Five Years' Expedition, Against the Revolted Negroes of Surinam, in Guiana, on the Wild Coast of South America; from the Year 1772, to 1777*, 2 vols. (London: 1796), 1:82.

7. Mason, *Preservation of Life*, 2–3; Anonymous, "Swimming," 152; Dalton, *How to Swim*, 1–4.

8. Digby, *Swimme*; Percey, *Compleat Swimmer*; Thévenot, *Nager*; Tegg, *Art of Swimming*; Frost, *Art of Swimming*; Orme, *British Swimming*; Anonymous, "Swimming," 152; Mandell, *Sport*, 112–113, 179–180; Sinclair and Henry, *Swimming*; Nelligan, *Swimming*, frontispiece, 12–14, 129; Captain Webb, *The Art of Swimming* (London: 1873), 24, 31–32; Dalton, *How to Swim*, 20–27; Annette Kellerman, *How to Swim* (New York: 1918), 49, 107–112.

9. Orme, *British Swimming*; Mandell, *Sport*, 112–113.

10. Digby, *Swimme*; Thévenot, *Nager*; Sinclair and Henry, *Swimming*, 18.

11. Benjamin Franklin, *The Art of Swimming Rendered Easy* (Glasgow: 1840?), 15; Richard Ligon, *A True and Exact History of the Island of Barbadoes* (1673; Portland: 1998), 53; P. E. H. Hair, Adam Jones, and Robin Law, eds., *Barbot on Guinea: The Writings of Jean Barbot on West Africa, 1678–1712*, 2 vols. (London: 1992), 2:545n50; R. S. Rattray, *Ashanti* (Oxford: 1923), 63; George Catlin, *Letters and Notes on the Manners, Customs, and Conditions of the North American Indian*, 2 vols. (London: 1841), 1:97.

12. Frost, *Art of Swimming*, 9; Orme, *British Swimming*, 164; Franklin, *Swimming*, 14; Digby, *Swimme*; Mason, *Preservation of Life*; Nelligan, *Swimming*, 12–17.

13. Catlin, *Letters*, 1:176, 186, 196, plate 70, esp. 96–97 (italics added); Charles Mckenzie, "Some Account of the Mississouri [sic] Indians in the years 1804, 5, 6, & 7," in W. Raymond Wood and Thomas D. Thiessen, eds., *Early Fur Trade on the Northern Plains: Canadian Traders Among the Mandan and Hidatsa Indians, 1738–1818: The Narratives of John Macdonell, David Thompson, François-Antoine Larque, Charles W. McKenzie* (Norman: 1999), 239. Thanks to Elizabeth Fenn for these sources.

14. Digby, *Natandi*, chap. 1, esp. 3; Frost, *Art of Swimming*, 52–53; Kellerman, *Swim*, 80–92; Dalton, *How to Swim*, 17–19.

15. Lynn Sherr, *Swim: Why We Love the Water* (New York: 2012), 44; Kellerman, *Swim*, 13–15, 38–53, esp. 37, 53; Annette Kellermann, *Physical Beauty: How to Keep It* (New York: 1918), 83–90; William Wilson, *The Swimming Instructor: A Treatise on the Arts of Swimming and Diving* (London: 1883), v, 1, 5.

16. G. R. Crone, ed., *The Voyages of Cadamosto and Other Documents on Western Africa in the Second Half of the Fifteenth Century* (London, 1937), 34, 37; Hugh Crow, *Memoirs of the Late Captain Hugh Crow, of Liverpool; Comprising a Narrative of his Life* (London: 1830), 39–40.

17. Pieter de Marees, *Description and Historical Account of the Gold Kingdom of Guinea*, Albert Van Dantzig and Adam Jones, trans. (1602; New York: 1987), 26, 32, esp. 186–187; Hair, Jones, and Law, eds., *Barbot on Guinea*, 2:532; Rattray, *Ashanti*, 63; Pieter Van den Broecke, *Pieter Van den Broecke's Journal of Voyages to Cape Verde, Guinea and Angola, 1605–1612*, J. D. La Fleur, trans. (1634; London, 2000), 37.

18. Adam Jones, ed., *German Sources for West African History, 1599–1669* (Weisbaden: 1983), 12; Thomas J. Hutchinson, *Ten Years' Wanderings Among the Ethiopians: With Sketches of the Manners and Customs of the Civilized and Uncivilized Tribes, from Senegal to Gaboon* (London: 1861), 90, 228–229, 309; Francisco Travassos Valdez, *Six Years of a Traveller's Life in Western Africa*, 2 vols. (London: 1861), 1:212; de Azurara, *Chronicle*, 2:227–228; Charles Jones Stewart, "The Diary of Chas. J. Stewart: New York to Monrovia, West Coast Africa," 50; Hair, Jones, and Law, *Barbot on Guinea*, 2:532, Zamba, *The Life and Adventures of Zamba, an African Negro King; and His Experience of Slavery in South Carolina*, in Peter Neilson, ed. (London: 1847), 169; Thompson, *Palm Land*, 184; M. French-Sheldon, *Sultan to Sultan: Adventures Among the Masai and Other Tribes of East Africa* (London: 1892), 36, 76; James Holman, *Travels in Madeira Sierra Leone, Teneriffe, St. Jago, Cape Coast, Fernando Po, Princes Island, Etc.* (London: 1840), 192–193; D. B. Waters, "How the Krooboys Come Home After a Year's Work," *The Graphic: An Illustrated Weekly Newspaper*, July 7, 1900.

19. Edward Sullivan, *Rambles and Scrambles in North and South America* (London: 1852), 284; George Pinckard, *Notes on the West Indies: Written During the Expedition Under the Command of the Late General Sir Ralph Abercromby: Including Observations on the Island of Barbadoes, and the Settlements Captured by the British Troops, upon the Coast of Guiana*, 3 vols. (London: 1806), 2:148–149; Stedman, *Expedition*, 1:11. Chapter 3 considers how comparisons to aquatic creatures were used to racialize African-descended people.

20. Horatio Bridge, *Journal of an African Cruiser: Comprising Sketches of the Canaries, the Cape Verds, Liberia, Madeira, Sierra Leone, and Other Places of Interest on the West Coast of Africa* (New York: 1853), 76–77, 103–104, 174; Robin Law, ed., *The English in West Africa, 1681–1683: The Local Correspondence of the Royal African Company of England, 1681–1699*, 3 vols. (Oxford: 1997), 1:97; Holman, *Travels*, 231–232, 381, 414; Elizabeth Helen Melville, *A Residence at Sierra Leone. Described from a Journal kept on the spot, and from Letters Written to Friends at Home* (1849; London, 1968), 197; Hair, Jones, and Law, *Barbot on Guinea*, 2:531; Peter C. W. Gutkind, "Trade and Labor in Early Precolonial African History: The Canoemen of Southern Ghana," in Catherine Coquery-Vidrovitch and Paul Lovejoy, eds., *The Workers of the African Trade* (Beverly Hills: 1985), 32.

21. A. B. Ellis, *The Tshi-Speaking Peoples of the Gold Coast of West Africa* (London: 1887), 44–48; Mary H. Kingsley, *Travels in West Africa: Congo Français, Corisco and Cameroons* (London: 1897), 448, 513; Martha G. Anderson, "Enchanted Rivers: True Stories About Water Spirits from the Niger Delta," in Henry John Drewal, ed., *Sacred Waters: Arts for Mami Wata and Other Divinities in Africa and the Diaspora* (Bloomington: 2008), 27–48, esp. 30. For spiritual beliefs, see Adam Jones, ed., *Olfert Dapper's Description of Benin (1668)* (Madison: 1998), 26; Law, *Ouidah*, 88, 93, 95, 152; Melville J. Herskovits, *Dahomey: An Ancient West*

African Kingdom, 2 vols. (Evanston: 1967), 1:194–205; John Duncan, *Travels in Western Africa, in 1845 & 1846, Comprising a Journey from Whydah, Through the Kingdom of Dahomey, to Adofoodia, in the Interior*, 2 vols. (1847; New York: 1967), 1:126; Bosman, *Accurate Description*, 368a, 383; A. B. Ellis, *The Ewe-Speaking Peoples of the Slave Coast of West Africa* (London: 1890), 63–64.

22. Richard Jobson, *The Golden Trade: or; a Discovery of the River Gambra and the Golden Trade of the Aethiopians* (London: 1623), 91; F. Harrison Rankin, *The White Man's Grave: A Visit to Sierra Leone in 1834*, 2 vols. (London: 1836), 2:200.

23. French-Sheldon, *Sultan to Sultan*, 76. See Chapter 3 for racialization of aquatics.

24. De Marees, *Gold Kingdom*, 186–187; Rattray, *Ashanti*, 63; William Snelgrave, *A New Account of Some Parts of Guinea and the Slave-Trade* (London: 1734), 101–104; Holman, *Travels*, 297; Samuel P. Verner, *Pioneering in Central Africa* (Richmond: 1903), 412–413; Hair, Jones, and Law, *Barbot on Guinea*, 2:532, 501n16, 639–640; Crow, *Memoirs*, 44; John Adams, *Remarks on the Country Extending from Cape Palmas to the River Congo, Including Observations on the Manners and Customs of the Inhabitants* (1823; London: 1966), 138–139.

25. Hair, Jones, and Law, *Barbot on Guinea*, 2:501n16; Ligon, *Barbadoes*, 53; John Lawson, *A New Voyage to Carolina* (Chapel Hill: 1709), 158; Octavia V. Rogers, *Albert, The House of Bondage, or, Charlotte Brooks and Other Slaves, Original and Life Like, As They Appeared in Their Old Plantation and City Slave Life* (New York: 1890), 24; Belle Kearney, *A Slaveholder's Daughter* (New York: 1900), 37–38; Stedman, *Expedition*, 2:323, 359.

26. Henry Francis Fynn, *The Diary of Henry Francis Fynn: Compiled from Original Sources*, James Stuart, ed. (Pietermaritzburg: 1950), v, 81–82; David Northrup, *Africa's Discovery of Europe, 1450–1850* (Oxford: 2002), 14.

27. For Muslim slaves, see Gomez, *Country Marks*, 71–72, 75, 79, 85; Mary C. Karasch, *Slave Life in Rio de Janeiiro, 1808–1850* (Princeton: 1987), 26, 90, 215, 219, 219n15, 225, 284–285, 322; João José Reis, *Slave Rebellion in Brazil: The Muslim Uprising of 1835 in Bahia*, Arthur Brakel, trans. (1986; Baltimore: 1995), 93, 98–101, 105–110; Sultana Afroz, "The Jihad of 1831–1832: The Misunderstood Baptist Rebellion in Jamaica," *Journal of Muslim Minority Affairs* 21, no. 2 (2001): 227–243; Alberto da Costa e Silva, "Buying and Selling Korans in Nineteenth-Century Rio de Janeiro," *Slavery and Abolition*, 22, no. 1, (2001): 72–82; Sylvaine A. Diouf, *Servants of Allah: African Muslims Enslaved in the Americas* (New York: 1998); Yacine Daddi Addoun and Paul E. Lovejoy, "The Arabic Manuscript of Muhammad Kaba Saghanughu of Jamaica, c. 1820," in Annie Paul, ed., *Creole Concerns: Essays in Honour of Kamau Brathwaite*, (Kingston: 2005); Yacine Daddi Addoun and Paul E. Lovejoy, "Muhammad Kaba Saghanughu and the Muslim Community of Jamaica," in Paul E. Lovejoy, ed. *Slavery on the Frontiers of Islam* (Princeton: 2004); Yacine Daddi Addoun and Paul E. Lovejoy, "The Arabic Manuscript of Muhammad Kaba Saghanughu of Jamaica," in Annie Paul and Kamau Brathwaite, eds., *Caribbean Culture: Soundings on Kamau Brathwaite* (Kingston: 2007), 313–341; Omar Ibn Said, *A Muslim American Slave: The Life of Omar Ibn Said*, Ala Alryyes, trans. (Madison: 2011).

28. William Hubert Miller, *Nassau, Bahamas, 1823–4: The Diary of a Physician from the United States Visiting the Island of Providence* (Nassau: 1960), 26, 34, 41; quoted in Peter Earle, *Treasure Hunt: Shipwreck, Diving, and the Quest for Treasure in an Age of Heroes* (New York: 2008), 11; Daniel McKinnen, *A Tour Through the British West Indies, in the Years 1802 and 1803* (London: 1804), 142–143.

29. J. G. Clinkscales, *On the Old Plantation: Reminiscences of his Childhood* (Spartanburg: 1916), 16–19; Stedman, *Expedition*, 1:81–82, 84, 2:341; Virginia Bernhard, *Slaves and Slaveholders in Bermuda, 1616–1782* (Columbia: 1999), 23, 107, 178; Cynric R. Williams, *A Tour Through the Island of Jamaica: From the Western to the Eastern End in the Year 1823* (London: 1827), 7–9, 26–29, 35–36. Also see Charles E. Whitehead, *Camp-Fires of the Everglades; or Wild Sports in the South* (1860; Gainesville: 1991), 11; and see James Battle Avirett, *The Old Plantation: How We Lived in Great House and Cabin* (New York: 1901), viii, 91; Nina Hill Robinson, *Aunt Dice: The Story of a Faithful Slave* (Nashville: 1897), 28; John S. Wise, *The End of an Era* (Boston: 1899), 52; Zamba, *Life and Adventures*, 1, 86, 168–170.

30. Robert Robinson, "description of Bermuda," July 1687, CO 40/1A, fol. 103; Philip Freneau, "Account of the Island of Bermuda," [May 10, 1778] in *The Bermuda Historical Quarterly* 5, no. 2 (April, May, June 1948), 98–99; Michael J. Jarvis, *In the Eye of All Trade: Bermuda, Bermudians, and Maritime Atlantic World, 1680–1783* (Chapel Hill: 2010), 284, 578n50; Michael J. Jarvis, "The Binds of the Anxious Mariner: Patriarchy, Paternalism, and the Maritime Culture of Eighteenth-Century Bermuda," *Journal of Early Modern History* 14, no. 1/2 (2010): 84; Bernhard, *Slaves and Slaveholders*, 23–25.

31. Bernhard, *Slaves and Slaveholders*, 18–19, 23–25, 152, 273–274; J. H. Lefroy, *Memorials of the Discovery and Early Settlement of the Bermudas or Somers Islands, 1515–1687*, 2 vols. (London: 1877), 1:56–61, 72, esp. 115–116; Vernon A. Ives, ed., *The Rich Papers: Letters from Bermuda, 1615–1646* (London: 1984), 16n4; Ligon, *Barbadoes*, 52; David Buisseret, ed., *Jamaica in 1687: The Taylor Manuscript at the National Library* (Kingston: 2008), 105; Jarvis, *Eye of All Trade*, 102–103, 111–112, 155–156, 284; Bernhard, *Slaves and Slaveholders*, 23–25 90, 98.

32. Robert Robinson, "description of Bermuda," July 1687, CO 40/1A, fol. 103; Freneau, "Account of the Island of Bermuda," 98–99; John Hope, "description of Bermuda," 1722, CO 37/10, fol. 218; Jarvis, *Eye of All Trade*, 284.

33. Herbert S. Klein, *Atlantic Slave Trade* (Cambridge: 1999), 176–177.

34. Ligon, *Barbadoes*, 15–16, 53; Stephanie M. H. Camp, *Closer to Freedom: Enslaved Women and Everyday Resistance in the Plantation South* (Chapel Hill: 2004), 60–92. Ligon's admiration of a nude Barbadian swimmer discussed in Chapter 3 perhaps explains his request that she receive preferential treatment.

35. Holman, *Travels*, 297; de Marees, *Gold Kingdom*, 187; Hair, Jones, and Law, *Barbot on Guinea*, 2:501n16; Ligon, *Barbadoes*, 53; A. C. de C. M. Saunders, *A Social History of Slaves and Freemen in Portugal, 1441–1555* (Cambridge: 1982), 39–40.

36. Cynric Williams, *Jamaica*, 296; Hall, ed., *Miserable Slavery*, 20, 29; Camp, *Closer to Freedom*, 60–92. For examples of scholarship on sexual abuse, see Wilma King, *Stolen Childhood: Slave Youth in Nineteenth-Century America* (1995; Bloomington: 2011), 17–18, 41–41, 178–179, 247–248, 254–255, 270–273; Jennifer Morgan, *Laboring Women: Reproduction and Gender in New World Slavery* (Philadelphia: 2004); Marie Jenkins Schwartz, *Born in Bondage: Growing Up Enslaved in the Antebellum South* (Cambridge: 2000), 44–46, 154, 172–174, 188–189, 206–207; Marie Jenkins Schwartz, *Birthing a Slave: Motherhood and Medicine in the Antebellum South* (Cambridge: 2006), 26–27, 314–315; Bernard Moitt, *Women and Slavery in the French Antilles, 1635–1848* (Bloomington: 2001), 99–100; Barbara Bush, *Slave Women in Caribbean Society, 1650–1838* (Bloomington: 1990), 110–118; Sweet, *Recreating Africa*, 72–74; Walter Hawthorne, *From Africa to Brazil: Culture, Identity, and an Atlantic Slave Trade, 1600–*

1800 (New York: 2010), 173–174, 191–206. Harriet Jacobs explained how rape caused slave girls to understand their predicaments. Harriet Ann Jacobs, *Incidents in the Life of a Slave Girl* (Boston: 1861), 45–48.

37. N. T. Hall, *Slave Society in the Danish West Indies: St. Thomas, St. John, and St Croix.* (Mona: 1992), 128–138; Jorge Chinea, "A Quest for Freedom: The Immigration of Maritime Maroons into Puerto Rico, 1656–1800," *Journal of Caribbean History* 31 (1997): 51–87; Jerome S. Handler, "Escaping Slavery in a Caribbean Plantation Society: Maronage in Barbados, 1650s–1830s," *New West Indian Guide* 71 (1997): 183–225; Hilary Beckles, "From Land to Sea: Runaway Barbados Slaves and Servants, 1630–1700," *Slavery and Abolition* 6, no. 3 (December 1985), 79–94. For an overview of resistance, see Gad J. Heuman, *Out of the House of Bondage: Runaways, Resistance and Maroonage in Africa and the New World* (London: 1986); Michael Craton, *Testing the Chains: Resistance to Slavery in the British West Indies* (Ithaca: 1982); John Hope Franklin and Loren Schweninger, *Runaway Slaves: Rebels on the Plantation* (New York, 1999), 98–109.

38. N. Hall, *Danish West Indies*, 124–138, esp. 135; David Turnbull, *Travels in the West Indies: Cuba; with Notices of Porto Rico, and the Slave Trade* (London: 1840), 565; Christian Georg Andreas Oldendorp, *A Caribbean Mission: History of the Mission of the Evangelical Brethren on the Caribbean Islands of St. Thomas, St. Croix, and St. John* (1777; Ann Arbor: 1987), 234; Chinea, "Quest for Freedom."

39. Clinkscales, *Old Plantation*, 16–19; quoted in Ira Berlin, Barbara J. Fields, Steven F. Miller, Joseph P. Reidy, and Leslie S. Rowland, eds. *Free at Last, A Documentary History of Slavery, Freedom and the Civil War* (New York: 1992), 52; John Andrew Jackson, *The Experience of a Slave in South Carolina* (London: 1862), 23–24; Allen Parker, *Recollections of Slavery Times* (Worcester: 1895), 29, 47–48; Isaac Johnson, *Slavery Days in Old Kentucky* (Ogdensburg: 1901), 29–30.

40. Benjamin Drew, *A North-Side View of Slavery. The Refugee: or the Narratives of Fugitive Slaves in Canada* (Boston: 1856), 19, 25, 105, 107, 206, 215, 221; North Carolina Narratives, vol. 11, part 2—Hattie Rogers, 227–228. Also see Frederick Douglass, *Narrative of the Life of Frederick Douglass, an American Slave* (Boston: 1845), 85; Solomon Bayley, *A Narrative of Some Remarkable Incidents in the Life of Solomon Bayley Formerly a Slave in the State of Delaware* (London: 1825), 5–6; Moses Roper, *Narrative of the Adventures and Escape of Moses Roper from American Slavery* (Philadelphia: 1838), 64, 71; Leonard Black, *The Life and Sufferings of Leonard Black, A Fugitive From Slavery* (New Bedford: 1847), 28; Charles Ball, *Fifty Years in Chains; or, The Life of an American Slave* (New York: 1859), 310–312, 338–339, 343, 345, 352; J. D. Green, *Narrative of the Life of J. D. Green, a Runaway Slave, from Kentucky* (Huddersfield: 1864), 32–33.

41. James W. C. Pennington, *A Narrative of Events of the Life of J. H. Banks, an Escaped Slave, from the Cotton State, Alabama, in America* (Liverpool: 1861), 37–41; Hall, ed., *Miserable Slavery*, 54–55; William Wells Brown, *Narrative of William W. Brown, An American Slave* (London: 1849), 58–60; Bayley, *Narrative*, 5–7; James Lindsay Smith, *Autobiography of James L. Smith, Including, Also, Reminiscences of Slave Life, Recollections of the War, Education of Freedmen, Causes of the Exodus, Etc.* (Norwich: 1881), 16–20. For domestic slave trade, see Johnson, *Soul by Soul*; Steven Deyle, *Carry Me Back: The Domestic Slave Trade in American Life* (Oxford: 2005).

42. Douglass, *My Bondage*, 122–123; Douglass, *Narrative*, 22–24; Kenneth S. Greenberg, *Honor & Slavery: Lies, Duels, Noses, Masks, Dressing as a Woman, Gifts, Strangers, Humanitarianism, Death, Slave Rebellions, the Proslavery Argument, Baseball, Hunting, and Gambling in*

the Old South (Princeton: 1996), esp. xi–xii, 7–9, 11, 34–35, 80–82; Jack R. Williams, *Dueling in the Old South: Vignettes of Social History* (1980; College Station: 2000).

Chapter 2

1. De Marees, *Gold Kingdom*, 26; Hair, Jones, and Law, *Barbot on Guinea*, 2:501n16, 532, 640; Bosman, *Accurate Description*, 121–122; Jones, *German Sources*, 109; William Smith, *A New Voyage to Guinea: Describing the Customs, Manners, Soil, Climate, Habits, Buildings, Education, Manual Arts, Agriculture, Trade, Employment, Languages, Ranks of Distinction, Habitations, Diversions, Marriages, and Whatever else is Memorable among the Inhabitants* (1774; London: 1967), 210. For nursing, see Patrick Manning, *Slavery and African Life: Occidental, Oriental, and African Slave Trades* (Cambridge: 1990), 55.

2. Benjamin Franklin Prentiss, *The Blind African Slave, or Memoirs of Boyrereau Brinch, Nick-named Jeffrey Brace. Containing an Account of the Kingdom of Bow-Woo, in the Interior of Africa* (St. Albans: 1810), 70, 96, 124, esp. 68–69; Thomas Winterbottom, *An Account of the Native Africans in the Neighborhood of Sierra Leone*, 2 vols. (London: 1803), 2:256; Kingsley, *West Africa*, 448; Vickers with Walsh, *Young Men*, 3. For Brinch, see Dickson D. Bruce, *The Origins of African American Literature, 1680–1865* (Charlottesville: 2001), 98–102.

3. Rankin, *White Man's Grave*, 2:200; Henry Stanley, *Through the Dark Continent: Or The Source of the Nile Around the Great Lakes of Equatorial Africa and Down the Livingston River to the Atlantic*, 2 vols. (New York: 1878), 1:172, 260, esp. 467–468.

4. Richard Burton, *Wanderings in West Africa*, 2 vols. bound as one (1863; New York: 1991), 1:245; Canneau, *Log Book*, 138.

5. Canneau, *Log Book*, 136, 138: de Marees, *Gold Kingdom*, 23, 39, 52, 68, 73; Hair, Jones, and Law, *Barbot on Guinea*, 2:512; George Tams, *Visit to the Portuguese Possessions in South-Western Africa*, 2 vols. (New York: 1845), 1:103–104; Olaudah Equiano, *The Interesting Narrative of the Life of Olaudah Equiano, or Gustavus Vassa, the African, Written by Himself*, 2 vols. (London: 1789), 1:13, 31–33, 40; Isert, *Letters*, 115; Stanley, *Dark Continent*, 1:172, 260, esp. 467–468: Thomas Bluett, *Some Memoirs of the Life of Job* (London: 1734), 43; Caillié, *Timbuctoo*, 1:163, 351: Van den Broecke, *Journal*, 38, 99; Bosman, *Accurate Description*, 122; William Smith, *New Voyage*, 211; Nicolas Villault, *A Relation of the Coast of Africk Called Guinee* (London: 1670), 156, Ludewig Ferdinand Rømer, *A Reliable Account of the Coast of Guinea* (1760; New York: 2000), 237; Ellis, *Tshi-Speaking Peoples*, 232–233; Alfred Ellis, *The Yoruba-Speaking Peoples of the Slave Coast* (1894; New York: 1970), 152–153.

6. Hair, Jones, and Law, *Barbot on Guinea*, 2:532; George Thompson, *The Palm Land or West Africa, Illustrated: Being a History of Missionary Labors and Travels* (London: 1858), 184; Réné Caillié, *Travels Through Central Africa to Timbuctoo; and Across the Great Desert, to Morocco; Performed in the Years 1824–1828*, 2 vols. (1830; London: 1992), 2:5–6; Jones, *German Sources*, 219; William Smith, *New Voyage*, 210; John Matthews, *A Voyage to the River Sierra-Leone: Containing an Account of the Trade and Productions of the Country* (London: 1788), 51.

7. King, *Stolen Childhood*, 107–115; Nick Ford and David Brown, *Surfing and Social Theory: Experience, Embodiment and Narrative of the Dream Glide* (London: 2006), esp. 3, 7–14; Michael A. Coronel, "Fanti Canoe Decoration," in *African Arts* 13, no. 1 (November 1979), 54.

8. See note 32 for liminality.

9. Vance Packard, *Our Endangered Children: Growing Up in a Changing World* (Boston: 1983), 64–66; Jacqueline S. Reinier, *From Virtue to Character: American Childhood, 1775–1850* (London: 1996), 60–61; my observation of West African children in 1998 and 1999.

10. Bernard Mergen, *Play and Playthings: A Reference Guide* (Westport: 1982), 3, 22; Vickers with Walsh, *Young Men*, 3.

11. French-Sheldon, *Sultan to Sultan*, 75–76.

12. Harms, *Games Against Nature*, 28.

13. Equiano, *Narrative*, esp. 1:54, 79; Rattray, *Ashanti*, 61–65; Verner, *Central Africa*, 122, 126, 222, 306, 413.

14. Rattray, *Ashanti*, 61–65.

15. Mungo Park, *Travels in the Interior Districts of Africa: Performed Under the Direct Patronage of the African Association, in the Years 1795, 1796, and 1797* (1799; New York: 1971), 71–72, 210–211; Mungo Park, *Travels of Mungo Park* containing *Book One, The First Journey: Travels in the Interior districts of Africa. and Book Two, The Second Journey: The Journal of a Mission to the Interior of Africa in the Year 1805* (London: 1954), 53–54, 161, 336; Verner, *Central Africa*, 126.

16. Park, *Travels*, esp. 319–320, 352, 365–366, 368–372.

17. John H. Weeks, *Among the Congo Cannibals:* Experiences, Impressions, and Adventures During a Thirty Years' Sojourn Amongest the Boloki and Other Congo Tribes (London: 1913), 99, 109, 333; E. J. Glave, *In Savage Africa: Or Six Years of Adventure in Congo-Land* (New York: 1892), 129, 195, 200; H. E. Crocker, "A Canoe Voyage on the Congo," *Journal of the Royal African Society* 42 (April 1943): 71; Stanley, *Dark Continent*, 1:172, 260, esp. 467–468; Dixon Denham, Hugh Clapperton, Walter Oudney, and Abraham V. Salamé, *Narrative of Travels and Discoveries in Northern and Central Africa in the Years 1822, 1823, and 1824*, 2 vols. (London: 1826), 2:4–5, 188–190; Caillié, *Timbuctoo*, 2:6, 31, 35–36.

18. Harms, *Games Against Nature*, 22–24, 28–56; Glave, *Savage Africa*, 117, 194–195, 199–200, 206, 238–239; Weeks, *Congo Cannibals*, 98–99, 109, 333; Verner, *Central Africa*, 126; Kingsley, *West Africa*, 280.

19. Elisée Soumonni, "Lacustrine Villages of South Benin as Refuges from the Slave Trade," in Sylviane Anna Diouf, ed., *Fighting the Slave Trade: West African Strategies* (Athens: 2003), 3–14, esp. 4, 6; author's observations in 1998; David and Charles Livingston, *Narratives of Expedition to the Zambezi* (New York: 1866), 413–414; Richard Francis Burton and Verney Lovett Cameron, *To the Gold Coast for Gold: A Personal Narrative*, 2 vols. (London: 1883), 2:149–153.

20. Verney Lovett Cameron, *Across Africa*, 2 vols. (New York: 1877), 2:163, 166; *The Illustrated London News, An Illustrated Weekly Newspaper*, April 22, 1876; Glave, *Savage Africa*, 199–200.

21. Peter Leonard, *Records of a Voyage to the Western Coast of Africa, in His Majesty's Ship Dryad* (Edinburgh: 1833), 138–143, 233–235; Richard Drake, *Revelations of a Slave Smuggler: Being the Autobiography of Capt. Rich'd Drake, An African Trader for Fifty Years—From 1807–1857* (Northbrook: 1972), 59–62; Holman, *Travels*, 104.

22. Valdez, *Traveller's Life*, 2:44–45; Tony Hodges and Malyn Newitt, *São Tomé and Prícipe: From Plantation Colony to Microstate* (Boulder: 1988), 59–60; Jan Vansina, "Quilombos on São Tome or in Search of Original Sources," *History of Africa*, 23 (1996): 456–457; Fernando Castelo-Branco, "Subsidios para o Estudo do Angolares de S. Tomé," *Studia,*

(1973), 149–159; Robert Garfield, *A History of São Tomé Island, 1470–1655: The Key to Guinea* (San Francisco: 1992), 121–122. There is speculation that Angolares were runaway slaves. For other communities, see William Allen, *Accounts of Shipwreck and Other Disasters at Sea: Designed to be Interesting and useful to Mariners* (Brunswick: 1823), 176–178; Isert, *Letters*, 176–177.

23. William Young, *An Account of the Black Charibs in the Island of St. Vincent's with the Charib Treaty of 1773* (London: 1795), 6–8; Charles Shepard, *An Historical Account of the Island of Saint Vincent* (London: 1831), 20–27; Christopher Taylor, *The Black Carib Wars: Freedom, Survival, and the Making of the Garifuna* (Jackson: 2012).

24. Jones, *German Sources*, 98, 109; Ben Finney, "Surfboarding in West Africa," *Wiener Volkerkundliche Mitteilungen*, 5 (1962): 41–42; C. Béart, "Jeux et Jouets de L'Oust African: VII. Le Surf-Riding," *Mémoires de L'Institut Français D'Afrique Noire* 1, no. 42 (1955): 329–331; Jean Fouch, "Surf-Riding sur la Côte d'Afrique," *Notes Africaines: Bulletin D'Information et de Correspondence de l'Institut Francais d'Afrique Noir*" 42 (April 1942): 50–53. For Oceanian surfing, see Finney and Houston, *Surfing*, 24–25, 97; Beaglehole, *Captain James Cook*, 3:1, 628, 3:2, 1164–1165; Hawkesworth, *Account of the Voyages*, 1:475. Hawaiians used oral traditions and pictographs to document surfing centuries before Europeans did.

25. Finney and Houston, *Surfing*, 24–25; Ben Finney, "Surfboarding in Oceania: Its Pre-European Distribution," *Wiener Velkerkundliche Mitteilungen*, 2 (1959): 23–36.

26. Jack London, "Riding the South Seas Surf," *Woman's Home Companion*, 34, no. 10 (October 1907), 9–10. London changed "black Mercury" to "brown." Jack London, *The Cruise of the Snark* (New York: 1911), 75–90, esp. 76.

27. Jones, *German Sources*, 98, 109; Hair, Jones, and Law, *Barbot on Guinea*, 2:532.

28. James Edward Alexander, *Narrative of a Voyage of Observation Among the Colonies of Western Africa*, 2 vols. (London, 1837), 1:192.

29. Hutchinson, *Ten Years' Wanderings*, 227–228.

30. For Western accounts of Hawaiian surfing, see Twain, *Roughing It*, "Chap. LXXIII"; Charles Nordhoff, "Hawaii-Nei," *Harper's New Monthly Magazine* 47, no. 279 (August 1873): 399, 402; Finney and Houston, *Surfing*, 21, 97–113; Moser, *Pacific Passages*, 49–131.

31. Honor will be discussed in Chapter 4.

32. Greg Dening, *Islands and Beaches: Discourse on a Silent Land: Marquesas, 1774–1880* (Honolulu: 1980), esp. 3, 20, 31–32, 151, 157–158; Pearson, "Littoral Society," 356; Ford and Brown, *Surfing and Social Theory*, 7–8.

33. Vickers with Walsh, *Young Men*, esp. 3, 7–60, 248; Pearson, "Littoral Society," 353–373; Bolster, "Putting the Ocean"; Ford and Brown, *Surfing and Social Theory*, 7; Corbin, *Lure of the Sea*. For "contact Zone," see Mary Louise Pratt, "Arts of the Contact Zone" *Profession* 91 (1991): 33–40; Mary Louise Pratt, *Imperial Eyes: Travel Writing and Transculturation* (London: 1992), 7. For multiracial coastal communities, see Pernille Ipsen, *Daughters of the Trade: Atlantic Slavers and Interracial Marriage on the Gold Coast* (Philadelphia: 2015); George E. Brooks, *Eurafricans in Western Africa: Commerce, Social Status, Gender, and Religious Observance from the Sixteenth to the Eighteenth Century* (Athens: 2003); Peter Mark, *"Portuguese Style" and Luso-African Identity: Precolonial Senegambia, Sixteenth-Nineteenth Centuries* (Bloomington: 2002). The topic of children at the forefront of cultural encounters requires consideration.

34. Beaglehole, *Captain James Cook*, 3.2:1164–1165, 3.1:628; Hawkesworth, *Account of the Voyages*, 1:475; Warren Henry, *The Confessions of a Tenderfoot "Coaster": A Trader's Chronicle of Life on the West African Coast* (London: 1927), 109. Twentieth-century white Americans

increasingly valued beaches, transforming them into segregated spaces. Andrew W. Karhl, *The Land Was Ours: African American Beaches from Jim Crow to the Sunbelt South* (Cambridge: 2012).

35. Prentiss, *Blind African Slave*, 70. For play, see Wilma King, *Stolen Childhood: Slave Youth in Nineteenth-Century America* (1995; Bloomington: 2011), 107–115; J. Huizinga, *Homo Ludens: A Study of the Play-Element in Culture* (London: 1998), 1–27; Packard, *Endangered Children*, 65; Steven Mintz, *Huck's Raft: A History of American Childhood* (Cambridge: 2004), 18–19, 104–108; Kellerman, *Swim*, 36, 193–213.

36. Smallwood, *Saltwater Slavery*, 101–121; Marcus Rediker, *The Slave Ship: A Human History* (New York: 2007), 263–307, Alexander X. Byrd, *Captives and Voyagers: Black Migrants Across the Eighteenth-Century British World* (Baton Rouge: 2008), 32–56; Sidney W. Mintz and Richard Price, *The Birth of African American Culture: An Anthropological Perspective* (Boston: 1976), 42–51.

37. James Fairhead, Tim Geysbeek, Svend E. Holsoe, and Melissa Leach, eds., *African-American Exploration in West Africa: Four Nineteenth-Century Diaries* (Bloomington: 2003), 96, 98–99.

38. Anna Maria Falconbridge, *Narrative of Two Voyages to the River Sierra Leone During the Years 1791–1792–1793*; Christopher Fyye, ed. (1794; Liverpool: 2000), 215; Hair, Jones, and Law, *Barbot on Guinea*, 2:640. Also see Ligon, *Barbadoes*, 53.

39. Anonymous, *Narrative of Voyages to the Guinea Coast and the West Indies, 1713/4–1716, Followed by Items of West Indian News from Barbados, 1722–1723/4*, British Library, Add. MS. 39946, 8–9.

40. Matthews, *Voyage to the River Sierra-Leone*, 50; Alexander Falconbridge, *An Account of the Slave Trade on the Coast of Africa* (London: 1792), 30, 52. For example, also see Crow, *Memoirs*, 264–267; William Smith, *New Voyage*, 239; John Atkins, *A Voyage to Guinea, Brasil and the West Indies* (London: 1736), 46; Bosman, *Accurate Description*, 281–282, 452; Winterbottom, *Native Africans*, 2:256; Park, *Interior Districts*, 6; Rediker, *Slave Ship*, 37–40; Skertchly, *Dahomey*, 6.

41. Herman Melville, *Moby Dick; or The Whale* (New York: 1902), 255; Drake, *Revelations*, 49, 50, 88; *Norwich Packet, or, the Country Journal*, April 14, 1785; Crow, *Memoirs*, esp. 265–266; Bosman, *Accurate Description*, 281–282; Falconbridge, *Slave Trade*, 30–31; Rediker, *Slave Ship*, 37–40, 151, 368n24.

42. Snelgrave, *New Account*, 102–104, 177–178; Crow, *Memoirs*, 44; Falconbridge, *Slave Trade*, 30–31.

43. Anonymous, "Natural History of Sharks, from Dr. Goldsmith and Other Eminent Writers," *Universal Magazine of Knowledge and Pleasure* 43 (1778): 231–233; Nigel Tattersfield, ed., *The Forgotten Trade: Comprising the Log of the Daniel and Henry of 1700 and Accounts of the Slave Trade From the Minor Ports of England 1698–1725* (New York: 2011), 121, 409n57; Rediker, *Slave Ship*, 39–40; Anderson and Peek, *Ways of the River*. In ports, naval officers fed sharks to discourage their captives from desertion. *Connecticut Gazette*, January 30, 1789; Crow, *Memoirs*, 266; Samuel Jennings, *A Narrative of the Wonderful Deliverance of Samuel Jennings* (Sandwich: 1716), 4; Rediker, *Slave Ship*, 39. Some slavers reportedly used African bodies to catch sharks that were fed to slaves. Tattersfield, *Forgotten Trade*, 121, 409n57.

44. Drake, *Revelations*, 88.

45. For suicide, see Terri L. Snyder, "Suicide, Slavery, and Memory in North America," *Journal of American History* 97, no. 1 (June 2010): 42; Terri L. Snyder, *The Power to Die: Slavery and Suicide in Early North America, 1630–1830* (Chicago: 2015); Daniel E. Walker, "Suicidal Tendencies: African Transmigration in the History and Folklore of the Americas," *The Griot* 18 (1999): 10–15; Gomez, *Country Marks*, 116–131; Walter C. Rucker, *The River Flows On: Black Resistance, Culture, and Identity Formation in Early America* (Baton Rouge: 2006), 52–55.

46. Michael Brown, *African-Atlantic Cultures*, 95–100; T. J. Desche Obi, "Combat and Crossing the Kalunga," in Linda M. Heywood, ed., *Central Africans and Cultural Transformations in the American Diaspora* (Cambridge: 2002), 360.

47. Snyder, "Suicide," 39–62, esp. 40; Rediker, *Slave Ship*, 17–19, 120–121, 151, 212–213, 240, 289–291, 382n18; Stephanie E. Smallwood, *Saltwater Slaves: A Middle Passage from Africa to the American Diaspora* (Cambridge: 2007), 63, 145, 151, 186; Equiano, *Narrative*, 1:73–74; Snelgrave, *New Account*, 190; Drake, *Revelations*, 88, 91, 93; Falconbridge, *Slave Trade*, 30–31; Isert, *Letters on West Africa*, 176; Law, *English in West Africa*, 2:206.

48. Quoted in Rediker, *Slave Ship*, 289–291; *Pennsylvania Gazette*, May 21, 1788; Anonymous, "Natural History of Sharks," 231–232; Rediker, *Slave Ship*, 39–40; Brown, *Reaper's Garden*, 133–144.

49. Hair, Jones, and Law, *Barbot on Guinea*, 2:640; Briton Hammon, *A Narrative of the Uncommon Sufferings, and Surprizing Deliverance of Briton Hammon* (Boston: 1760), 6.

50. I asked several prominent swimmers how they would drown themselves and all reached this conclusion.

51. March 16, 1675, March 31, 1776, and April 17, 1767, Ship's log by Commander Peter Blake of a Royal African Company voyage from England to West Africa, trading along the Guinea coast from Cape Palmas to Accra for tooth, gold and slaves and thence to Barbados and Nevis, PRO T70/1211, 72, 75, 100, 101; "Extract from a Letter Aboard the *Prince of Orange*, April 7, 1737, *Boston News-Letter*, September 15, 1737; *New-York Journal or the Weekly Register*, February 16, 1786; Rediker, *Slave Ship*, 289.

52. Roderick A. McDonald, ed., *Between Slavery and Freedom: Special Magistrate John Anderson's Journal of St. Vincent During the Apprenticeship* (Philadelphia: 2001), 183; Sheila Lambert, ed., *House of Commons Sessional Papers of the Eighteenth Century* (Wilmington: 1975), 82:50; Oldendorp, *Caribbean Mission*, 589.

53. John Treadwell Norton to Lewis Tappan, Farmington, August 9, 1841, and A. F. Williams to Lewis Tappan, Farmington, August 18, 1841, ARC; Austin F. Williams Account Book, 1845–1881, CHS, 12. Marcus Rediker graciously shared these sources. For the *Amistad*, see Marcus Rediker, *The Amistad Rebellion: An Atlantic Odyssey of Slavery and Freedom* (New York: 2012), esp. 211–213; "The Mendian Negroes," *African Repository and Colonial Journal* 17, no. 23 (December 1, 1841): 361–362; John Warner Barber, *A History of the Amistad Captives: Being a Circumstantial Account of the Capture of the Spanish Schooner Amistad, by the Africans on Board* (New Haven: 1840), 4.

54. William Mein to Pierce Butler, May 24, 1803, box 6, folder 27, Plantation Management, Miscellaneous Correspondence 1802–1803, Butler Family Papers (Historical Society of Pennsylvania, Philadelphia); Snyder, "Suicide," 39–40; Gomez, *Country Marks*, 117–118; Malcolm Bell Jr., *Major Butler's Legacy: Five Generations of a Slaveholding Family* (Athens: 1987), 132; Walter Charlton Hartridge, ed., *Letters of Robert MacKay to His Wife: Written from Ports in America and England, 1795–1816* (Athens: 2010), 254n8.

55. Schwartz, *Born in Bondage*, 101, 130.

56. Solomon Northup, *Twelve Years a Slave: Narrative of Solomon Northup, a Citizen of New-York, Kidnapped in Washington City in 1841, and Rescued in 1853* (Auburn: 1853), 137; George P. Rawick, ed., *The American Slave: A Composite Autobiography, Supplement*, series 1, vol. 1—Alabama Narratives (Westport: 1972), 112; Buisseret, *Taylor Manuscript*, 294; McDonald, *Slavery and Freedom*, 183; William Dickson, *Letters on Slavery. To which is Added, Addresses to the Whites, and to the Free Negroes of Barbadoes* (London: 1789), 29; Schwartz, *Born in Bondage*, 101, 130.

57. Stedman, *Expedition*, 1:11–12, 106, 158; Frederick Douglass, *My Bondage and My Freedom* (New York: 1855), 33–37, 40, 42, 60, 65, 70; David W. Blight, ed., *A Slave No More: Two Men Who Escaped to Freedom, Including Their Own Narratives of Emancipation* (New York: 2007), 171, 175–176; Charles L. Perdue Jr., Thomas E. Barden, and, Robert K. Phillips, eds. *Weevils in the Wheat: Interviews with Virginia Ex-Slaves* (Charlottesville: 1976), 325.

58. Stedman, *Expedition*, 1:11–12, 2:323; John August Waller, *A Voyage in the West Indies: Containing Various Observations made During a Residence in Barbadoes, and Several of the Leward Islands; with some Notices and Illustrations Relative to the City of Paramarabo, in Surinam* (London: 1820), 1–3; Thomas Ewbank, *Life in Brazil; or, A Journal of a Visit to the Land of the Cocoa and the Palm* (New York: 1856), 249, 362; Maria Graham, *Journal of a Voyage to Brazil*, 155–156; McKinnen, *British West Indies*, 9.

59. Prentiss, *Blind African Slave*, 68–72, 124, 196.

60. For enslaved children, see Audra A. Diptee, "African Children in the British Slave Trade During the Late Eighteenth Century," *Slavery & Abolition* 27, no. 2 (2006), 183–196; Paul Lovejoy: "The Children of Slavery: The Transatlantic Phase," *Slavery & Abolition* 27, no. 2 (2006): 197–217, esp. 208; Jerome Teelucksingh, "The 'Invisible Child' in British West Indian Slavery," *Slavery & Abolition* 27, no. 2 (2006): 237–250. For children's role in passing traditions from one generation to the next, see King, *Born in Bondage*.

61. Brown, *Reaper's Garden*, esp. 3, 57; Stedman, *Expedition*, 1:11–12, 64, plates 4, 11, 35; Dawson, "Enslaved Ship Pilot," 87. For spectacles of violence, see Brown, *Reaper's Garden*, esp. 131–144; Saidiya Hartman, *Scenes of Subjection: Terror, Slavery, and Self-Making in Nineteenth-Century America* (Oxford: 1997). Also see Chapter 7.

62. King, *Stolen Childhood*, 169–211; Schwartz, *Born in Bondage*, 124, 167–169. Chapter 10 discusses plantations' waterside location.

63. Sidbury, *Becoming African in America*, esp. 6; Gomez, *Country Marks*. For culture as resistance, see Introduction, note 24.

64. T. J. Desch Obi, *Fighting for Honor: The History of African Martial Art Traditions in the Atlantic World* (Columbia: 2008), 78–82; Paul, "Wrestling Tradition," 29. For perceptions of gouging, see Eliott J. Gorn, " 'Gouge and Bite, Pull Hair and Scratch': The Social Significance of Fighting in the Southern Backcountry," *American Historical Review* 90 (February 1985): 18–43; Tom Parramore, "Gouging in Early North Carolina," *North Carolina Folklore Journal* 22 (May 1974): 55–62; Desch Obi, *Fighting for Honor*, 79–80; Jeff Forret, *Race Relations at the Margins: Slaves and Poor Whites in the Antebellum Southern Countryside* (Baton Rouge: 2006), 161; Bernhard, *Slaves and Slaveholders*, 274–275. Chapter 3 considers how Westerners racialized African swimming.

65. Stacy K. Close, *Elderly Slaves of the Plantation South* (New York: 1997), 14–26; Schwartz, *Born in Bondage*, 117, 123, 124, 143; Sweet, *Recreating Africa*, 69. For parents teaching children to endure bondage, see King, *Stolen Childhood*, 67–80; Deborah Gray White,

Ar'n't I a Woman? Female Slaves in the Plantation South (New York: 1985); Betty Wood, *Women's Work, Men's Work: The Informal Slave Economies of Lowcountry Georgia* (Athens: 1995), 31–34, 40–43; Schwartz, *Born in Bondage;* Herbert S. Klein and Ben Vinson III, *African Slavery in Latin America and the Caribbean* (Oxford: 2007), 169–178; Gail D. Saunders, *Slavery in the Bahamas, 1648–1838* (Nassau: 1985), 109–113; Bernhard, *Slaves and Slaveholders,* 258–261.

66. Gwendolyn Midlo Hall, *Social Control in Slave Plantation Societies: A Comparison of St. Domingue and Cuba* (Baton Rouge: 1996), 17–19, Dunn, *Sugar and Slaves,* 248–249; Dickson, *Letters on Slavery,* 116; Oldendorp, *Caribbean Mission,* 249.

67. Northup, *Twelve Years,* 137, 239; Thomas Chalkley, *A Journal of the Life, Travels and Christian Experiences of Thom. Chalkley* (London: 1818), 54; Jarvis, *Eye of All Trade,* 284, 578n50; Jarvis, "Binds of the Anxious Mariner," 84, 100; Michael J. Jarvis, "Maritime Masters and Seafaring Slaves in Bermuda, 1680–1783," *William and Mary Quarterly* 59, no. 3 (July 2002): 597; Bernhard, *Slaves and Slaveholders,* 18–19, 23–25, 50, 107, 152, 273–274.

68. Bernhard, *Slaves and Slaveholders,* 23–24, 40, 107, 274; Jarvis, *Eye of All Trade,* 102–103.

69. Francis Fedric, *Slave Life in Virginia and Kentucky; or, Fifty Years of Slavery in the Southern States of America* (London: 1863), 1–2; Robert Walsh, *Notice of Brazil in 1828 and 1829,* 2 vols. (Boston: 1831), 1:281.

70. Ligon, *Barbadoes,* 53; Stedman, *Expedition,* 7, 8, 10, 57, 214; Cynric R. Williams, *A Tour Through the Island of Jamaica: From the Western to the Eastern End in the Year 1823* (London: 1827), 296; Dunn, *Sugar and Slaves,* 13–17, 23–24, 152–153, 237–238, 249, 264, 270, 283–284, 286; Gwendolyn M. Hall, *Social Control,* 13–17, 23–24, 152–153; Benjamin Drew, ed., *A North-Side View of Slavery. The Refugee: or the Narratives of Fugitive Slaves in Canada* (Boston: 1856), 221; Albert, *House of Bondage,* 24; Kearney, *Slaveholder's Daughter,* 37–38; Jennifer Morgan, *Laboring Women,* 144–165; Daina Ramey Berry, *Swing the Sickle for the Harvest Is Ripe: Gender and Slavery in Antebellum Georgia* (Urbana: 2007); Michael Craton, *Searching for the Invisible Man: Slavery and Plantation Life in Jamaica* (Cambridge: 1978), 142–143.

71. February 4, 1799, Charles Drayton's Plantation Journals, 1784–1820, Drayton Hall, 228; Close, *Elderly Slaves,* 20; Perdue et al., *Weevils,* 325; Kate E. R. Pickard, *The Kidnapped and the Ransomed: Being the Personal Recollections of Peter Still and His Wife "Vina"* (Syracuse: 1856), 229–230; Chinea, "Quest for Freedom," 57; Eiliza Lucas Pinckney, *The Letterbook of Eiliza Lucas Pinckney, 1739–1762* (Columbia: 1997), 13; Schwartz, *Born in Bondage,* 101; H. C. Bruce, *The New Man: Twenty-Nine Years a Slave, Twenty-Nine Years a Free Man* (1895; Lincoln: 1996), 20; Hall, *Miserable Slavery,* 253.

72. Pickard, *Kidnapped,* 229–230; quoted in John W. Blassingame, *Slave Testimony: Two Centuries of Letters, Speeches, Interviews, and Autobiographies* (Baton Rouge: 1977), 139.

73. B. W. Higman, *Slave Populations of the British Caribbean, 1807–1834* (Baltimore: 1984), 218–223; Peter H. Wood, *Strange New Land: Africans in Colonial America* (Oxford: 2003), 60–72.

74. Kellerman, *Swim,* 53.

75. Pinckard, *West Indies,* 2:149, 318, 373–374, 381.

76. Camp, *Closer to Freedom,* 60–92, esp. 61, 83.

77. Albert, *House of Bondage,* 24–25; *South Carolina Narratives,* vol. 14, part 4—Manda Walker, 170–171.

78. *North Carolina Narratives*, vol. 14, part 1—Bill Crump, 208; Theodore Foulks, *Eighteen Months in Jamaica: With Recollections of the Late Rebellion* (London: 1833), 46; Close, *Elderly Slaves*, 20; Douglass, *My Bondage*, 36, 65; Clinkscales, *Old Plantation*, 26, 35, esp. 17; Perdue, et al., *Weevils*, 325; Pickard, *Kidnapped*, 229–230.

79. Stedman, *Expedition*, 2:376; *North Carolina Narratives*, vol. 14, part 1—Bill Crump, 208; Pinckard, *West Indies*, 2:148–149.

80. Pinckard, *West Indies*, 2:148–150.

81. Cynric Williams, *Jamaica*, 296; Pinckard, *West Indies*, 2:149–150.

82. Stedman, *Expedition*, 1: esp. 81–82, 84, 2:341.

Chapter 3

1. Christopher Marlow and George Chapman, *Hero and Leander: A Poem* (1598; Cheswick: 1821), passim; Homer, J. W. Mackail, trans., *The Odyssey* (London: 1903), 1:147–148; Moser, *Pacific Passages*, 17–47; David Kalakaua, *The Legends and Myths of Hawaii* (New York: 1888); Chauncey Brewster Tinker, trans., *Beowulf* (New York: 1912), 32–35; Sherr, *Swim*, 1–3, 15–20, 163–178; Dawn Elaine Bastian and Judy K. Mitchell, *Handbook of Native American Mythology* (Santa Barbara: 2004); Orme, *British Swimming*, 1–45; "Eora First People Exhibit," Australian National Maritime Museum; "Pacific Cultures Exhibit" and "Indigenous Australia Exhibit," Australian Museum.

2. John Iliffe, *Honour in African History* (Cambridge: 2005), 1–118, esp. 1–8, 11–13, 45, 67–69, 101, 103; T. J. Desch Obi, *Fighting for Honor: The History of African Martial Art Traditions in the Atlantic World* (Columbia: 2008), esp. 11–12, 32, 34, 54, 58–60, 111–121, 213, 239n98; Ras Michael Brown, " 'Walk in the Feenda': West-Central Africans and the Forest in the South Carolina–Georgia Lowcountry," in Linda M. Heywood, ed., *Central Africans and Cultural Transformations in the American Diaspora* (Cambridge: 2002), 306, 308–310, 313–314, 317; Frank Henderson Stewart, *Honor* (Chicago: 1994); Gordon Innes with Bakari Sidibe, eds., *Hunters and Crocodiles: Narratives of a Hunter's Bard* (Sandgate: 1990); Frank A. Salamone, "Gungawa Wrestling as an Ethnic Boundary Marker," in *Afrika und Übersee* 57, no. 3 (1973–1974): 193–202.

3. David D. Gilmore, *Manhood in the Making: Cultural Concepts of Masculinity* (New Haven: 1990), esp. 9–29; Paul Sigrid, "The Wrestling Tradition and Its Social Function," in William J. Baker and James A. Mangan, *Sport in Africa: Essays in Social History* (New York: 1987), 23–46; Iliffe, *Honour*.

4. Quoted in Thomas Astley, *A New General Collection of Voyages and Travels*, 4 vols. (London: 1745–1747), 2:370; René Claude Geoffroy de Villeneuve, *L'Afrique, ou Histoire, Moeurs, usages et Coutumes des Africains: le Sénégal* (Paris: 1814), 1:82–83; Glave, *Savage Africa*, 238–239; Weeks, *Congo Cannibals*, 333–334.

5. Quoted in Astley, *Collection of Voyages*, 4:362; Rankin, *White Man's Grave*, 2:200; Holman, *Travels*, 193.

6. Bridge, *African Cruiser*, 53, 62–64, 76, esp. 55; Holman, *Travels*, 193; Canneau, *Log Book*, 255; Brooks, *Kru Mariner*, 71–112; Anonymous, "Natural History of Sharks," 232.

7. J. G. Wood, *The Natural History of Man: Being an Account of the Manners and Customs of the Uncivilized Races of Men*, 2 vols. (London: 1874), 1:v, 379–384; Samuel White Baker, *In the Heart of Africa* (New York: 1884), 62, 74–76; Eric Jay Dolin, *Leviathan: The History of Whaling in America* (New York: 2007), 50, 391n29.

8. Sigrid, "Tradition," 27–29; Desch Obi, *Fighting for Honor*, 17–74; Salamone, "Gungawa Wrestling," 197.

9. Sweet, *Recreating Africa*, 34–35; Elizabeth Allo Isichei, *A History of the Igbo People* (London: 1976), 82; Iliffe, *Honour*, esp. 11–13, 100–102; Toyin Falola, *Igbo History and Society: The Essays of Adiele Afigbo* (Trenton: 2005), 314; Desch Obi, *Fighting for Honor*, esp. 17–74, 92–100; Michael Brown, "'Walk in the Feenda,'" 306, 308–314, 317; Gilmore, *Manhood*, esp. 11–12, 165–166; Sigrid, "Tradition," 31, 35; Salamone, "Gungawa Wrestling," 199; Innes with Sidibe, *Hunters and Crocodiles*.

10. Desch Obi, *Fighting for Honor*, 17–74, 92–93, esp. 215; Sigrid, "Tradition," 23–46; Salamone, "Gungawa Wrestling," 197–202.

11. Prentiss, *Blind African Slave*, 68–70; Sigrid, "Tradition," 24–25, 32–33, 40–41; Desch Obi, *Fighting for Honor*, 41, 31, 59; Salamone, "Gungawa Wrestling," 193–202, esp. 197.

12. Michael Brown, "'Walk in the Feenda,'" 289–317, esp. 306; Michael Brown, *African-Atlantic Cultures*.

13. Sigrid, "Tradition," 36–38.

14. Desch Obi, *Fighting for Honor*, esp. 59–60; Iliffe, *Honour*, esp. 3, 116; Robert Edgerton, *Warrior Women: The Amazons of Dahomey and the Nature of War* (Boulder: 2000), 23–25, 147; Kwame Arhin, "The Political and Military Roles of Akan Women," in Christine Oppong, ed., *Female and Male in West Africa* (London: 1983), 91–98; Stanley B. Alpern, *Amazons of Black Sparta: The Women Warriors of Dahomey* (New York: 1998).

15. Weeks, *Congo Cannibals*, 332–333; Park, *Travels*, 326, 332; Peter Wood, *Black Majority: Negroes in Colonial South Carolina from 1670 Through the Stono Rebellion* (New York: 1974), 123; Sweet, *Recreating Africa*, 34–35; Salamone, "Gungawa Wrestling," 199; Iliffe, *Honour*, 39, 102, 110–111, 142, 148, 236. For scars related to rites of passage, see Sweet, *Recreating Africa*, 34–35; George Balandier, *Daily Life in the Kingdom of the Kongo*, Helen Weaver, trans. (London: 1968), 215; Pigafeta, *Kingdom of Congo*, 25, 28, 125; Amadou Nouhou Diallo, *Male Circumcision and Initiation in Rural Africa: Autobiography, Culture and Traditions* (Bloomington: 2009); Godfrey B. Tangawa, "Circumcision: An African Point of View," in George C. Denniston, Frederick Mansfield Hodges, and Marilyn Fayre Milos eds., *Male and Female Circumcision: Medical, Legal and Ethical Considerations in Pediatric Practice* (New York: 1999), 183–193.

16. Stedman, *Expedition*, 1:82; R. Q. Mallard, *Plantation Life Before Emancipation* (Richmond: 1892), 26–28; Schaw, *Journal of a Lady*, 149–151; Ambrose E. Gonzales, *The Black Border: Gullah Stories of the Carolina Coast* (Columbia: 1922), 121–124.

17. William Elliott, *William Elliott's Carolina Sports by Land and Water: Including Incidents of Devil-Fishing, Wild-Cat, Deer & Bear Hunting, Etc.* (1846; Columbia: 1994), 15–19; Foulks, *Eighteen Months*, 36. For Southern honor, see Wyatt-Brown, *Southern Honor*; Wyatt-Brown, *Honor and Violence*; Wyatt-Brown, "Mask," 1228–1252; Greenberg, *Honor and Slavery*; Graham, "Honor Among Slaves," 201–228; Edward E. Baptist, "The Absent Subject: African American Masculinity and Forced Migration to the Antebellum Plantation Frontier," in Craig Thompson Friend and Korri Glover, eds., *Southern Manhood: Perspectives on Masculinity in the Old South* (Athens: 2004), 136–171.

18. Lawson, *New Voyage*, 158; Jean Crèvecoeur, "Description of Bermuda: Extract from 'Lettres d'un Cultivateur Americain,'" *Bermuda Historical Quarterly* 3, no. 4 (October, November, December 1946): 202–203; Anonymous, *A Short Journey in the West Indies, in*

Which Are Interspersed, Curious Anecdotes and Characters, 2 vols. (London: 1790), 1:27–30; Foulks, *Eighteen Months*, 36. Hawaiians similarly fought sharks: *Sailor's Magazine* 13, no. 1 (September 1840), 29; Hawai'i Maritime Center exhibit, Honolulu, Hawaii.

19. Quoted in Walter Edgar, *South Carolina: A History* (Columbia: 1998), 155; Corbin, *Lure of the Sea*, 1–18; esp. 7.

20. Schaw, *Journal*, 78, 149–151.

21. Ibid, 149.

22. Thomas Jefferson, *Notes on the State of Virginia* (London: 1887), 231; Edward Long, *The History of Jamaica; or, General Survey of the Antient and Modern State of that Island*, 3 vols. (London: 1774), 354; David Brion Davis, *The Problem of Slavery in Western Culture* (Ithaca: 1966), 446–482. For how race and slavery subjugated African-descended peoples, see David Eltis, *The Rise of African Slavery in the Americas* (Cambridge: 2000); Lacy K. Ford, *Deliver Us from Evil: The Slavery Question in the Old South* (Oxford: 2009); Bruce R. Dain, *A Hideous Monster of the Mind: American Race Theory in the Early Republic* (Cambridge: 2002); Colin Kidd, *The Forging of Races: Race and Scripture in the Protestant Atlantic World, 1600–2000* (Cambridge: 2006); George William Van Cleve, *A Slaveholders' Union: Slavery, Politics, and the Constitution in the Early American Republic* (Chicago: 2010); Matthew Mason, *Slavery And Politics in the Early American Republic* (Chapel Hill: 2008); Sweet, *Domingos Álvares*; Matthew Restall, *The Black Middle: Africans, Mayas, and Spaniards in Colonial Yucatan* (Stanford: 2009).

23. Henry M. Stanley, *Darkest Africa*, 2 vols. (London: 1890), 2:24–26.

24. Crèvecoeur, "Description of Bermuda," 202; Davis, *Problem of Slavery*; William B. Cohen, *The French Encounter with Africans: White Response to Blacks, 1530–1880* (Bloomington: 1980); Stephen R. Haynes, *Noah's Curse: The Biblical Justification of American Slavery* (Oxford: 2002); Larry E. Tise, *Proslavery; A History of the Defense of Slavery in America, 1701–1840* (Athens: 1987).

25. Douglass, *Life and Times*, 182; Saidiya V. Hartman, *Scenes of Subjection: Terror, Slavery, and Self-Making in Nineteenth-Century America* (New York: 1997), 17–48. For social hierarchy, see Isaac, *Transformation of Virginia*, 131–138; Olwell, *Masters, Slaves, and Subject*; Jarvis, "Binds of the Anxious Mariner," 75–117, esp. 98n26; Eltis, *Rise of African Slavery*; Ford, *Deliver Us*; Dain, *Hideous Monster*; Kidd, *Forging of Races*; Cleve, *Slaveholders Union*; Mason, *Slavery and Politics*. White participation in blood sports, like bear- and dog-baiting and "gouging" were not necessarily deemed proof of participants' racial, ethnic, or national inadequacies. Gorn, "'Gouge and Bite,'" 18–43; Parramore, "Gouging," 55–62; Desch Obi, *Fighting for Honor*, 79–80; Forret, *Race Relations*, 161.

26. Bernth Linfors, ed., *Africans on Stage: Studies in Ethnological Show Business* (Bloomington: 1999); Clifton C. Crais and Pamela Scully, *Sara Baartman and the Hottentot Venus: A Ghost Story and a Biography* (Princeton: 2009); Rachel Holmes, *The Hottentot Venus: The Life and Death of Saartjie Baartman: Born 1789–Buried 2002* (New York: 2008); Charles Forsdick, Eric Deroo, Gilles Boëtsch, Nicolas Bancel, Pascal Blanchard, and Sandrine Lemaire, eds., *Human Zoos: From the Hottentot Venus to Reality Shows* (Liverpool: 2008); Rolyn Poignant, *Professional Savages: Captive Lives and Western Spectacles* (New Haven: 2004); Sadiah Qureshi, *Peoples on Parade: Exhibitions, Empire, and Anthropology in Nineteenth-Century Britain* (Chicago: 2011); Alan Trachtenberg, *Shades of Hiawatha: Staging Indians, Making Americans, 1880–1930* (New York: 2004); Susan Brownell, ed., *The 1904 Anthropology Days and Olympic Games: Sport, Race, and American Imperialism* (Lincoln: 2008).

27. Mandell, *Sport*, 180; Stedman, *Expedition*, 2:375–376; Desch Obi, *Fighting for Honor*; Dawson, "Enslaved Swimmers."

28. For "community performance rituals," see Desch Obi, *Fighting for Honor*, 92–97. Captives anticipated the late nineteenth- and early twentieth-century exhibitions in which white daredevils leapt from objects into the water and swimmers performed in aquatic ballets, vaudeville shows, and movies. Kellerman, *How to Swim*, esp. 38–41, 177, 193; Paul E. Johnson, *Sam Patch, the Famous Jumper* (New York: 2003), x–xi, 42–77; Webb, *Art of Swimming*, 68–111, Dalton, *How to Swim*, 88–104.

29. Dawson, "Enslaved Ship Pilots; Robert Olwell, *Master, Slaves, and Subject: The Culture of Power in the South Carolina Low Country, 1740–1790* (Ithaca: 1998); Richard Follett, *Planter-Slave Relationships: The Sugar Masters: Planters and Slaves in Louisiana's Cane World, 1820–1860* (Baton Rouge: 2009), esp. 5; Ira Berlin, *Many Thousands Gone: The First Two Centuries of Slavery in North America* (London: 1998), esp. 2–6, 66, 142–176; William Dusinberre, *Them Dark Days: Slavery in the American Rice Swamps* (Oxford: 1996), esp. 179–210, 302–349; Philip D. Morgan, *Slave Counterpoint: Black Culture in the Eighteenth Century Chesapeake and Lowcountry* (Chapel Hill: 1998), 257–300, 377–437; Dawson, "Enslaved Swimmers," 1347–1348, 1352–1354.

30. Desch Obi, *Fighting for Honor*; Sergio Lussana, "To See Who Was Best on the Plantation: Enslaved Fighting Contests and Masculinity in the Antebellum South," *Journal of Southern History* 76, no. 4 (November 2010): 901–922; Frederick Douglass, *Life and Times of Frederick Douglass, Written by Himself: His Early Life as a Slave, His Escape from Bondage* (Boston: 1892), 181–182; David K. Wiggins, "Good Times on the Old Plantation: Popular Recreations of the Black Slave in the Antebellum South, 1810–1860," *Journal of Sport History* 4, no. 3 (1977): 273–274; Henry Bibb, *Narrative of the Life and Adventures of Henry Bibb, an American Slave* (1850; New York: 1869), 23; Mandell, *Sport*, 180; Betty Wood, *Women's Work*, 135; Kenneth S. Greenberg, *Honor & Slavery: Lies, Duels, Noses, Masks, Dressing as a Woman, Gifts, Strangers, Humanitarianism, Death, Slave Rebellions, the Proslavery Argument, Baseball, Hunting, and Gambling in the Old South* (Princeton: 1996), 34–35, Stedman, *Expedition*, 1:158, 2:323, 376. "Formal" sporting events are those announced in advance with invited spectators. Mandell, *Sport*, xiii, 180.

31. Ligon, *Barbadoes*, 52–53. Most Barbadian seventeenth-century slaves were born in Africa: Hilary McD. Beckles, *White Servitude and Black Slavery in Barbados, 1627–1715* (Knoxville: 1989), 31; Russell R. Menard, *Sweet Negotiations: Sugar, Slavery, and Plantation Agriculture in Early Barbados* (Charlottesville: 2006), 31, 53–60.

32. Dawson, "Enslaved Swimmers," 1341; Desch Obi, *Fighting for Honor*, esp. 99–100, 77–121; Lussana, "Who Was Best," 919–920; Camp, *Closer to Freedom*, 76–78; Wiggins, "Good Times." For wagering among planters, see Timothy H. Breen, "Horses and Gentlemen: The Cultural Significance of Gambling Among the Gentry of Virginia," *William and Mary Quarterly* 34 (April 1977): 329–347; Bertram Wyatt-Brown, *Southern Honor: Ethics and Behavior in the Old South* (New York: 1982), 350–360.

33. Desch Obi, *Fighting for Honor*, 27–28, 92–93, 98, 215, esp. 93; Lussana, "Who Was Best," 118–121, 913; Paul, "Wrestling Tradition," 23–46.

34. Stedman, *Expedition*, 2:323. One wonders if these bondmen were practicing a form of African martial arts generally called "foot-fighting." Desch Obi, *Fighting for Honor*, esp. 1–2, 14, 17, 46, 78, 141.

35. Berry, *Swing the Sickle*, 60–61; Mallard, *Plantation Life*, 26–28; Elliott, *Carolina Sports*, 15–19; Gonzales, *Black Border*, 121–124; LeConte, *Autobiography*, 27–29, esp. 29; Whitehead, *Camp-Fires*, 21.

36. Rawick, *American Slave: Georgia Narratives* 13:223–224; Proctor, *Bathed in Blood*, 159; Berry, *Swing the Sickle*, 60–61; White, *Ar'n't I a Woman*, 119–141.

37. For examples of scholarship on slaves maintaining ethnic traditions and blending similar customs, see Sweet, *Domingos Álvarez*, esp. 13–14; Sweet, *Recreating Africa*; Gomez, *Country Marks*, 1–185; Hawthorne, *Africa to Brazil*; Childs, *Aponte Rebellion*, 95–119; Thornton, *Africa and Africans*, 183–234; Hall, *Slavery and African Ethnicities*.

38. For slaveholders orchestrating fights, see Desch Obi, *Fighting for Honor*, 99, 133–134; Lussana, "Who Was Best," 907, 912; Greenberg, *Honor and Slavery*, 34–35. For honor in the Americas, see Desch Obi, *Fighting for Honor*; Lussana, "Who Was Best," 901–922; Baptist, "Absent Subject," 136–171; Sandra Lauderdale Graham, "Honor Among Slaves," in Lyman L. Johnson and Sonya Lipsett-Rivera, eds., *The Faces of Honor: Sex, Shame, and Violence in Colonial Latin America* (Albuquerque: 1998), 201–228; Wyatt-Brown, *Southern Culture*; Greenberg, *Honor and Slavery*. T.J. Desch Obi argues that saltwater slaves primarily maintained African concepts of honor. Obi, *Fighting for Honor*.

39. R. Q. Mallard, *Plantation Life Before Emancipation* (Richmond: 1892), 26–28; Stedman, *Expedition*, 1:82; Schaw, *Journal of a Lady*, 149–151; Gonzales, *Black Border*, 121–124.

40. Gomez documented how bondpeople reinterpreted white traditions to provide meanings they valued. Gomez, *Exchanging Our Country Marks*, passim, esp. 8–10. Friend and Glover, *Southern Manhood*, 136–171; Johnson and Lipsett-Rivera, *Faces of Honor*; Greenberg, *Honor and Slavery*, 11–12, 33–35, 40–43; Desch Obi, *Fighting for Honor*; Bertram Wyatt-Brown, "The Mask of Obedience: Male Slave Psychology in the Old South," *American Historical Review* 93, no. 5 (December 1988), 1228–1252; Wyatt-Brown, *Southern Culture*.

41. Rebecca Fraser, "Negotiating Their Manhood: Masculinity Amongst the Enslaved in the Upper-South, 1830–1861," in Lydia Plath and Sergio Lussana, eds., *Black and White Masculinity in the American South, 1800–2000* (Newcastle: 2009), 80.

42. Blood sports as expressions of honor probably mirrored slaves' use of African martial arts. Desch Obi, *Fighting for Honor*, esp. 99–100.

43. Lussana, "Who Was Best," 903–904; Fraser, "Negotiating Their Manhood," 81–85; Rebecca J. Fraser, *Courtship and Love Among the Enslaved in North Carolina* (Jackson: 2007), 69–87; West, *Chains of Love*, 43–79; Nicholas W. Proctor, *Bathed in Blood: Hunting and Mastery in the Old South* (Charlottesville: 2002), 150–153.

44. Proctor, *Bathed in Blood*, 61–75, 121–123, 147, 157–158, esp. 144; Greenburg, *Honor and Slavery*, 133–135; Elliott, *Carolina Sports*, 15–19; Schaw, *Journal*, 149–151; Gonzales, *Black Border*, 121–124.

45. Joseph LeConte, *The Autobiography of Joseph LeConte* (New York: 1903), 29, 27–29; Mallard, *Plantation Life*, 26–28.

46. Greenberg, *Honor and Slavery*, 35–36, 136–145, esp. 143, 145; quoted in Blassingame, *Slave Testimony*, 52; Breen, "Horses and Gentlemen," 329–347; Wyatt-Brown, *Southern Honor*, Wyatt-Brown, *Honor and Violence*; Friend and Glover, *Southern Manhood*; Fraser, "Manhood," 76; Baptist, "Absent Subject," 136–173. White peoples' refusal to extend honor to slaves is considered later in this chapter.

47. Clinkscales, *Old Plantation*, 7, 10–17; Desch Obi, *Fighting for Honor*, 94–100; Lussana, "Who Was Best," 903–904, 913–914; Proctor, *Bathed in Blood*, 150–153. Chapter 8

considers how canoemen similarly exhibited their seminude physiques. For courtship, see Desch Obi, *Fighting for Honor*, 96–100; White, *Ar'n't I a Woman?*,104–106, 142–145; Schwartz, *Born in Bondage*, 177–205, esp. 181–183, 189; Anthony E. Kaye, *Joining Places: Slave Neighborhoods in the Old South* (Chapel Hill: 2007), 51–82; Emily West, *Chains of Love: Slave Couples in Antebellum South Carolina* (Champaign: 2004), 19–39, esp. 26; Damian Pargas, *The Quarters and the Fields: Slave Families in the Non-Cotton South* (Gainesville: 2011), esp. 98, 152–170; Bernard Moitt, *Women and Slavery in the French Antilles, 1635–1848* (Blooming-ton: 2011), 80–99; Brenda E. Stevenson, *Life in Black and White: Family and Community in the Slave South* (New York: 1996), 226–257; Frances Smith Foster, *'Til Death or Distance Do Us Part: Love and Marriage in African America* (New York: 2010); Fraser, *Courtship*.

48. Fraser, "Manhood," 84–85; Greenberg, *Honor and Slavery*, 33–36; Fraser, *Courtship*, 69–87; West, *Chains of Love*, 43–79.

49. Proctor, *Bathed in Blood*, 61, 147. For examples of scholarship on how slaves maintained African traditions as a form of resistance, see Gomez, *Exchanging Our Country Marks*, passim; esp. 8–10; Sweet, *Recreating Africa*; Young, *Rituals of Resistance*.

50. Johnson, *Soul by Soul*, 19–22, 31, 113–114, 164; Dusinberre, *Dark Days*, 269; Michael Tadman, *Speculators and Slaves: Masters, Traders, and Slaves in the Old South* (1989; Madison: 1996), 269; Zamba, *Life and Adventures*, 152–155; Equiano, *Interesting Narrative*, 256–257; Douglass, *Narrative*, 12–13; 19–20.

51. Greenberg, *Honor and Slavery*, 7–9, 11, 34–35, 81–82, esp. xi–xii, 7; Camp, *Closer to Freedom*, 71, 92; Desch Obi, *Fighting for Honor*, esp. 96, 77–121; Lussana, "Who Was the Best," 911; Baptist, "Absent Subject," 146, Graham, "Honor Among Slaves," 204; Wyatt-Brown, "Mask," 1233–1234, Wyatt-Brown, *Honor and Violence*, 143–153; Wyatt-Brown, *Southern Honor*, 350–360; Jack R. Williams, *Dueling in the Old South: Vignettes of Social History* (1980; College Station: 2000); Forret, *Race Relations*, 161–163. For slaves' appropriating control of their bodies, see Camp, *Closer to Freedom*, esp. 60–92; Lussana, "Who Was Best," 915–917.

52. Proctor, *Bathed in Blood*, 145. For men and boys hunting together, see Gonzales, *Black Border*, 96–127.

53. Forret, *Race Relations*, 161; Greenberg, *Honor and Slavery*, 15; Gorn, " 'Gouge and Bite,' " 43.

54. Shane White and Graham White, *The Sounds of Slavery: Discovering African American History through Songs, Sermons, and Speech* (Boston: 2005), 72–96; Camp, *Closer to Freedom*, 76–87; Paul, "Wrestling Tradition," 29, 33; King, *Stolen Childhood*, 117, 141–142; Charles Joyner, *Down by the Riverside: A South Carolina Slave Community* (Urbana: 1984), 131, 190–195; Desch Obi, *Fighting for Honor*, 94; Pollard, *Black Diamonds Gathered in the Homes of the South* (New York: 1859), 99–105; Brooke Baldwin, "The Cakewalk: A Study in Stereotype and Reality," *Journal of Social History* 15, no. 2 (Winter 1981): 205–218.

55. Childs, *Aponte Rebellion*, 105–116; Elizabeth W. Kiddy, "Who Is the King of Congo? A New Look at African and Afro-Brazilian Kings in Brazil," in Linda M. Heaywood, ed., *Central Africans in North America and the Caribbean* (Cambridge: 2002), 153–182; William D. Piersen, *Black Yankees: The Development of Afro-American Subculture in Eighteenth-Century New England* (Amherst: 1988), 105, 117–124, 130, 136, 139; Bolster, *Black Jacks*, 110–119; Desch Obi, *Fighting for Honor*, 95–97.

56. Desch Obi, *Fighting for Honor*, 27–28, 92–93, 98, 215, esp. 93; Lussana, "Who Was Best," 913, 118–121; Paul, "Wrestling Tradition," 23–46.

Chapter 4

1. Robin Blackburn, *The Making of New World Slavery: From the Baroque to the Modern, 1492–1800* (London: 1997), 82; Thornton, *Africa and Africans*, 7–8, 21, 36, esp. 42.

2. Theophilus Canneau, *A Slaver's Log Book, or 20 Years' Residence in Africa* (Englewood Cliffs: 1976), 256, 285. For profits, see Herbert Klein, *The Atlantic Slave Trade* (Cambridge: 1999), 98–100, 132; William Darity Jr., "British Industry and the West Indies Plantations," in Joseph E. Inikori and Stanley L. Engerman, eds., *The Atlantic Slave Trade: Effects on Economies, Societies and Peoples in Africa, the Americas, and Europe* (Durham: 1998), esp. 11, 215, 247–279; David Eltis, *Economic Growth and the Ending of the Transatlantic Slave Trade* (Cambridge: 1987), 269–282; Johannes Postma, *The Atlantic Slave Trade* (Gainesville: 2003), 56–58, 61n13; P. C. Emmer, *The Dutch Slave Trade, 1500–1850* (New York: 2006), 82–84, 106–110.

3. Hair, Jones, and Law, *Barbot on Guinea*, 2:497n3, 501, 510n20, 529–532, 544n45, 545n46, 550, 573n8, 640; de Marees, *Gold Kingdom*, 26, 32, 186–187; Jones, *German Sources*, 12, 103, 109, 219; Crow, *Memoirs*, 34, 39–40.

4. Robert Baker, *The Travails in Guinea of an unknown Tudor poet in verse* (1568; Liverpool: 1999), 42; Paul Erdmann Isert, *Letters on West Africa and the Slave Trade: Paul Erdmann Isert's Journey to Guinea and the Caribbean Islands in Columbia* (1788), in Selena Axelrod Winsnes, trans. and ed. (1788; Oxford: 1992), 89; J. P. L. Durand, *A Voyage to Senegal; or Historical, Philosophical, and Political Memoirs, Relative to the Discoveries, Establishments, and Commerce of Europeans in the Atlantic Ocean* (London: 1806), 110–111.

5. Burton, *West Africa*, 1:195; Thompson, *Palm Land*, 240; Melville, *Residence at Sierra Leone*, 113.

6. Linda M. Heywood and John K. Thornton, *Central Africans, Atlantic Creoles, and the Foundation of the Americas, 1585–1660* (Cambridge: 2007), 53; Fillipo Pigafetta, *A Report of the Kingdom of Congo and the Surrounding Countries Drawn out of the Writings and Discourses of the Portuguese Duarte Lopes* (London: 1818), 18–19; Bosman, *Accurate Description*, 83, 119, 120, 230, 437, 527, 535.

7. Hair, Jones, and Law, *Barbot on Guinea*, 2:338; Olfert Dapper, *Description de l'Afrique: Contenant les noms, la Situation et les Confins de Toutes ses Parties, leurs Rivieres, Leurs Villes & Leurs Habitations, Leurs Plantes & Leurs Animaux* (Amsterdam: 1686), 293; John Ogilby, *Africa: Being an Accurate Description of the Regions of Aegypt, Barbary, Lybia, and Billedulgerid, the Land of Negroes* (London: 1670), 449.

8. Stewart, "Diary," 51–52; G. R. Crone, *Voyages of Cadamosto*, 37.

9. George E. Brooks Jr., *The Kru Mariner in the Nineteenth Century: An Historical Compendium* (Newark: 1972), 4, 71; George E. Brooks, *Eurafricans in Western Africa: Commerce, Social Status, Gender, and Religious Observance from the Sixteenth to the Eighteenth Century* (Athens: 2003), 18–19; Stewart, "Diary," 51.

10. Bosman, *Accurate Description*, 491; Holman, *Travels*, 297, 321; Stewart, "Diary," 52; French-Sheldon, *Sultan to Sultan*, 36. Also see Verner, *Central Africa*, 307; Denham, Clapperton, Oudney, and Salamé, *Narrative*, 2:188–190.

11. C. Herbert Gilliland, ed., *Voyage of a Thousand Cares: Master's Mate Lawrence with the African Squadron, 1844–1846* (Annapolis: 2004), 64.

12. Charles Abbott, *A Treatise of the Law Relative to Merchant Ships and Seamen* (1802; Newburyport: 1810), 557–597; Geoffrey Brice, *Maritime Law of Salvage* (Est Kilbride, Scotland: 1983), 1–41; Francis H. Upton, *Maritime Warfare and Prize* (New York: 1863), 234–235, 232–246.

13. Isert, *Letters on West Africa*, 177; Frederick Shobel, ed., *The World in Miniature; Africa, Containing a Description of the Manners and Customs*, 4 vols. (London: 1821), 3:27–30; Rodney, *Upper Guinea Coast*, 86–87; A. Brasio, *Monumenta Missionaria Africana. Africa Ocidental*, 1500–1569 (2nd series; Lisboa: 1963), 2:467; Valentim Fernandes, *Description de la côte occidentale d'Afrique (Sénégal du Cap de Monte, Archipels), par Valentim Fernandes 1506–1510*, in Th. Monod, A. Teixeira da Mota, R. Mauny, eds. (Bissau: 1951), 96.

14. André Álvares de Almada, *Brief Treatise on the Rivers of Guinea. Being an English Translation of a Variorum Text of Tratado breve dos Rios de Guiné, c.1594*, in P. E. H. Hair and Jean Boulègue, trans. and eds. (c.1595; Liverpool: 1984), 1:100; Manuel Álvares, *Ethiopia Minor and a Geographical Account of the Province of Sierra Leone (c. 1615)*, in P. E. H. Hair, trans. and ed. (Liverpool: 1990), chap. 9:3, chap. 11:4; Valdez, *Traveller's Life*, 1:211.

15. Álvares, *Ethiopia Minor*, chap. 3:11–12; Walter Hawthorne, *Planting Rice and Harvesting Slaves: Transformations along the Guinea-Bissau Coast, 1400–1900* (Portsmouth: 2003), 96; Brooks, *Eurafricans*, 75; Diouf, *Fighting the Slave Trade*.

16. Robert Baker, *Travails in Guinea*, 42; Caillié, *Timbuctoo*, 2:31, 35–36; Philip D. Curtin, *Africa Remembered: Narratives by West Africans from the Era of the Slave Trade* (Prospect Heights: 1967) 179, 179n29.

17. Hutchinson, *Ten Years' Wanderings*, 92–105; Webb, *Art of Swimming*, 16–17; C. R. Boxer, ed., *The Tragic History of the Sea, 1589–1622* (Cambridge: 1959), 119. For Isuwu, see Austen and Derrick, *Cameroons Rivers*, esp. 37.

18. Quoted in Jones, *German Sources*, 12; de Marees, *Gold Kingdom*, 187; Holman, *Travels*, 261, 329–330.

19. Slaveholders probably exploited African artisanal skills, including carpentry and metalworking, which scholars have yet to consider.

20. Follett, *Sugar Masters*, 127–128; Morgan, *Laboring Women*, 144–165, esp. 146–147; Berry, *Swing the Sickle*, 14–19.

21. Pinckard, *West Indies*, 2:321; Clinkscales, *Old Plantation*, 26.

22. Robert Haynes, *The Barbadian Diary of General Robert Haynes, 1787–1836* (Hampshire: 1934), 26; H. G. Adams, ed., *God's Image in Ebony: Being a Series of Biographical Sketches, Facts, Anecdotes, etc., Demonstrative of the Mental Powers and Intellectual Capacities of the Negro Race* (London: 1854), 159–160; Zamba, *Life and Adventures*, 1, 86, esp. 168–170; Frederic W. N. Bayley, *Four Year's Residence in the West Indies, During the Years 1826,7,8, and 9* (London: 1833), 486.

23. Zamba, *Life and Adventures*, 169–170.

24. *Columbian Herald*, May 12, 1785. For slaves wading and swimming to clear canals and irrigation trenches, see Matthew Lewis, *Journal of a West Indian Proprietor: Kept During a Residence in the Island of Jamaica* (1834; New York: 1999), 119–120.

25. Edelson, *Plantation Enterprise*, 62–63, 97, 156–158, esp. 84; Carney, *Black Rice*, esp. 81; Fields-Black, *Deep Roots*, 157–160, 179. For an opposing view, see David Eltis, Philip Morgan, and David Richardson, "Black, Brown, or White? Color-Coding American Commercial Rice Cultivation with Slave Labor," *American Historical Review* 115, no. 1 (February 2010): 164–171.

26. José de Acosta, *Historia natural y moral de las Indias: en que se tratan de las cosas notables del cielo, elementos, metales, plantas y animals dellas*, in Emundo O'Gorman, ed. (1590; Mexico City, 1962), chap. 15; Linda A. Newson and Susie Minchin, *From Capture to*

Sale: The Portuguese Slave Trade to Spanish South America in the Early Seventeenth Century (Leiden: 2007), 5; Enrique Otte, *Las Perlas del Caribe: Nueva Cádiz de Cubagua* (Caraca: 1977), 48–49, 355–362; R. A. Donkin, *Beyond Price: Pearls and Pearl-Fishing, Origins to the Age of Discoveries* (Philadelphia: 1998), 321–322; Thornton, *Africa and Africans*, 135; Bartholomé de Las Casas, *Bartholomew de Las Casas: His Life, His Apostolate and His Writings*, in Francis Augustus MacNutt, trans. and ed. (New York: 1909), 374–383. For the pearl industry, see Molly Warsh, "Enslaved Pearl Divers in the Sixteenth Century Caribbean," *Slavery & Abolition*, 31 no.3 (September 2010): 345–362; "A Political Ecology in the Early Spanish Caribbean." *William & Mary Quarterly*, 3d ser., 71, no. 4 (October 2014): 517–548; *American Baroque: Pearls and the Nature of Empire 1492–1700* (forthcoming: Chapel Hill, 2018).

27. For example, Littlefield, *Rice and Slaves*; Carney, *Black Rice*; Fields-Black, *Deep Roots*, esp. 171–186; Lorena S. Walsh, *From Calabar to Carter's Grove: A History of a Virginia Slave Community* (Charlottesville: 1997), esp. 63–64; Stuart B. Schwartz, *Sugar Plantations in the Formation of Brazilian Society: Bahia, 1550–1835* (Cambridge: 1985), 66; Herbert S. Klein and Francisco Vidal Luna, *Slavery in Brazil* (Cambridge: 2010), 28; Kathleen J. Higgins, *"Licentious Liberty" in a Brazilian Gold-Mining Region: Slavery, Gender, and Social Control in Eighteenth-Century Sabará, Mina Geras* (University Park: 1999), 73–75, 147n4; Sluyter, *Black Ranching Frontiers*; Sweet, *Domingos Álvares*; Sweet, *Recreating Africa*, 120–134, 145, 146; Fett, *Working Cures*, 100–108; Weaver, *Medical Revolutionaries*, esp. 54, 59, 66, 72, 128.

28. Enrique Otte, ed., *Cédulas de la Monarquía Española Relativas a la Parte Oriental de Venezuela, 1520–1561* (Caracas: 1965), 171–172, 401; Enrique Otte, ed., *Cedularios de la Monarquía Española de Margarita, Nueva Andalucía y Caracas, 1553–1604* (Caracas: 1961), 1:201–203, 260, 376, 381.

29. de Marees, *Gold Kingdom*, 186. De Marees seemingly visited South America; read extensively about the region; and was tuned into Dutch, Portuguese, and French discussions. E-mail correspondence with Adam Jones, December 3, 2011, and Ernst van den Boogaart, December 5, 2011.

30. Otte, *Margarita*, 1:171–172.

31. Visayans (a Filipino ethnicity), "chinos," and Aboriginal Australians were renowned freedivers forced into pearl diving. James Warren, *The Sulu Zone, 1768–1898: The Dynamics of External Trade, Slavery and Ethnicity in the Transformation of a Southeast Asian Maritime State* (Singapore: 2007), xxxv, 187, 201; conversations with James Warren during the *Sea Stories: Maritime Landscapes, Cultures and Histories Conference*, University of Sydney. Sydney, Australia, June 12–14, 2013; Michael J. McCarthy, *Iron and Steamship Archaeology: Success and Failure on the SS Xantho* (London: 2002), 37–40; Sanford Alexander Mosk, "Spanish Voyages and Pearl Fisheries in the Gulf of California: A Study in Economic History" (Ph.D. diss., University of California, Berkeley, 1927), 131.

32. Marion Clayton Link, *Sea Diver: A Quest for History Under the Sea* (Miami: 1964), 279; de Espinosa, *Compendium*, 51. Bernard documented how divers transmitted generational wisdom. H. Russell Bernard, "Kalymnian Sponge Diving," in *Human Biology* 39, no. 2 (May 1967), 118–119. For training skilled slaves, see Bolster, *Black Jacks*; Dawson, "Enslaved Ship Pilots;" Follett, *Sugar Masters*, 5, 118–150, esp. 126; Dusinberre, *Dark Days*, 87, 94, 179–210, esp. 190; Richard Sheridan, *Sugar and Slavery: An Economic History of the British West Indies, 1623–1775* (Baltimore: 1973), 115–117; Dunn, *Sugar and Slaves*, 192–195; King, *Stolen Childhood*, 71–106; Schwartz, *Born in Bondage*, 115–130; Charles B. Dew, *Bond of Iron: Master and*

Slave at Buffalo Forge (New York: 1994), 26, 171–219; Charles B. Dew, *Ironmaker to the Confederacy: Joseph R. Anderson and the Tredegar Iron Works* (Richmond: 1999), 23–27.

33. Antonio Vázquez de Espinosa, *Compendium and Description of the West Indies*, Charles Upson Clark, trans. (c.1634; Washington, DC: 1942), iv–v, 50–52; Donkin, *Beyond Price*, 320–324, 331; Sanford Alexander Mosk, "Spanish Pearl-Fishing Operations on the Pearl Coast in the Sixteenth Century," *Hispanic American Historical Review* 18 (August 1938): 400; Otte, *Las Perlas*, 45–48.

34. de Espinosa, *Compendium*, 51–52; Clements Markham, ed., *Hawkins' Voyages during the Reigns of Henry VIII, Queen Elizabeth, and James I* (1847; New York: 1970), 313–315; Gonzlo Fernandez de Oviedo, *Natural History of the West Indies*, Sterling A. Stoudemire, trans. and ed. (1555; Chapel Hill: 1959), 116; John Ogilby, *America: Being the Latest and Most Accurate Description of the New World; Containing the Original Inhabitants, and the Remarkable Voyages Thither* (London: 1671), 227; R. W. H. Hardy, *Travels in the Interior of Mexico, in 1825, 1826, 1827, and 1828* (London: 1829), 253; Samuel de Champlain, *Narrative of a Voyage to the West Indies and Mexico in the Years 1599–1602* (London: 1859), 7; Donkin, *Beyond Price*, 323.

35. For "diving negroes," see the rest of this chapter.

36. Claes E. G. Lundgren, "The Science of Breath-Hold Diving: Past, Present and Future," in *Breath-Hold Diving 2006 Workshop Proceedings* (Durham: 2006), 2–16; Lindholm and Lundgren, "Physiology and Pathophysiology of Human Breath-Hold Diving," 284–292; Massimo Ferrigno and Claes E. G. Lundgren, "Human Breath-Hold Diving," in Claes E. G. Lundgren and John Noel Miller, eds. *The Lung at Depth* (New York: 1999), 529–585; D. F. Speck, and D. S. Bruce, "Effects of Varying Thermal and Apneic Conditions on the Human Diving Reflex," *Undersea Biomedical Research Journal* 5, no. 1 (March 1978), 9–14; Terry Maas, *Bluewater Hunting and Freediving* (Ventura: 1995), esp. 50–51, 58; Umberto Pelizzari and Stefano Tovaglieri, *Manual of Freediving: Underwater on a Single Breath* (Reddick: 2004), 38–92; "Defying Free Dives: Pushing Boundaries," January 13, 2013 episode of *CBS' 60 Minutes*. My observations. Also see Undersea and Hyperbaric Medical Society Charles W. Shilling Library at Duke University Medical Center and Undersea and Hyperbaric Medical Society, Inc. (www.uhms.org).

37. Anna Gislén, Marie Dacke, Ronald H. Kröger, Maths Abrahamsson, Dan-Eric Nilsson, and Eric J Warrant, "Superior Underwater Vision in a Human Population of Sea Gypsies," *Current Biology* 13, no. 10 (May, 13, 2003), 833–836; McCarthy, *Iron and Steamship Archaeology*, 31; Megan Lane, "What Freediving Does to the Body," *BBC News* (January 12, 2011), www.bbc.co.uk/news/science-environment-12151830; Brian Handwerk, "Sea Gypsies of Asia Boast 'Incredible' Underwater Vision" *National Geographic Ultimate Explorer* (May 14, 2004); http://news.nationalgeographic.com/news/2004/05/0514_040514_seagypsies.html; www.bbc.co.uk/nature/humanplanetexplorer/environments/oceans; "The 'Sea-Nomad' Children Who See Like Dolphins," *BBC World News* (March 1, 2016) www.bbc.com/future/story/20160229-the-sea-nomad-children-who-see-like-dolphins.

38. de Marees, *Gold Kingdom*, 186 (italics added).

39. Noel Roydhouse, "Ear Drum Rupture in Scuba Divers," *South Pacific Underwater Medicine Society Journal* 28, no. 2 (June 1998): 81–83; Pelizzari and Tovaglieri, *Manual of Freediving*, 95–145, 195–214; Maas, *Bluewater Hunting*, 58–59; "Death-Defying Free Dives"; author interview with Tanya Streeter, May 16, 2014. Tanya Streeter is a world champion freediver.

40. Lundgren, "The Science of Breath-Hold Diving," 2–17; Peter Lindholm, "Physiological Mechanisms Involved in the Risk of Loss of Consciousness During Breath-Hold Diving," in *Breath-Hold Diving 2006 Workshop Proceedings*, Jointly Sponsored by the Undersea and Hyperbolic Medical Society and Divers Alert Network (Durham: 2006), 26–31; Tanya Streeter, "Nitrogen Narcosis During No Limits Freediving World Record Dive To 160 M (525 Ft)," in *Breath-Hold Diving 2006 Workshop Proceedings* (Durham: 2006), 17–25; M. Hobbs, "Subjective and Behavioural Responses to Nitrogen Narcosis and Alcohol," *Undersea & Hyperbaric Medicine: Journal of the Undersea and Hyperbaric Medical Society, Inc.* 35, no. 3 (2008): 175–184; Pelizzari and Tovaglieri, *Manual of Freediving*, 96–135. Tanya Streeter stressed that "so much of freediving is mental," requiring one to push oneself to the limits of his or her "full physical and physiological capabilities." Streeter interview.

41. Based on my observations during decades of freediving and spearfishing.

42. "Carta del presidente Pedro Carrillo de Guzmán," March 14, 1655, Archivo General de Indias-Panama, leg. 21, exp. 9, n. 54; Antonio de Ulloa, *A Voyage to South America: Describing at Large the Spanish Cities, Towns, Provinces, &c. on that Extensive Continent: Undertaken, by Command of the King of Spain*, 2 vols. (1748; London: 1760), 1:126–128; Alexander von Humbolt, *Political Essay on the Kingdom of New Spain*, 4 vols. (1811: London: 1966), 2:328–329; George Frederick Kunz and Charles Hugh Stevenson, *The Book of the Pearl: Its History, Art, Science, and Industry* (Mineola: 1993), 235–246; Mosk, "Spanish Voyages." De Ulloa's account indicates that Panamanian divers were treated the same as Pearl Coast captives and was republished numerous times, alerting whites to this form of exploitation. *The London General Gazetteer, or Geographic Dictionary*, 3 vols. (London: 1825), 1:339; *The Jersey Magazine; Or, Monthly Recorder*, 2 vols. (1809), 1:133. There is no evidence of pearl diving off California's Pacific Coast, though accounts suggest Spaniards searched there for pearl oysters and mother of pearl.

43. Tomas de Cardona, Señor, El Capitan Tomas de Cardona, por si, y en nôbre de los demas participes en el assiento que con V. Magestad se hizo el año de 1612, de nueuos descubrimientos de perlas (Madrid?, 1820?), British Library, 725.k.18(43.); Tomas de Cardona, Señor Tomas de Cardona desseoso del seruicio de V. M. y del bien publico, y restauracion destos Reynos (Seville?, 1620?), British Library, 1322.1.7.(2.); Asiento con Tomas de Cardona y Sancho de Meras, (December 22, 1610), Archivo General de Indias, Indiferente 428, L. 34, ff. 62r–69v; Nicolás de Cardona, *Geographic and Hydrographic Descriptions of Many Northern Lands and Seas of the Indies, Specifically of the Discovery of the Kingdom of California* (1632; Los Angeles: 1974); Sanford A. Mosk, "The Cardona Company and the Pearl Fisheries of Lower California, *Pacific Historical Review* 3, no. 1 (March 1934): 50–61; W. Michael Mathes, eds., *The Pearl Hunters in the Gulf of California 1668: Summary Report of the Voyage Made to the Californias by Captain Francisco de Lucenilla* (Los Angeles: 1966), 14; Peter Gerhard, "Pearl Diving in Lower California, 1553–1830," *Pacific Historical Review* 25 (August 1956): 240–241; Samuel Purchas, *Hakluytus Posthumus, or Purchas his Pilgrimes: Contayning a History of the World in Sea Voyages and Lande Travells by Englishmen and Others*, 4 vols. (London: 1625), book 1, book 2:84; Mosk, *Pearl Fisheries*, 92–98.

44. For 1534 law, see Otte, *Margarita*, 1:171–172. For 1540 law, see Genaro Rodríguez Morel, ed., *Cartas de la Real Audiencia de Santo Domingo, 1530–1546* (Santo Domingo: 2007), 392, 399. For 1602 letter, see Mosk, "Pearl-Fishing," 400. Also see Morel, *Cartas*, 177; de Marees, *Gold Kingdom*, 186.

45. Francisco López de Gómara, *Historia general de las Indias con la conquista de Mexico y de la Nueva España*, 2 vols. (1551; Madrid: 1922), 1:187; Acosta, *Historia,* chap. 15; de Espinosa, *Compendium*, 51; de Las Casas, *Bartholomew de Las Casas*, 382; Otte, *Margarita*, 1:191–192; Ogilby, *America*, 227–278; Mosk, "Pearl-Fishing," 395, 399; Donkin, *Beyond Price*, 321–329; Hardy, *Travels*, 237; Kunz and Stevenson, *Pearl*, 231–232; Mass, *Bluewater Hunting*, 25–47, 59. For drowning, see Lundgren, "Breath-Hold Diving," 298–290; Robert M. Wong, "Decompression Sickness in Breath-Hold Diving," in *Breath-Hold Diving 2006 Workshop Proceedings* (Durham: 2006), 119–129; Bernard, "Sponge Diving," 113; Terry L. Maas, "Shallow Water Blackouts: The Problem of and a Potential Solution," in *Breath-Hold Diving 2006 Workshop Proceedings* (Durham: 2006), 76; my experiences. Streeter believes shallow-water blackouts would have been the leading cause of death. Streeter interview.

46. Henry Stevens and Fred W. Lucas, eds., *The New Laws of the West Indies for the Good Treatment and Preservation of the Indians Promulgated by the Emperor Charles the Fifth, 1542–1543* (1893; London: 1971), xiii–xiv; Las Casas, *Bartholomew de Las Casas*, 374–383; Donkin, *Beyond Price*, 321–322; Mosk, "Pearl-Fishing," 395.

47. For hallucinatory "rapture" effects of narcosis, see "Death-Defying Free Dives;" Bernard, "Sponge Diving," 119–120.

48. J. H. Parry, *The Spanish Seaborne Empire* (Berkeley: 1990), 51; Donkin, *Beyond Price*, 318–24; Mosk, "Pearl-Fishing," 397; Dunn, *Sugar and Slaves*, 10; Van den Broecke, *Journal of Voyages*, 27, 58; Kunz and Stevenson, *Pearl*, 231–232.

49. De Espinosa, *Compendium*, 51–52; Champlain, *Narrative*, 7; Donkin, *Beyond Price*, 320; Mosk, "Pearl-Fishing," 400.

50. David Eltis and David Richardson, *Atlas of the Transatlantic Slave Trade* (New Haven: 2010), 299.

51. Kenneth Scott, ed. "City of Wreckers: Key West Letters of 1838," in *Florida Historical Quarterly* 25, no. 2 (October 1946): 195; Sullivan, *Rambles*, 284; John Hope, "description of Bermuda," 1722, CO 37/10, fol. 218; Miller, *Nassau, Bahamas*, 34; Schoepff, *Travels*, 184–185.

52. Alejandro de la Fuentes, *Havana and the Atlantic in the Sixteenth Century* (Chapel Hill: 2011), 11–79, esp. 16; Parry, *Spanish Seaborne Empire*, esp. 134–135, 251–271; Roger C. Smith, *The Maritime Heritage of the Cayman Islands* (Gainesville: 2000), 170–176.

53. Sloane, *Voyage*, 1:lxxx–lxxxi.

54. Anonymous, *A True Relation of that which lately hapned to the Great Spanish Fleet, and Galeons of Terra Firma in America. With Many Strange Deliveries of Captaines, and Souldiers in the Tempest* (London: 1623); John Viele, *The Florida Keys: The Wreckers*, 3 vols. (Sarasota: 2001), 3:xii, 5–9; John Christopher Fine, *Lost on the Ocean Floor: Diving the World's Ghost Ships* (Annapolis: 2005), 2–3.

55. Viele, *Florida Keys*, xii, 5–10; Fine, *Lost*, 5–10; Eugene Lyon, *The Search for Atocha* (New York: 1974), 73–77; Jedwin Smith, *Fatal Treasure: Greed and Death, Emeralds and Gold, and the Obsessive Search for the Legendary Ghost Galleon Atocha* (Hoboken: 2003), 15–16.

56. April 22, 1627?, Gonzalez de Ribero, "Begin, Señor, Francisco Nuñez Melián, Tesorero de la Santa Cruzada en las Islas de Barlovento, Etc." [A Memorial on Behalf of F. Nuñez Melián, Setting Forth His Services in Cuba] (April 22, 1627?), Eugene Lion, trans., Mel Fisher Maritime Heritage Society, Key West, FL, and British Library; "Contratacion," Archivo General de Indias, Seville, 93B; Fine, *Lost*, 1–10; Lyon, *Atocha*, 75–77; Viele, *Florida Keys*, xii, 5–10.

57. John Hope, "description of Bermuda," 1722, CO 37/10, fol. 218; Johann David Schoepff, *Travels in the Confederation*, Alfred J. Morrison, ed. (Philadelphia: 1911), 284–285; Bernhard, *Slaves and Slaveholders*, 24; Viele, *Florida Keys*, 24, 26, 71–72. For scholarship on these colonies, see Jarvis, *Eye of All Trade*; Sandra Riley, *Homeward Bound: A History of the Bahama Islands to 1850 with a Definitive Study of Abaco in the American Loyalist Plantation Period* (Miami: 2000); Michael Craton and Gail Saunders, *Islanders in the Stream: A History of the Bahamian People from Aboriginal Times to the End of Slavery* (Athens: 1999); Saunders, *Slavery in the Bahamas*; Smith, *Cayman Islands*.

58. Ligon, *Barbadoes*, 52.

59. J. H. Lefroy, *Memorials of the Discovery and Early Settlement of the Bermudas, 1515–1685: Compiled from the Colonial Records and Other Original Sources*, 2 vols. (London: 1877), 1:60–61, 72, 115–116, 159–160, esp. 115–116; Sloane, *Voyage*, lxxx–lxxxi; John Smith, *The Generall Historie of Virginia, New-England, and the Summer Isles: With the Names of the Adventurers, Planters, and Governours* (London: 1632), 198; Vernon A. Ives, ed., *The Rich Papers: Letters from Bermuda, 1615–1646* (London: 1984), 401; David Marley, *Sack of Vera-cruz: The Great Pirate Raid of 1683* (Ontario: 1993); Law, *English in West Africa, 1681–1683*, 1:273; Jarvis, *Eye of All Trade*, 80–82; Bernhard, *Slaves and Slaveholders*, 6–7, 23–24; Law, *English in West Africa, 1681–1683*, 1: 273.

60. Jarvis, *Eye of All Trade*, 80–82, 502n34; William Phipps Papers, 7:14, Frederick Lewis Gay Transcripts, Massachusetts Historical Society; Enoch Pond, *The Lives of Increase Mather and Sir William Phipps* (Boston: 1870), 228–230; Peter Earle, *The Wreck of the Almiranta: Sir William Phips and the Search for the Hispaniola Treasure* (London: 1979), 155, 168–180; U1515/O10, William Yarway, A Journal of our Voyage Intended by Divine Asistance in the Ship Henry, Frances Rogers Com: Bound for Ambroshia Banks on ye North Side off Hispan-iola, in Company with ye James & Mary, Cap: W.ᵐ· Phips Comᵉʳ: Both in Pursuits of a Spanish Wreck in Search with God for our Guide Henry, Kent History and Library Centre, February 27, 1686 (hereafter, "Yarway, Journal of the Henry"); Inventory of Abraham Adderley, April 4, 1690, Bermuda Wills, 3:107–111. Thanks to archivist Betsy Boyle for help with Phipps's papers.

61. John Knepp's Journal of a Voyage from the Downes to Boston in the Ship Rose, William Phipps Commander, 1683, Frederick Lewis Gay Transcripts, Massachusetts Historical Society, 86–87 (hereafter, John Knepp's Journal); Cotton Mather, *Pietas in Patriam the life of His Excellency Sir William Phips, Knt. Late Captain General and Governour in Chief of the Province of the Massachusetts-Bay, New England* (London: 1697), sect. 6, 10–15.

62. Yarway, Journal of the Henry, September 24–November 16, 1686.

63. Yarway, Journal of the Henry, September 24, 1685–March 16, 1686, esp. January 20, 1686. The *James and Mary*'s ship log states the wreck was found on February 8, 1686/1687, Phipps Papers, 7:7, 12. For Phipps's endeavors off New Providence and Hispaniola, see Emerson W. Baker and John G. Reid, *New England Knight: Sir William Phips, 1651–1695* (Toronto: 1998).

64. Yarway, Journal of the Henry.

65. Phipps Papers, 6: 66–68; Lieutenant's logbooks for HMS FORESIGHT 1687–1690; HMS FOWEY 1696–1716; HMS FALCON 1778–1782, ADM/L/F/198; Peter Earle, *Treasure Hunt: Shipwreck, Diving, and the Quest for Treasure in an Age of Heroes* (New York: 2007), 72.

66. Phipps Papers, book 7: esp. 12, 14, 17, 20; Yarway, Journal of the Henry, September 24, 1685–March 16, 1686; esp. January 20, 1686; Jarvis, *Eye of All Trade*, 80–82, 502n34,

503n36; Enoch Pond, *The Lives of Increase Mather and Sir William Phipps* (Boston: 1870), 228–230; Earle, *Almiranta*, 155, 168–180.

67. Dive times are based on Miller, *Nassau, Bahamas*, 34; my observations; Streeter interview.

68. Bermuda Colonial Records, 1615–1713, 8:190, Bermuda Archives, Jarvis, *Eye of All Trade*, 503n36; Yarway, Journal of the Henry.

69. Phipps Papers, book 6, book 7:esp. 20.

70. Phipps Papers, book 4, book 7:14, 19, 22, 24, esp. 1:14–15; Jarvis, *Eye of All Trade*, 80–82, 502n34, 503n36.

71. Phipps Papers, book 7:25, 40; Inventory of Abraham Adderley, April 4, 1690, Bermuda Wills, book 3:107–111, Bermuda Archives; Jarvis, *Eye of All Trade*, 503n36. For the more modest Virginian material culture, see Isaac, Transformations of Virginia, 30–42, 58–87. On May 23, 1687, Hans Sloan reported that a Bahamian ship arrived in London "some few days ago" with silver from the *Concepción*. Phipps reached London on June 4. Gavin de Beer, *Sir Hans Sloane and the British Museum* (Oxford: 1953), 29–30. Adderley's slaves included an Indian girl, a woman, and apparently an older or disabled man.

72. Dunn, *Sugar and Slaves*, 21, 36, 43–45, 177–179, esp. 36; Robert F. Marx, "Divers of Port Royal," *Jamaica Journal* 2, no. 1 (March 1968): 15–23, esp. 21; "A Letter from Hans Sloane, M.D., with Accounts of the Earthquakes in Peru, Oct. 20. 1687; and at Jamaica, Feb. 19. 1687–8; and June 7. 1692," in *Philosophical Transactions, Giving Some Account of the Present Undertakings, Studies and Labors of the Ingenious in Many Considerable Parts of the World* 18, no. 207–214 (London: 1695): 77–100; J. W. Fortescue, ed., *Calendar of State Papers, Colonial Series: America & West Indies 1689–1692* (London: 1902), 651–711.

73. Hunter to Lord of Trades, 4 July 1730, September 19, 1730, December 24, 1730, PRO, CO 137/18, fols. 70–71, 120–122; Proclamation of September 26, 1730, list of treasure, PRO, CO 137/19, fols. 3, 5.

74. ADM I/1871/12, September 22, 1699, December 7, 1699, February 28, 1700; Collin Hunter Log, 1700/1701–1701/1702, ADM I/1872; Dolphin Log, ADM 52/25/8, April 16, 1700; Earl, *Treasure Hunt*, 133–165.

75. ADM I/1871/12, December 7, 1699; Collin Hunter Log, 1700/1701–1701/1702, ADM I/1872; Dolphin Log, ADM 52/25/8, April 10, 11, 12, 1700.

76. ADM I/1872 Collin Hunter Log, 1700/1701–1701/1702; Dolphin Log, ADM 52/25/8, April 11, 12, 1700. For tricksters, see Mamacar M'Baye, *The Trickster Comes West: Pan African Influences in Early Black Diaspora Narratives* (Jackson: 2009); John W. Roberts, *From Trickster to Badman: The Black Folk Hero in Slavery and Freedom* (Philadelphia: 1989); Dawson, "Enslaved Ship Pilots," 76–77.

77. Basil Hall, *Fragments of Voyages and Travels: Including Anecdotes of a Naval Life: Chiefly for the Use of Young Persons*, 3 vols. (Edinburgh: 1831), 1:116–117.

78. *London Chronicle*, August 11–14, 14–16, 16–18, 1787; *The Times* (London), August 13, 1787, October 22, 1787, November 11, 1788, January 5, 1789, April 24, 1790, esp. February 15, 1787; *The Times* (London), October 22, 1787.

79. Quoted in Earle, *Treasure Hunt*, 255–276, esp. 266, 267; "Short Journal of Commodore Inglefield's Transactions on the Coast of Africa," *The Times* (London), June 1, 1790.

80. ADM 1/2488/12, Henry Savage to Philip Stephens, May 27, 1790, "Narrative of the Capture of the Pirate Sloop Brothers"; ADM 51/703/2, log of the *Pomona*, October 230,

1789, Kent History and Library Centre. Freshwater salvage work was also performed. Rawick, *American Slave: Texas Narratives*, parts 1 and 2, 4:204; Rawick, *Texas Narratives*, part 2, 24:35–66.

81. "Short Journal of Commodore Inglefield's Transactions on the Coast of Africa," *The Times*, June 1, 1790; *Oxford English Dictionary*; "Voyage from Halifax to Bermuda," in *The Mariner's Chronicle of Shipwrecks, Fires, Famines and Other Disasters at Sea*, 2 vols. (Boston: 1834), 1:326–327.

82. Smith, *Cayman Islands*, 174; A. H. Wightwick, Haywood, "Sam Lord and His Castle," *The Journal of Barbados Museum and Historical Society* 30, no. 4 (May 1964): 114–125; Neville Connell, "Sam Lord's Castle," *Journal of Barbados Museum and Historical Society* 30, no. 4 (May 1964): 126–129; Anonymous, *A Guide to Sam Lord's Castle* (Barbados: 197?); Anonymous, *Sam Lord's Castle* (Barbados: 1952); Derek Bickerton, "Sam Lord: Fact? or Fiction?" *Barbados Advocate*, April 30, 1961; Earle, *Treasure Hunt*, 266; "Voyage from Halifax to Bermuda," 326–327; Jarvis, *Eye of All Trade*, 217–218.

83. Schoepff, *Travels*, 283; Long, *History of Jamaica*, 1:313; Waddell, *Twenty-Nine Years*, 214–215; Smith, *Cayman Islands*, 170–176; Michael Craton, *Founded upon the Sea: A History of the Cayman Islands and Their People* (Kingston: 2003), 56, 146–147; Charles Vigoles, *Observations upon the Floridas* (New York: 1823), 127.

84. Neville Williams, *A History of the Cayman Islands* (Grand Cayman: 1970), 21; Voyages: The Trans-Atlantic Slave Trade Database, retrieved June 22, 2010, http://www.slave voyages.org/voyage/82894/variables; Gomer Williams, *History of the Liverpool Privateers and Letters of Marque with an Account of the Liverpool Slave Trade* (London: 1897), 566. Gomer Williams wrote that the *Nelly* wrecked in the "Grand Canaries," which seems to be Gran Canaria in the Canary Islands. It is improbable that the *Nelly* passed through the Canary Islands. Passing by Grand Cayman is also an unlikely route but probably occurred if the captain were lost.

85. Waddell, *Twenty-Nine Years*, 212–217.

86. Sullivan, *Rambles*, 283–285; McKinnen, *British West Indies*, 140.

87. Griffith Hughes, The *Natural History of Barbados* (London: 1750), 276–277; Schoepff, *Travels*, 295, 303; Douglass Hall, ed., *Miserable Slavery*, 75. In 2004, I observed men harvesting conch in waters eight and thirty feet deep.

88. Anonymous, *Short Journey in the West Indies*, 2:107–108.

89. Miller, *Nassau, Bahamas*, 16–17; McKinnen, *British West Indies*, 140; Edward Sullivan, *Rambles and Scrambles in North and South America* (London: 1852), 283–285.

90. James H. Stark, *Stark's History of and Guide to the Bahama Islands* (Boston: 1891), 218, 223–227; Schoepff, *Travels*, 285–286.

91. Schoepff, *Travels*, 293; Jarvis, *Eye of All Trade*, 284; Riva Berlean-Schiller, "Environment, Technology, and the Catch: Fishing and Lobster Diving in Barbuda," in Bela Gunda, ed., *The Fishing Cultures of the World: Studies in Ethnology, Cultural Ecology and Folklore* (Budapest: 1984), 803–817.

92. Interviews with Barbadian fishermen in July and August 2004. The names of the interviewed fishermen are not provided as octopus was out of fishing season, making it illegal to catch them at that time.

93. Buisseret, *Jamaica*, 171; C. C. Nutting, "Some Notes on the Echinoderms (Starfish, Sea-Eggs) of Barbados," *Journal of the Barbados Museum and Historical Society*, 4, no. 1

(November 1936), 70; Sloane, *Voyage*, 2:267; H. H. Brown, *The Sea Fisheries of Barbados* (Barbados: Report to the Comptroller for the Development and Welfare in the West Indies by the director of the Fisheries Investigation, 1997), 15–16; Christopher Parker, "A Bajan Delicacy: The Seaegg Fishery of Barbados," in *Ins & Outs of Barbados*, (2003), 177; Jerome S. Handler and Frederick W. Lange, *Plantation Slavery in Barbados: An Archaeological and Historical Investigation* (Cambridge: 1978), 15; Ministry of Agriculture and Rural Development, Fisheries Division, *Barbados Sea Eggs: Past, Present, Future. Barbados Fisheries Management Plan: Public Information Document No. 1* (Barbados, 1999), 2–5; Morris Greenidge, *Holetown, Barbados: Settlement Revisited and Other Accounts* (Cave Hill: 2004), 32.

94. Ministry of Agriculture, *Barbados Sea Eggs*, 6; John Lewis, "Sea Eggs," *The Bajan* (Barbados) 5, no. 1 (September 1957): 27–28; Parker, "A Bajan Delicacy," 177; H. Brown, *Fisheries of Barbados*, 15–16; Mark D. Alleyne, "Crisis Among the Sea-Eggs," *The Bajan & South Caribbean* 324 (November 1980), 4; Nutting, "Echinoderms," 69–70; Willoughby et al., *Fishing Industry of Barbados*, 6.

95. Ministry of Agriculture, *Sea Eggs*, 6; Lewis, "Sea Eggs," 27; Greenidge, *Holetown*, 124.

96. Ministry of Agriculture, *Sea Eggs*, 7; Lewis, "Sea Eggs," 28; Rey, *Amplified Polymorphic DNA*, 15–20; H. Brown, *Sea Fisheries*, 16.

97. H. Brown, *Sea Fisheries*, 16; Alleyne, "Sea-Eggs," 4; Nutting, "Echinoderms," 69–70; Lewis, "Sea Eggs," 27; Ministry of Agriculture, *Sea Eggs*, 8; Karl Watson, *The Civilised Island of Barbados: A Social History 1750–1816* (Ellerton: 1975), 50; Handler and Lange, *Plantation Slavery*, 15.

98. Ball, *Fifty Years*, 206–240.

99. Frederick Law Olmsted, *A Journey in the Seaboard Slave States; With Remarks on Their Economy* (London: 1856), 351–355; "The Fisheries of Albermarle and Pamlico Sounds, North Carolina," *Harper's Weekly*, September 28, 1861; David S. Cecelski, *The Waterman's Song: Slavery and Freedom in Maritime North Carolina* (Chapel Hill: 2001), 74–75.

100. Olmsted, *Slave States*, 353–354; Edmund Ruffin, *Agricultural, Geological, and Descriptive Sketches of Lower North Carolina, and the Similar Adjacent Lands* (Raleigh: 1861), 183.

101. Olmsted, *Slave States*, 354.

102. Ibid., 353–355.

Chapter 5

1. Dawson, "Enslaved Ship Pilots"; Olwell, *Masters, Slaves, and Subjects*, esp. 7; Follett, *Sugar Masters*, esp. 5, 124–130; Berlin, *Many Thousands Gone*, esp. 2–6, 66, 142–176; Dusinberre, *Dark Day*, 179–210, 302–349; Dawson, "Enslaved Swimmers," 1347–1348, 1352–1354; Stewart B. Schwartz, *Slaves, Peasants, and Rebels: Reconsidering Brazilian Slavery* (Urbana: 1992), 48.

2. Dawson, "Enslaved Ship Pilots"; Follett, *Sugar Masters*, 5, 118–150, esp. 126; Dusinberre, *Dark Days*, 179–210, esp. 190; Sheridan, *Sugar and Slavery*, 107–118, 339–340; Dunn, *Sugar and Slaves*, 192–195; Charles B. Dew, *Bond of Iron: Master and Slave at Buffalo Forge* (New York: 1994), 26, 171–219; Charles B. Dew, *Ironmaker to the Confederacy: Joseph R. Anderson and the Tredegar Iron Works* (Richmond: 1999), 23–27; Menard, *Sweet Negotiations*, 17; Bayly Marks, "Skilled Blacks in Antebellum St. Mary's County, Maryland," *Journal of Southern History* 53, no. 4 (November 1987), 553–564; Daniel C. Littlefield, *Rice and Slaves: Ethnicity and the Slave Trade in Colonial South Carolina* (Chicago: 1991), 93–95, 106; Judith

A. Carney, *Black Rice: The African Origins of Rice Cultivation in the Americas* (Cambridge: 2001), 94–97.

3. Dusinberre, *Dark Days*, 192, 196–201; Follett, *Sugar Masters*, 124–130; Dawson, "Enslaved Ship Pilots"; Sheridan, *Sugar and Slavery*, 112–118.

4. Dawson, "Enslaved Swimmers"; Dawson, "Enslaved Ship Pilots;" Bolster, *Black Jacks*, esp. 133.

5. Dusinberre, *Dark Days*, 178–210.

6. Dawson, "Enslaved Pilots"; Dawson, "Enslaved Swimmers," 1351–1352; Jonathan D. Martin, *Divided Mastery: Slave Hiring in the American South* (Cambridge: 2009); Pedro L. V. Welch, *Slave Society in the City: Bridgetown, Barbados, 1680–1834* (Kingston: 2003); Higman, *Slave Populations*; N. A. T. Hall, "Slavery in Three West Indian Towns: Christiansted, Fredericksted and Charlotte Amalie in the late Eighteenth and Early Nineteenth Century," in B. W. Higman, *Trade, Government and Society in Caribbean History, 1700–1920* (Kingston: 1983).

7. Hope, "description of Bermuda," 1722, CO 37/10, fol. 218; McKinnen, *British West Indies*, 140–141; Vigoles, *Floridas*, 125–126; Jarvis, *Eye of All Trade*, 217, 281, 283; Dawson, "Enslaved Ship Pilots"; Anonymous, "Voyage from Halifax to Bermuda," in *The Mariner's Chronicle of Shipwrecks, Fires, Famines and Other Disasters at Sea*, 2 vols. (Boston: 1834), 1:326–327. For how smuggling and piracy facilitated maritime commerce, see Wim Klooster, "Inter-Imperial Smuggling in the Americas, 1600–1800," Bailyn and Denault, *Soundings in Atlantic History*, 141–180; Bailyn, *Atlantic History*, 88–92; Wim Klooster, *Illicit Riches: Dutch Trade in the Caribbean, 1648–1795* (Leiden: 1998); Kenneth J. Banks, "Official Duplicity: The Illicit Slave Trade of Martinique," in Peter A. Coclanis, ed., *The Atlantic Economy During the Seventeenth and Eighteenth Centuries: Organization, Operation, Practice, and Personnel* (Columbia: 2005), 229–252; Mark G. Hanna, *Pirate Nests and the Rise of the British Empire, 1570–1740* (Chapel Hill: 2015); Kevin P. McDonald, *Pirates, Merchants, Settlers, and Slaves: Colonial America and the Indo-Atlantic World* (Oakland: 2015); Dawson, "Enslaved Ship Pilots," 75; Eve Tavor Bannet, *Transatlantic Stories and the History of Reading, 1720–1810: Migrant Fictions* (Cambridge: 2011), 65–86.

8. Miller, *Nassau, Bahamas*, 25, 43; Anonymous, "Halifax to Bermuda," 326–327; Jarvis, *Eye of All Trade*, 30–31, 147–151; Jarvis, "Maritime Masters," 608, Jarvis, "Anxious Mariner," 86, Bernhard, *Slaves and Slaveholders*, 50–52, 123, 238–272; Dawson, "Enslaved Ship Pilots;" Bolster, *Black Jacks*, esp. 268–269; Saunders, *Slavery in the Bahamas*; Riley, *Homeward Bound*, 203–204, 213–214; Craton and Saunders, *Islanders*, 179–396; Craton, *Founded on the Sea*, 52–53, 111, 146–147, 217; Roger Smith, *Cayman Islands*, 73–74; Higman, *Slave Populations*, 64–65, 76, 307, 376, 379–380; McKinnen, *British West Indies*, 140–141.

9. Menard, *Sweet Negotiations*, esp. 30, 44–45, 48; Dunn, *Sugar and Slavery*, 3–187.

10. For hiring out, see Dawson, "Enslaved Pilots."

11. Dawson, "Enslaved Pilots," 354–355.

12. Ibid.

13. Phipps Papers, 6: 33–38; Vigoles, *Floridas*, 125.

14. Bermuda Colonial Records, 1615–1713, 8:190, Bermuda Archives. Adderley died in 1690.

15. For other Barbadian ships, see Phipps Papers, book 6, book 8.

16. For Phipps's treatment of white mariners, see John Knepp's journal. For treatment of ill divers, see Phipps Papers, 7:14, 17, 20. The pirates who plundered the *Hartwell* apparently lost one diver. ADM 1/2488/12, Henry Savage to Philip Stephens, May 27, 1790, "Narrative of the Capture of the Pirate Sloop Brothers"; ADM 51/703/2, log of the *Pomona*, October 26, 1789, Kent History and Library Centre.

17. Dunn, *Sugar and Slaves*, 301; Sheridan, *Sugar and Slavery*, 243–245; Menard, *Sweet Negotiations*, 26, 83–84.

18. Phipps Papers, 7: 3, 6–8; U1515/O10, Yarway, Journal of the Henry, January 9, 1687, May 28, 1686; Earle, *Almiranta*, 184. For time off when ill, see Phipps Papers, 7:14, 17, 20; U1515/O10, Yarway, Journal of the Henry. For dive conditions, see Phipps Papers, book 6, book 7; U1515/O10, Yarway, Journal of the Henry, September 24, 1685–March 16, 1686. The *Concepción* wreck seemingly illustrates the improbability of quickly training divers. The Mosquito divers had apparently worked shallower water and had difficulty adapting to the wreck's depths. Phipps Papers, 7:14, 17.

19. For labor informing life, see Richard S. Dunn, *A Tale of Two Plantations: Slave Life and Labor in Jamaica and Virginia* (Cambridge: 2014); Follett, *Sugar Master*; Dusinberre, *Dark Day*; Martin, *Divided Mastery*; Welch, *Slave Society*; Dawson "Enslaved Ship Pilots;" Dawson, "Enslaved Swimmers."

20. Dunn, *Sugar and Slaves*, 194; quoted in Sheridan, *Sugar and Slavery*, 107–118, 339–340; Follett, *Sugar Masters*, 118–194; Oldendorp, *Caribbean Mission*, 225–226; Johan Christian Schmidt, *Various Remarks collected on and about the Island of St. Croix in America* (1788; St. Croix: 1998), 4–12; Reimert Haagensen, *Description of the Island of St Croix in America in the West Indies* (1758; St Croix: 1995), 23–31.

21. Dew, *Ironmaker*, 27; Dew, *Bond of Iron*, 26, 171–219.

22. Dusinberre, *Dark Days*, esp. 175, 198; Berlin, *Many Thousands Gone*, 1–6, 66, 142–176.

23. Follett, *Sugar Masters*, 128; Martin, *Divided Mastery*, 1–9, 161–166, esp. 161; Dusinberre, *Dark Days*, 196–197; Emma Hart, *Building Charleston: Town and Society in the Eighteenth-Century British Atlantic World* (Charlottesville: 2010), esp. 110–112, 231n33; Dew, *Ironmaker*, 24–26; Dawson, "Enslaved Ship Pilots."

24. Berry, *Swing the Sickle*, 1–10, 60–61; Wiggins, "Good Times," 278–280.

25. Interrogation of and Deposition made by Jacques Francis on Tuesday, February 8, 1548 (O.S.), February 18, 1548 (D.S.), PRO, HCA 13/93/202v–203r (hereafter, Jacques Francis); Deposition made by Anthonius de Nicholao Rimero on May 28, 1548, PRO, HCA 13/93, ff. 275–276 (hereafter, Nicholao Rimero). Miranda Kaufmann, "Africans in Britain, 1500–1640" (Ph.D. diss., Oxford University, 2005), 67–68, 130, 182–183; Miranda Kaufmann, *Black Tudors: The Untold Story* (London: 2017). Thanks to Miranda Kaufmann for insights and sources on Francis. For sixteenth-century English concepts of race and slavery, see note 28.

26. Jacques Francis; Nicholao Rimero, 275–276; Azurara, *Chronicle of Discovery*, I, 58; II, xi, 104, 107, esp. 320; Duarte Pacheco Pereira, *Esmeraldo de Situ Orbis* (1892; London: 1937), 72–78, esp. 72; 77; John William Blake, *Europeans in West Africa: 1450–1560* (1942; London: 1967), 14, 22, 88, 132–133, 139–140; Gustave Ungerer, "Recovering a Black Africans' Voice in an English Lawsuit: Jacques Francis and the Salvage Operations of the *Mary Rose* and the *Sancta Maria and Sanctus Edwardus*, 1545–c. 1550," *Mediaeval and Renaissance Drama in England* 17 (2005), 255–271; A. C. de C. M. Saunders, *A Social History of Slaves and Freemen in Portugal, 1441–1555* (Cambridge: 1982), 5; 20–25.

27. William Mussen, PRO, HCA 13/93, ff. 193v–194; John Westcott PRO, HCA 13/93, ff.192v–193r; Jacques Francis; Nicholao Rimero. The divers' ability to communicate with each other but apparently not in English suggests they were from the same African region. HCA 13/93, ff. 203–204.

28. Deposition made by Niccolo de Marini on June 5, 1548, PRO, HCA 13/5/191; Nicholao Rimero; Deposition made by Domenico de Milanes on May 23, 1548, PRO, HCA 13/93/

242–243; Ungerer, "Africans' Voice," 263, 270n36. For perceptions of race, see Kaufmann, "Africans in Britain," 67–68, 130, 182–183, 271–283; T. F. Earle and K. J. P. Lowe, eds., *Black Africans in Renaissance Europe* (Cambridge: 2005); Kate Lowe, "Visible Lives: Black Gondoliers and Other Black Africans in Renaissance Venice," *Renaissance Quarterly* 66, no. 2 (Summer 2013), 412–452; Anthony Barthelemy, Black Face, Maligned Race: The Representation of Blacks in English Drama from Shakespeare to Southerne (Baton Rouge: 1987).

29. Jacques Francis; Nicholao Rimero. For problems with assuming sixteenth-century Africans in England were slaves, see Michael Guasco, *Slaves and Englishmen: Human Bondage in the Early Modern Atlantic World* (Philadelphia: 2014), 11–79, 115, esp. 108; Kaufmann, "Africans in Britain," 269–278. Guasco explains that sixteenth-century English people understood slavery but did not accept it "as a labor system or a way of organizing human populations in terms of superficial phenotypical categories" and even when labeling Africans "slaves" it was often "a label of convenience rather than a true indication of their condition." Guasco, *Slaves and Englishmen*, 14, 67. For previous scholarship on Francis, see Ungerer, "Black Africans' Voice," 255–271; Ray Costello, *Black Salt: Seafarers of African Descent on British Ships* (Liverpool: 2012), 3–9.

30. For manipulation of legal systems, see Thelma Wills Foote, *Black and White Manhattan: The History of Racial Formation in Colonial New York City* (Oxford: 2004), 23–88; Graham Russell Hodges, *Root and Branch: African Americans in New York and East Jersey, 1613–1863* (Chapel Hill: 1999), 7–68; Anthony S. Parent Jr., *Foul Means: The Formation of a Slave Society in Virginia, 1660–1740* (Chapel Hill: 2003), 105–172; Katherine Howlett Hayes, *Slavery Before Race: Europeans, Africans, and Indians at Long Island's Sylvester Manor Plantation, 1651–1884* (New York: 2013); T. H. Breen and Stephen Innes, *"Myne Owne Ground": Race and Freedom on Virginia's Eastern Shore, 1640–1676* (Oxford: 1980); Lander, *Spanish Florida*; Sweet, *Domingos Álvares*; Dawson, "Enslaved Ship Pilots."

31. Jacques Francis; *King James Bible*, Songs of Solomon 1:5. For racial and social inversion, see Dawson, "Enslaved Ship Pilots."

32. Bernard, "Sponge Diving," 103–130, esp. 119; Mac Marshall, *Weekend Warriors: Alcohol in a Micronesian Culture* (Palo Alto: 1979), 59, 89–93; Gilmore, *Manhood*, esp. 9–23; "Death-Defying Free Dives"; my observations.

33. Markham, *Hawkins' Voyages*, 314; Kunz Stevenson, *Pearl*, 231; Otte, *Margarita*, 1:218–221; Donkin, *Beyond Price*, 323.

34. Hawthorne, *Africa to Brazil*, 20, 140; Fraser, "Negotiating Their Manhood," 76–94, 84–85; Olwell, *Masters, Slaves, and Subject*, esp. 6–10, 166–219; Follett, *Sugar Masters*, esp. 5, 124–130; Dusinberre, *Dark Days*, 179–210, 302–349; Peter A. Coclanis, "How the Low Country Was Taken to Task: Slave-Labor Organization in Coastal South Carolina and Georgia," in Robert L. Paquette and Louis A. Ferleger, eds., *Slavery, Secession, and the Southern History* (Charlottesville: 2000), 59–80.

35. Like other enslaved mariners, divers probably "measured possibilities for freedom in hours or days without white interference." Bolster, *Black Jacks*, 133; Dawson, "Enslaved Ship Pilots."

Chapter 6

1. Thornton, *Africa and Africans*, 17–21; Ferreira, *Cross-Cultural Exchange*.

2. For example, see Smith, "Palaver Islands," 3–25; Smith, "Canoe," 515–533; Harms, *River of Wealth*, 48–49, 72; Miller, *Way of Death*; Green, *Gender, Ethnicity, and Social Change*;

Akyeampong, *Sea and the Lagoon*; Law, *Ouidah*; Mann, *Birth of an African City*; Searing, *West African Slavery*; Austen and Derrick, *Middlemen*; Ray and Rich, *African Maritime History*; J. A. Alago, "Long-Distance Trade in the Niger Delta," *Journal of African History* 13, no. 3 (1970): 319–329; Robin Horton, "From Fishing Village to Trading State," in Mary Douglas and Phyllis Kaberry, eds., *Man in Africa* (London: 1969); Peter C. W. Gutkind, "The Boatmen of Ghana: The Possibilities of a Pre-Colonial African Labor History," in Michael Hanagan and Charles Stephenson, eds., *Confrontation, Class Consciousness, and the Labor Process: Studies in Proletarian Class Formation* (Westport: 1986), 130; Gutkind, "Trade and Labor"; Thornton, *Africa and Africans*, 14–21; Finmore, *Maritime History*; Weeks, *Congo Cannibal*, 18, 23.

3. André Álvares de Almada, *Rivers of Guinea: Being an English Translation of a Variorum Text of Tratado breve dos Rios de Guiné, c.1594*; P. E. H. Hair and Jean Boulègue, trans. and eds. (c. 1595; Liverpool: 1984), 1:78, 2:2, 10, 18; Atkins, *Voyage to Guinea*, 59.

4. Quoted in Smith, "Canoe," 521; Thornton, *Africa and Africans*, 17–19; Searing, *West African Slavery*; Austen and Derrick, *Middlemen*; Akyeampong, *Sea and the Lagoon*; Law, *Ouidah*; Mann, *Birth of an African City*; Harms, *River of Wealth*; Miller, *Way of Death*.

5. Thornton, *Africa and Africans*, 19.

6. Searing, *West African Slavery*; Rodney, *Upper Guinea*; Barry, *Senegambia*; George E. Brooks, *Eurafricans in Western Africa: Commerce, Social Status, Gender, and Religious Observance from the Sixteenth to the Eighteenth Century* (Athens: 2003); David Wright, *The World and a Very Small Place: A History of Globalization in Niumi, The Gambia* (London: 2004).

7. Quoted in Law, *English in West Africa*, 1:234; Law, *Ouidah*, 29; Thornton, *Africa and Africans*, 18–19; K. Onwuka Dike, *Trade and Politics in the Niger Delta, 1830–1885* (Oxford: 1956), passim, esp. 19–46; Mann, *Birth of an African City*, esp. 24; Akyeampong, *Sea and the Lagoon*, esp. 29–30; Greene, *Gender, Ethnicity, and Social Change*.

8. Thornton, *Africa and Africans*, 18–19; Searing, *West African Slavery*; Brooks, *Eurafricans*, Wright, *World and a Very Small Place*.

9. Thornton, *Africa and Africans*, 19; Harms, *River of Wealth*, 1; Harms, *Games Against Nature*, Miller, *Way of Death*; Heywood and Thornton, *Central Africans*, 52–57.

10. Tams, *Portuguese Possessions*, 1:81.

11. Patrick Manning, "Merchants, Porters, and Canoemen in the Bight of Benin: Links in the West African Trade Network," in Catherine Coquery-Vidrovitch and Paul Lovejoy, eds., *The Workers of the African Trade* (Beverly Hills: 1985), 62; Smallwood, *Saltwater Slaver*, 42; Ray A. Kea, *Settlements, Trade, and Polities in the Seventeenth-Century Gold Coast* (Baltimore: 1982), 40, passim, esp. 37–50, 41, 42, 57, 206–247; Law, *Ouidah*, 18, 28; Gutkind, "Trade and Labor," 25; Akyeampong, *Sea and the Lagoon*, 75, 75n1; R. Earle Anderson, *Liberia: America's African Friend* (Chapel Hill: 1952), 11.

12. Olaf U. Janzen, "A World-Embracing Sea: The Oceans as Highways, 1604–1815," in Finmore, *Maritime History*, 104.

13. Law, *Ouidah*, 5; Miller, *Way of Death*; Greene, *Gender, Ethnicity, and Social Change*; Akyeampong, *Between the Sea and the Lagoon*; Mann, *Birth of an African City*; Searing, *West African Slavery*; Austen and Derrick, *Middlemen of the Cameroon Rivers*; Ray and Rich, *African Maritime History*; G. I. Jones, *The Trading States of the Oil Rivers: A Study of Political Development in Eastern Nigeria* (Oxford: 1963); Dike, *Trade and Politics*; Robin Law, "Ouidah as a Multiethnic Community," in Cañizares-Esguerra, Childs, and Sidbury, eds., *Black Urban Atlantic*, 42–62; Roquinaldo Ferreira, "Slavery and the Social and Cultural Landscapes of Luanda," in Cañizares-Esguerra, Childs, and Sidbury, *Black Urban Atlantic*.

14. Hawthorne, *Harvesting Slaves*, 40; George E. Brooks, *Landlords and Strangers: Ecology, Society, and Trade in Western Africa, 1000–1630* (Oxford: 1993), 80–87; Harms, *Games Against Nature*; Wright, *World Is a Small Place*, esp. 63–77, 301n40; Robert Smith, "To the Palaver Islands: War and Diplomacy on the Lagos Lagoon in 1852–1854," *Journal of the Historical Society of Nigeria* 5, no. 1 (December 1969): 3, 3n1.

15. Snelgrave, *New Account*, 99; Bolster, *Black Jacks*, 48; Smith, "Canoe," 518; James Hornell, "The Kru Canoes of Sierra Leone," *The Mariner's Mirror: The Journal of the Society for Nautical Research* 15 (1929): 231, 233; Thornton, *Africa and Africans*, 37; John Barbot, *A Description of the Coasts of North and South Guinea* (London, 1746), 382; Hair, Jones, and Law, *Barbot on Guinea*, 1:229n/13; Thomas Phillips, "The Voyage of the Ship *Hannibal* of London, in 1693," in George Frances Dow, ed., *Slave Ships and Slaving* (Cambridge: 1968), 73; Atkinson, *Voyage to Guinea*, 59; Isert, *Letters*, 27.

16. Rodney, *Upper Guinea*, 17, esp. 18; A. P. Brown, "The Fishing Industry in the Labadi District," in F. R. Irvine, *The Fishes and Fisheries of the Gold Coast* (London: 1947), 32–33, 38–39; Smith, "Canoe," 520–521; Harms, *River of Wealth*, 69; Bolster, *Black Jacks*, 49; Kea, *Settlements, Trade, and Polities*, 40; Gutkind, "Trade and Labor," 43.

17. Rodney, *Upper Guinea*, 16–17, 80–82, 159; Brooks, *Kru Mariner*, 15; Burton, *Wanderings*, 284; Canneau, *Slaver's Logbook*, 255; de Marees, *Gold Kingdom*, 119. For portaging, see Canneau, *Slaver's Logbook*, 255; de Marees, *Gold Kingdom*, 119; Hair, Jones, and Law, *Barbot on Guinea*, 1:181, 194n11; Wm. R. Smith, *Africa Illustrated* (New York: 1889), 179, 187.

18. Bolster, *Black Jacks*, 48; Michel Adanson, *A Voyage to Senegal, the Isle of Goree, and the River Gambia* (London: 1759), 94; Gutkind, "Boatmen of Ghana," 130.

19. Barbot, *Barbot on Guinea*, 2:267, 278n1.

20. Great Britain Hydrographic Office, *Africa Pilot*, 3 vols. (London: 1893), 2:35, 42, 142, 181, 208, esp. 36, 37; W. E. F. Ward, *My Africa* (1970; Accra: 1991), 112.

21. Barbot, *Barbot on Guinea*, 2;529–530; Hornell, "Kru Canoes," 231, 237; Markham, ed., *Hawkins' Voyages*, 18.

22. Crone, *Voyages of Cadamosto*, 59; Chas. W. Thomas, *Adventures and Observations on the West Coast of Africa, and Its Islands: Historical and Descriptive Sketches of Madeira, Canary, Biafra, and Cape Verd Islands* (Macon: 1860), 104; Robert Baker, *Travail in Guinea*, 27–29.

23. E. J. Glave, *In Savage Africa: Or Six Years of Adventure in Congo-Land* (London, 1893), 129; Harms, *River of Wealth*, 208, 216–217.

24. De Marees, *Gold Kingdom*, 15, 118–119; Weeks, *Congo Cannibals*, 94–95; Jones, *German Sources*, 66; Hair, Jones, and Law, *Barbot on Guinea*, 2:341; Canneau, *Slaver's Logbook*, 255; Nicolas Villault, *A Relation of the Coasts of Africk called Guinee* (1669; London: 1670): 214–215; Hornell, "Kru Canoes," 231, 237; Ward, *My Africa*, 112; Adanson, *Voyage to Senegal*, 94.

25. De Marees, *Gold Kingdom*, 119; Jones, *German Sources*, 254; Barbot, *Barbot on Guinea*, 2:341, 528–529; Smith, "Canoe," 520; Irvine, *Fisheries*, 32; Hornell, "Kru Canoes," 231; Coronel, "Fanti Canoe Decoration," 54; Richard B. Nunoo, "Canoe Decoration in Ghana," *African Arts* 7, no. 3 (Spring 1974), 32; Harms, *River of Wealth*, 69; F. R. Irvine, *Woody Plants of Ghana: With Special Reference to Their Uses* (Oxford: 1961), 191, plate 16. For scaffolds and platforms, see Richard Price, *Alabi's World* (Baltimore: 1990), 137 ; Chevalier de Préfontaine, *Maison rustique, a l'usage des habitans de la partie de la France équinoxiale, connue sous le nom de Cayenne* (Paris, 1763), plate 6.

26. C. K. Meek, *A Sudanese Kingdom: An Ethnographical Study of the Jukan-Speaking Peoples of Nigeria* (London: 1931), 427; Harms, *River of Wealth*, 69; Smith, "Canoe," 520n31.

27. Smith, "Canoe," 520; Irvine, *Woody Plants*, 190–193; Hornell, "Kru Canoes," 232; Brown "Fishing Industry," 32; Rodney, *Upper Guinea*, 17; Frederick Edwin Forbes, *Six Months' Service in the African Blockade, from April to October, 1848, in Command of H.M.S. Bonetta.* (1949; London: 1969), 22; Bosman, *Accurate Description*, 544; Hydrographic Office, *Africa Pilot*, vol. 2; Meredith, *Gold Coast*, 25, 59; Almada, *Rivers of Guinea*, 1:38; Atkins, *Voyage to Guinea*, 59; Brooks, *Landlords and Strangers*, 209.

28. Bosman, *Accurate Description*, 129, 544n, esp. 294–295; Barbot, *Barbot on Guinea*, 2:544n43.

29. Smith, "Canoe," 520; Irvine, *Woody Plants*, 184–185; Nunoo, "Canoe Decoration in Ghana," 32.

30. Harms, *River of Wealth*, 7, 169; Glave, *Savage Africa*, 114, 117; Meek, *Sudanese Kingdom*, 426; Irvine, *Woody Plants*, 270–271, 520–524.

31. Rodney, *Upper Guinea*, 18; Brown, "Fishing Industry," 24; Smith, "Canoe," 520; Harms, *River of Wealth*, 59–60, 69; Meek, *Sudanese Kingdom*, 426; Nunoo, "Canoe Decoration in Ghana," 32; Rankin, White Man's Grave, 1:227.

32. Quoted in Shobel, *World in Miniature*, 2:78–79. Kea discussed Gold Coast-craft villages, and Harms documented those in the Congo River basin. Kea, *Settlements, Trade, and Polities*, 48, 64–65, 76; Harms, *River of Wealth*, 22, 59–60, 69; Cronel, "Fante Canoe Decoration," 54; Jean-Marie Gibbal, *Genii of the River Niger*, Beth G. Raps, trans. (Chicago: 1994), 6.

33. Harms, *River of Wealth*, 69; Cronel, "Fante Canoe Decoration," 54; Meek, *Sudanese Kingdom*, 425.

34. Weeks, *Congo Cannibals*, 81, 95; Brown, "Fishing Industry," 24; Smith, "Canoe," 520; Harms, *River of Wealth*, 59–60, 69; Meek, *Sudanese Kingdom*, 426; Nunoo, "Canoe Decoration in Ghana," 32; Rankin, *White Man's Grave*, 1:227.

35. Kea, *Settlements, Trade, and Polities*, 48, 64–65, 84, esp. 76; quoted in Law, *English in West Africa*, 3:4, 13–14, 27, 47, 55, 67, esp. 28; Barbot, *North and South Guinea*, 266; Kwamina B. Dickson, *A Historical Geography of Ghana* (Cambridge: 1971), 93; de Marees, *Gold Kingdom*, 118; Jones, *German Sources*, 254, 254n516.

36. De Marees, *Gold Kingdom*, 118; Bosman, *Accurate Description*, 19; Jones, *German Sources*, 254, 254n516.

37. Jones, *German Sources*, 254, 254n516; Hair, Jones, and Law, *Barbot on Guinea*, 2:528–529, 543n43; Barbot, *North and South Guinea*, 266, 268. Adam Jones explained that there was probably already a scarcity of large trees close to Cape Coast. Jones, *German Sources*, 254n516.

38. Kea, *Settlements, Trade, and Polities*, 84; Smith, "Canoe," 520; Kwame Yeboa Daaku, *Trade and Politics on the Gold Coast, 1600–1720: A Study of the African Reaction to European Trade* (Oxford: 1970), 200; Harvey M. Feinberg, *Africans and Europeans in West Africa: Elminans and Dutchmen on the Gold Coast During the Eighteenth Century* (Philadelphia: 1989), 11.

39. Quoted in Law, *English in West Africa*, 1:96; Hair, Jones, and Law, *Barbot on Guinea*, 2:341, 364n51, 528–529.

40. Daaku, *Trade and Politics*, esp. 7, 103; Gutkind, "Boatmen of Ghana," 143; Law, *Ouidah*, Mann, *Birth of an African City*; Thornton, *Warfare in Atlantic Africa*; Brown, "Fishing Industry," 24; Smith, "Canoe," 520.

41. Daaku, *Trade and Politics*, 7, 79, 103–104; Harms, *River of Wealth*, 48–49, 69, 103, 169–170; A. P. Brown, "Fishing Industry," 24, Robert Smith, "Canoe," 520; Gutkind, "Boatmen of Ghana," 143.

42. Brown, "Fishing Industry," 24; Smith, "Canoe," 520; Harms, *River of Wealth*, 48–49, 69.

43. Brown, "Fishing Industry," 24; Smith, "Canoe," 520; Harms, *River of Wealth*, 69; Meek, *Sudanese Kingdom*, 427; Coronel, "Fanti Canoe Decoration," 54; C. Béart, "Jeux et Jouets de L'Oust African: 7 Les Courses," *Mémoires de L'Institut Français D'Afrique Noire* 1, no. 42 (1955): 331–332.

44. De Marees, *Gold Kingdom*, 118; Hair, Jones, and Law, *Barbot on Guinea*, 2:528–529, 543n43; Barbot, *North and South Guinea*, 266, 268, 286, 289, 304; Jones, *German Sources*, 254; Law, *English in West Africa*, 2:51–52, 54–55, 81, 88, 3:4, 13, 14, 27, 95, 183, 224.

45. Smith, "Canoe," 520n32; Kea, *Settlements, Trade, and Polities*, 84.

46. Feinberg, *Africans and Europeans*, 8, 11, 70; Meredith, *Gold Coast*, 78–79; Albert van Dantzig, *Forts and Castles of Ghana* (Accra; 1980), 19; de Marees, *Gold Kingdom*, 79n4, 203n5; Daaku, *Trade and Politics*, 202; Bosman, *Accurate Description*, 20–23; Law, *English in West Africa*, 1:48; Great Britain Hydrographic Office, *The African Pilot, or Sailing Directions for the Western Coast of Africa*, 3 vols. (London: 1856), 1:148–149.

47. Meredith, *Gold Coast*, 1:78–79; T. Edward Bowdich, *Mission from Cape Coast to Ashantee* (London: 1824), 214; de Marees, *Gold Kingdom*, 79n4; van Dantzig, *Forts and Castles*, 19; Verrips, "Canoe Decorations," 46.

48. E. J. Alogoa, "Long-Distance Trade and States in the Niger Delta," *Journal of African History* 11, no. 3 (1970): 323–325, esp. 324.

49. Jones, *German Sources*, 254, 254n516.

50. Alogoa, "Long Distance Trade," 323–324; Meek, *Sudanese Kingdom*, 425; Harms, *River of Wealth*, 69. For barn-raising, see Randy Leffingwell, *American Barn* (St. Paul: 2003), 11–25; Doug Ohman and Will Weaver, *Barns of Minnesota* (St. Paul: 2004), 37–50; John Fitchen and Gregory D. Huber, *The New World Dutch Barn: The Evolution, Forms, and Structure of a Disappearing Icon* (Syracuse: 2001); Robert F. Ensminger, *The Pennsylvania Barn: Its Origin, Evolution, and Distribution in North America* (Baltimore: 2003).

51. Jones, *German Sources*, 254; de Marees, *Gold Kingdom*, 119; Hair, Jones, and Law, *Barbot on Guinea*, 2:341, 364n51, 528–529.

52. Kea, *Settlements, Trade, and Polities*, 293–294; Law, *Ouidah*, Manning, "Merchants, Porters, and Canoemen," 62, 65, 71–72.

53. Harms, *River of Wealth*, 69, 169–170; Weeks, *Congo Cannibals*, 94; Rodney, *Upper Guinea Coast*, 18; Joseph C. Miller, *Way of Death: Merchant Capitalism and the Angolan Slave Trade, 1730–1830* (Madison: 1988), 48.

54. Hornell, "Kru Canoes," 231, 237; Ward, *My Africa*, 112.

55. Hornell, "Kru Canoes," 231–232, 233, 237; Brown, "Fishing Industry," 39; de Marees, *Gold Kingdom*, 15, 118–119.

56. Jones, *German Sources*, 11; de Marees, *Gold Kingdom* 15; Villault, *Coasts of Africk*, 78; Canneau, *Slaver's Logbook*, 106, 249n1, 255; Great Britain Hydrographic Office, *African Pilot, or Sailing Directions for the Western Coast of Africa. Part I, From Cape Spartel to the River Cameroon*, 2 vols. (London: 1856), 1:106. Alexander Kup stated that a "Bullom canoe, called *sala*, is narrower than the so-called Bullom boat of today, although it is of a similar design."

Alexander Peter Kup, *A History of Sierra Leone, 1400–1787* (London: 1961), 140; George Thompson, *The Palm Land; or, West Africa, Illustrated: Being a History of Missionary Labors and Travels* (London: 1858), 189–190.

57. Brown, "Fishing Industry," 32–33.

58. Ibid.; Brown, *The Endless Summer*, Scene 5, The First Leg: Ghana; my observations of the coast and surf conditions from 1998 through 1999.

59. Brown, "Fishing Industry," 32–33.

60. Brown, "Fishing Industry," 38–39; Law, *English in West Africa*, 2:362.

61. De Marees, *Gold Kingdom*, 118–119; Tams, *Portuguese Possessions*, 1:236; Hair, Jones, and Law, *Barbot on Guinea*, 2:380, 387n25; Villault, *Coasts of Africk*, 219; Brown, "Fishing Industry," 38–39; Hornell, "Kru Canoes," 231–232; Adam Jones, *Remarks on the Country Extending from Cape Palmas to the River Congo* (London: 1823), 130; Gutkind, "Trade and Labor," 38; Stewart, "Diary," 52, Ogilby, *Africa*, 454.

62. Meek, *Sudanese Kingdom*, 426; Smith, "Canoe," 520n31; James Fairhead, Tim Geysbeek, Svend E. Holsoe, and Melissa Leach, eds., *African-American Exploration in West Africa: Four Nineteenth-Century Diaries* (Bloomington: 2003), 99.

63. Smith, "Canoe," 520; Harms, *River of Wealth*, 69; Rodney, *Upper Guinea*, 18; Hornell, "Kru Canoes," 231–232; Brown, "Fishing Industry," 32–33; Mann, *Birth of an African City*, 67, 351n57.

64. Barbot, *North and South Guinea*, 266; Gutkind, "Trade and Labor," esp. 25, 42, 44; Adanson, *Voyage to Senegal*, 26; Gutkind, "Boatmen of Ghana," 133–135; Manning, "Merchants, Porters, and Canoemen," 61; Hair, Jones, and Law, *Barbot on Guinea*, 2:347, 364n51, 531.

65. Smith, "Canoe," 515n2; my observations while in Ghana, Togo, Benin, Senegal, and The Gambia.

66. Thornton, *Africa and African*, 19–20; Kea, "Settlements," 223, 234; Brooks, *Eurafricans*, 1–20; Brooks, *Landlords and Strangers*, 80–87; Hawthorne, *Harvesting Slaves*, 40–41.

67. Villault, *Coasts of Africk*, 219; Van den Broecke, *Journal*, 37; Hair, Jones, and Law, *Barbot on Guinea*, 2:519; Brooks, *Eurafricans*, 7–8. For how prevailing winds and currents inhibited oceanic travel, see Brooks, *Eurafricans*, 5–7. I observed wind patterns while traveling throughout West Africa.

68. Pereira, *Esmeraldo*, 113; G. R. Crone, ed., *Voyages of Cadamosto*, 76, 91, 97; John William Blake, ed., *Europeans in West Africa, 1450–1560: Documents to Illustrate the Nature and Scope of Portuguese Enterprise in West Africa*, 2 vols. (London: 1942), 2:372.

69. De Marees, *Gold Kingdom*, 118, 118n6; Gutkind, "Boatmen of Ghana," 134–135; Brown, "Fishing Industry," 32–39; Gutkind, "Trade and Labor," 25; Manning, "Merchants, Porters, and Canoemen," esp. 60–61. In scientific terms, surf and breakers break on beaches or bars at river mouths; waves do not break. This book uses the common definition of "wave" interchangeably with "surf," and "breaker."

70. Irvine, *Fisheries*, 33; Hornell, "Kru Canoes," 232, 233. Canoes still required bailers. Hair, Jones, and Law, *Barbot on Guinea*, 2:530; Hornell, "Kru Canoes," 235; Durand, *Voyage to Senegal*, 111.

71. Álvares, *Ethiopia Minor*, chap. 9:2; Almada, *Rivers of Guinea*, 1:56, 92, 97, 121. George Brooks used "Bijago" when referring to the ethnic group and "Bissago" when referring to the archipelago. George E. Brooks, *Western Africa and Cabo Verde, 1790s–1830s: Symbiosis of Slave and Legitimate Trades* (Bloomington: 2010), 60.

72. Duarte Pacheco Pereira, *Esmeraldo de Situ Orbis* (1892; London: 1937), 116; Hair, Jones, and Law, *Barbot on Guinea*, 1:382; Zamba, *Life and Adventures*, 40. For other modifications, see Glave, *Savage Africa*, 129, 210–211; Barbot, *North and South Guinea*, 382; Smith, "Canoe," 518–520; Rodney, *Upper Guinea*, 17; Hornell, "Kru Canoes," 232; Irvine, *Fisheries*, 33; Thornton, *Africa and Africans*, 37; R. Earle Anderson, *Liberia: America's African Friend* (Chapel Hill: 1952), 15; Harms, *River of Wealth*, 215.

73. Meredith, *Gold Coast*, 58; Jamie Bruce Lockhart and Paul E. Lovejoy, eds., *Hugh Clapperton into the Interior of Africa: Records of the Second Expedition, 1825–1827* (1829; Boston: 2005), 105; Waddell, *Twenty-Nine Years*, title page, 242, 287.

74. Law, *English in West Africa*, 1:185, 222, 2:362.

75. Phillips, "Ship *Hannibal*," 64, 72; C. W. Newbury, ed. *A Mission to Gelele, King of Dahomey by Sir Richard Burton* (1864; London: 1966), 44; Manning, "Merchants, Porters, and Canoemen," 60–61, 65; Gutkind, "Boatmen of Ghana," 134; Law, ed., *English in West Africa*, 1:27n125, 3: 27, 27n125, 95; Robin Law, "Between the Sea and the Lagoons: The Interaction of Maritime and Inland Navigation on the Pre-Colonial Slave Coast," *Cahiers d' Études africaines* 29, no. 2 (1989): 227–228.

76. Law, *English in West Africa*, 3:4n26, 13–14, 41, 43, 95, 161, 2:319, 319n103, esp. 1: 4–5, 27, 27–28, 95; Law, "Sea and the Lagoons," 227–228.

77. Law, "Sea and the Lagoons," 227–228; Law, *English in West Africa*, 3:4–5, 27–28, 95; Phillips, "Ship *Hannibal*," 64, 72; Newbury, *Mission to Gelele*, 44.

78. Brooks, *Landlords and Stranger*, 209; D. P. Gamble, *The Wolof of Senegambia: Together with Notes on the Lebu and the Serer* (London: 1957), 94; Adanson, *Voyage to Senegal*, 94, 231–232, 273; Van den Broecke, *Journal*, 37. See Chapter 8 for *pirogue*'s etymology.

79. Brooks, *Eurafricans*, 5–7; Wright, *World and a Very Small Place*, passim, esp. 58, 63, 73. This area is also known as the Siné-Saloum Delta.

80. Van den Broecke, *Journal*, 37; Almada, *Rivers of Guinea*, sect. 1:38; Brooks, *Landlords and Strangers*, 209–210; Brooks, *Eurafricans*, 7; Adanson, *Voyage to Senegal*, 94, 231–232, 273; Durand, *Voyage to Senegal*, 111; Gamble, *Wolof of Senegambia*, 94.

81. Stewart, "Diary," 43; University of Virginia Library, Special Collections, MSS 14357, no 20.

Chapter 7

1. Smith, "Canoe," 515–533.

2. Dike, *Trade and Politics*, 5, 19–46; Smith, "Canoe," 521–525; Harms, *River of Wealth*, 92–93; 111; Randy J. Sparks, "Two Princes of Calabar: An Atlantic Odyssey from Slavery to Freedom," *William and Mary Quarterly*, 3rd ser. 59, no. 3 (July 2002), 560; Miller, *Way of Death*, 16; Thornton, *Africa and Africans*, 189–190, 191–192, 194; Searing, *West African Slavery*, 60, 76, 95; Hawthorne, *Harvesting Slaves*, 58; Karasch, *Slave Life in Rio de Janeiro*, 215.

3. C. Fayle, *A Short History of the World's Shipping Industry* (London: 1933), 21–22.

4. Patrick Manning, "Merchants, Porters, and Canoemen in the Bight of Benin: Links in the West African Trade Network," in Catherine Coquery-Vidrovitch and Paul Lovejoy, eds., *The Workers of the African Trade* (Beverly Hills: 1985), 51–72, esp. 56, 60, 61; Law, *Ouidah*, 259; Robin Law, ed., *From Slave Trade to "Legitimate" Commerce: The Commercial Transition in Nineteenth-Century West Africa* (Cambridge: 1995), 10–11; Smith, "Canoe," 521–525; Thornton, *Africa and Africans*, 14–15. For West-Central Africa, see Miller, *Way of Death*,

59–60, 102–103, 191–194, 266, esp. 191–192; Harms, *River of Wealth* 48–49, 72, 103; Harms, *Games Against Nature*, 26; Weeks, *Congo Cannibals*, 160.

5. Law, *"Legitimate" Commerce*, 10–13; Bosman, *Accurate Description*, 129; Harms, *River of Wealth*, 3; Glave, *Savage Africa*, 129.

6. Bolster, *Black Jacks*, 48; Rodney, *Upper Guinea Coast*, 17; Harms, *River of Wealth*.

7. Thornton, *Africa and Africans*, 22–24; Ward, *My Africa*, 112.

8. Law, *"Legitimate" Commerce*, 10–13; Bosman, *Accurate Description*, 129; Harms, *River of Wealth*, 3; Glave, *Savage Africa*, 129.

9. George E. Brooks Jr., ed., "A. A. Adee's Journal of a Visit to Liberia in 1827," *Liberian Studies Journal* 2 (1968): 61, 62; Leonard, *Western Coast of Africa*, 257–258; Ludewig Ferdinand Rømer, *Reliable Account of the Coast of Guinea, 1760* (1760; New York: 2000), 192; Foote, *Africa and the American Flag*, 51; Atkins, *Voyage to Guinea*, 69, 77–78; Anonymous, *West Africa*, 43; Isert, *Letters*, 27–28; William Smith, *New Voyage*, 167, 238–239; Adam Jones, *German Sources*, 11, 66; Rankin, *White Man's Grave*, 2:7–8; Adams, *Remarks on the Country*, 4.

10. Great Britain Hydrographic Office, *African Pilot* (1856), 148–149, esp. 160; Hydrographic Office, *African Pilot*, 2:35–37, 42, 142, 208, esp. 36, 37, 181, 182, 183; Manning, "Merchants, Porters, and Canoemen," 62; Bolster, *Black Jacks*, 48.

11. Pereira, *Esmeraldo*, 108, 108n6, 113, 132; Bosman, *Accurate Description*, 287; Snelgrave, *New Account*, vix–x, quoted in Adam Jones, *German Sources*, 11; Blake, *Europeans in West Africa*, 1:40, 240, 2:240, 372–374; Crone, *Voyages of Cadamosto*, 76; Meredith, *Account of the Gold Coast*, 22, 57–58, Villault, *Coasts of Africk*, 33, 66–67, 78, 115, 214–216.

12. Kea, *Settlements, Trade, and Polities*, 40–41; Hawthorne, *Harvesting Slaves*, 127; Akyeampong, *Between the Sea and the Lagoon*; Sandra Greene, *Gender, Ethnicity, and Social Change*.

13. Harms, *River of Wealth*, 93–98; Glave, *Savage Africa*, 128–129; Lovejoy, *Transformations in Slavery*, 103. For discussion of dependents, see Kea, *Settlements, Trade, and Politie*, 40; Manning, "Merchants, Porters, and Canoemen," 62, 65, 71–72; Horton, "Fishing Village," 47–48; Miller, *Way of Death*, 48, 266.

14. Jones, *Trading States*, 19, 55–57, 62–64, 66, 100, 159–162, 167, 170–176, 181–185, 207–215, esp. 55; Nimi Wariboko, "A Theory of the Canoe House Corporation," *African Economic History* 26 (1998), esp. 145; Sparks, *Two Princes*; Smith, "Canoe," 522, 528; Mary H. Kingsley, *West African Studies* (New York: 1901), 365; Miller, *Way of Death*, 45, 48, 101, 201; Dike, *Trade and Politics*, 36, 42; G. Ugo Nwokeji, *The Slave Trade and Culture in the Bight of Biafra* (Cambridge: 2010), passim, esp. 30, 65, 179; Robin Horton, "From Fishing Village to City-State: A Social History of New Calabar," in Mary Douglas and Phyllis M. Kaberry, eds., *Man in Africa* (New York: 1971), 38–60, esp. 47–48; Lovejoy, *Transformations in Slavery*, 102–103.

15. Harms, *River of Wealth*, 93–96, 103; Jones, *Trading States*, 55–57, 62, 169; Crocker, "Canoe Voyage," 69, 71.

16. Adam Jones, *Olfert Dapper's Description of Benin* (1668; Madison: 1998), 17; Glave, *Savage Africa*, 128; Alagoa, "Niger Delta," 270, 294–295, 303; Miller, *Way of Death*, 45, 101, 201.

17. H. E. Crocker, "A Canoe Voyage on the Congo," *Journal of the Royal African Society* 42 (April 1943), 69, 71; de Marees, *Gold Kingdom*, 26–27; Hair, Jones, and Law, *Barbot on Guinea*, 2:519.

18. Brown, "Fishing Industry," 24; Coronel, "Fanti Canoe Decoration," 54; Smith, "Canoe," 520; my observations in Ghana.

19. Harms, *River of Wealth*, esp.17–18, 43, 69, 113–115; Harms, *Games Against Nature*, 29, 33–34; Glave, *Savage Africa*, 193, 194, 199–200, esp. 145–146.

20. Law, *Ouidah*, 83–84; Mann, *Birth of an African City*, passim, esp. 24, 31, 53–55.

21. Duke, *Efik Traders*, 32; Manning, "Merchants, Porters, and Canoemen," 59; Hawthorne, *Harvesting Slaves*, 127; Leonard, *Western Coast of Africa*, 166; Stewart, "Diary," 52; Crocker, "Canoe Voyage," 187.

22. Harms, *River of Wealth*, 97; Hawthorne, *Harvesting Slaves*, 131–132; Lovejoy, *Transformations in Slavery*, 103; Horton, "Fishing Village." Also see earlier discussion of Bijago.

23. Robin Law, *The Slave Coast of West Africa, 1550–1750: The Implications of the Atlantic Slave Trade on an African Society* (Oxford: 1991), 47, 52, 310, 315.

24. Harms, *River of Wealth*, 97; Miller, *Way of Death*, 48, 266.

25. Dike, *Trade and Politics*, 42; Jones, *Trading States*, 55; Wariboko, "Canoe House Corporation," 142; Horton, "Fishing Village," 47–48.

26. Manning, "Merchants, Porters, and Canoemen," 51, 61, 72, 73; Gutkind, "Trade and Labor," 27–29, 41, 44; Gutkind, "Boatmen of Ghana," 133–139.

27. Meredith, *Gold Coast*, 22; Gutkind, "Trade and Labor," 30, 31, 34–42; Manning, "Merchants, Porters, and Canoemen," 61, 63–64, 72; Gutkind, "Boatmen of Ghana," 133, 135, 138–139, 163n49.

28. De Marees, *Gold Kingdom*, 121, 151; Ellis, *Tshi-Speaking Peoples*, 220–221; Brown "Fishing Industry," 41; Gutkind, "Boatmen of Ghana," 139, 163n49; Barbot, *North and South Guinea*, 269; Hair, Jones, and Law, *Barbot on Guinea*, 2:519.

29. Gutkind, "Boatmen of Ghana," 132; Gutkind, "Trade and Labor," 32; Law, *English in West Africa, 1681–1683*, 1:72, 77, 224, 254.

30. Matthew Bishop, *The Life and Adventures of Matthew Bishop* (London: 1744), 78; Rediker, *Devil and the Deep Blue Sea*, 205–253, esp. 208–209; Ralph Davis, *The Rise of the English Shipping Industry in the Seventeenth and Eighteenth Centuries* (London: 1962), 131–132; Herbert Compton, ed., *A Master Mariner: Being the Life and Adventures of Captain Robert William Eastwick* (London: 1891), 25.

31. Gutkind, "Boatmen of Ghana," 139; Law, *English in West Africa*, 1:72.

32. Kingsley, *Travels in West Africa*, 72, 514–515.

33. Quoted in Gutkind, "Trade and Labor," esp. 38; Manning, "Merchants, Porters, and Canoemen," 63–64; M. Priestly, "An Early Strike in Ghana," *Ghana Notes and Queries* 7 (1965): 25; Ellis, *Land of the Fetish*, 36. For strike, see C. R. Dobson, *Masters and Journeymen: A Prehistory of Industrial Relations, 1717–1800* (London, 1980), 19, 25–26, 154–170; Bolster, *Black Jacks*, 87–88; Rediker, *Devil and the Deep Blue Sea*, 110, 205–206.

34. Law, *English in West Africa*, 1:221, 224, 226, esp. 1:221, 2:336; Manning, "Merchants, Porters, and Canoemen," 61, 72; Gutkind, "Trade and Labor," 27, 34, 40; Gutkind, "Boatmen of Ghana," 137, esp. 136; Jones, *German Sources*, 12; de Marees, *Gold Kingdom*, 187; Meredith, *Gold Coast*, 22–23.

35. Gutkind, "Trade and Labor," 30, 31, 34–42; Ellis, *Land of the Fetish*, 36.

36. Manning, "Merchants, Porters, and Canoemen"; Gutkind, "Trade and Labor"; Gutkind, "Boatmen of Ghana"; de Marees, *Gold Kingdom*, 151; Ellis, *Tshi-Speaking Peoples*, 220–221; Brown "Fishing Industry," 41.

37. Ellis, *Land of the Fetish*, 5; Wright, *World Is a Very Small Place*, 58, 61, 63; Rodney, *Upper Guinea Coast*, 17–20; 149; Almada, *Rivers of Guinea*, 1:93, 122, 2:7, 10, 19–20.

38. Hair, Jones, and Law, *Barbot on Guinea*, 2:529; Smith, "Canoe," 522; R. Anderson, *Liberia*, 15; Forbes, *Six Months' Service*, 22; Falconbridge, *Slave Trade*, 53. It seems unlikely that canoemen voyaged between Ghana and Angola.

39. Hawthorne, *Harvesting Slaves*, 40–41; Almada, *Rivers of Guinea*, 1:38, 93; Brooks, *Landlords and Strangers*, 80–87; Rodney, *Upper Guinea Coast*, 17, 149.

40. Bridge, *African Cruiser*, 116.

41. Anonymous, *West Africa*, 197; Law, *Ouidah*, 29, 45; Great Britain Hydrographic Office, *African Pilot* (1856), 1:172–173; Hair, Jones, and Law, *Barbot on Guinea*, 2:382, 390n43; Law, *English in West Africa, 1681–1683*, 1: 219, 219n22, 234.

42. Hair, Jones, and Law, *Barbot on Guinea*, 2:382, 529; Robert Norris, *Memoirs of the Reign of Bossa Ahadee of Dahomey, King of Dahomy an Inland Country of Guineay* (London: 1789), 61–62; Meredith, *Gold Coast*, 78, 78n, 80; Phillips, "Voyage of the Ship *Hannibal*," 73.

43. Meredith, *Gold Coast*, 80; Law, *Ouidah*, 29, 45, 45n177, 191; Phillips, "Voyage of the Ship *Hannibal*," 73; Hair, Jones, and Law, *Barbot on Guinea*, 2:382; Law, *English in West Africa, 1681–1683*, 1: 219, 219n22; Meredith, *Gold Coast*, 59n, 80; Gutkind, "Trade and Labor"; Gutkind, "Boatmen of Ghana," 132; Manning, "Merchants, Porters, and Canoemen."

44. Phillips, "Voyage of the Ship *Hannibal*," 73; Hair, Jones, and Law, *Barbot on Guinea*, 2:382, 390n43; Meredith, *Gold Coast*, 80; Law, *English in West Africa, 1681–1683*, 1:219, 219n22, 234.

45. Law, *Slave Coast*, 24–26, 145, 244–245, 251, 258, 289, 315, 322; Akyeampong, *Between the Sea and the Lagoon*, 38, 41–44; Bosman, *Accurate Description*, 330–331; A. B. Ellis, *The Ewe-Speaking Peoples of the Slave Coast of West Africa* (London: 1890), 305.

46. Law, *Ouidah*, 45, 75, 74n12, 75n13, 75n14. These residents of Little Popo were from Elmina or Accra. Law, *Slave Coast*, 25; Law, *Ouidah*, 61.

47. Smith, "Palaver Islands," 3, 3n1; Dike, *Trade and Politics*, 19–20. Robin Law states that Badagry "is more correctly [called] Agbadarigi." Law, *Slave Coast*, 310.

48. Harms, *River of Wealth*, 93; Law, "Introduction," in Law, *"Legitimate" Commerce*, 10–11; Mann, *Birth of an African City*, 56; Dike, *Trade and Politics*, 19–20.

49. Pereira, *Esmeraldo*, 132; Glave, *Savage Africa*, 128; Adam Jones, *Remarks on the Country*, 130; Barbot, *North and South Guinea*, 266, 383; Hair, Jones, and Law, eds., *Barbot on Guinea*, 1:222, 229n13, 273, 2:529, 533.

50. Hair, Jones, and Law, eds., *Barbot on Guinea*, 2:618–619.

51. Dike, *Trade and Politics*, 19–20, quoted on 19; Sparks, "Two Princes," 559.

52. Sparks, "Two Princes," 557; www.slavevoyages.org/tast/database/search.faces, accessed May 3, 2013.

53. Pereira, *Esmeraldo*, 132; Smith, "Canoe," 523; Adams, *Remarks on the Country*, 129–131, 245; Dike, *Trade and Politics*, 41–43; Lovejoy, *Transformations in Slavery*, 102–103.

54. Duke, *Efik Traders*, vii; Sparks, "Two Princes," 557–565; Lovejoy, *Transformations in Slavery*, 103.

55. Sparks, "Two Princes," 557, 559, 562–564; Duke, *Efik Traders*, vii, 32, 33, 46, 48; Smallwood, *Saltwater Slavery*, 35.

56. Miller, *Way of Death*, 16–18, 45, 186, 217, 224, 228, 278, 297, 389, 649, esp. 37; T. E. Bowdich, *An Account of the Discoveries of the Portuguese in the Interior of Angola and Mozambique* (London: 1824), 98; Tams, *Portuguese Possessions*, 2:130, 208–209, 234; Ferreira, *Cross-Cultural Exchange*.

57. Hair, Jones, and Law, *Barbot on Guinea*, 1:183, esp. 182; Rømer, *Reliable Account*, 208–209; Ellis, *Land of the Fetish*, 5; Valdez, *Traveller's Life*, 1:227; Rankin, *White Man's Grave*, 2:89–90, 94; George Thompson, *Palm Land*, 186–188.

58. Álvares, *Ethiopia Minor*, chap. 11:1; Hawthorne, *Harvesting Slaves*, esp. 40–41, 43; Almada, *Rivers of Guinea*, 1: 86–87, 93, 121, 122, 2:2, 4–7, 19–20, 30.

59. Smith, "Canoe," 522; Harms, *River of Wealth*, 71–72, 74–75; Dike, *Trade and Politics*, 42–43; Jones, *Trading States*, 56, 92–101, 143–144; Crow, *Memoirs*, 43, 216–217; Atkins, *Voyage to Guinea*, 77.

60. Waddell, *Twenty-Nine Years*, 320; Harms, *River of Wealth*, 75; Searing, *West African Slavery* 95.

61. Anonymous, *West Africa*, 28–30, 32, 43; Hawthorne, *Harvesting Slaves*, 43–44.

62. Valdez, *Traveller's Life*, 1:227; Manning, "Merchants, Porters, and Canoemen," 60–61; Jones, *Trading States*, 56, 92–93, 95, 99–101, 143–144, 181; Adams, *Remarks on the Country*, 248; Canneau, *A Slaver's Logbook*, 256; Dochard, *Travels in Western Africa*, 182.

63. Hutchinson, *Ten Year's Wanderings*, 18; Duke, *Efik Traders*, 6, 33. African rulers also recast traditional duties to extract revenues from white merchants. Hair, Jones, and Law, *Barbot on Guinea*, 1:320; Jones, *Trading States*, 95; Adams, *Remarks on the Country*, 245, 248; Dochard, *Travels in Western Africa*, 72.

64. Zamba, *Life and Adventures*, 1, 17, 35, 39, 40, 44, 46–66, esp. 1, 17, 35, 40, 55. Also see James L. Sims, "Scenes in the Interior of Liberia: Being a Tour Through the Countries of the Dey, Goulau, Pessah, Barlain, Kpellay, Suloany and King Boatwains Tribes, in 1758" in James Fairhead, Tim Geysbeek, Svend E. Holsoe, and Melissa Leach, eds., *African-American Exploration in West Africa: Four Nineteenth-Century Diaries* (Bloomington: 2003), 98–99; Jones, *German Sources*, 63; Miller, *Way of Death*; Harms, *River of Wealth*, 16–18, 30–39, 45, 217, 224, 228, 278, 297, 389, 649; Searing, *West African Slavery*, 60, 115, 146.

65. Pereira, *Esmeraldo*, 132; Hair, Jones, and Law, *Barbot on Guinea*, 2:675, 691; Anonymous, *West Africa in the Mid-Seventeenth Century: An Anonymous Dutch Manuscript*, in Adam Jones, trans. and ed. (Piscataway: 1995), 28–30, 32; Atkins, *Voyage to Guinea, Brazil, & the West Indies*, 40, 62–67; Law, *English in West Africa, 1681–1699*, 1:43, 103, 120, 220, 224, 271, 300, 324; Antera Duke, *Efik Traders of Old Calabar, Containing the Diary of Antera Duke an Efik Slave-Trading Chief of the Eighteenth Century*, in Darylle Forde, ed. (New York: 1956), vii; E. J. Alagoa, "The Niger Delta States and Their Neighbors, 1600–1800," in J. F. A. Ajayi and Michael Crowder eds., *History of West Africa*, 2 vols. (Cambridge: 1972), 1:319–329; Horton, "Fishing Village," 37–58.

66. Law, "Introduction," in Law, *"Legitimate" Commerce*, 10–11; Mann, *Birth of an African City*, 55–56.

67. Harms, *River of Wealth*, 37–38; Miller, *Way of Death*, 203; Herbert S. Klein, *The Middle Passage: Comparative Studies in the Atlantic Slave Trade* (Princeton: 1978), 56, 84–85.

68. Anonymous, *West Africa*, 33; Marcus Rediker, *The Slave Ship: A Human History* (New York: 2007), 39–40; Bosman, *Accurate Description*, 281–282; Snelgrave, *New Account*, 177–178; Crow, *Memoirs*, 44.

69. Law, *English in West Africa*, 2:269n15, 329; Tams, *Portuguese Possessions*, 1:324; Patrick Manning, *Slavery and African Life: Occidental, Oriental, and African Slave Trades* (Cambridge: 1990), 116; Lovejoy, *Transformations in Slavery*, 188, 243.

70. Waddell, *Twenty-Nine Years*, 319–320; Lovejoy, *Transformations in Slavery*, 188, 243; Jones, *Trading States*, 169, 172–173.

71. Falconbridge, *Slave Trade*, 14–15; Law, *English in West Africa*, 1:97, 109, 126, 225, esp. 113–114, 221, 263, 263n8; Kea, *Settlements, Trade, and Politics*, 243; Gutkind, "Trade and Labor," 30, 36; Villault, *Coasts of Africk*, 48, 123; Sparks, "Two Princes," 559; Miller, *Way of Death*, 101, 201; Harms, *River of Wealth*, 94, 185; Lovejoy, *Transformations in Slavery*, 10, 188, 243; Dike, *Trade and Politics*, 36; Gutkind, "Boatmen of Southern Ghana," 136; Searing, *West African Slavery*, 95; Austen and Derrick, *Cameroons Rivers*, 33; Glave, *Savage Africa*, 128; Weeks, *Congo Cannibals*, 186; Lovejoy, *Transformations in Slavery*, 188.

72. Kea, *Settlements, Trade, and Politics*, 243; Gutkind, "Trade and Labor," 36–38; Austen and Derrick, *Cameroons Rivers*, 33; Kea, *Settlements, Trade, and Politics*, 243. For an example of how customs and laws became corrupted, see Hawthorne, *Harvesting Slaves*, 65, 91–94, 100–101, 124, 207.

73. Venture Smith, *A Narrative of the Life and Adventures of Venture, a Native of Africa* (New London: 1798), 13; Equiano, *Interesting Narrative*, 67–68; Chandler B. Saint and George A. Krimsky, *Making Freedom: The Extraordinary Life of Venture Smith* (Middleton: 2009), 9, 17.

74. Atkins, *Voyage to Guinea*, 69; Snelgrave, *New Account*, 102; Anonymous, *West Africa*, 28.

75. Chas. Thomas, *Adventures and Observations*, vi, 80–83, 193, 212, 205, 321.

76. Rømer, *Reliable Account*, 192; Nicholas Owen, *Journal of a Slave-Dealer: "A view of some Remarkable Axcedents in the life of Nics. Owen on the Coast of Africa and America from the year 1746 to the year 1757"* (London: 1930), 105; Kingsley, *West African Studies*, 36; A. B. Ellis, *The Land of Fetish* (London: 1833), 36; Henry, *Confessions of a Tenderfoot*, 48, 109. During months of surfing in Ghana, I never saw waves larger than five feet.

77. Adanson, *Voyage to Senegal*, 30.

78. Isert, *Letters*, 27–28.

79. Adanson, *Voyage to Senegal*, 30.

80. Atkins, *Voyage to Guinea*, 69, 77–78; Robert Harms, *The Diligent: A Voyage Through the Worlds of the Slave Trade* (New York: 2002), 228–229; Hair, Jones, and Law, *Barbot on Guinea*, 2:530; Meredith, *Gold Coast*, 57–58; Rømer, *Reliable Account*, 192; Henry, *Confessions of a Tenderfoot*, 37–39, 47–48.

81. Phillips, "Voyage of the Ship *Hannibal*," 72; Kingsley, *Travels in West Africa*, 72, 514–515; Durand, *Voyage to Senegal*, 111; Hair, Jones, and Law, *Barbot on Guinea*, 2:531; Meredith, *Gold Coast*, 22.

82. Smith, "Canoe," 525. For example, see John K. Thornton, "African Soldiers in the Haitian Revolution," *Journal of Caribbean History* 25 (1991): 58–80; Thornton, *Warfare in Atlantic Africa*; Thornton, *Africa and Africans*; Manning, *Slavery and African Life*, esp. 126–148; Patrick Manning, *Slavery, Colonialism and Economic Growth in Dahomey, 1640–1960* (Cambridge: 1982); Kea, *Settlements, Trade, and Politics*; Law, *Slave Coast*; Law, *Ouidah*; Rodney, *Upper Guinea Coast*; Barry, *Senegambia*; Lovejoy, *Transformations in Slavery*; Paul E. Lovejoy, "The Impact of the Atlantic Slave Trade on Africa: A Review of the Literature," *Journal of African History* 30 (1989); J. E. Inikori, ed., *Forced Migration: The Impact of the Export Slave Trade on African Societies* (London: 1982); Nwokeji, *Slave Trade and Culture*.

83. Thornton, *Warfare in Atlantic Africa*, 47–49, 83–83; Smith, "Canoe," 525–532; Smith, *Warfare and Diplomacy*, 51; Harms, *River of Wealth*, 36–37, 94–97; Miller, *Way of Death*, 266.

84. Glave, *Savage Africa*, 53–55, 71–72, 104–107, 198; Harms, *River of Wealth*, 94–95; Stanley, *Through the Dark Continent*, 1:328, 331–332, 333, 338, 341; Thornton, *Warfare in Atlantic Africa*, 29.

85. Thornton, *Africa and Africans*, 36–39; Azurara, *Chronicle*, 2:253–254; Thornton, *Africa and Africans*, 36–37; Thornton, *Warfare in Atlantic Africa*, 11, 27; Glave, *Savage Africa*, 53–54, 71–72, 104–107, 173.

86. Hawthorne, *Harvesting Slaves*, 77–78, 104, 131–132.

87. Almada, *Rivers of Guinea*, 1:38.

88. Álvares, *Ethiopia Minor*, chap. 8:1; Hawthorne, *Harvesting Slaves*, 77–78, 109, 121, 131–132.

89. Hawthorne, *Harvesting Slaves*, 131–132; Harms, *River of Wealth*, 96–97,187; Hair, Jones, and Law, *Barbot on Guinea*, 1:170–171.

90. Almada, *Rivers of Guinea*, sect. 1:96, 97; Edward Stallibrass, "The Bijaouga or Bissago Islands, West Africa," in *Proceedings of the Royal Geographic Society and Monthly Record of Geography* 11 (1889): 596; Rodney, *Upper Guinea Coast*, 17, 103; Álvares, *Ethiopia Minor*, chap. 9:1; Valdez, *Traveller's Life*, 1:210–212; Philip Beaver, *African Memoranda: Relative to an Attempt to Establish a British Settlement on the Island of Bulama, on the West Coast of Africa, in the year 1792* (London: 1805), 47–53,74, 335–336; Hawthorne, *Harvesting Slaves*, 101–104, esp. 103; Thornton, *Warfare in Atlantic Africa*, 42. Almada provides the names of the islands comprising the Bijago Archipelago. Almada, *Rivers of Guinea*, sect. 1:96.

91. G. Mollien, *Travels in the Interior of Africa to the Sources of the Senegal and Gambia Performed by the French Government in the Year 1818* (London: 1820), 336; Almada, *Rivers of Guinea*, sect. 1:64, 92, 97, 98; Hawthorne, *Harvesting Slaves*, 102, 104; Rodney, *Upper Guinea Coast*, 17, 103–104; Boubacar Barry, *Senegambia*, 43, 65, 117; Hair, Jones, and Law, *Barbot on Guinea*, 1:319; Beaver, *African Memoranda*, 335–336.

92. Almada, *Rivers of Guinea*, sect. 1:97; Álvares, *Ethiopia Minor*, chap. 9:1, 2; Stallibrass, "Bijouga," 599; Beaver, *African Memoranda*, 48–53, 69, 74, 82, 339; Thornton, *Warfare in Atlantic Africa*, 48; Brooks, *Eurafricans*, 47, 48, 70. Guinala is on the Grande River. Brooks, *Eurafricans*, 42, 78–79. "Biguda" is apparently the Baïnuk commercial center of Buguando. Barry, *Senegambia*, 20, 42.

93. Álvares, *Ethiopia Minor*, chap. 9:2; Valdez, *Traveller's Life*, 1:210–211.

94. Álvares, *Ethiopia Minor*, chap. 9:1, 2; Almada, *Rivers of Guinea*, sect. 1:96–97; Hair, Jones, and Law, *Barbot on Guinea*, 1:319; Rodney, *Upper Guinea Coast*, 17, 103.

95. Stallibrass, "Bijaouga," 596–600; Hair, Jones, and Law, *Barbot on Guinea*, 1:171, 316–319; Beaver, *African Memoranda*, 335–336; Valdez, *Traveller's Life*, 1:212; Almada, *Rivers of Guinea*, sect. 1:97; Álvares, *Ethiopia Minor*, chap. 9:2.

96. Brooks, *Eurafricans*, 165.

97. Álvares, *Ethiopia Minor*, chap. 8, esp. 2, 3, 6, 7; Hawthorne, *Harvesting Slaves*, 107–109; esp. 108–109.

98. Mollien, *Interior of Africa*, 336; Beaver, *African Memoranda*, 337, 345; Hair, Jones, and Law, *Barbot on Guinea*, 1:171.

99. Hawthorne, *Harvesting Slaves*, 78, 101–102, 104, 131–132.

100. Hawthorne, *Harvesting Slaves*, 73; Rodney, *Upper Guinea Coast*, 17, 109; Almada, *Rivers of Guinea*, sect. 1:98–99, 2:1, 2; Álvares, *Ethiopia Minor*, chap. 9:2; Crone, *Voyages of Cadamosto*, 77–78.

101. Barry, *Senegambia*, 65; Brooks, *Eurafricans*, 165.

102. Thornton, *Warfare in Atlantic Africa*, 9–11; Smith, "Canoe," 518; Dike, *Trade and Politics*, 42. Smith noted that there is no evidence that crossbows or rifles were adopted by

African navies. Thomas Hutchinson provides a confusing account of canoemen using rifles. Smith, "Canoe," 526–257; Hutchinson, *Ten Years' Wanderings*, 49–50.

103. Dalzel, *History of Dahomey*, 183; quoted in Thomas Hodgkin, *Nigerian Perspective: An Historical Anthology* (Oxford: 1975), 226; G. Robertson, *Notes on Africa*, 283; Thornton, *Warfare in Atlantic Africa*, 84; Mann, *Birth of an African City*, 67.

104. Mann, *Birth of an African City*, esp. 67–68; Lockhart and Lovejoy, *Hugh Clapperton into the Interior of Africa*, 105; Richard Lander and John Lander, *Journal of an Expedition to Explore the Course and Termination of the Niger: With a Narrative of a Voyage Down That River to Its Termination in Two Volumes* (New York: 1832), 1:71–72; Mann, *Birth of an African City*, 67; Smith, "Canoe," 526–527; Smith, "Canoe in West African History," 526–527; Charles Henry Vidal Gollmer, *Charles Andrew Gollmer: His Life and Missionary Labours in West Africa, Compiled from His Journals and the Church Missionary Society's Publications* (London: 1889), 48–53.

105. Dike, *Trade and Politics*, 41–43; Adams, *Remarks on the Country*, 129–131, 135–136.

106. Thornton, *Warfare in Atlantic Africa*, 84.

107. Miller, *Way of Death*, esp. 16–18, 45, 105–139, 217, 224, 228, 278; Harms, *River of Wealth*, 36–37, 95.

108. For example, see Searing, *West African Slavery*, 95; Hawthorne, *Harvesting Slaves*; Lovejoy, *Transformations in Slavery*; Austen and Derrick, *Cameroons Rivers*.

109. Stanley, *Through the Dark Continent*, 1:326–341, esp. 328.

110. Law, *Ouidah*, 2.

Chapter 8

1. William Bright, *Native American Placenames of the United States* (Norman: 2004), 80; Edwin Tappan Adney and Howard I. Chapelle, *The Bark Canoes and Skin Boats of North America* (Washington, DC: 1964), 13; Terence T. Quirke, *Canoes the World Over* (Urbana: 1952), 9.

2. Gonzalo Fernández de Oviedo y Valdés, *Coronica de las Indias: La hystoria general de las Indias agora nueuamente impressa corregida y emendada* (1535; Salamanca: 1547), book 6, chap. 4:50, lxi; Gonzalo Fernández de Oviedo y Valdés, *The Conquest and Settlement of the Island of Boriquen or Puerto Rico*, Daymond Turner, trans. and ed. (Avon: 1975), 115; Adanson, *Voyage to Senegal*, 94, 231–232, 273; Van den Broecke, *Journal*, 37; Gamble, *Wolof of Senegambia*, 94; John Michael Vlach, *The Afro-American Tradition in Decorative Arts* (Cleveland: 1978), 98, 101; Ignacio Olazagasti, "The Material Culture of the Taino Indians," in Samuel M. Wilson, ed., *The Indigenous People of the Caribbean* (Gainesville: 1997), 134; R. Mauny, *Glossaire de expressions et terms locaux employés dans l'Ouest Africain* (Dakar: 1952), 56; Brooks, *Landlords and Strangers*, 209.

3. Crone, *Voyages of Cadamosto*, 34; Blake, *Europeans in West Africa*, 1:40, 240, 2:372, 408; de Marees, *Gold Kingdom* 117, 117n1, 117 n2; R. Mauny, *Glossaire de expressions*, (Dakar: 1952), 18.

4. Marshall B. McKusick, "Aboriginal Canoes in the West Indies," *Yale University Publications in Anthropology* 63 (New Haven: 1970): 4; Walter Raleigh, *The Discovery of Guiana and the Journal of the Second Voyage Thereto* (London: 1901), 143.

5. Jean Baptiste Du Tertre, *Histoire générale des Antilles habitées par les François*, 4 vols. (Paris: 1667), 2:397; Long, *History of Jamaica*, 3:737; Jose Toribio Medina, *The Discovery of*

the Amazon: According to the Account of Friar Gaspar de Carvajal and Other Documents, Bertram T. Lee, trans., H. C. Heaton, ed. (New York: 1934), 440; McKusick, "Aboriginal Canoes," 6; Bright, *Placenames*, 80; F. W. Clonts, "Travel and Transportation in Colonial North Carolina," *North Carolina Historical Review* 3 (1926): 19–20.

6. William C. Fleetwood Jr., *Tidecraft: The Boats of South Carolina, Georgia and Northeastern Florida, 1550–1950* (Tybee Island, GA: 1995), 31; John Michael Vlach, *Afro-American Tradition in Decorative Arts* (London: 1990), 101; Bolster, *Black Jacks*, 14; M. V. Brewington, *Chesapeake Bay Log Canoes* (Newport News: 1937), 27–29.

7. James Hungerford, *The Old Plantation, and What I Gathered There in an Autumn Month* (New York: 1859), 79; Adanson, *Voyage to Senegal*, 94, 231, 273; "Pirogues des Nègres," in René Claude Geoffroy de Villeneuve, *L'Afrique, ou Histoire, Moeurs, Usages et Coutumes des Africains: Le Sénégal*, 4 vols. (Paris: 1814), 3:facing 60; Gwendolyn Hall, *Africans in Colonial Louisiana*, esp. 76, 216; Carl W. Mitman, ed., *Catalogue of the Watercraft Collection in the United States National Museum* (Washington, DC: 1923), 205; Howard I. Chapelle, *The National Watercraft Collection* (Washington, DC: 1960), 296–297.

8. De Marees, *Gold Kingdom*, 116–117, 117n1, 117n2; William Falconer, *An Universal Dictionary of the Marine: or, A Copious Explanation of the Technical Terms and Phrases Employed in the Construction, Equipment, Furniture, Machinery, Movements, and Military Operations of a Ship* (London: 1784), pages not numbered; William Falconer, *New Universal Dictionary of the Marine 1815*, William Burney, ed. (1815; London: 2006), 31; Albert Von Sak, *Narrative of a Voyage to Surinam: Of a Residence There During 1805–07* (London: 1810), 52, 73; Stedman, *Expedition*, 1:55, 57, 58, 164, 166, 169, 174, 202, plate 10, plate 17, esp. 13, 2:253, 260, 387, 406, plate 41; Palgrave, *Dutch Guiana*, 74–75; Walter Raleigh, *The Discovery of Guiana and the Journal of the Second Voyage Thereto* (London: 1901), 143.

9. Frances Anne Kemble, *Journal of a Residence on a Georgia Plantation in 1838–1839*, John A. Ascott, ed. (1863; New York: 1970), passim, 72, 86, 90, 114, 118, 144–145, 192–193; D. Drinkwater and Hugh Finlay, *Finlay's Journals and Drinkwater's Letters*, (Washington, DC: 1867), 54; Stedman, *Expedition*, 1:13.

10. De Marees, *Gold Kingdom*, xv, 117, 244–245; Adkin, *Voyage to Guinea*, 59, 226–228. There is no evidence that de Marees traveled to the Americas, but, due to detailed descriptions, Adam Jones believes he visited Brazil before his 1590s Africa voyage. E-mail correspondence with Adam Jones and Ernst van den Boogaart between December 3 and December 5, 2011.

11. For scholarship briefly considering the African origins of dugouts, see Bolster, *Black Jacks*, 60–61; Wood, *Black Majority*,123–124, 123n107; Vlach, *Afro-American Tradition*, 98, 103–104.

12. Adney and Chapelle, *Bark Canoes*, 30. For Amerindian dugouts, see Adney and Chapelle, *Bark Canoes*, 3, 5–6, 7, 10, 13, 30, 36, 72, 154, 174, 176, 213; McKusick, "Aboriginal Canoes;" Jeanne E. Arnold, "Credit Where Credit Is Due: The History of the Chumash Oceangoing Canoe," *American Antiquity* 72, no. 2 (2007): 196–209; William E. Engelbrecht and Carl K. Seyfert, "Paleoindian Watercraft: Evidence and Implications," *North American Archaeologist* 15 no. 3 (1994): 221–234; David Gidmark, "Algonquian Birchbark Canoe Construction," in William Cowan and Christina A. Thiele, eds., *Papers of the Sixteenth Algonquian Conference* (Ottawa: 1985), 25–46; MacCracken, "An 'Indian' Dugout Canoe from Wyoming County, Pennsylvania," *Pennsylvania Archaeologist* 32 (1962): 35–38; Nicholas N. Smith, "The

Wabanaki as Mariners," in William Cowan and Christina A. Thiele, eds., *Papers of the Twenty-Fourth Algonquian Conference* (Ottawa: 1993): 364–380; Robert F. Heizer, "The Frameless Plank Canoe of the California Coast," in *Primitive Man* 13, no. 3/4 (July–October 1940), 80–90.

13. Miles Harvey, *Painter in a Savage Land: The Strange Saga of the First European Artist in North America* (New York: 2008), 84–86; Olazagasti, "Material Culture," 133–134; Heizer, "Frameless Plank Canoe," 81.

14. Oviedo, *Coronica de las Indias*, book 6, chap. 4:50, lx–lxi; Gonzalo Fernández de Oviedo y Valdés, *Historia General y Natural de las Indias, Islas y Tierra-Firme del Mar Océano*; D. José Amador de los Ríos, ed., 4 vols. (Madrid: 1851–1855), 1:170–171, 343–344, 634[Lam. 2], 2:657[Lam. a.2.a]; Oviedo, *Conquest*, 113–116; Kathleen Ann Myers, *Fernandez de Oviedo's Chronicle of America*, Nina M. Scott, trans. (Austin: 2007), esp. 5, 79, 124, 199, 250; Olazagasti, "Material Culture," 133–134.

15. Stefan Lorant, *The New World: The First Pictures of America Made by John White and Jacques Le Moyne and Engraved by Theodore de Bry, With Contemporary Narratives of the French Settlements in Florida, 1562–1565, and the English Colonies in Virginia, 1585–1590* (New York: 1965), 33, 49, 79, 107, 119; Harvey, *Painter*, esp. xvi, 228. For analysis of Le Moyne's painting and De Bry's etchings of them, see Todd P. Olsen, "Markers: Le Moyne de Morgues in Sixteenth-Century Florida," in Dana Leibsohn and Jeanette Favrot Peterson, eds., *Seeing Across Cultures in the Early Modern World* (Farnham: 2012), 193–212; Harvey, *Painter*, 42, 84–86, 179–181, 194, 220–221, 251.

16. Thomas Harriot, *A Briefe and True Report of the new found Land of Virginia* (London: 1588; 1590), vii–viii, 23, 45, 47–51, 53–55, 57. The first edition of *Brief and True Report*, published in 1588, did not include etchings, which were first included in the 1590 edition.

17. Robert Beverley, *The History and Present State of Virginia in Four Parts* (London: 1705), book 2:34, 3:7, 62. This is seemingly the earliest image to depict bark and dugout canoes.

18. Peter (Pehr) Kalm, *Travels into North America; Containing Its Natural History, and a Circumstantial Account of its Plantations and Agriculture in General*, 3 vols. (London: 1771), 2:37–39; Oviedo, *Coronica de las Indias*, book 6, chap. 4:50, lx–lxi; Quirke, *Canoes the World Over*, 42.

19. Beverley, *Virginia*, book 3, chap. 13:60–61; Timothy Silver, *A New Face on the Countryside: Indians, Colonists, and Slaves in the South Atlantic Forests, 1500–1800* (Cambridge: 1990), 59.

20. Thomas Harriot, *Briefe and True Report*, 23, 55; John Smith, *The Generall Historie of Virginia, New England, and the Summer Isles* (London: 1632), 31; John de Verazzano, *The Voyage of John de Verazzano a Florentine to the Coast of Florida*, in Richard Hakluyt, ed., *The Principal Navigations, Voyages, Traffiques & Discoveries of the English Nation*, 10 vols. (Glasgow: 1904), 8:429; Strachey, *Travell into Virgnia*, 82; Kalm, *Travels*, 2:37–39; Silver, *New Face*, 57.

21. Oviedo, *Historia General*, 1:470–471; Olazagasti, "Material Culture," 133–134; McKusick, "Aboriginal Canoes," 6; Silver, *New Face*, 59; Jack D. Forbes, *The American Discovery of Europe* (Urbana: 2007), 61.

22. Du Tertre, *Histoire générale*, 2:397; McKusick, "Aboriginal Canoes," 6; Paul Johnstone, *The Sea-Craft of Prehistory* (Cambridge: 1980), 28, 46, 235.

23. Jean Baptiste Labat, *Nouveau Voyage aux Isles de l'Amerique: Contenant l'histoire Naturelle de ces Pays*, 11 vols. (Paris: 1724), 2:553; Ball, *Fifty Years*, 211; Hall, *Miserable Slavery*, 144–145.

24. Martha Warren Beckwith, *Black Roadways: A Study of Jamaican Folk Life* (New York: 1929), 30.

25. Brewington, *Chesapeake Bay*, 19, 22, 23.

26. Robert Kerr, ed., *A General History and Collection of Voyages and Travels, Arranged in Systematic Order*, 18 vols. (Edinburgh: 1824), 3:57; Bright, *Placenames*, 80; Oviedo, *Coronica de las Indias*, book 6, chap. 4:50, lxi; Oviedo, *Historia General*, 1:470–471; Oviedo, *Conquest*, 114, 116; Olazagasti, "Material Culture," 133–134; Harriot, *Briefe and True Report*, 23; Smith, *Generall Historie*, 31–32; Henry Spelman, *Relation of Virginia*, in John Smith, *Travels and Works of Captain John Smith*, 2 vols. (Edinburgh: 1910), 1:cxiv.

27. Brewington, *Chesapeake Bay*, 19.

28. Strachey, *Historie*, 23; Eben. Cook, *The Sot-Weed Factor: Or a Voyage to Maryland. A Satyr.* (London: 1708), 3; Brewington, *Chesapeake Bay*, 21.

29. Wood, *Black Majority*, 123–124, 123n107: Bolster, *Black Jacks*, 45–47, 60–61; Vlach, *Afro-American Tradition*, 98, 103–104; Joyner, *Down by the Riverside*, 76, 270n93.

30. Erik Gilbert, *Dhows and the Colonial Economy of Zanzibar, 1860–1970* (Athens: 2004), 4–6, 4n5, esp. 5; Bolster, *Black Jacks*, 60–61; Erik Gilbert, "The Dhow as Cultural Icon," in *International Journal of Heritage Studies* 17, no. 1 (January 2011), 66–68; Richard Price, "Caribbean Fishing and Fishermen: A Historical Sketch," *American Anthropologist* 68, no. 6 (December 1966), 1364, 1369, 1380n4, esp. 1371. Richard Price and Arthur Middleton have contributed mightily to our historical understanding, while stripping slaves of their maritime accomplishments. Middleton appropriated the Chesapeake from Indians, calling colonists "natives," suggesting canoes were a European contrivance. Noting that boats "appear with monotonous regularity in the records," he ignored the slaves mentioned in the same "monotonous" breath. Middleton, *Tobacco Coast*, 242, 287.

31. Fleetwood, *Tidecraft*, 313–314, 316, Johnstone, *Sea-Craft*; James Hornell, *Water Transport: Origins and Early Evolution* (Cambridge: 1946), 190–191; Howard Irving Chapelle, *American Small Sailing Craft, Their Design, Development, and Construction* (New York: 1951); Price, "Caribbean Fishing," esp. 1371, 1375–1376; Seán McGrail, *Boats of the World: From the Stone Age to Medieval Times* (Oxford: 2004); William S. Dudley, *Maritime Maryland: A History* (Baltimore: 2010).

32. Kevin Dawson, "Slave Culture"; Robert Paquette and Mark M. Smith, eds., *The Oxford Handbook of Slavery in the Americas* (Oxford: 2010), 467–468; Joanna Brooks, *American Lazarus: Religion and the Rise of African-American and Native American Literatures* (Oxford: 2003), 158–159; Lydia Parrish, *Slave Songs of the Georgia Sea Islands* (1942; Athens: 1992), 45; Joyce Chaplin, *The First Scientific American: Benjamin Franklin and the Pursuit of Genius* (New York: 2007), 22–23; Littlefield, *Rice and Slaves*, 107; Duncan Clinch Heyward, *Seed from Madagascar* (Chapel Hill: 1937), 8–10.

33. White, *Ar'n't I a Woman?*, 4; Carney, *Black Rice*, 12–15, 29, 48–49, 75, 79–80, 97–98, esp. 12, 32, 81, Bolster, *Black Jacks*, 60–61.

34. Bolster, *Black Jacks*, 60–61.

35. Europeans largely stopped building dugouts during the medieval period. Johnstone, *Sea-Craft*, 45–49, 140–155; Hornell, *Water Transport*, 189–195.

36. Castiglioni, *Viaggio*, 126; Oviedo, *Coronica de las Indias*, book 6, chap. 4:50, lxi; Oviedo, *Conquest*, 115; Wood, *Black Majority*, 123, 123n107; Vlach, *Afro-American Tradition*, 101; Eddis, *Letters from America*, 402; Henry Nelson Coleridge, *Six Months in the West Indies* (London: 1826), 158–160, 163–164, 178; Anonymous, "Observations in Several Voyages and Travels in America in the Year 1736," *William and Mary Quarterly* 15, no. 4 (April 1907); 217–218; A. J. Morrison, "Virginia Patents," *William and Mary Quarterly*, 2nd ser. 2, no. 3 (July 1922), 154; Bolster, *Black Jacks*, 47; Cynric Williams, *Jamaica*, 114–138; Elkanah Watson, *Men and Times of the Revolution; or Memoirs of Elkanah Watson* (New York: 1856), 247. For a good analysis of North American Indian dugouts, see Andrew Lipman, *The Saltwater Frontier: Indians and the Contest for the American Coast* (New Haven: 2015), 54–84.

37. Oviedo, *Coronica de las Indias*, book 6, chap. 4:50, lxi; Oviedo, *Conquest*, 115; Anonymous, "Observations in Several Voyages and Travels in America 217–218; R. P. Raymond Breton, *Dictionnaire Caraïbe-Français of 1665* (1665; Leipzeg: 1892), 331; quoted in Peter Wood, *Black Majority*, 123n107, 124; Price, "Caribbean Fishing," 1369; Lawson, *New Voyage*, 16–17; Vickers with Walsh, *Young Men and the Sea*, 14, 17.

38. Brewington, *Chesapeake Bay*, 23–24, 26–27, esp. 20–21; Susan Myra Kingsbury, ed., *Records of the Virginia Company of London*, 4 vols. (Washington, DC: 1906–1935), 4: xvii, 144, 230, 260; Lipman, *Saltwater Frontier*, 72–76; Vlach, *Afro-American Tradition*, 98; Vickers with Walsh, *Young Men and the Sea*, 14.

39. Patricia Seed, *Ceremonies of Possession in Europe's Conquest of the New World, 1492–1640* (Cambridge: 1995), 16–40; Colin G. Calloway, *New Worlds for All: Indians, Europeans, and the Remaking of Early America* (Baltimore: 1997), esp. 8–23; Colin G. Calloway, *White People, Indians, and Highlanders: Tribal Peoples and Colonial Encounters in Scotland and America* (Oxford: 2008), esp. 60–87; Cañizares-Esguerra, *Puritan Conquistador*; Alida C. Metcalf, *Go-Betweens and the Colonization of Brazil, 1500–1600* (Austin: 2005); William Cronan, *Changes to the Land: Indians, Colonists, and the Ecology of New England* (New York: 1983); Joyce E. Chaplin, *An Anxious Pursuit: Agricultural Innovation & Modernity in the Lower South, 1730–1815* (Chapel Hill: 1993); April Lee Hatfield, *Atlantic Virginia: Intercolonial Relations in the Seventeenth Century* (Philadelphia: 2004), 8–38; Karen O. Kupperman, *Indians and English: Facing off in Early America* (Ithaca: 2000); Silver, *New Face*; Parent, *Foul Means*; Isaac, *Transformation of Virginia*, 11–57; David Watts, *Man's Influence on the Vegetation of Barbados, 1627–1899* (Hull: 1966), 38–64; Larry Gragg, *Englishmen Transplanted: The English Colonization of Barbados, 1627–1660* (Oxford: 2003); Dunn, *Sugar and Slaves*, 263–264; Edelson, *Plantation Enterprise*, 13–165; Jill Lepore, *Name of War: King Philip's War and the Origins of American Identity* (New York: 1999); Emma Hart, *Building Charleston, Town and Society in the Eighteenth-Century British Atlantic World* (Charlottesville: 2010), 17–64; Welch, *Slave Society in the City*, esp. 31–50.

40. Strachey, *Historie*, 17.

41. Henry Glassie, *Folk Housing in Middle Virginia: A Structural Analysis of Historical Artifacts* (Knoxville: 1983), 130; Vlach, *Afro-American Tradition*, 102–104; Finch, *Bodies of Dissent*, esp. 185–189, 200–202; Brewington, *Chesapeake Bay*, 20–24. Europeans did not claim African dugouts were uncivilized and many were impressed by their aesthetic design and extolled their craftsmanship. Adam Jones, ed., *German Sources*, 66; de Marees, *Gold Kingdom*, 15, 118–119; Hair, Jones, and Law, *Barbot on Guinea*, 2:341; Canneau, *Slaver's Logbook*, 255; Hornell, "Kru Canoes," 231, 237; Ward, *My Africa*, 112.

42. Aluminum and fiberglass canoes, popular in America and Europe, are modeled after Indian bark canoes.

43. Brewington, *Chesapeake Bay*, 23–24; A. J. Morrison, "Virginia Patents," *William and Mary Quarterly* 2, no. 3 (July 1922), 154; William Chauncy Langdon, *Everyday Things in American Life, 1776–1876*, 2 vols. (London: 1941), 2:10; Virginia Genealogical Society, *Albemarle County Road Orders, 1725–1816: Published With Permission from the Virginia Transportation Research Council* (Westminster: 2008), 49; Ralph E. Fall, ed., *The Diary of Robert Rose: A View of Virginia by a Scottish Colonial Parson, 1746–1751* (Verona: 1977), 250–251.

44. Quoted in Ann Maury, ed., *Memoirs of a Huguenot Family: Translated and Compiled from the Original Autobiography of Re. James Fontoine, and other Family Manuscripts, Comprising an Original Journal of Travels in Virginia, New-York etc., in 1716 and 1716* (New York: 1872), 388–389; Morrison, "Virginia Patents," 154; Herndon, *William Tatham*, 62–64, 473; Alexander Brown, *The Cabells and Their Kin: A Memorial Volume of History, Biography, and Genealogy* (New York: 1895), 51–52, 215; Wayland Fuller Dunaway, *History of the James River and Kanawha Company* (New York: 1922), 21n1; Brewington, *Chesapeake Bay*, 23; Fall, *Robert Rose*, viii; 250–251.

45. Oviedo, *Coronica de las Indias*, book 6, chap. 4:50, lxi; Fernández de Oviedo y Valdés, *L'histoire naturelle et génèralle des Indes, isles, et terre ferme de la grand mer oceane. Tradvicte de Castillan en Francois*, Jean Poleur, ed. (Paris, 1556), 79, 89; Oviedo, *Historia General*, 3:335–340, 654[Lam. a.2.a]; Gonzalo Solís de Menéndez Avilés, *Pedro Menédez de Avilés, Adelantado, Governor and Captain-General of Florida: Memorial by Gonzalo Solís de Merás* (Gainesville: 1964), 193; Barbara A. Purdy, "American Indians After A.D. 1492: A Case Study of Forced Cultural Change," *American Anthropologist*, New Series 90, no. 3 (September 1988), 642.

46. A. C. Haddon, "The Outrigger Canoe of East Africa," *Man* 18 (April 1918), 49–54; James Hornell, "The Affinities of East African Outrigger Canoes," *Man* 19 (July 1919): 97–100; James Hornell, "Common Origin of the Outrigger Canoes of Madagascar and East Africa," *Man* 20 (September 1920): 134–139; E. Torday, "Outrigger Canoes of the Congo," *Man* 18 (May 1918): 72. Slaves sometimes lashed canoes together. George Gardner, *Travels in the Interior of Brazil, Principally Through the Northern Provinces, and the Gold and Diamond Districts, During the Years 1836–1841* (London: 1846), 321.

47. Fall, *Robert Rose*, xiii–xv, 53, 75, 250–251, 310; Brown, *Cabells and Their Kin*, 52; "Notes from the Records of Albemarle County," *Virginia Magazine of History and Biography* 26 (1918): 317.

48. Du Tertre, *Histoire générale*, 2:397; Raymond Breton, *Relations de l'île de la Guadeloupe* (Guadalupe: 1978), 69; McKusick, "Aboriginal Canoes," 6; Brewington, *Chesapeake Bay*, 23–24.

49. Kalm, *Travels*, 37–39.

50. Mitman, *Catalogue of the Watercraft Collection in the United States National Museum*, 205; Chapelle, *National Watercraft Collection*, 301–302; United States National Museum, *Bulletin of the United States National Museum*, "Collections Sent from the United States to the International Fisheries Exhibition, London, 1883, Consisting of a Report Upon the American Section," 27 (1884): 708.

51. Van Tilburg, "Vessels of Exchange," 38–52; Robert J. Schwendinger, *Ocean of Bitter Dreams: Maritime Relations Between China and the United States, 1850–1915* (Tuscan: 1988); Linda Bentz, "Redwood, Bamboo, and Ironwood: Chinese Junks of San Diego," *Mains'l Haul*

35, no. 2 and 3 (1999), 14–21; Marray K. Lee, "The Chinese Fishing Industry of San Diego," *Mains'l Haul* 35, no. 2 and 3 (1999): 6–13.

52. Gilbert, *Dhows*, esp.1–2, 38–39, 41, 46, 48; Erik Gilbert, "The Mtepe: Regional Trade and the Late Survival of Sewn Ships in the East African Waters," *International Journal of Nautical Archaeology* 27, no. 1 (February 1998), 43–50; Gilbert, "Dhow as Cultural Icon," 62–80; Prins, *Sailing from Lamu*, 97, 100–102, 126–128, 254.

53. Gomez, *Country Marks*, 18–22; Heywood and Thornton, *Central Africans*, 242–248; Robin Blackburn, *American Crucible: Slavery, Emancipation and Human Rights* (London: 2011), 24.

54. Joseph Miller, "Central Africa During the Era of the Slave Trade, c. 1490–1850s," in Heywood, *Cultural Transformations*, 28; Heywood and Thornton, *Central Africans*, 248; T. H. Breen and Stephen Innes, *"Myne Owne Ground": Race and Freedom on Virginia's Eastern Shore, 1640–1676* (Oxford: 1980), 17, 45, 111.

55. Walsh, *Calabar to Carter's Grove*, 54–55; Gwendolyn Hall, *Slavery and African Ethnicities*, 94–95; Edda L. Fields-Black, *Deep Roots: Rice Farmers in West Africa and the African Diaspora* (Bloomington: 2008), 6–7, 33, 75, 137; Anderson and Peek, "Ways of the Rivers," 12–13.

56. Gwendolyn Hall, *Slavery and African Ethnicities*, 130–133, 142, esp. 136; Douglass B. Chambers, *Murder at Montpelier: Igbo Africans in Virginia* (Jackson: 2005), 22–24, 250n1; Walsh, *Calabar to Carter's Grove*, 55–56, Heywood and Thornton, *Central Africans*, 247; Nwokeji, *Slave Trade and Culture*, 58.

57. For examples of water people, see Rodney, *Upper Guinea*; Barry, *Senegambia*; Hawthorne, *Harvesting Slaves*; Searing, *West African Slavery*; Fields-Black, *Deep Roots*, 6–7, 33, 137; Harms, *River of Wealth*; Harms, *Games Against Nature*; Miller, *Way of Death*; Alagoa, "Long-Distance Trade," 323–325; Anderson and Peek, "Ways of the Rivers," 12–13; Thornton, *Warfare Atlantic Africa*, 75–98; Law, *Ouidah*; Mann, *Birth of an African City*; Dike, *Trade and Politics*; Jones, *Trading States*.

58. Gwendolyn Hall, *Slavery and African Ethnicities*, 129–131; Chambers, *Murder at Montpelier*, 22–23; Paul E. Lovejoy and David Richardson, " 'This Horrid Hole': Royal Authority, Commerce and Credit in Bonny, 1690–1840," *Journal of African History* 45, no. 3 (2004): 363–392"; David Northrup, *Trade Without Rulers: Pre-Colonial Economic Development in South-Eastern Nigeria* (Oxford: 1978). For Ibo/Igbo identity, see Gwendolyn Hall, *Slavery and African Ethnicities*, 129–133; David Northrup, "Igbo and Myth Igbo Culture and Ethnicity in the Atlantic World, 1600–1850," *Slavery and Abolition* 21, no. 3 (December 2000): 1–20; Alexander X. Byrd, *Captives and Voyagers: Black Migrants Across the Eighteenth-Century British Atlantic World* (Baton Rouge: 2008), 17–56; Femi J . Kolapo, "The Igbo and their Neighbours during the Era of the Atlantic Slave-Trade," *Slavery and Abolition* 25, no. 1 (2004): 114–133.

59. Thornton, *Africa and Africans*, 320; Joyner, *Down by the Riverside*, 39.

60. Gomez, *Country Marks*, 40–41, 66–70, 106–107, 115, 149–153, 225–227, 283, esp. 149–150, 194; Littlefield, *Rice and Slaves*, esp. 8–32; Wood, *Black Majority*, 36–37, 58–62; Michael Brown, *African-Atlantic Cultures*, 42–82; Gwendolyn Hall, *Africans in Colonial Louisiana*, 34, 40–41, 195–196, 288–289. Thornton argued against the premise of cruising, which purportedly "randomized" slaves. Thornton, *African and Africans*, 183–184, 191–196, 209–210.

61. Sweet, *Recreating Africa*, esp. 47, 58; Gomez, *Country Marks*, 283; Matt D. Childs, " 'The Defects of Being a Black Creole': The Degrees of African Identity in Cuban *Cabildos de*

Nación, 1790–1820," in Jane G. Landers and Barry M. Robinson, eds., *Slaves, Subjects, and Subversives: Blacks in Colonial Latin America* (Albuquerque: 2006), 209–245; Young, *Rituals of Resistance*; Brown, *Reaper's Garden*; Hawthorne, *Africa to Brazil*; Ferreira, *Cross-Cultural Exchange*.

62. Michael Brown, *African-Atlantic Cultures*, 11.

63. *Virginia Gazette*, (Purdie and Dixon) December 24, 1772; Equiano, *Interesting Narrative*, 2:178, 211–212; Peter Wood, *Black Majority*, 203; James Sidbury, *Becoming African in America: Race and Nation in the Early Black Atlantic* (Oxford: 2007), 50–52.

64. Gwendolyn Hall, *Slavery and African Ethnicities*, 166; Gomez, *Country Marks*, 8.

65. For example, see Sweet, *Recreating Africa*; Gomez, *Country Marks*; Peter Wood, *Black Majority*; Gwendolyn Hall, *Africans in Colonial Louisiana*; Gwendolyn Hall, *Slavery and African Ethnicities*; Heywood and Thornton, *Central Africans, Atlantic Creoles*; Hawthorne, *Africa to Brazil*.

66. William D. Pierson, *Black Yankees: The Development of an Afro-American Subculture in Eighteenth-Century New England* (Amherst: 1988), esp. 14, 49–61, Graham Russell Hodges, *Root & Branch: African Americans in New York & East Jersey, 1613–1836* (Chapel Hill: 1999), esp. 2, 53–60; Foote, *Black and White Manhattan*, esp. 47–49, 124–147; Berlin, *Many Thousands Gone*, 369–375.

67. Samuel M. Wilson, "The Legacy of the Indigenous People of the Caribbean," in Wilson, *Indigenous People of the Caribbean*, 218–219.

68. Price, "Caribbean Fishing," 1364, 1368, 1369, 1371, 1380n4; Labat, *Nouveau Voyage*, 2:550–553; Dale W. Tomich, *Slavery in the Circuit of Sugar: Martinique and the World Economy, 1830–1848* (Baltimore: 1990), 1; Léo Elisabeth, "The French Antilles" in David W. Cohen and Jack P. Greene, eds., *Neither Slave Nor Free: The Freedman of African Descent in the Slave Societies of the New World* (Baltimore: 1974), 147. For Caribs' refusal to associate with slaves, see Price, "Caribbean Fishing," 1368; Labat, *Nouveau Voyage*, 2:75; Du Tertre, *Histoire générale*, 2:489–492. Rivièr Capo is on the eastern side of the island, north of Fort-de-France. Richard Price claimed that Labat's account was proof that Island Caribs taught slaves to make dugouts. Price did not consider African maritime traditions, claiming Africans were merely subsistence fishermen. Price, "Caribbean Fishing."

69. Matthew Restall, ed., *Beyond Black and Red: African-Native Relations in Colonial Latin America* (Albuquerque: 2005); Tiya Miles and Sharon P. Holland, eds., *Crossing Waters, Crossing Worlds: The African Diaspora in Indian Country* (Durham: 2006), 4–12; Hammon, *Uncommon Sufferings*, 5–8; Jean Baptiste Labat, *The Memoirs of Père Labat, 1693–1705* (London: 1970), 137–139; Anonymous, *Authentic Papers Relative to the Expedition Against the Charibbs*, 6, 26; Young, *Account of the Black Charaibs*, 7–8; Virginia Kerns, *Women and the Ancestors: Black Carib Kinship and Ritual* (Champaign: 1997), 17–20; Young, *Black Charibs*, 7–8; Jerome S. Handler, "Escaping Slavery in a Caribbean Plantation Society: Maroonage in Barbados, 1650s–1830s," *New West Indian Guide/Nieuwe West-Indische Gids* 71 (1997): 198–202; Beckles, "From Land to Sea," 86.

70. Labat, *Nouveau Voyage*, 2:75, 394–396; Du Tertre, *Histoire générale*, 2:490–492; Price, "Caribbean Fishing," 1368–1369; Miles and Holland, *Crossing Waters, Crossing Worlds*, 10; Prentiss, *Blind African Slave*, 176; Love, *Life and Adventures*.

71. Wilson, "Legacy," 208; Blackburn, *American Crucible*, 51; Schwartz, *Sugar Plantations*, 49, 62, 65–70; Hawthorne, *Africa to Brazil*, 25–60.

72. Robin Blackburn, *American Crucible: Slavery, Emancipation and Human Rights* (London: 2011), 31–48; Blackburn, *Making of New World Slavery*, 129–184; Hawthorne, *Africa to Brazil*, 25–53.

73. Philip D. Curtin, *The Rise and Fall of the Plantation Complex: Essays in Atlantic History* (Cambridge: 1990), 42–85, esp. 42; Eltis, *Rise and Fall of African Slavery*; Kenneth Morgan, *Slavery, Atlantic Trade and the British Economy, 1660–1800* (Cambridge: 2000); Kenneth Morgan, *Slavery and the British Empire: From Africa to America* (Oxford: 2007), esp. 11–33; 54–83; Blackburn, *Making of New World Slavery*; Blackburn, *American Crucible*, esp. 29–96; www.slavevoyages.org/assessment/estimates, accessed October 15, 2012.

74. Bernhard, *Slaves and Slaveholders*; Jerome S. Handler and Frederick W. Lange, *Plantation Slavery in Barbados: An Archaeological and Historical Investigation* (New York: 1999), 15, 160, 229, 290n4; Dunn, *Sugar and Slaves*, 18; Craton, *Founded Upon the Seas*, 1–2; Neville Williams, *A History of the Cayman Islands* (Grand Cayman: 1970), 1–6.

75. Las Casas, *Destruction of the Indies*; J. H. Bernardin de Saint-Pierre, *A voyage to the Isle of Mauritius, (or, Isle of France), the Isle of Bourbon, and the Cape of Good Hope, &c.* (London; 1775), 105; Blackburn, *American Crucible*, 1, 31–48; Wilson, "Legacy," 208; Hawthorne, *Africa to Brazil*, 25–53.

76. Paul Kelton, *Epidemics and Enslavement: Biological Catastrophe in the Native Southeast, 1492–1715* (Lincoln: 2007), xvii–xviii; David Jones, "Virgin Soils Revisited," *William and Mary Quarterly*, 3rd ser. 60, no. 4 (October 2003), 703–742, esp. 703; Alfred W. Crosby, "Virgin Soil Epidemics as a Factor in the Aboriginal Depopulation of America," *William and Mary Quarterly*, 3rd ser. 33, no. 2 (April 1976), 289–299; Hawthorne, *Africa to Brazil*, 33.

77. McKusick, "Aboriginal Canoes," 4; Brown, *Reaper's Garden*, 6; Douglas M. Taylor, *The Black Carib of British Honduras* (New York: 1951), 15–20; Craton and Saunders, *Islanders in the Stream*, 1, 48–55; Thornton, *Africa and Africans*, 141–142.

78. Natalie A. Zacek, *Settler Society in the English Leeward Islands, 1670–1776* (Cambridge: 2010), 28–29; Sheridan, *Sugar and Slavery*, 84–85, 148–158; Dunn, *Sugar and Slaves*, 18, 119–123; Waldemar Westergaard, *The Danish West Indies Under Company Rule (1671–1754): With a Supplementary Chapter, 1755–1917* (New York: 1917), 23; V. S. Naipaul, *The Loss of El Dorado* (London 1969), 95; Edward Arber, ed., *Travels and Works of Captain John Smith, of Willoughby by Alford, Lincolnshire; President of Virginia, and Admiral of New England. Works, 1580–1631*, 2 vols. (London: 1884), 1:900–901.

79. Cornelis Goslinga, *The Dutch in the Caribbean and on the Wild Coast 1580–1680* (Assen: 1971), 425, 433–456; Henry Iles Woodcock, *A History of Tobago* (London: 1867), 23–68; Eric Williams, *History of the People of Trinidad and Tobago* (London: 1964), esp. 59–60, 66–86; Gertrude Carmichael, *The History of the West Indian Islands of Trinidad and Tobago, 1498–1900* (London: 1961): 302–317.

80. Westergaard, *Danish West Indies*, 2, 33; N. Hall, *Danish West Indies*, 3, 6–7; Haagensen, *St. Croix*, xii–xv; Arnold R. Highfield, *St. Croix 1493: An Encounter of Two Worlds* (St. Thomas: 1995).

81. Frank Cundall and Joseph L. Pirtersz, *Jamaica Under the Spaniards: Abstracted from the Archives of Seville* (Kingston: 1919), 34; Michael Craton, *Testing the Chains: Resistance to Slavery in the British West Indies* (Ithaca: 1982), 67–70, 75, 352n5; Dunn, *Sugar and Slaves*, 35–36; 151–156; Emmanuel Kofi Agorsah, *Maroon Heritage: Archaeological, Ethnographic, and Historical Perspectives* (Kingston: 1994); Nicholas J. Saunders, *The Peoples of the Caribbean: An Encyclopedia of Archeology and Traditional Culture* (Santa Barbara: 2005), 197.

82. Mavis C. Campbell, *The Maroons of Jamaica, 1655–1796* (Trenton: 1990), 9, 14; Joseph John Williams, *The Maroons of Jamaica* (Chestnut Hill: 1938), 379, 379n1.

83. For complexities of Indians' relationships with American colonists, see Kulikoff, *Tobacco and Slaves*, 9, 27–29, esp. 23; Parent, *Foul Means*, 16–79, esp. 19; Hatfield, *Atlantic Virginia*, 8–38; James Axtell, *Natives and Newcomers: The Cultural Origins of North America* (Oxford: 2001), 233–258; Calloway, *White People, Indians, and Highlanders*, 43–59; Michael Brown, *African-Atlantic Cultures*, 33–89, Wood, *Black Majority*, 95–166; James H. Merrell, *The Indians' New World: Catawbas and Their Neighbors from European Contact Through the Era of Removal* (Chapel Hill: 2012); Eve Tavor Bannet, *Transatlantic Stories and the History of Reading, 1720–1810: Migrant Fictions* (Cambridge: 2011), 152–154; John Marrant, *A Narrative of the Lord's Wonderful Dealings with John Marrant: A Black, Born in New-York, in North-America. Taken Down from His Own Relation* (London: 1785); Kenneth Wiggins Porter, *The Black Seminoles: History of a Freedom-Seeking People* (Gainesville: 1996); Kevin Mulroy, *The Seminole Freedmen: A History* (Norman: 2016).

84. For examples of scholarship, see Alan Gallay, *The Indian Slave Trade: The Rise of the English Empire in the American South, 1670–1717* (New Haven: 2002); Robbie Franklyn Ethridge and Sheri Marie Shuck-Hall, *Mapping the Mississippian Shatter Zone: The Colonial Indian Slave Trade and Regional Instability in the American South* (Lincoln: 2009); William L. Ramsey, *The Yamasee War: A Study of Culture, Economy, and Conflict in the Colonial South* (Lincoln: 2008), 26–32, 60–61, 69; Paul Kelton, *Epidemics and Enslavement: Biological Catastrophe in the Native Southeast, 1492–1715* (Lincoln: 2007); Christina Snyder, *Slavery in Indian Country: The Changing Face of Captivity in Early America* (Cambridge: 2010), 46–79; Wendy Warren, *New England Bound: Slavery and Colonization in Early America* (New York: 2016); Larry E. Ivers, *This Torrent of Indians: War on the Southern Frontier, 1715–1728* (Columbia: 2016).

85. Herbert S. Klein, *African Slavery in Latin America and the Caribbean* (Oxford: 1986), 21–26, 40–42, 47–49, 68, esp. 42; Schwartz, *Slaves, Peasants, and Rebels*, 110–111, 119; Schwartz, *Sugar Plantations*, 15–22, 28–50, 65–72, esp. 62; Klein and Luna, *Slavery in Brazil*, 19–28; Sweet, *Recreating Africa*, 22–23; Hawthorne, *Africa to Brazil*, 28, Herbert Klein, "The Atlantic Slave Trade to 1650," in Stuart B. Schwartz, ed., *Tropical Babylons: Sugar and the Making of the Atlantic World, 1450–1680* (Chapel Hill: 2004), 207–208. Also see, Herman L. Bennett, *Africans in Colonial Mexico: Absolutism, Christianity, and Afro-Creole Consciousness, 1570–1640* (Oxford: 2003), 19–23, 29; David Eltis, *Rise and Fall of African Slavery*, 7, 24–27; Las Casas, *Destruction of the Indies*; Blackburn, *American Crucible*, 31–48.

86. Hawthorne, *Africa to Brazil*, 25–60, esp. 47.

87. Malcolm Letts, trans. and ed., *Hans Staden: The True History of His Captivity, 1557* (New York: 1929), 14; Jean de Léry, *History of a Voyage to the Land of Brazil, Otherwise Called America*, Janet Whatley, trans. and ed. (1599; Berkeley: 1992), 97, 116.

88. Adney and Chapelle, *Bark Canoes*, Johnstone, *Sea-Craft*, 19–23.

89. Las Casas, *Destruction of the Indies*; Blackburn, *American Crucible*, 1, 31–48; Blackburn, *Making of New World Slavery*, 129–184.

90. Byrd, *Captives and Voyagers*, 2; Klein, "Atlantic Slave Trade to 1650," 201–236, esp. 208–215, 230–231; David Eltis, *Rise of African Slavery in the Americas* (Cambridge: 2000), 8–28; Klein and Luna, *Slavery in Brazil*, 16; Thomas Benjamin, *The Atlantic Worlds: Europeans, Africans, Indians and Their Shared History, 1400–1900* (Cambridge: 2009), 326–327; Blackburn, *American Crucible*, 1, 24, 77; Voyages: The Trans-Atlantic Slave Trade Database, www.slavevoyages.org/assessment/estimates, accessed July 30, 2010.

91. Klein and Luna, *Slavery in Brazil*, 170–171; Sweet, Recreating Africa, 59–64; Dunn, *Sugar and Slaves*, 301, 323, 330–334.

92. David Eltis, "Coverage of the Slave Trade, (2007)" on Voyages: The Trans-Atlantic Slave Trade Database, http://www.slavevoyages.org/voyage/understanding-db/methodology -02, accessed July 30, 2010.

93. Michael Brown, *African-Atlantic Cultures*, 35. For scholarship on African cultural transmissions, see Wood, *Black Majority*; Littlefield, *Rice and Slaves*; Landers, *Black Society in Spanish Florida*; Gwendolyn Hall, *Slavery and African Ethnicities*; Gomez, *Country Marks*; Heywood and Thornton, *Central Africans*; Heywood, *Cultural Transformations*; Sweet, *Recreating Africa*; Young, *Rituals of Resistance*; Ferreire, *Cross-Cultural Exchange*.

Chapter 9

1. Hall, *Miserable Slavery*, x–xii, xvi, 13, 21–22, 115–116.

2. Berry, *Swing the Sickle*, esp. 3; Thomas Thistlewood, Thistlewood's Diaries, 18:59, 73, 86, 92, 102, esp. 66, 79, 102, 104; Lincolnshire Archives, MON/31/18; Hall, *Miserable Slavery*, 78, 139–140, 163–164, 249, esp. 144–146. On Saturday, March 21, 1767, "Young Cunningham the carpenter of Pen" provided some assistance in constructing the canoe. Thistlewood, Thistlewood's Diaries, 18:79. South Carolinian colonists similarly used canoes to help establish estates. George C. Rogers, Jr., David R. Chestnut, Peggy J. Clark, eds., *The Papers of Henry Laurens*, 16 vols. (Columbia: 1976), 5:104.

3. Hall, *Miserable Slavery*, 78, esp. 154.

4. Charles Lyell, *A Second Visit to the United States of North America*, 2 vols. (London: 1849), 1:357; Ball, *Fifty Years*, 110, 206–239, esp. 212.

5. James Kelly, *Jamaica in 1831: Being a Narrative of Seventeen Years Residence in That Island, with Extracts from Sturge and Harvey's "West Indies in 1837"* (Belfast: 1838), 25; Lewis, *West India Proprietor*, 44, 45; Charles Kingsley, *At Last: A Christmas in the West Indies* (1871; London: 1874), 153.

6. Fall, *Robert Rose*, vii, 53, 57–58, 75, 291n734.

7. Haagensen, *St. Croix*, ix, xiii–xiv, 9–10; Karen Fog Olwig, "African Cultural Principles in Caribbean Slave Societies: A View from the Danish West Indies," in Stephan Palmié, ed., *Slave Cultures and the Cultures of Slavery* (Knoxville: 1995), 34; Karen Fog Olwig, *Cultural Adaption and Resistance on St. John: Three Centuries of Afro-Caribbean Life* (Gainesville: 1985), 50, 53–54. For sugar production, see Ligon, *Barbadoes*, 90; Sheridan, *Sugar and Slavery*, 115; Dunn, *Sugar and Slaves*, 194; Schwartz, *Sugar Plantations*, 117, 145.

8. Haagensen, *St. Croix*, ix, xiii–xiv, 10.

9. November 6, 1767, and November 13, 1767, Thistlewood's Diaries, 18:254, 259, Lincolnshire Archives, MON/31/18; Hall, *Miserable Slavery*, 124–125, 152, 155, 157, 198, 303. While I was writing this book, Thistlewood's Diaries were pulled from the Lincolnshire Archives and held at Christie's Auction House, preventing examination of them.

10. For boatbuilding and tools needed, see Gardner, *Building Classic Small Craft*, Chapelle, *Boatbuilding*, esp. 588–598; Steward, *Boatbuilding Manual*, esp. 19–35; Herbert Ashcroft, *Boatbuilding Simplified: Being a Practical Guide to the "Simplex" Method* (New Haven: 1917).

11. Hall, *Miserable Slavery*, 27, 39, 148, 234, 249, 282; Chinard, *Huguenot Exile*, 133.

12. Hall, *Miserable Slavery*, 140, 145, 146, 162; James Henderson, *A History of the Brazil; Comprising Its Geography, Commerce, Colonization, Aboriginal Inhabitant* (London; 1821), 389.

13. Hall, *Miserable Slavery*, 35–37, 40.

14. Ibid., 22, 26–27, 29, 30–31, 39, 40, 44, 68, 74–75, 95, 103, 108, esp. 34, 47–48, 62.

15. Ibid., 22, 28, 43–44, 71, 75.

16. Ibid., 21–22, 30–31, 34–36, 40–41, 96, 109.

17. Ibid., 21–22, 35–36.

18. Ibid., 22, 35, 38, 42.

19. Ibid., 140, 145–146, 162, 249.

20. Dawson, "Enslaved Swimmers," 1347; Dusinberre, *Them Dark Days*, 179–210.

21. Based on my decades of surfing and bringing kayaks and canoes through surf.

22. Lawson, *New Voyage*, 16, 103–104; D. Smith, *Charlestonian's Recollections*, 45; Betty Wood, *Women's Work*, 74–75. For boatbuilding, see Gardner, *Building Classic Small Craft*; Chapelle, *Boatbuilding*, esp. 588–598; Steward, *Boatbuilding Manual*, esp. 19–35; my observations of canoe-making in Ghana and boat-making at Mystic Seaport, The Museum of America and the Sea in Connecticut.

23. Paul A. Kube, Carriage Museum of America, *Wagon-Making in the United States During the Late-19th Through Mid-20th Centuries: A Study of the Gruber Wagon Works at Mt. Pleasant, Pennsylvania* (Newark: 2005); Don Peloubet, Carriage Museum of America, *Wheelmaking: Wagon Wheel Design and Construction* (Mendham: 1996); Bruce Morrison and Joyce Morrison, *Wheelwrighting: A Modern Introduction* (Parkersville: 2003).

24. J. Bryan Grimes, ed., *North Carolina Wills and Inventories. Copied from Original and Recorded Wills and Inventories* (Baltimore: 1967), 522–524, 553, 572, esp. 574–575; Hall, *Miserable Slavery*, 118, 123, 145, 160, 162, 215, 228, 230, 258; George C. Rogers Jr., David R. Chestnut, and Peggy J. Clark, eds., *The Papers of Henry Laurens*, 16 vols. (Columbia: 1976), 8:101; June 26, 1765, Ravenel Day Book, in Henry Ravenel Ledger, 12/313/03, South Carolina Historical Society; Lyell, *Second Visit*, 1:357; Thomas Newe, "Letters of Thomas Newe, 1682," in Alexander S. Sally Jr., ed., *Narratives of Early Carolina, 1650–1708* (New York: 1911), 184; Anonymous, "A Gentleman's Account of His Travels, 1733–34," in H. Roy Merrens, ed., *The Colonial South Carolina Scene: Contemporary Views, 1697–1774* (Columbia: 1977), 112–113; Drinkwater and Finlay, *Finlay's Journal & Drinkwater's Letters*, 54; Long, *History of Jamaica*, 3:737, 2:105–106.

25. Inventory of Estate of Francis Howard 1748, May 16, Inventory of Estate of William Bakers 1777, December 15, Inventory of Estate of John Tenham 1770, November 19, in Mary Marshall Brewer, ed., *York County, Virginia Wills, Inventories, and Court Orders*. Colonial Williamsburg. Also see Lyell, *Second Visit*, 1:357; Betty Wood, *Women's Work*, 47.

26. Inventory of Estate of John Kerby 1778, February 16; Inventory of Estate of John Kerby 1796, July 18, in Brewer, *York County*; Grimes, *North Carolina Wills and Inventories*, 574–575; Lyell, *Second Visit*, 1:357.

27. *Virginia Gazette* (Parks), December 17, 1736; *South Carolina Gazette and Country Journal*, January 26, 1768, August 8, 1769.

28. Long, *History of Jamaica*, 3:737, 2:105–106; Thistlewood, 16, 35, 37, 93, 170, 299, esp. 162. Thistlewood valued goods in Jamaican pounds, Long used the British pound sterling, which had a greater value than colonial currencies.

29. Basil Hall, *Travels in the United States in the Years 1827 and 1828*, 3 vols. (London: 1829), 3:212–214, 216.

30. Edelson, *Plantation Enterprise*, 131; Federal Writers' Project, *The Oregon Trail: The Missouri River to the Pacific Ocean* (New York: 1939), 72; Dale Lowell Morgan, ed., *Overland*

in 1846: Diaries and Letters of the California-Oregon Trail, 2 vols. (Lincoln: 1993), 1:178, 182–187, 205; Osburn Winther, *The Old Oregon Country: A History of Frontier Trade, Transportation and Travel* (Stanford: 1950), 224.

31. Clonts, "Travel and Transportation," 18; Edmund Ruffin, *Agricultural, Geological, and Descriptive Sketches of Lower North Carolina, and the Similar Adjacent Lands* (Raleigh: 1861), 200–201; Long, *History of Jamaica*, 3:736; Marsden, *Account of the Island of Jamaica*, 32–33; Cynric Williams, *Island of Jamaica*, 35; Palgrave, *Dutch Guiana*, 29; Clonts, "Travel and Transportation," 18; Renny, *An History of Jamaica*, 89.

32. James M. Clifton, ed., *Life and Labor on Argyle Island: Letters and Documents of a Savannah River Rice Plantation, 1833–1867* (Savannah: 1978), passim, 78; Joyner, *Down by the Riverside*, 76, 270n93; Frances Butler Leigh, *Ten Years on a Georgia Plantation Since the War* (London: 1883), 114; Klein and Luna, *Slavery in Brazil*, 295–296; Kemble, *Journal*, 62.

33. Ball, *Fifty Years*, 9–10, 15–17, 99, 211; Berry, *Swing the Sickle*, 60–61; Rawick, *American Slave*, 13:223–224. See Chapter 6 in this book for barn-raising and community canoe-making.

34. Hall, *Miserable Slavery*, 144–145; Clifton, *Argyle Island*, 4, 7, 8, 20, 31, 65, 67–68, 77–78, 86–87, 95–96, 152–153, 184, 193–194, 220, 248–249, 288, 295, esp. 82, 86, 123; Rosengarten, *Tombee*, 237, 330, 331, 428, 439; Fall, *Robert Rose*, 53, 75; *Virginia Gazette* (Purdie and Dixon), January 3, April 11, 1771; *Republic* (Baton Rouge, Louisiana), July 30, 1822; "List of Negroes taken at Hampton, May 11, 1793," Box 10, Folder 11, Butler Plantation Papers: The Papers of Piers Butler (1744–1822) and Successors [hereafter, Butler Plantation Papers]; "Return of Negroes belonging to the Honorable Pierce Butler, January 5, 1803," Butler Plantation Papers, Box 10, Folder 12; "Births & Deaths," June 1 to January 1, 1803, Butler Plantation Papers, Box 10, Folder 12; "List of Births and Deaths for 1820," Butler Plantation Papers, Box 10, Folder 13; "Inventory and Appraisements of the Estate of Capt. John Butler dec'd," Butler Plantation Papers, Box 11, Folder 10; Johan Martin Bolzius, "Reliable Answer to Some Submitted Questions Concerning the Land Carolina," in *William and Mary Quarterly*, 3rd series, vol. 14, no. 2 (April 1957), 260; Stewart, *"What Nature Suffers to Groe,"* 127; Leigh, *Georgia Plantation*, 114.

35. Pierce Butler to John Potter, August 12, 1809, Butler Plantation Papers, Box 16, Folder 17; "Lists of Negroes taken at Hampton, May 4, 1793," Butler Plantation Papers, Box 10, Folder 11; "Hampton Plantation Negroes, January 5, 1803," Butler Plantation Papers, Box 10, Folder 12; Bell, *Major Butler's Legacy*, 111–112, 116–117, 118–119, 155, 174, 560. Also see "Inventory and Appraisement of the Estate of Capt. John Butler dec'd, February 13, 1849," Butler Plantation Papers: The Papers of Piers Butler (1744–1822) and Successors, Box 11, Folder 10.

36. Bell, *Major Butler's Legacy*, 147–148, 167, 425; "Inventory and Appraisement of the Estate of Capt. John Butler dec'd, February 13, 1849," Butler Plantation Papers, Box 11, Folder 10; Kemble, *Journal*, 62, 86, 96, 174, 192–194, 333; *Darien Gazette*, December 21, 1818.

37. June 26, 1765, Ravenel Day Book, in Henry Ravenel Ledger, 12/313/03, South Carolina Historical Society; Roswell King Jr., "On the Management of the Butler Island Estate, and the Cultivation of Sugar Cane," *Southern Agriculturalist* (December 1828), 524; Long, *History of Jamaica*, 3:737; Lyell, *Second Visit*, 1:357.

38. Ball, *Fifty Years*, 205–212 (italics added).

39. Ibid., 99, 211, 206–213, 240–241. For captives' ability to use skills to invert social and racial hierarchies, see Dawson, "Enslaved Ship Pilots."

40. Federal Writers' Project, *Slave Narratives: A Folk History of Slavery in the United States from Interviews with Former Slaves*, 17 vols., Alabama Narratives (Washington, DC: 1941), 1:421; Arkansas Narratives, 2: part 1, 120, Arkansas Narratives, 2: part 3, 256, part 6, 126; North Carolina Narratives, 11: part 2, 416, Tennessee Narratives, 15:34.

41. Berry, *Swing the Sickle*, 104–128, 110, esp. 105–106; John Luffman, *A Brief Account of the Island of Antigua* (London: 1789), 94–94, 138–141; Richard Graham, *Feeding the City: From Street Market to Liberal Reform in Salvador, Brazil, 1780–1860* (Austin: 2010), passim, esp. 33–53, 74–91. For internal economy, see Sidney W. Mintz and Douglass Hall, *The Origins of the Jamaican Internal Marketing System* (New Haven: 1960); N. A. T. Hall "Slaves' Use of Their 'Free' Time in the Danish Virgin Islands in the later Eighteenth and Early Nineteenth Century," in Hilary Beckles and Verne Shepherd, eds., *Caribbean Slave Society and Economy* (New York: 1991), 335–344; Ira Berlin and Philip D. Morgan, eds., *The Slaves' Economy: Independent Production by Slaves in the Americas* (London: 1991); Wood, *Women's Work*; Dylan C. Penningroth, *The Claims of Kinfolk: African American Property and Community in the Nineteenth-Century South* (Chapel Hill: 2003); Timothy James Lockley, *Lines in the Sand: Race and Class in Lowcountry Georgia, 1750–1860* (Athens: 2004); Forret, *Race Relations at the Margins*. For recent consideration of slaves' internal economy, see Kathleen M. Hilliard, *Masters, Slaves, and Exchange: Power's Purchase in the Old South* (Cambridge, 2014).

42. Berry, *Swing the Sickle*, 14–19, esp. 150.

43. King, "Management," 524 (italics added); Luffman, *Island of Antigua*, 94–94, Wood, *Women's Work*, 45, 47, 54, 89, 90–92, 132, 183, 216n59; Dusinberre, *Dark Days*, 140, 145; October 24, 1830, personal diary, Moses Ashley Curtis Papers; N. Hall, *Danish West Indies*, 90–91; *South Carolina Gazette*, September 24, 1772; Stewart, *"What Nature Suffers to Groe,"* 136.

44. Wood, *Women's Work*, esp. 75, 90–92.

45. South Carolina Council Journal, no. 17, part 1, 160–161, South Carolina Department of Archives and History; Clifton, *Argyle Island*, 62, 99 135–136; Pierce Butler to William Page, June 6, 1799, Pierce Butler Letterbook, 1787–1822, 289, Historical Society of Pennsylvania; Dusinberre, *Dark Days*, 141; Stewart, *"What Nature Suffers to Groe,"* 132–134.

46. Wetherell, *Stray Notes*, 27. "Bicho" broadly means "beast" and can describe any creature.

47. Wood, *Women's Work*, esp. 84–85; McDonald, *Between Slavery and Freedom*, 117; Highfield, *Hans West's Accounts*, 38, 213n58; Luffman, *Island of Antigua*, 94–95, 138–141; Graham, *Feeding the City*, 33–120; N. Hall, *Danish West Indies*, 114–115.

48. Gardner, *Interior of Brazil*, 93, 98–99, 119–121; Wetherell, *Stray Notes*, 26–27; Nishida, *Slavery and Ethnicity*, 41–42; Graham, *Feeding the City*, 74–91.

49. Wetherell, *Stray Notes*, 26–27; Nishida, *Slavery and Identity*, 41.

50. Johann Moritz Rugendas, *Voyage Pittoresque dans le Bresil* (Paris: 1835), reprinted in João Maurício Rugendas, *Viagem Pitoresca Através do Brasil* (Rio de Janeiro: 1967), plate 4/12; Gardner, *Interior of Brazil*, 120–121; Luffman, *Island of Antigua*, 139.

51. Wood, *Women's Work*, 57, 128; Higman, *Slave Populations*, 210–212; Highfield, *Hans West's Accounts*, 80.

52. Lyell, *Second Visit*, 2:1–2; Kemble, *Journal*, 90; Clifton, *Argyle Island*, 123, 151.

53. Joyner, *Down by the Riverside*, 126; Higman, *Slave Populations*, 204, 210–212, 219–223; Walsh, *Calabar to Carter's Grove*, 19–20; Handler and Lange, *Plantation Slavery*, 30–33; Mary Turner, *Slaves and Missionaries: The Disintegration of Jamaican Slave Society, 1787–1834* (Urbana: 1982), 44–47; Sweet, *Recreating Africa*, 31–58.

54. Hall, *Miserable Slavery*, 27, 34, 145, 238.

55. N. Hall, *Danish West Indies*, 115; Wood, *Women's Work*, 31–34, 40–43, 84–85, 168; Turner, *Slaves and Missionaries*, 44–45; Barbara Bush, *Slave Women in the Caribbean Societies, 1650–1838* (Bloomington: 1990), 46–50; Sidney Mintz, *Tasting Food, Tasting Freedom: Excursions into Eating, Culture, and the Past* (Boston: 1996), 43; Simmonds, "Internal Marketing," 275; Woodville K. Marshall, "Provision Ground and Plantation Labour on Four Windward Islands: Competition for Resources During Slavery," in Berlin and Morgan, *Slaves' Economy*, 48–67; Beckles, "Economic Life," 31–47; William Beckford, *A Descriptive Account of the Island of Jamaica: With Remarks upon the Cultivation of the Sugar-Cane Throughout the Different Seasons of the Year*, 2 vols. (London: 1790), 2:150–156; Sally Price, *Co-Wives and Calabashes* (Ann Arbor: 1993), 1, 28, 29, 41, 83, 192. For gendered labor, see Edna G. Bay, *Women and Work in Africa* (Boulder: 1982); Fields-Black, *Deep Roots*, 16, 36–41, 50; Carney, *Black Rice*; Wood, *Women's Work*.

56. Simmonds, "Internal Marketing," 274–275; Martin, *Divided Mastery*; B. W. Higman, *Montpelier Jamaica: A Plantation Community in Slavery and Freedom, 1739–1912* (Kingston: 1998), 2.

57. Dusinberre, *Dark Days*, 140, 145, 175; Kemble, *Journal*, 90; Wood, *Women's Work*, 45, 46, 47; N. Hall, *Danish West Indies*, 126, 128.

58. Sally Price, *Co-Wives*, 1, 13, 201n3; Higman, *Slave Populations*, 212; Wood, *Women's Work*, esp. 32–33; Jacqueline Jones, *Labor of Love, Labor of Sorrow Black Women, Work, and the Family from Slavery to the Present* (New York: 2010), 9–41; Wilma King, *Stolen Childhood*; Schwartz, *Born in Bondage*, esp. 50–53, 123–124, 139, 191–192, 198; Jennifer Morgan, *Laboring Women*; Bernard Moitt, *Women and Slavery in the French Antilles, 1635–1848* (Bloomington: 2001); Bush, *Slave Women*, 46–50.

59. *The Jamaica Magistrate's and Vestryman's Assistant* (Jamaica: 1828), 209, 292, 295; Hall, *Miserable Slavery*, 258; Simmonds, "Internal Marketing," 283, 289n37; *The Gentleman's Magazine, and Historical Chronicle* 51(London: 1791): 537; Wood, *Women's Work*, 74–78.

60. Alexander Barclay, *Practical View of the Present State of Slavery in the West Indies* (London: 1827), 273; Turner, *Slaves and Missionaries*, 44–45; Olwig, *Cultural Adaptation*, 53–54.

61. Berry, *Swing the Sickle*, 107–110; Olwell, " 'Idle and Disorderly,' " 97–110; esp. 99, 102.

62. Berry, *Swing the Sickle*, 3, 60–61; Turner, *Slaves and Missionaries*, 46–47; Kidder and Fletcher, *Brazil*, 16, 475; Kemble, *Journal*, 90; Lyell, *Second Visit*, 2:1–2; D'Orbigny, *Voyage Pittoresque*, image opposite page 59; Rugendas, *Voyage Pittoresque*, plate 4/12; South Carolina Council Journal, no. 17, part 1, 160–161.

63. South Carolina Council Journal, no. 17, part 1, 160–161.

64. Wood, *Women's Work*, 71, 92, 108, 144; Olwell, *Slaves and Subjects*, 141–180; Handler and Lange, *Plantation Slavery*, 31, 90–91; *South Carolina Gazette*, September 24, 1772.

65. Ball, *Fifty Years*, 220–227; Dusinberre, *Dark Days*, 140, 145; Labat, *Memoirs*, 171; Bolster, *Black Jacks*, 17.

66. Kelly, *Jamaica in 1831*, 28; Wetherell, *Stray Notes*, 26–27; Simmonds, "Internal Marketing," 282–283; Graham, *Feeding the City*, 60, 75.

67. Pierre Jacques Benoit, *Journey Through Suriname: Adopted from Voyage à Suriname*, Silvia W. de Groot, trans. (Amsterdam: 1980), 89; J. B. Moreton, *West India Customs and*

Manners (London: 1793), 16; Susette Harriet Lloyd, Sketches of *Bermuda* (London: 1835), 21; Wetherell, *Stray Notes*, 26–27; Nishida, *Slavery and Identity*, 41; Philip Wright, ed., *Lady Nugent's Journal: Her Residence in Jamaica from 1801 to 1805* (1839; Mona, Jamaica: 2002), 8; Stedman, *Expedition*, 1:13, 158; Mrs. Houston, *Texas and the Gulf of Mexico* (Philadelphia: 1845), 35–36; Agassiz, *Journey in Brazil*, 47; Lewis, *West India Proprietor*, 35; Handler and Lange, *Plantation Slavery*, 31; Lorena Elaine Simmonds, "The Afro-Jamaican and the Internal Marketing System: Kingston, 1780–1834," in Kathleen E. A. Monteith and Glen Richards, eds., *Jamaica in Slavery and Freedom: History, Heritage and Culture* (Kingston: 2002), 282.

68. Wetherell, *Stray Notes*, 27; October 25, 1830, personal diary, Moses Ashley Curtis Papers; "Bum Boat in Carlisle Bay," Edwin Stocqueler, artist, n.d., Barbados Museum and Historical Society.

69. "Narrative of Mr. Caulkins," in Theodore Weld, *American Slavery as It Is: Testimony of a Thousand Witnesses* (New York: 1839), 13; David S. Cecelski, *Waterman's Song: Slavery and Freedom in Maritime North Carolina (Chapel Hill: 2001)*, 70.

70. For ports' demographics and hiring out, see Martin, *Divided Mastery*; Dawson, "Enslaved Ship Pilots," 9–10; Higman, *Slave Populations*, 175, 226–225, 235–236, 245–246, 258; Wade, *Slavery in the Cities*, 16–19, 48–49, 243–244; Welch, *Slave Society in the City*, 18, 95; Robert S. Shelton, "Slavery in a Texas Seaport: The Peculiar Institution Galveston," *Slavery and Abolition*, 28, no. 1 (August 2007), 155–156; N. Hall, *Danish West Indies*, 87.

71. Benoit, *Journey Through Suriname*, 89; Lloyd, *Bermuda*, 21; Graham, *Feeding the City*, 89.

72. Robert Renny, *An History of Jamaica. With Observations on the Climate, Scenery, Trade, Production, Negroes, Slave Trade, Disease of Europeans, Customs, Manners, and Dispositions of the Inhabitants* (London: 1807), 241. For mortality, see Brown, *Reaper's Garden*, esp. 1–4; Dunn, *Sugar and Slaves*, 300–334.

73. Charles Campbell, *Memoirs of Charles Campbell, at Present Prisoner in the Jail of Glasgow: Including His Adventures as a Seaman, and as an Overseer in the West Indies* (Glasgow: 1828), 11–12.

74. Campbell, *Memoirs*, 12; Obi, *Fighting for Honor*, 100–101; Dawson, "Enslaved Ship Pilots," 8.

75. Wood, *Women's Work*, esp. 81, 84–85, 93; Olwell, *Slaves and Subjects*, 141–180, esp. 172; Robert Olwell, " 'Loose, Idle and Disorderly': Slave Women in the Eighteenth-Century Charleston Marketplace," in David Barry Gaspar and Darlene Clark Hine, eds. *More Than Chattel: Black Women and Slavery in the Americas* (Bloomington: 1996), 218–238; Simmonds, "Internal Marketing," esp. 274, 276; Graham, *Feeding the City*, 35, 111, Wetherell, *Stray Notes*, 21, 27; Kidder, *Travels*, 2:24–25; Nishida, *Slavery and Ethnicity*, 45–46; Richard Cotter, *Sketches of Bermuda, or Somers' Islands* (London: 1828), 58–59, 58n.

76. Schmidt, *Island of St. Croix*, 25; N. Hall, *Danish West Indies*, 103, 114; Alcide Dessalines d'Orbigny, *Voyage Pittoresque dans les deux Amériques Résumé général de tous les Voyages* (Paris: 1836), image opposite 59; 80–81; Highfield, *Hans West's Accounts*, 17, 38, 79–83, 166–167, 177, 183; Kemble, *Journal*, 90; Kidder and Fletcher, *Brazil*, 16, 475, 552; Hall, *Miserable Slavery*, 35, 340; Mintz and Hall, *Internal Marketing*, Tomich, "Other Face of Slave Labor," N. Hall, "Slaves Use of Their 'Free' Time."

77. Simmonds, "Internal Marketing," 277–278; Hilary McD. Beckles "An Economic Life of Their Own: Slaves as Commodity Producers and Distributors in Barbados," in Berlin and Morgan, *Slaves' Economy*, 31–47.

78. Luffman, *Island of Antigua*, 128; *South Carolina Gazette*, September 24, 1772.

79. *The Laws of the Island of Antigua: Consisting of the Acts of the Leeward Islands, Commencing 8th November 1690, ending 21st April 1798; and the Acts of Antigua, Commencing 10th April 1668, ending 7th May 1804*, 2 vols. (London: 1805), 1:55, 425; Elsa V. Goveia, *Slave Society in the British Leeward Islands at the end of the Eighteenth Century* (New Haven: 1965),162; N. Hall, *Danish West Indies*, 126, 128; C. S Higham, *The Development of the Leeward Islands Under the Restoration, 1660–1688* (Cambridge: 1921), 176.

80. Wood, *Black Majority*, 124, 216–217, 320–325; Morgan, *Laboring Women*, 188–189; Olwell, *Slaves and Subjects*, 62–71.

81. "Management of a Southern Plantation; Rules Enforced on the Rice Estate of P. C. Weston, Esq., of South Carolina," *DeBow's Review and Industrial Resources* (January 1857), 41, 43; Pierce Butler to William Page, June 6, 1799, Pierce Butler Letterbook, 1787–1822, 289; Clifton, ed., *Argyle Island*, 62, 135–136; Dusinberre, *Dark Days*, 141; Mart Stewart, *"What Nature Suffers to Groe,"* 132–134.

82. Oldendorp, *Caribbean Mission*, 234; Highfield, *St. Thomas*, 28–29; N. Hall, *Danish West Indies*, 128; Wood, *Black Majority*, 325; Ball, *Fifty Years*, 211; Cecelski, *Waterman's Song*, 68–69, 70.

83. Clifton, *Argyle Island*, 123.

84. Roswell King to Pierce Butler, December 31, 1808, Butler Family Papers, Historical Society of Philadelphia, Box 2, Folder 17; Bell, *Butler's Legacy*, 167; Hungerford, *Old Plantation*, 154.

85. Clifton, *Argyle Island*, 95, 99, 151.

86. "Narrative of Mr. Caulkins," 13; South Carolina Council Journal, no. 17, part 1, 160–161; Kemble, *Journal*, 90. For captives producing goods, see Higman, *Slave Populations of the British Caribbean*, 204–218; Wood, *Women's Work*, 31–46, 168, 179; Mintz, *Tasting Food*, 176–177; Tomich, "Other Face of Slave Labor," N. A. T. Hall "Slaves Use of their 'Free' Time."

87. Hall, *Miserable Slavery*, 21–22, 30–31, 78; Trevor Burnard, *Master, Tyranny, & Desire: Thomas Thistlewood and His Slaves in the Anglo-Jamaican World* (Chapel Hill: 1999), 44, 59, 61, 165, 196.

88. Martin, *Divided Mastery*, esp. 161–187; Dawson, "Enslaved Ship Pilots," 9–10.

89. Kemble, *Journal*, 90; Lyell, *Second Visit*, 7:1–2; Kidder and Fletcher, *Brazil*, 16.

Chapter 10

1. Dening, *Islands and Beaches*, esp. 142; Westerdahl, "Fish and Ships," 206–209; Gilbert, *Dhows*; Prins, *Sailing from Lamu*.

2. Ralph Waldo Emerson, "History," in *Essays: First Series* (1865; Boston: 1883), 21–22 (italics added).

3. Hans Konrad Van Tilburg, "Vessels of Exchange: The Global Shipwright in the Pacific," in Jerry H. Bentley, Renate Bridenthal, and Karen Wigens, eds., *Seascapes: Maritime Histories, Littoral Cultures, and Transoceanic Exchanges* (Honolulu: 2007), 38–52, esp. 38; Bolster, *Black Jacks*, 45–47. For Western refusals to adopt other people's watercraft, see Ben Finney, "Playing with Canoes," in Robert C. Kiste and Bril V. Lal, eds., *Pacific Places, Pacific Histories: Essays in Honor of Robert C. Kiste* (Honolulu: 2004), 290–308; George Turner, *Nineteen Years in Polynesia: Missionary Life, Travels, and Researches in the Islands of the Pacific* (London: 1861), 267–269; John Gardner, *The Dory Book* (Camden: 1978), 25–29. For Western

beliefs in the superiority of their regional watercraft, see Geoffrey M. Footner, *Tidewater Triumph: The Development and Worldwide Success of the Chesapeake Bay Pilot Schooner* (Annapolis: 1998); David Roy MacGregor, *British & American Clippers: A Comparison of Their Design, Construction and Performance in the 1850s* (Annapolis: 1993); Middleton, *Tobacco Coast*, 287.

4. Dening, *Islands and Beaches*, esp. 142; Westerdahl, "Fish and Ships," 206–209; Gilbert, *Dhows*; Prins, *Sailing from Lamu*.

5. Weeks, *Congo Cannibals*, 95; Meek, *Sudanese Kingdom*, 427; Bolster, *Black Jacks*, 49.

6. Bolster, *Black Jacks*, 49; Skertchly, *Dahomey*, 467; Harms, *Games Against Nature*, 35, 234–235; Karasch, *Slave Life*, 319, 319n50.

7. Brooks, *Eurafricans*, 21, 23–24; Winterbottom, *Native Africans*, 1:xiv, 4–5, 18, 225–226, 258; Rodney, *Upper Guinea*, 16; Irvine, *Woody Plants*, 193; Meek, *Sudanese Kingdom*, 426–427. For spiritual beliefs about the forest, see Winterbottom, *Native Africans*, 1:225–226; Michael Brown, "'Walk in the Feenda.'" The Bullom were also called the Sherbro and Sapes. Brooks, *Eurafricans*, 21, 23, 167. Bolster explained that *blom* was a noun derived from the same root as the Bullom's name for themselves, and Winterbottom noted that Bullom meant "low land," referring to the tidal region they inhabited. Bolster, *Black Jacks*, 49; Winterbottom, *Native Africans*, 1:xiv, 18; Skertchly, *Dahomey*, 467; Ellis, *Land of Fetish*, 14–15; 48.

8. Winterbottom, *Native Africans*, 1:225–226.

9. Carol P. MacCormack, "Proto-Social to Adult: A Sherbro Transformation," in Carol P. MacCormack and Marilyn Strathern, ed., *Nature, Culture and Gender* (Cambridge: 1980), 99; Brooks, *Eurafricans*, 23.

10. Chinua Achebe, *Things Fall Apart* (London: 1958), 46, 138–139; Ellis, *Land of Fetish*, 48; Rattray, *Ashanti*, 210; MacCormack, "Proto-Social to Adult," 106–110, esp. 106; de Marees, *Gold Kingdom*, 66, 68, 68n6, 82n20, 85, 95, 238.

11. Brooks, *Eurafricans*, 23; MacCormack, "Proto-Social to Adult"; Bosman, *Accurate Description*, 368a, 382. For honor associated with canoe-borne trading, fishing, and whaling, see Austen and Derrick, *Middlemen of the Cameroons Rivers*, 21; Harms, *River of Wealth*, 94–97; Meek, *Sudanese Kingdom*, 426; Glave, *Savage Africa*, 130; Michael Brown, "'Walk in the Feenda,'" 306–310.

12. Meek, *Sudanese Kingdom*, 426; Irvine, *Woody Plants*, 271. For mahogany and other types of woods, also see Harms, *Games Against Nature*, 114; Harms, *River of Wealth*, 7, 169; Glave, *Savage Africa*, 117; Weeks, *Congo Cannibals*, 94.

13. Meek, *Sudanese Kingdom*, 425–427, esp. 426.

14. Weeks, *Congo Cannibals*, 95; Meek, *Sudanese Kingdom*, 427.

15. Brown, "Fishing Industry," 42; Verrips, "Canoe Decoration," 47–49; Nunoo, "Canoe Decoration in Ghana," 32; Meek, *Sudanese Kingdom*, 427.

16. Brown, "Fishing Industry," 42; Jojada Verrips, "Ghanaian Canoe Decorations," *MAST*, 1, no. 1 (2002), 49–50, 62. For Jukun beliefs, see Meek, *Sudanese Kingdom*, 427.

17. David Northrup, *Africa's Discovery of Europe, 1450–1850* (Oxford: 2002), 18–19; Brooks, *Eurafricans*, 27; Harms, *River of Wealth*, 2, 122; Bolster, *Black Jacks*, 49; Law, *Ouidah*, 88, 93, 95, 99; Desche Obe, "Crossing the Kalunga," 360; Miller, *Way of Death*, 4–5; Winterbottom, *Native Africans*, 1:224, 229–230; Forbes, *Six Months' Service*, 22; Isert, *Letters on West Africa*, 28; Michael Brown, *African-Atlantic Cultures*.

18. Law, *Ouidah* 88, 93, 95, esp. 152; Melville J. Herskovits, *Dahomey: An Ancient West African Kingdom*, 2 vols. (Evanston: 1967), 1:194–205; John Duncan, *Travels in Western Africa*,

in 1845 & 1846, 2 vols. (1847; New York, 1967), 1:126; Bosman, *Accurate Description*, 368a, 383; Ellis, *Land of Fetish*, 47.

19. Skertchly, *Dahomey as it Is*, 468, 472, 478; C. W. Newbury, ed. *A Mission to Gelele, King of Dahomey by Sir Richard Burton* (1864; London: 1966), 295; Ellis, *Land of Fetish*, 47.

20. Winterbottom, *Native Africans*, 1:229: Law, *Ouidah*, 99; Desch Obi, "Crossing the Kalunga," 360.

21. Chas. Thomas, *Adventures and Observations*, 109; Burton, *Wanderings*, 284–285; Brooks, *The Kru Mariner*, 97–99; Rankin, *White Man's Grave*, 310–311; Ellis, *Tshi-Speaking Peoples*, 44–48; Murphy and Sanford, *Oṣun Across the Waters*; Henry John Drewal, ed., *Sacred Waters: Arts for Mami Wata and other Divinities in Africa and the Diaspora* (Bloomington: 2008); Anderson and Peek, *Ways of the River*.

22. Villault, *Coasts of Africk*, 219; Waddell, *Twenty-Nine Years*, 256, 287; Hair, Jones, and Law, *Barbot on Guinea*, 1:292; Brown, "Fishing Industry," 32; Hornell, "Kru Canoes," 236; Coronel, "Fanti Canoe Decoration," 54–100; Jojada Verrips, "Ghanaian Canoe Decorations," *MAST* 1, no. 1 (2002): 43–66; my observations while in Togo, Benin, Ghana, Côte d'Ivoire, The Gambia, and Senegal.

23. Coronel, "Fanti Canoe Decoration," 54, 55, 59; Verrips, "Canoe Decorations," 57; Brown, "Fishing Industry," 24; Smith, "Canoe," 520.

24. Coronel, "Fanti Canoe Decoration," 54–55, 56; Verrips, "Canoe Decorations," 50.

25. Coronel, "Fanti Canoe Decoration," 54–55; Verrips, "Canoe Decorations," 49, 51; my observations while in Ghana, Togo, and Côte d'Ivoire.

26. Coronel, "Fanti Canoe Decoration," 55–59; Verrips, "Canoe Decorations," 51, 62; Peter Adler and Nicholas Barnard, *Asafo! African Flags of the Fante* (London: 1992), 7, 9; my observations.

27. Coronel, "Fanti Canoe Decoration," 54–59.

28. John Barbot, *A Description of the Coasts of North and South-Guinea; and of Ethiopia Inferior, vulgarly Angola: Being a New and Accurate Account of the Western Maritime Countries of Africa. In six books* (London: 1746), book 3, 268; Peter Leonard, Records of a Voyage to the *Western Coast of Africa in His Majesty's Shyp Dryad: During the Years 1830, 1831, and 1831* (Edinburgh: 1833), 163.

29. Coronel, "Fanti Canoe Decoration," 59; Verrips, "Canoe Decorations," 51.

30. Brown, "Fishing Industry," 32; Coronel, "Fanti Canoe Decoration," 56; R. Anderson, *Liberia: America's African Friend*, 15; Hydrographic Office, *Africa Pilot*, 2:36; my observations.

31. Quoted in Markham, *Hawkins' Voyages*, 18.

32. Georgia W. Hamilton, *Silent Pilots: Figureheads in Mystic Seaport Museum* (Mystic: 1984), 14–18; "Figureheads Exhibit," Mystic Seaport: The Museum of America and the Sea; John Ogilby, *Africa*, image opposite 453.

33. Thornton, *Warfare in Atlantic Africa*, 83.

34. De Marees, *Gold Kingdom*, 119; Hair, Jones, and Law, *Barbot on Guinea*, 2:531; Barbot, *North and South Guinea*, 268; Ogilby, *Africa*, 455; Villault, *Coasts of Africk*, 44, 219; Robert C. Helmholz, "Traditionally Bijago Statuary, *African Arts* 6, no. 1 (Autumn 1972), 53.

35. Stallibrass, "Bijaouga," 600; Álvares, *Ethiopia Minor*, chap. 9:3, 3nf., 4, chap. 10:3, chap. 11:3; Robert C. Helmholz, "Traditional Bijago Statuary," *African Arts* 6, no. 1 (Autumn 1972): 53; Georges Louis Leclerc Buffon, *Natural History, General and Particular, by the Count de Buffon* (London: 1791), 6:294; George Thompson, *Palm Land*, 88.

36. *Ceiba pentandra* is found in much of West Africa and *Ceiba samauma* and *Cieba pentandra* are indigenous to South America. United States Department of Agriculture [hereafter, USDA], *Encyclopedia of Wood* (New York: 2007), 1–20, 3–10, 4–16, 4–20; James A. Duke and Rodolfo Vásquez, *Amazonian Ethnobotanical Dictionary* (Boca Raton, 1994), 48; Marsden, *Account of the Island of Jamaica*, 32; Lewis, *West India Proprietor*, 35, 101; Cynric Williams, *Island of Jamaica*, 35; Long, *History of Jamaica*, 3:736–737.

37. Arnold R. Highfield, ed., *Carsten's St. Thomas in Early Danish Times: A General Description of the Danish American or West Indian Islands* (St. Croix: 1997), 28–29.

38. Lawson, *New Voyage*, 16, 103–104; Wood, *Black Majority*, 124; Basil Hall, *Travels*, 3:216, 356; Lyell, *Second Visit*, 1:357; William Bartram, *Travels Through North & South Carolina, Georgia, East & West Florida, the Cherokee Country, the Extensive Territories of the Muscogulges, or Creek Confederacy, and the Country of the Chactaws* (Philadelphia: 1791), 48, 91–92; Roger, Chestnut, and Clark, *Papers of Henry Laurens*, 5:151–155, 10:91n1; Whitehead, *Everglades*, 133; J. C. Loudon, *Arboretum et Fruticetum Britannicum: or, The Trees and Shrubs of Britain, Native and Foreign, Hardy and Half-Hardy*, 8 vols. (London: 1854), 4:2464–2488; USDA, *Encyclopedia of Wood*, 1–10, 4–2, 4–3, 7–21.

39. Castiglioni, *Viagio*, 401; Chambers, *Murder at Montpelier*, 164, 173.

40. Ball, *Fifty Years*, 99, 211; Harms, *River of Wealth*, 7, 169.

41. Stedman, *Narrative of Five Year's Expedition*, 2:364; Martha Warren Beckwith, *Black Roadways: A Study of Jamaican Folk Life* (New York: 1929), 89, 101, 145–146, 158; Karasch, *Slave Life*, 319; Orlando Patterson, *The Sociology of Slavery: An Analysis of the Origins, Development and Structure of Negro Slave Society in Jamaica* (London: 1975), 203–206; Joseph J. Williams, *Psychic Phenomena of Jamaica* (New York: 1934), 29–30, 50, 55, 127, 134, 138–139, 142, 155, 237; Desch Obi, "Crossing the Kalunga," 354–355; Robert W. Slenes, "The Great Porpoise-Skull Strike: Central African Water Spirits and Slave Identity in Early-Nineteenth-Century Rio de Janeiro," in Linda M. Heywood, ed., *Central Africans and Cultural Transformation in the American Diaspora* (Cambridge: 2002), 190; Terry Rey, "Kongolese Catholic Influences on Haitian Popular Catholicism: A Sociohistorical Exploration," in Linda M. Heywood, *Central Africans*, 283–284; Lewis, *West India Proprietor*, 156–157; Michael Brown, *Atlantic African Cultures*; Michael Brown, "Walk in the Feenda," 307, 312. For white misconceptions on spiritual beliefs, see Palgrave, *Dutch Guiana*, 127; Benoit, *Journey Through Suriname*, 93.

42. Joseph Williams, *Psychic Phenomena in Jamaica*, 29. Williams incorrectly stated that "odum" is the Akan term for cottonwood trees. The correct term is "onyina" or "onyaa." Odum (*Chlorophora excelsa*) and onyina trees are both buttressed and possessed spiritual valuations. Thanks to Kwasi Konadu for the clarification, July 7, 2011, e-mail. Also see Irvine, *Woody Plants*, 190, 427; R. Sutherland Rattray, *Ashanti Proverbs (The Primitive Ethics of a Savage People) Translated from the Original with Grammatical and Anthropological Notes* (Oxford: 1916), 49.

43. Benoit, *Journey Through Suriname*, 64, 93, 96–97, plate 58; Kingsley, *At Last*, 153–154; Bolster, *Black Jacks*, 49; Lewis, *West India Proprietor*, 156–157.

44. Palgrave, *Dutch Guiana*, 127; Dianne Stewart, *Three Eyes for the Journey*, 11, 102–103, 128–129, 173–174; Monica Schuler, *"Alas, Alas, Kongo": A Social History of Indentured African Immigration into Jamaica, 1841–1865* (Baltimore: 1980), 73–74; Billy Hall, "George Liele: Should Be a National Hero," *Jamaica Gleaner*, April 8, 2003; John W. Davis, "George Liele

and Andrew Bryan, Pioneer Negro Baptist Preachers," *Journal of Negro History* 3, no. 2 (April 1918): 119–127; Clement Gayle, *George Liele: Pioneer Missionary to Jamaica* (Kingston: 1982), 1–32; Milton C. Sernett, "George Liele," in Henry Louis Gates Jr. and Evelyn Brooks Higginbotham, eds., *African American Lives* (Oxford: 2004), 534; Beckwith, *Black Roadways*, 145–146, 160; Konadu, *Akan Diaspora*, 135.

45. Edward Brathwaite, "Kumina: The Spirit of African Survival in Jamaica," *Jamaica Journal* 42 (1978): 47; Dianne Stewart, *Three Eyes for the Journey*, 146–147.

46. Kingsley, *At Last*, 153; Patterson, *Sociology of Slavery*, 203–206.

47. Palgrave, *Dutch Guiana*, 10; Kingsley, *At Last*, 101, 153, 226; Schuler, "*Alas, Alas, Kongo*," 73–75, Georgia Writers' Project, *Drums and Shadows*, 148; Patterson, *Sociology of Slavery*, 203–206; Beckwith, *Black Roadways*, 89, 101, 145–146, 158, 160; Joseph Williams, *Psychic Phenomena of Jamaica*, 29–30, 50, 55, 129–130, 134, 138–139, 172, 237.

48. Karasch, *Slave Life*, 319; Michael Brown, "'Walk in the Feenda,'" 312–313; Slenes, "Porpoise-Skull Strike," Murphy and Sanford, *Ọṣun Across the Water*; Drewal, *Sacred Waters*; Beckwith, *Black Roadways*, 89, 101–102, 145–146, 160; Patterson, *Sociology of Slavery*, 205; MacGaffey, *Religion and Society*, passim; Karl Edvard Laman, *The Kongo*, 3 vols. (1953), 3: 33–34; Joseph Williams, *Psychic Phenomena of Jamaica*, 10, 127, 142–143, 150, 159,165, 170, 173; William James Gardner, *A History of Jamaica from Its Discovery by Christopher Columbus to the Year 1872* (London: 1873), 379. John Iliffe discusses how suicide in Africa could be honorable. Iliffe, *Honour*, passim.

49. Aimery P. Caron and Arnold R. Highfield, trans and eds., *The French Intervention in the St. John Slave Revolt of 1733–34* (Charlotte Amalie: 1981), 51n13; Ray A. Kea, "When I die, I shall return to my own land: An 'Amina' Slave Rebellion in the Danish West Indies 1733–1734," in John Hunwick and Nancy Lawler, eds., *The Cloth of Many Colored Silks: Papers on History and Society Ghanaian and Islamic in Honor of Ivor Wilks* (Evanston: 1997), 159–160; Anonymous, *The Importance of Jamaica to Great-Britain, Consider'd. With Some Account of that Island, from its Discovery in 1492 to this Time* (London: 1741), 19; Brown, *Reaper's Garden*, 133–134; Pinckard, *West Indies*, 1:274–275. Also see Chapter 2.

50. Lewis, *West India Proprietor*, 65; J. Stewart, *A View of the Past and Present State of the Island of Jamaica; with Remarks on the Moral and Physical Conditions of the Slaves, and on the Abolition of Slavery in the Colonies* (London: 1823), 280–281; John Stewart, *An Account of Jamaica, and Its Inhabitants.* (London: 1808), x, 249; "African Dirge," in M. J. Chapman, *Barbados, and Other Poems* (London: 1833), 153–154; *Great Newes From the Barbadoes. Or, A True and Faithful Account of the Grand Conspiracy of The Negroes against the English. and the Happy Discovery of the same* (London: 1676), 12; Pinckard, *West Indies*, 1:274–275; Gomez, *Country Marks*, 133–134; Terri L. Snyder, "Suicide, Slavery, and Memory in North America," *Journal of American History* 97, no. 1 (June 2010), 54; Daniel E. Walker, "Suicidal Tendencies: African Transmigration in the History and Folklore of the Americas," *The Griot*, 19 (1999): esp. 10, 13, 15; Charles Leslie, *A New History of Jamaica, from the Earliest Accounts to the Taking of Porto Bello by Vice-Admiral Vernon* (London: 1740), 307; G. Ugo Nwokeji, *The Slave Trade and Culture in the Bight of Biafra: As African Society in the Atlantic World* (Cambridge: 2010), 132–134; Walter C. Rucker, *The River Flows On: Black Resistance, Culture, and Identity Formation in Early America* (Baton Rouge: 2008), 52–55.

51. Snyder, "Suicide, Slavery, and Memory," 39–62; Karasch, *Slave Life*, 59, 319, 319n50; Desch Obi, "Crossing the Kalunga," 354; Schuler, "*Alas, Alas, Kongo*," 73–74, 93–96; Gomez,

Country Marks, 117–120; Daniel Walker, "Suicidal Tendencies," 11; William Mein to Pierce Butler, March 15, 1803, and March 24, 1803, Butler Plantation Papers, Box 6, Folder 27; Wyatt MacGaffey, "The Westin Congolese Experience," in Philip D. Curtin, ed., *Africa and the West* (Madison: 1972), 51–57, 61.

52. Ball, *Fifty Years*, 193, 197–198; Daniel Walker, "Suicidal Tendencies," 10, 11; Philip M. Peek, "The Isoko as a Delta People," in Anderson and Peek, *Ways of the River*, 179.

53. Benoit, *Journey Through Suriname*, 64, 97. For seashells, see MacGaffey, *Religion*, 96–99, 121; Laman, *Kongo*, 3:37; Slenes, "Porpoise-Skull Strike," 204–206.

Chapter 11

1. Creighton and Norling, *Wooden Women*, esp. 125–137; Bolster, *Black Jacks*, esp. 75, 82; Paul Gilje, *Liberty on the Waterfront: American Maritime Culture in the Age of Revolution* (Philadelphia: 2004), esp. 13, 81, 94, 109; Simon Finger, "'A Flag of Defyance at the masthead': The Delaware River Pilots and the Sinews of Philadelphia's Atlantic World in the Eighteenth Century," *Early American Studies*, 8, no. 2 (Spring 2010), 319; Klein and Mackenthun, *Sea Changes*; Cheryl A. Fury, *Tides in the Affairs of Men: The Social History of Elizabethan Seamen, 1580–1603* (Westport: 2002); Ricardo Rodriguez-Martos, *The Merchant Vessel: A Sociological Analysis* (Barcelona: 2009); Alison Games, *Migration and the Origins of the English Atlantic World* (Cambridge: 1999), Richard Burg, *Sodomy and the Pirate Tradition: English Sea Rovers in the Seventeenth Century Caribbean* (New York: 1995); Rediker, *Deep Blue Sea*; Linebaugh and Rediker, *Many-Headed Hydra*; Dawson, "Cultural Geography of Enslaved Ship Pilots."

2. Margaret S. Creighton, "Davy Jones' Locker Room: Gender and the American Whaleman, 1830–1870," Creighton and Norling, *Wooden Women*, 127.

3. Winterbottom, *Native Africans*, 1:212, 212–213n; Stewart, *Present State of Jamaica*, 250n; Lewis, *West India Proprietor*, 64, 137, 219; Rediker, *Slave Ship*, 8, 120, 122, 130, 154, 263–305, 325, 346; Smallwood, *Saltwater Slavery*, 174, 185, 190, 196–197; Chambers, *Murder at Montpelier*, 76, 89, 94; Emma Christopher, *Slave Ship Sailors and Their Captive Cargoes, 1730–1807* (Cambridge: 2006), 54; Sowande' M. Mustakeem, "Shipmates," in Toyin Falola and Amanda Warnock, eds., *Encyclopedia of the Middle Passage* (Westport: 2007), 341–342; Henry Koster, *Travels in Brazil* (London: 1816), 417, 443; Sweet, *Recreating Africa*, 33, 50; Nishida, *Slavery and Identity*, 32, 39; Paul E. Lovejoy, "Background of Rebellion: The Origins of Muslim Slaves in Brazil," *Slavery and Abolition* 15, no. 2 (1994): 155.

4. Mustakeem, "Shipmates," 341–342; Smallwood, *Saltwater Slavery*, 174, 185, 196–197; Rediker, *Slave Ship*, 8, 120, 122, 130, 154, 263–305, 304–306, 325, 346; Chambers, *Murder at Montpelier*, 75–76, 89, 94; Christopher, *Slave Ship Sailors*, 54.

5. For whipsaw, see Wood, *Black Majority*, 97. Ira Berlin labels this "sawbuck equality." Berlin, *Many Thousands Gone*, 66, 399n101.

6. Bolster, *Black Jacks*, 45–47.

7. *South Carolina Gazette*, January 12–19, 1738; Bolster, *Black Jacks*, 45; Stedman, *Expedition*, 1:55.

8. *Virginia Gazette* (Parks), July 14–12, 1738; *South Carolina Gazette*, February 16, 1734, August 8, 1769.

9. *Virginia Gazette* (Parks), May 9–16, 1745; Marks, *"Portuguese" Style*, passim, esp. 13–18; Brooks, *Eurafricans*, esp. xxi; Cynric Williams, *Jamaica*, 31, 79–81.

10. Koster, *Travels*, 135–136; Elizabeth W. Kiddy, "King of Congo," in Linda M. Heywood, ed., *Central Africans and Cultural Transformation in the American Diaspora* (Cambridge: 2002), 153–155.

11. Koster, *Travels*, 158–160; Kiddy, "King of Congo," 172.

12. Cécile Fromont, "Dancing for the King of Congo from Early Modern Central Africa to Slavery-Era Brazil," *Colonial Latin American Review* 22, no. 2 (July 2013), 188, 197; Elizabeth W. Kiddy, *Blacks of the Rosary: Memory and History in Minas Gerais, Brazil* (University Park: 2007), esp. 46–47, 77–78; Desch Obi, "Crossing the Kalunga," 353–370, esp. 359, 361; Kiddy, "King of Congo," 172; Koster, *Travels* 136, 159–160.

13. Dawson, "Enslaved Swimmers," 1340–1343.

14. Daniel P. Kidder, *Sketches of Residence and Travels in Brazil: Embracing Historical and Geographical Notices of the Empire and Its Provinces*, 2 vols. (Philadelphia: 1945), 2:153.

15. John Luccock, *Notes on Rio de Janeiro, and the Southern Parts of Brazil; Taken During a Residence of Ten Years in That Country* (London: 1820), 334, 335, 344, 364–366; Slenes, "Porpoise-Skull Strike," 183–209; Wyatt MacGaffey, *Religion and Society in Central Africa: The Bakongo of Lower Zaire* (Chicago: 1986), 96–99, 121.

16. Adèle Tousaint-Samson, *A Parisian in Brazil: The Travel Account of a Frenchwoman in Nineteenth-Century Rio de Janeiro* (Wilmington: 2001), 27–28; Palgrave, *Dutch Guiana*, 75; Koster, *Travels*, 82–83; Kidder, *Sketches*, 2:217; Pinckard, *West Indies*, 1:326.

17. Maturin M. Ballou, *History of Cuba; or, Notes of a Traveller in the Tropics. Being a Political, Historical, and Statistical Account of the Island, from its First Discovery to the Present Time* (Boston: 1854), 94, 181. See Chapter 1 for nudity.

18. Dawson, "Cultural Geography of Enslaved Ship Pilots," 173–175; Childs, *Aponte Rebellion*, 166–169, esp. 167; Camp, *Closer to Freedom*, 78–85; Shane White and Graham White, "Slave Clothing and African-American Culture in the Eighteenth and Nineteenth Centuries," *Past & Present* 148 (August 1995), esp. 164–165, 174; Pierson, *Black Yankees*, 11, 120–121, 154–155; Dunn, *Sugar and Slaves*, 263; Isaac, *Transformation of Virginia*, 43–46; Wood, *Women's Work*, 137.

19. Stedman, *Expedition*, 1:13, 55; Whitehead, *Everglades*, 133. For clothing, see Higman, *Slave Populations*, 257; Mary Karasch, "From Porterage to Proprietorship: African Occupations in Rio de Janeiro, 1808–1850," in Stanley L. Engerman and Eugene D. Genovese, eds., *Race and Slavery in the Western Hemisphere* (Princeton: 1975), 384; Pierson, *Black Yankees*, 120; Saunders, *Black Slaves*, 63–64, 82, 93–95.

20. Pinckard, *West Indies*, 2:149, 373–374, 381; Stedman, *Expedition*, 1:55, 81–82.

21. Edmond Buerkely Jr., ed., *The Diary, Correspondence, and Papers of Robert "King" Carter of Virginia, 1701–1732*, July 14 and 17, 1727 (Virginia Historical Society); Kulikoff, *Tobacco and Slaves*, 328.

22. *South-Carolina and American General Gazette*, January 20–27, 1775; *South Carolina Gazette*, February 16, 1734; *South Carolina Gazette; And Country Journal*, December 5, 1769, November 21, 1769; *Virginia Gazette* (Purdie and Dixon), September 12, 1771.

23. *South-Carolina Gazette*, December 8, 1758; F. Dabadie, *A Travers L'Am rique du Sud* (Paris: 1858), 49–50.

24. For examples of maritime mobility and channels of communication, see Bolster, *Black Jacks*; Dawson, "Enslaved Ship Pilots"; Julius S. Scott, "Afro-American Sailors and the International Communication Network: The Case of Newport Bowers," in Colin Howell and

Richard Twomey, eds., *Jack Tar in History: Essays in the History of Maritime Life and Labour* (Fredericton: 1991), 37–52; James Dator, "Frank Travels: Space, Power and Slave Mobility in the British Leeward Islands, c. 1700–1730," *Slavery and Abolition* 36, no. 2 (2015): 335–359; esp. 339; Robert S. Shelton, "Slavery in a Texas Seaport: The Peculiar Institution Galveston," *Slavery and Abolition* 28, no. 1 (August 2007), 155–156.

25. Hau'ofa, "Our Sea of Islands," 31.

26. N. Hall, *Danish West Indies*, 128–138; Oldendorp, *Caribbean Mission*, 28, 234, 430, 490, 611; Haagensen, *St. Croix*, 34–37; Chinea, "Quest for Freedom," 51–87.

27. James Thome, *Emancipation in the West Indies: A Six Month's Tour in Antigua, Barbados, and Jamaica* (New York: 1838), 212.

28. December 15, 1789, "The Memorial and humble petition of the Council and Assembly of Jamaica," National Archives, Kew, Colonial Records Office, 137/88, 96, "14th December 1809.—An Act for the protection, subsisting, clothing, and for the better order, regulation and government of Slaves, and for other purposes," in, *Colonial Laws Respecting Slaves. Return made in Pursuance of an Address of the House of Commons to His Royal Highness the Prince Regent* (London: 1816), 128; Byrd, *Captives and Voyagers*, 110–111.

29. Handler, "Escaping Slavery," 198–202; Beckles, "From Land to Sea," 86; Labat, *Memoirs*, 137; Anonymous, *Authentic Papers Relative to the Expedition Against the Charibbs, and the Sale of Lands in the Island of St. Vincent* (London: 1773), 26; Young, *Black Charaibs*, 7–8.

30. "1796.—An Act to consolidate and bring into one Act several laws relating to Slaves, and for giving them further protection and security; for altering the mode of trial of Slaves charged with capital offenses," in *Colonial Laws Respecting Slaves*, 23.

31. *South Carolina Gazette*, August 8, 1769; *South Carolina Gazette*, April 18, 1748.

32. Lander, *Black Society in Spanish Florida*, esp. 7–60, 113–114, 296n21; Wood, *Black Majority*, 295–296, 303–312; Young, *Rituals of Resistance*, 68–70; Mark M. Smith, "Remembering Mary, Shaping Revolt: Reconsidering the Stono Rebellion," *Journal of Southern History* 67, no. 3 (August 2001), 513–534; J. H. Easterby, ed., *Journal of the Commons House of Assembly, May 18, 1741–July 10, 1742* in *The Colonial Records of South Carolina* (Columbia: 1953), 1:595–596, 2: 81–84; *Stephens' Journal, 1737–1740*, in Allen D. Candler, ed., *Colonial Records of the State of Georgia* (Atlanta: 1904), 4:247–248.

33. Easterby, *Journal of the Commons House of Assembly*, 2:esp. 83. Also see *Stephens' Journal*, 595–596; Lander, *Black Society in Spanish Florida*, 33, 296n21; Fraser, *Charleston!*, 80. For newspaper accounts, see *South-Carolina Gazette*, September 7, 1765; *South Carolina and American General Gazette*, September 19 and 26, 1766, October 3, 1766; *South Carolina and American General Gazette*, July 17 and 24, 1767, August 7, 1767.

34. Rosalyn Howard, "The 'Wild Indians' of Andros Island: Black Seminole Legacy in the Bahamas," *Journal of Black Studies* 37, no. 2 (November 2006): 275–298; Porter, *Black Seminoles*, 26. Some of southern Florida remained a haven until the Second Seminole War ended in 1842. Daniel F. Littlefield Jr., *Africans and Seminoles: From Removal to Emancipation* (Jackson: 1977), 9–31; John K. Mahon, *History of the Second Seminole War, 1835–1842* (1967; Gainesville: 1991), esp. 321.

35. Pierre Jacques Benoit, *Voyage à Surinam: Description des Possessions Néerlandaises dans la Guyane* (Brussels: 1839), 59; Equiano, *Interesting Narrative*, 2:178, 211–212; *South Carolina Gazette*, February 16, 1734; Richard Price, *Alabi's World* (Baltimore: 1990).

36. *Laws of the Island of Antigua*, 1:55, 425; Goveia, *British Leeward Islands*, 162.

37. "An Act against running away with Boats and Canoes," no. 27, March 25, 1699, confirmed October 22, 1700, in *Acts of Assembly: Passed in the Island of Nevis, from 1664 to 1739, Inclusive* (London: 1740), 74, 76, 133, esp. 21, 160; Cedil Headlam, ed., *Calendar of State Papers, Colonial Series, American and the West Indies, 1699* (London: 1908), 116; David Barry Gaspar, *Bondmen & Rebels: A Study of Master-Slave Relations in Antigua, with Implications for Colonial British America* (Baltimore: 1985), 174, 305; Dator, "Frank Travels," esp. 342–343.

38. N. Hall, *Danish West Indies*, 126–128; C. S. Higham, *The Development of the Leeward Islands Under the Restoration, 1660–1688* (Cambridge: 1921), 176; Arnold R. Highfield, ed., *J. L. Carsten's St. Thomas in Early Danish Times. A General Description of all the Danish, American or West Indian Islands* (St. Croix: 1992), 29; Hall, *Miserable Slavery*, 258.

39. Peter Wood, *Black Majority*, 124, 216–217, 320–325; Jennifer Morgan, *Laboring Women*, 188–189; Olwell, *Slaves and Subjects*, 62–71.

40. Ball, *Fifty Years*, 226; Roswell King to Pierce Butler, December 31, 1808, Butler Family Papers, Box 2, Folder 17; *Georgia Gazette*, September 22, 1763; Bell, *Butler's Legacy*, 167; South Carolina Council Journal, no. 17, part 1, 159–161; King, *Stolen Childhood*, 17–18; Marc R. Matrana, *Lost Plantations of the South* (Jackson: 2009), 97. For how Surinamese Maroons used dugouts, see Price and Price, *Maroon Arts*, 20, 27, 64, 133.

41. James M. Simms, *The First Colored Baptist Church in North America Constituted at Savannah, Georgia, January 20, A.D. 1788. With Biographical Sketches of the Pastors* (Philadelphia: 1888), 19; Kemble, *Journal*, 90; Wood, *Women's Work*, 163; Lyell, *Second Visit*, 2:2, Davis; "George Liele and Andrew Bryan," 119–127; Milton C. Sernett, "Andrew Bryan," in Henry Louis Gates Jr. and Evelyn Brooks Higginbotham, eds., *African American Lives* (Oxford: 2004), 122–123.

42. Albert J. Raboteau, *Slave Religion: The "Invisible Institution" in the Antebellum South* (Oxford: 1978), 141–142, 189–190; Emanuel King Love, *History of the First African Baptist Church, from its Organization, January 10th, 1788, to July 1st, 1888* (Savannah: 1888), 38–40, esp. 2, 39; Whittington B. Johnson, *Black Savannah, 1788–1864* (Fayetteville: 1998), 9–18. As noted in Chapter 10, Bryan's mentor George Liele could not divest many of his Jamaican followers of their African spiritual beliefs concerning cottonwood trees.

43. Gomez, *Country Marks*, 15–16, 250–256, esp. 10, 250–251; Olwell, *Slaves and Subjects*, 105.

44. Gomez, *Country Marks*, 15–16, 250–256, esp. 10.

45. Wood, *Women's Work*, 168.

46. Bolster, *Black Jacks*, esp. 68–101; Rediker, *Deep Blue Sea*; Linebaugh and Rediker, *Many-Headed Hydra*; Dawson, "Enslaved Ship Pilots"; Paul Gilje, *Liberty on the Waterfront: American Maritime Culture in the Age of Revolution* (Philadelphia: 2004); Cecelski, *Waterman's Song*. For differing social standards ashore and afloat, see Barry Richard Burg and Philip Clayton Van Buskirk, *An American Seafarer in the Age of Sail: The Erotic Diaries of Philip C. Van Buskirk, 1851–1870* (New Haven: 1994); Jonathan Ned Katz, *Love Stories: Sex Between Men Before Homosexuality* (Chicago: 2001), 78; Burg, *Boys at Sea*.

47. Kemble, *Journal*, 212–213; Caroline Howard Gilman, *Recollections of a Southern Matron* (New York: 1838), 69–70. For differing social standards ashore and afloat, see Burg and Van Buskirk, *American Seafarer*; Katz, *Love Stories*, 78; Burg, *Boys at Sea*.

48. Tousaint-Samson, *Parisian in Brazil*, 27–28; *King James Bible*, Songs of Solomon 1:5; Caroline Couper Lovell, *The Golden Isles of Georgia* (Boston: 1932), 189–190; Pinckard, *West*

Indies, 1:326; Palgrave, *Dutch Guiana,* 75; Koster, *Travels,* 82–83. For bondmen touching white women, see Mark M. Smith, *How Race Is Made: Slavery, Segregation, and the Senses* (Chapel Hill: 2006), passim, esp. 24–25, 59, 83–84, 86; Martha Hodes, *White Women, Black Men: Illicit Sex in the 19th-Century South* (New Haven: 1997), 203; Wright, *Lady Nugent's Journal,* 156; Anonymous, *The Story of a Slave. A Realistic Revelation of a Social Relation of Slave Times* (Chicago: 1894), 84–85, 116–117, 145, 150–152, 157.

49. Kemble, *Journal,* 109.

50. Ibid., 90, 109, 159, 161, 172, 173, 177, 258, esp. 144–145 (italics added). For inversion, see Dawson, "Enslaved Ship Pilots;" Dawson, "Cultural Geography of Enslaved Ship Pilots."

51. Kemble, *Journal* 159.

52. Ibid., 84, 90, 161.

53. Ibid., 84–85. Also see relationship between Hector and Louis Manigault. Clifton, *Argyle Island,* passim, esp. 320–321, 360–363.

54. Kemble, *Journal,* 84–85, 343–344; Douglass, *Narrative,* 32–33, 40, 159.

55. LeConte, *Autobiography,* 27–28; Burnette Vanstory, *Georgia's Land of the Golden Isles* (Athens: 1981), 48–49; John S. Haller, *Outcasts From Evolution: Scientific Attitudes of Racial Inferiority, 1859–1900* (Carbondale: 1995), 154–156, Whitehead, *Everglades,* 8, 11, 133, 232.

56. LeConte, *Autobiography,* 27–31.

57. Ibid., 27.

Chapter 12

1. Paul E. Lovejoy, "The African Diaspora: Revisionist Interpretations of Ethnicity, Culture and Religion Under Slavery," *Studies in the World History of Slavery, Abolition and Emancipation,* 2, no. 1 (1997), ejournalofpoliticalscience.org/diaspora.html, accessed August 3, 2007.

2. Joyner, *Down by the Riverside,* 1.

3. Nicholas George Julius Ballanta, "Music of the African Races," *West Africa, a Weekly Newspaper* (London) June 14, 1930, 752–753.

4. Jon Cruz, *Culture on the Margins: The Black Spiritual and the Rise of American Cultural Interpretation* (Princeton: 1999), 64; Joyner, *Down by the Riverside,* 128.

5. Carney, *Black Rice,* 31, 135, esp. 124.

6. Ballanta, "Music," 753; Dena Epstein, *Sinful Tunes and Spirituals: Black Folk Music to the Civil War* (Chicago: 2003), 170–171; Stedman, *Expedition,* 2:321, 321n, 362; Joyner, *Down by the Riverside,* 15; Pinckard, *West Indies,* 323; William Francis Allen, Charles Pickard Ware, and Lucy McKim Garrison, *Slave Songs of the United States* (New York: 1867), passim, iii–viii.

7. Margaret Davis Cate, *Our Todays and Yesterdays: A Story of Brunswick and the Coastal Islands* (Brunswick: 1930), 158; Nicholas George Julius Ballanta-(Taylor), *Saint Helena Island Spirituals: Recorded and Transcribed at Penn Normal, Industrial and Agricultural School* (New York: 1925), xvii; Epstein, *Sinful Tunes,* 166–172; John Lambert, *Travels Through Canada and the United States, in the Years 1806, 1807, 1808, to which is added, Biographical Notices and Anecdotes of Some of the Leading Characters in the United States,* 2 vols. (London: 1816), 2:254; Stedman, *Expedition,* 2:321, 321n, 362; Pinckard, *West Indies,* 323; Allen, Ware, and Garrison, *Slave Songs,* iii–viii, J. K. Jr., "Who Are Our National Poets?" *The Knickerbocker; Or New York Monthly Magazine* 26, no. 4 (October 1845): 338; Richard J. Calhoun, ed., *Witness to Sorrow:*

The Antebellum Autobiography of William J. Grayson (Columbia: 1990), 57–58; Kemble, *Journal*, 259; Pearson, *Letters from Port Royal*, 19, 28–30, 134; Wetherell, *Stray Notes*, 97; W. Faux, *Memorable Days in America: Being a Journal of a Tour to the United States* (London: 1823), 78; Joyner, *Down by the Riverside*, 128; William Wyndham Malet, *Errand to the South in the Summer of 1862* (London: 1863), 114–115; Maximilian, *Recollections of My Life by Maximilian I, Emperor of Mexico*, 3 vols. (London: 1868), 3:164–165; Nishida, *Slavery and Ethnicity*, 41. Oars will be discussed below.

8. Lambert, *Canada and the United States*, 2:254.

9. Calhoun, *Witness to Sorrow*, 58; J. K., "National Poets," 338; Kemble, *Journal*, 162–164, 259; Lambert, *Canada and the United States*, 2:254; Adolph B. Benson, ed., *America in the Fifties: Letters of Fredrika Bremer* (New York: 1924), 142, 150; Faux, *Memorable Days*, 78; Epstein, *Sinful Tunes*, 66–67, 241–242; Lydia Parrish, *Slave Songs of the Georgia Sea Islands* (1942; Athens: 1992), 238; Malet, *Errand*, 114–115; Joyner, *Down by the Riverside*, 128.

10. Allen, Ware, and Garrison, *Slave Songs*, xvi–xvii, 21, 21n, 23–24; Epstein, *Sinful Tunes*, 170, 172; Kemble, *Journal*, 163–164; Parrish, *Slave Songs*, 172, 180, 216–217. For paddling mentioned in songs, see Pinckard, *West Indies*, 3:322–323; Trelawney Wentworth, *The West India Sketch Book*, 2 vols. (London: 1834), 1:241; Caroline Howard Gilman, *Recollections of a Southern Matron* (New York: 1838), 69–70; Jay B. Hubbell, "Boatmen's Songs," *Southern Folklore Quarterly* 18, no. 1 (March 1954): 244–245.

11. Allen, Ware, and Garrison, *Slave Songs*, 24.

12. Hubbell, "Boatmen's Songs," 244–245. Unfortunately, no copies of the August 13 and 27, 1842, editions of *The Chicora, or, Messenger of the South* containing "An Editorial Voyage to Edisto Island" seem to exist.

13. *The Chicora, or, Messenger of the South*, August 13 and 27, 1842; quoted in Hubbell, "Boatmen's Songs"; Berry, *Swing the Sickle*, 27.

14. Allen, Ware, and Garrison, *Slave Songs*, xvi–xvii, 21–22, 21n; quoted in Henry Edward Krehbiel, *Afro-American Folk Songs: A Study in Racial and National Music* (New York: 1914), 50; Parrish, *Slave Songs*, 80–81, 158–159, 199, 240, 243.

15. Hungerford, *Old Plantation*, 190–192; J. K., "National Poets," 338; Lambert, *Canada and the United States*, 2:254; Epstein, *Sinful Tunes*, 167–171; Cate, *Our Todays*, 158; Malet, *Errand*, 114–115. Hungerford's account is provided in his autobiographical novel, which is set in 1832. For corn songs, see Epstein, *Sinful Tunes*, 172.

16. October 22, 1830, personal diary, Moses Ashley Curtis Papers.

17. Pinckard, *West Indies*, 3:272–323, esp. 292, 321–322; Ballanta, "Music," 753; Sack, *Narrative of a Voyage to Suriname*, 52; Watson, *Men and Times*, 43; J. K., "National Poets," 338; Marvin L. Michael Kay and Lorin Lee Cary, *Slavery in North Carolina, 1748–1775* (Chapel Hill: 1999), 319n85; Koster, *Travels*, 4; Kidder and Fletcher, *Brazil*, 194; Thornton, *Africa and Africans*, 190–191. Special thanks to Carina Ray for her insights on "*gnyaam gnyaam* row."

18. Allen, Ware, and Garrison, *Slave Songs*, 21–22, 21n; Krehbiel, *Folk Songs*, 5; Wetherell, *Stray Notes from Bahia*, 97; Stedman, *Expedition*, 2:321, 321n; Sack, *Narrative of a Voyage to Suriname*, 52. Also see Kidder, *Sketches*, 2:153.

19. Maximilian, *Recollections*, 3:164; Cruz, *Culture on the Margins*, 55, 64; Cate, *Our Todays*, 158; Henry Martyn, *Memoir of the Late Rev. Henry Martyn* (London: 1819), 144–145; Graham, *Feeding the City*, 102.

20. Epstein, *Sinful Tunes*, 170–171; Martyn, *Memoir*, 145; Allen, Ware, and Garrison, *Slave Songs*; Laurence Oliphant, *Patriots and Filibusters, or, Incidents of Political and Exploratory Travel* (London: 1860), 141–143.

21. Koster, *Travels*, 4; Martyn, *Memoir*, 136, 144–145; Graham, *Feeding the City*, 26; McDonald, *Between Slavery and Freedom*, 5, 186; Wood, *Black Majority*, 202–203; Stedman, *Expedition*, 2:362. For lingua francas, see Rodney, *Upper Guinea Coast*, 86, 105; Thornton, *Africa and Africans*, 188, 191, 212–214, 216; Gwendolyn Hall, *Slavery and African Ethnicities*, 29, 37, 107, 170; Gomez, *Country Marks*, 171–172, 180; Searing, *West African Slavery*, 60, 76; Brooks, *Eurafricans*, 18, 39, 53, 60, 125, 152; Austen and Derrick, *Cameroon Rivers*, 2; Smallwood, *Saltwater Slavery*, 118; Walsh, *Calabar to Carter's Grove*, 35; Northrup, *Africa's Discovery of Europe*, 130.

22. Sack, *Voyage to Suriname*, 52; Wetherell, *Stray Notes from Bahia*, 97; Lambert, *Canada and the United States*, 2:254; Stedman, *Expedition*, 2:321, 321n; Parrish, *Slave Songs*, 81, 82.

23. Parrish, *Slave Songs*, 81, 82; Allen, Ware, and Garrison, *Slave Songs*, 22.

24. Quoted in Genevieve W. Chandler, Kincaid Mills, and Genevieve Chandler Peterkin, eds., *Coming Through: Voices of a South Carolina Gullah Community from WPA Oral Histories* (Columbia: 2008), 1, 8–9; Joyner, *Down by the Riverside*, 15–16.

25. Pinckard, *West Indies*, 3:321–323; Stedman, *Expedition*, 1:55; Sack, *Voyage to Suriname*, 52, 73; Joyner, *Down by the Riverside*, 128.

26. Douglass, *Narrative of the Life*, 12–13, 19–20; Zamba, *Life and Adventures*, 152–155; Equiano, *Interesting Narrative*, 1:256–257; Johnson, *Soul by Soul*, 19–22, 31.

27. Cate, *Our Todays*, 157–158; Lovell, *Golden Isles of Georgia*, 229–230; Kemble, *Journal*, 141–142; Epstein, *Sinful Tunes*, 167.

28. Clifton, *Argyle Island*, 93; Edward McCrady, *The History of South Carolina Under the Royal Government, 1719–1776* (New York: 1899), 516; Kemble, *Journal*, 162; Epstein, *Sinful Tunes*, 167. For interplantation competition, see Dawson, "Enslaved Swimmers," 1341.

29. Clifton, *Argyle Island*, 93; McCrady, *South Carolina*, 516; Kemble, *Journal*, 162.

30. Pinckard, *West Indies*, 323; Lambert, *Canada and the United States*, 254–255; Calhoun, *Witness to Sorrow*, 58. John Cruz considered how slaves similarly used songs to voice other desires. Cruz, *Culture on the Margins*, chap. 2, esp. 54, 64.

31. Faux, *Memorable Days*, 78; Hungerford, *Old Plantation*, 190–192; J. K., "National Poets," 338; Epstein, *Sinful Tunes*, 168–170; Calhoun, *Witness to Sorrow*, 58; Voorhoeve and Lichtveld, *Creole Drum*, 15.

32. Gilman, *Recollections*, 69–70; J. K., "National Poets," 338.

33. Maximilian, *Recollections*, 3:164–165. Many thanks to James Sweet for translating this song.

34. Epstein, *Sinful Tunes*, 161; Benson, *America in the Fifties*, 143.

35. Anonymous, "Gentleman's Account of His Travels," 114; Lewis, *West India Proprietor*, 101–102.

36. Basil Hall, *Travels in the United States*, 3:214, 216; Lyell, *Second Visit*, 1:327–328; Avirett, *Old Plantation*, 104; J. K., "National Poets," 338; Kemble, *Journal*, 162–164, 212, 259–261; Watson, *Men and Times*, 43; Lovell, *Golden Isles of Georgia*, 189.

37. McDonald, *Between Slavery and Freedom*, 5, 186.

38. Wentworth, *Sketch Book*, 1:238–242. Also see Pinckard, *West Indies*, 3:323; Hungerford, *Old Plantation*, 190–192.

39. Abbot, *Letters Written in the Interior of Cuba*, xiii, 51; J. K. Jr., "National Poets," in *The Knickerbocker; Or New York Monthly Magazine* 26, no. 4 (October 1845), 338; Lovell, *Golden Isles of Georgia*, 189; Constance Rourke, *American Humor: A Study of the National*

Character (New York: 1931), 71; Cate, *Our Todays*, 158; Francis, Ware, and Garrison, *Slave Songs*, viii; Pearson, *Letters from Port Royal*, 29–30; Benson, *America in the Fifties*, 143; J. W. Leigh, *Other Days* (London: 1921), 187.

40. McCrady, *South Carolina Under the Royal Government*, 516; Clifton, *Argyle Island*, 357. For songs of agricultural slaves providing a similar function, see Smith, *Listening*, 23; Parthenia Antoinette Hague, *A Blockade Family: Life in Southern Alabama During the Civil War* (Boston: 1888), 125–126; Avirett, *Old Plantation*, 31, 58, 129, 144–146, 176, 193; Stedman, *Expedition*, 2:362.

41. C. G. [Caroline Howard Gilman?] "A Ballad," *The Rose Bud, Or Youth's Gazette*, Charleston, (May 18, 1833), 149. Also see William J. Grayson, *The Hireling and the Slave, Chicora, and Other Poems* (Charleston: 1856), 61; Epstein, *Sinful Tunes*, 168.

42. J. K. "National Poets," 331–332, 338; Benson, *America of the Fifties*, 132; Calhoun, *Witness to Sorrow*, 57–58.

43. Calhoun, *Witness to Sorrow*, 58; McDonald, *Between Slavery and Freedom*, 186; Wentworth, *Sketch Book*, 1:238–242; Pinckard, *West Indies*, 3:322.

44. Alexander, *Transatlantic Sketches*, 1:130–131; Benson, *America in the Fifties*, 143; Pinckard, *West Indies*, 3:321–323; Wentworth, *Sketch Book*, 1:168, 238–241; October 23, 1830, personal diary, Moses Ashley Curtis Papers.

45. Smith, *Listening*, esp. 20, 98, 117–126.

46. Smith, *Listening*, 1–2; Megan Vaughan, *Creating the Creole Island: Slavery in Eighteenth-Century Mauritius* (Durham: 2005), 178; Henderson, *History of Brazil*, 10.

47. Malet, *Errand*, 47–48, 114–115.

48. Smith, *Listening*, 23, 36–38, 67–71.

49. Basil Hall, *Travels*, 3:216; McDonald, *Between Slavery and Freedom*, 186; Pinckard, *West Indies*, 3:321–323; Alexander, *Transatlantic Sketches*, 1:130–131; Lyell, *Second Visit*, 1:327–328; Cruz, *Culture on the Margins*, 64; Oliphant, *Patriots and Filibusters*, 141.

50. Miss Hart, *Letters from the Bahama Islands. Written in 1823–4* (Philadelphia: 1827), 17; Clifton, *Argyle Island*, 93; Stedman, *Expedition*, 2:362.

51. Bell, *Major Butler's Legacy*, 148.

52. Smith, *Listening*, 20; Frederick Douglass, *My Bondage and My Freedom* (New York: 1855), 97; Cruz, *Culture on the Margins*, 52.

53. Douglass, *Narrative*, 13–15; Smith, *Listening*, 66–69, 88–91, esp. 20; Epstein, *Sinful Tunes*, 161–162; Berry, *Swing the Sickle*, 27; Karasch, *Slave Life in Rio de Janeiro*, 238–239.

54. Ballanta, "Music," 753; Joyner, *Down by the Riverside*, 1.

55. Kemble, *Journal*, 162–163, 259–264; J. K., "National Poets," 238; Lambert, *Canada, and the United States*, 254; Calhoun, *Witness to Sorrow*, 57–58; Lovell, *Golden Isles of Georgia*, 189; Benson, *America in the Fifties*, 141, 143; Faux, *Memorable Days*, 78.

56. Ballanta-(Taylor), *Saint Helena Island Spirituals*, xviii; Ballanta, "Music," 752–753; Parrish, *Slave Songs*, 199.

57. Kemble, *Journal*, 163–164; Parrish, *Slave Songs*, 235; Gilman, *Recollections*, 69–70 (italics added). Brooke Baldwin, "The Cakewalk: A Study in Stereotype and Reality," in *Journal of Social History* 15, no. 2 (Winter 1981): 205–218; Marshall Stearns, *Jazz Dance: The Story of American Vernacular Dance* (New York: 1968), 123–124; Shane White and Graham White, "Slave Clothing and African-American Culture in the Eighteenth and Nineteenth Centuries," *Past & Present* 148 (August 1995): 162–164; Dawson, "Enslaved Ship Pilots," 174–176.

58. Elkanah Watson, *Men and Times of the Revolution; or, Memoirs of Elkanah Watson* (New York: 1856), 43, 247. For waterman's song overwhelming rural and urban soundscapes, see Henderson, *History of Brazil*, 10; Daniel McKinnen, *Tour of the British West Indies*, 9; Bayley, *Four Years' Residence*, 29; October 23, 1830, personal diary, Moses Ashley Curtis Papers. For culture as a form of resistance, see Sweet, *Recreating Africa*, 7, 229, chap. 8; Sweet, *Domingos Álvares*, esp. 6; Young; *Rituals of Resistance*; Gomez, *Country Marks*; Ferreira, *Cross-Cultural Exchange*, 242; Creel, *Peculiar People*; Fett, *Working Cures*; Rucker, *River Flows On*; Beckles, Natural Rebels; Moitt, *Women in Slavery*; Jennifer Morgan, *Laboring Women*; Weaver, *Medical Revolutionaries*.

59. Martyn, *Memoir*, 136, 144–145, 287, 405; Pinckard, *West Indies*, 3:322.

60. Isert, *Letters on West Africa*, 27; Darold D. Wax, "A Philadelphia Surgeon on a Slaving Voyage to Africa, 1749–1751," *Pennsylvania Magazine of History and Biography* 92 (October 1968), 478; Epstein, *Sinful Tunes*, 69.

61. Winterbottom, *Native Africans*, 1:112–113; Leonard, *Western Coast of Africa*, 58; Álvares, *Ethiopia Minor*, chap. 9:2; Atkins, *Voyage to Guinea*, 59; Glave, *Savage Africa*, 130.

62. Atkins, *Voyage to Guinea*, 59; Álvares, *Ethiopia Minor*, chap. 9:2; Rankin, *White Man's Grave*, 2:199–202.

63. Weeks, *Congo Savages*, 92, 160; Glave, *Savage Africa*, 130; Winterbottom, *Native Africans*, 1:112; Kingsley, *Travels in West Africa*, 181.

64. Tams, *Visit to the Portuguese Possessions*, 1:234–235. For Luanda's multicultural and patriarchal dynamics, see Ferreira, *Cross-Cultural Exchange*, esp. chap. 5; Martin, "Cabinda and Cabindans: Some Aspects of an African Maritime Society," in Jeffrey C. Stone, ed., *Africa and the Sea* (Aberdeen: 1985), 80–95.

65. Weeks, *Congo Savages*, 92; Kingsley, *Travels in West Africa*, 180–181; Winterbottom, *Native Africans*, 1:112–113.

66. Weeks, *Congo Savages*, 93.

67. Rankin, *White Man's Grave*, 2:201; Adanson, *Voyage to Senegal*, 273.

68. Martha G. Anderson, "From River Horses to Dancing Sharks: Canoe and Fish in Ijo Ritual," in Anderson and Peek, *Ways of the River*, 133.

69. Weeks, *Congo Cannibals*, 92–93.

70. Winterbottom, *Native Africans*, 1:112–113; Anna Maria Falconbridge, *Narrative of Two Voyages to the River Sierra Leone During the Years 1791–1792–1793*, Christopher Fyye, ed. (1794; Liverpool: 2000), 26, 30; Atkins, *Voyage to Guinea*, 59; Weeks, *Congo Savages*, 93; Rankin, *White Man's Grave*, 2:201–202.

71. Rankin, *White Man's Grave*, 2:201–202; Weeks, *Congo Savages*, 93; Anderson, "River Horses," in Anderson and Peek, *Ways of the River*, 154.

72. Winterbottom, *Native Africans*, 1:112–113; Rankin, *White Man's Grave*, 2:201–202.

73. Valdez, *Traveller's Life*, 2:74–77.

74. Weeks, *Congo Cannibals*, 93; Rankin, *White Man's Grave*, 2:201; Falconbridge, *Narrative of Two Voyages*, 30.

75. Álvares, *Ethiopia Minor*, chap. 9:2; Leonard, *Western Coast of Africa*, 58, 257–258; Ellis, *Land of the Fetish*, 2; Glave, *Savage Africa*, 130.

76. Rankin, *White Man's Grave*, 2:199 (italics added).

77. Kingsley, *Travels in West Africa*, 164–165, 239; Winterbottom, *Native Africans*, 1:112–113.

78. Kingsley, *Travels in West Africa*, 180–181.

79. For porters' songs, see Kidder, *Sketches*, 1:69, 2:21–22; Tousaint-Samson, *Parisian in Brazil*, 30–31; Elizabeth Agassiz, *A Journey in Brazil by Professor and Mrs. Louis Agassiz* (New York: 1888), 48–49; Koster, *Travels*, 4–5, 10; Henderson, *History of the Brazil*, 10; Alfred J. Pairpoint, *Uncle Sam and His Country, or, Sketches of America, in 1854–55–56* (London: 1857), 219. For slaves carrying offloaded passengers in chairs, see Kidder, *Sketches*, 2:21–22.

Conclusion

1. Michael A. Gomez, ed., *Diasporic Africa: A Reader* (New York: 2006), 1–3; Gwendolyn Hall, *Slavery and African Ethnicity*; Young, *Rituals of Resistance*, 184–188; Dawson, "Slave Culture."

2. Gillis, "Atlantic Oceania," 21.

3. Hau'ofa, "Sea of Islands," 32; Bolster, "Putting the Ocean in Atlantic History."

4. Vickers with Walsh, *Young Men and the Sea*, 3–24, esp. 3, 7–8; Norling, *Ahab Had a Wife*; Creighton and Norling, *Wooden Women*.

5. Richard Campanella, *Lincoln in New Orleans: The 1828–1831 Flatboat Voyages and Their Place in History* (Urbana: 2012); Vickers with Walsh, *Young Men and the Sea*, 248–251.

Epilogue

1. My observations.

2. R. L. Allen and David Nickel, "The Negro and Learning to Swim: The Buoyancy Problem Related to Reported Biological Difference," *Journal of Negro Education* 38 (Autumn 1969): 404–411; Jack Shafer, "Lost in the Flood: Why No Mention of Race or Class in TV's Katrina Coverage?" *Slate*, August 31, 2005, http://slate.com/id/2124688/, accessed November 18, 2005; *Washington Post*, November 16, 1993, A14; ibid., August 27, 1998, D4; *Miami Herald*, April 22, 2004, 1B.

3. Jeff Wiltse, *Contested Waters: A Social History of Swimming Pools in America* (Chapel Hill: 2007); E. B. Henderson, "The Participation of Negro Youth in Community and Educational Programs," *Journal of Negro Education* 9 (July 1940): 416–424; *Miami Herald*, April 22, 2004, 1B; *Washington Post*, August 27, 1998, D4.

4. Andrew W. Karhl, *The Land Was Ours: African American Beaches from Jim Crow to the Sunbelt South* (Cambridge: 2012); William Tuttle, *Chicago in the Red Summer of 1919* (Champaign: 1970), 5–7; Saidiya V. Hartman, *Scenes of Subjection: Terror, Slavery, and Self-Making in Nineteenth-Century America* (New York, 1997); Chicago Commission on Race Relations, *The Negro in Chicago: A Study of Race Relations and a Race Riot* (Chicago: 1922), 4–5. I have heard accounts of how racial violence and real and imagined lynchings made local waterways in the Northeast, South, and Midwest taboo swimming places.

5. *Miami Herald*, April 22, 2004, 1B; David Crary, "New Study: 58 Percent of Black Children Can't Swim," *Boston Globe*, May 28, 2008; "Swimming and Recreational Water Safety," www.cdc.gov/homeandrecreationalsafety/water-safety/waterinjuries-factsheet.html, accessed August 22, 2008; "Nonfatal and Fatal Drownings in Recreational Water Settings— United States, 2001–2002," www.cdc.gov/mmwr/preview/mmwrhtml/mm5321a1.htm, accessed August 22, 2008; "Unintentional Drowning: Get the Facts," www.cdc.gov/home andrecreationalsafety/water-safety/waterinjuries-factsheet.html, accessed August 24, 2008.

6. Tony Thomas, "Why African Americans Put the Banjo Down," in Diane Pecknold, ed., *Hidden in the Mix: The African American Presence in Country Music* (Duke: 2013), 143–170.

Index

Figures and their captions are indicated by an italicized page number followed by the letter *f*.

Acknowledgements

The roots of this book extend back to my youth when being a "black surfer" and "black swimmer" were far more paradoxical than they are today. My affinity for water goes back to about the age of three months when I started learning how to swim and it intensified when I began surfing at ten years old. Surf-zones, pools, and beaches were my constant playground and scenes for lifetime lessons that informed this book's development. My earliest memory of racism occurred while playing along the water's edge in Long Beach, California during the 1970s when I was about six years old. I asked my white playmates if they wanted to swim and a slightly older boy informed me that "colored people don't swim." Not knowing what a colored person was, I, nonetheless, recognized his remark as an insult. Being a strong swimmer I challenged him to a race. Despite my impressive Afro and tie-died speedo I easily restored my youthful honor. Yet, indelibly engraved upon my psyche was the lingering anxiety that aquatics were somehow not meant for African Americans like me even as my lived experiences in a multiracial community filled with backyard pools where I routinely swam with white, black, Asian, and Latino family members and friends told me otherwise. As my friends and I approached adolescence, we became a motley crew of dedicated surfers. When wintery storms churned up big surf, we voyaged northward to the Santa Monica Bay, passing through Compton on the RTD bus, the acronym for Regional Transit District, which, during the 1980s, was colloquially known as the "Rough, Tough, and Dangerous." Along this route issues of race and aquatics were occasionally raised as African American bus riders jokingly reminded me that black people don't surf. I politely laughed, but never found that joke amusing.

Having spent a considerable amount of time in African American communities in California and New York City I was continually reminded of the words of my racist playmate and fellow bus riders. Rarely did I encounter black people on a beach and, by my count, I was one of six black surfers to frequent the approximately sixty miles of coastline stretching from San Clemente to Manhattan Beach, though there were rumors of a Black Surfers Alliance further north. Beyond the borders of my youthful community I seldom encountered black swimmers. Jackie Robinson Park, across the street from my grandmother's Harlem apartment had a pool, but, during summer months, it was often so full one could not properly swim. During the winter, it stood cold and empty.

My aquatic pursuits and intellectual curiosities began to intertwine while working on my undergraduate senior history thesis at California State University, Fullerton. There, under the generous guidance of Ronald Reitveld I considered slavery during the American Civil War. Researching this topic, I found numerous accounts of captives' swimming and boating skills, which resonated as they cut across the grain of contemporary assumptions, motivating me to begin amassing an archive on the topic.

My research for this book began at the University of South Carolina. There, the Department of History nurtured and supported my intellectual pursuits. Special thanks are due to Daniel C. Littlefield, my advisor and friend. He mentored me through careful guidance, while giving me the space to chart my own intellectual waters as I situated myself in the fields of Atlantic history and the African diaspora. Comments provided by Mark M. Smith, Ronald Atkinson, and Kenneth Kelly, as well as Lacey Ford and Paul Johnson, continually directed my eye to unexamined regions and topics of consideration while Smith challenged me to creativity defy intellectual boundaries. While working with Valinda Littlefield and Bobby Donaldson's I became familiar with several archives during research trips throughout the Carolinas as they kindly allowed me to conduct further research. I was fortunate to have Kathleen Hilliard, Rebecca Shrum, Aaron Marrs, Melissa Jane Taylor, Tyler Boulware, Michael Reynolds, and David Prior as colleagues. Their friendship was encouraging, the citations they provided broadened this book's horizons, and their invaluable insights, often consumed while sharing pimento cheese fries, will always be fondly remembered and deeply appreciated.

Over the years Matt Childs, James Sweet, and Jane Landers have critiqued articles, essays, and conference papers that contributed to the development of this book while kindly answering a slew of questions. Much was gained through scholarly discussions with Terri Snyder, Sharla Fett, Wilma

King, Lisa Norling, Charles Joyner, Ted DeLaney, Marcus Rediker, Tyler Parry, Chaz Yingling, Sowande' Mustakeem, Jeff Fortin, and Eric Kimball, as well as the far-flung citations they offered. W. Jeffery Bolster kindly answered numerous maritime-related questions and shared sources. Fellow swimmers and historians Carina Ray and Elizabeth Fenn provided obscure sources on swimming and suggestions on how to interpret them. James Sidbury deserves specially thanks. As a blind reader, Sidbury thoughtfully critiqued the manuscript before kindly revealing his identity, facilitating exchanges that challenged me to further clarify and nuance my analyses and arguments.

Financial support was generously provided by the Department of History at the University of South Carolina; the University of South Carolina; the Institute for Southern Studies at the University of South Carolina; and the School of Social Sciences and Humanities at the University of California, Merced. The following fellowships greatly facilitated my research: the Ford Fellowship; the John Haskell Kemble Fellowship through the Huntington Library; the Fletcher Jones Foundation through the Huntington Library; and the Paul Cuffe Memorial Fellowship through Frank C. Munson Institute of American Maritime Studies at Mystic Seaport: Museum of America and the Sea.

I am especially thankful for the support and encouragement my family has provided throughout this process. From an early age, my mother cultivated my intellectual curiosity during, among other things, numerous trips throughout the United States and the world that always included cultural immersion and historical exploration. My wife, Liliana, has supported my research endeavors while grudgingly accompanying me on tropical research trips and my children Ariella and Matteo help keep life fun during the grim task of studying slave experiences.

Finally, I must thank the water for affording so many hours of sublime reflection. There is perhaps no better way to consider African-descended people's aquatic traditions than while gliding through the water in swimming pools, oceans, rivers, and lakes or sitting on a surfboard scanning Atlantic, Pacific, and Caribbean horizons for incoming waves. Much of this book was mentally transcribed while suspended in the drink.

Printed in the USA
CPSIA information can be obtained
at www.ICGtesting.com
JSHW022131311024
72774JS00004B/123